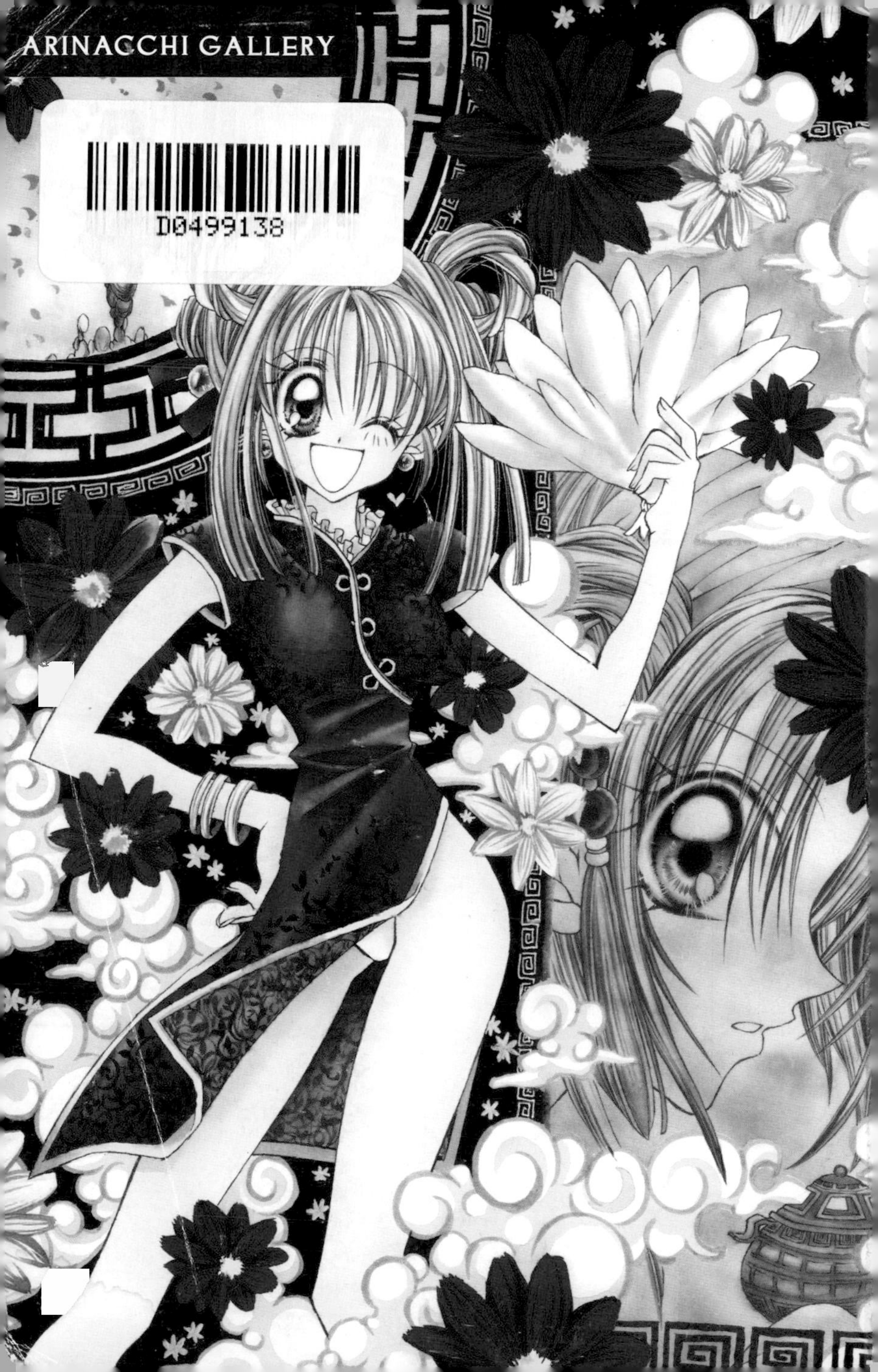
ARINACCHI GALLERY

COMMENT FROM **CURATOR ARINACCHI**

The contrasting red and black looks very nice.
Several of my mangaka friends have told me I
make a distinct use of the color red. I do have a
strong preference for that color. At times, I'll add
black, brown or yellow to it too.

PHANTOM THIEF
Jeanne

4

STORY AND ART BY
Arina Tanemura

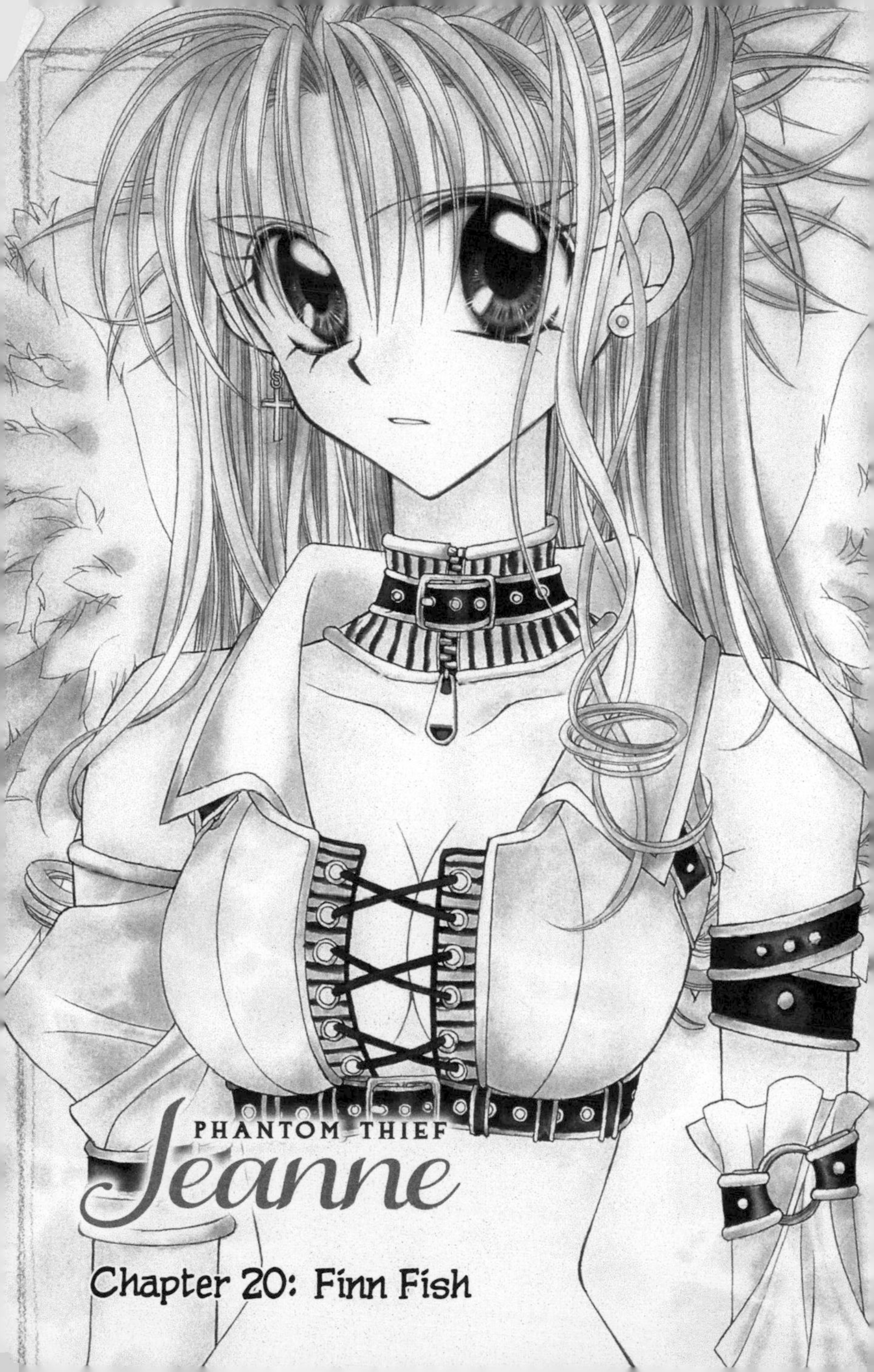
PHANTOM THIEF
Jeanne
Chapter 20: Finn Fish

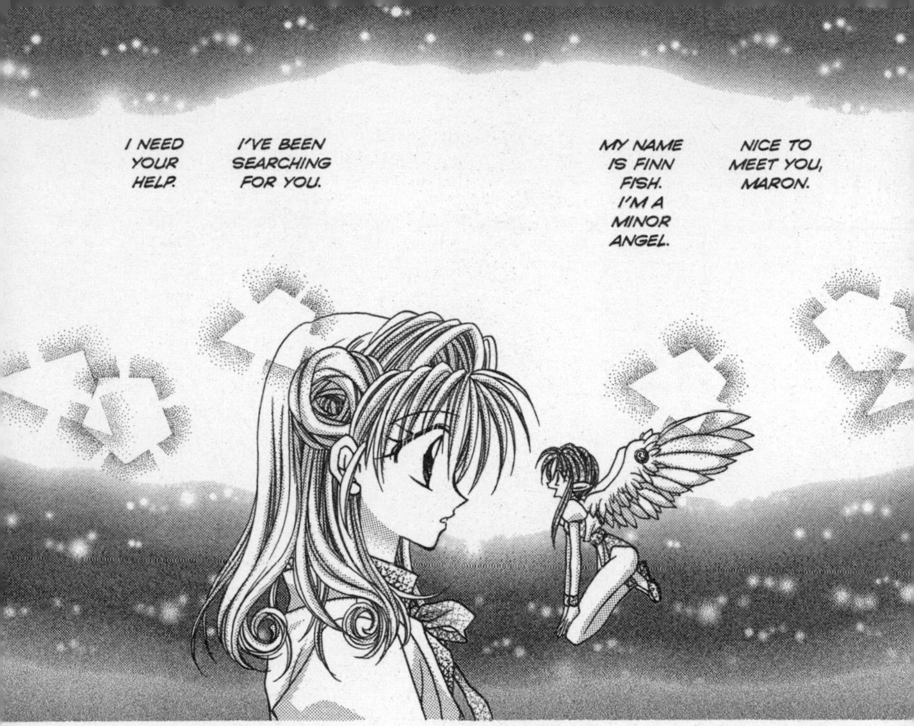
NICE TO MEET YOU, MARON.
MY NAME IS FINN FISH. I'M A MINOR ANGEL.
I'VE BEEN SEARCHING FOR YOU.
I NEED YOUR HELP.

PHANTOM
THIEF
JEANNE

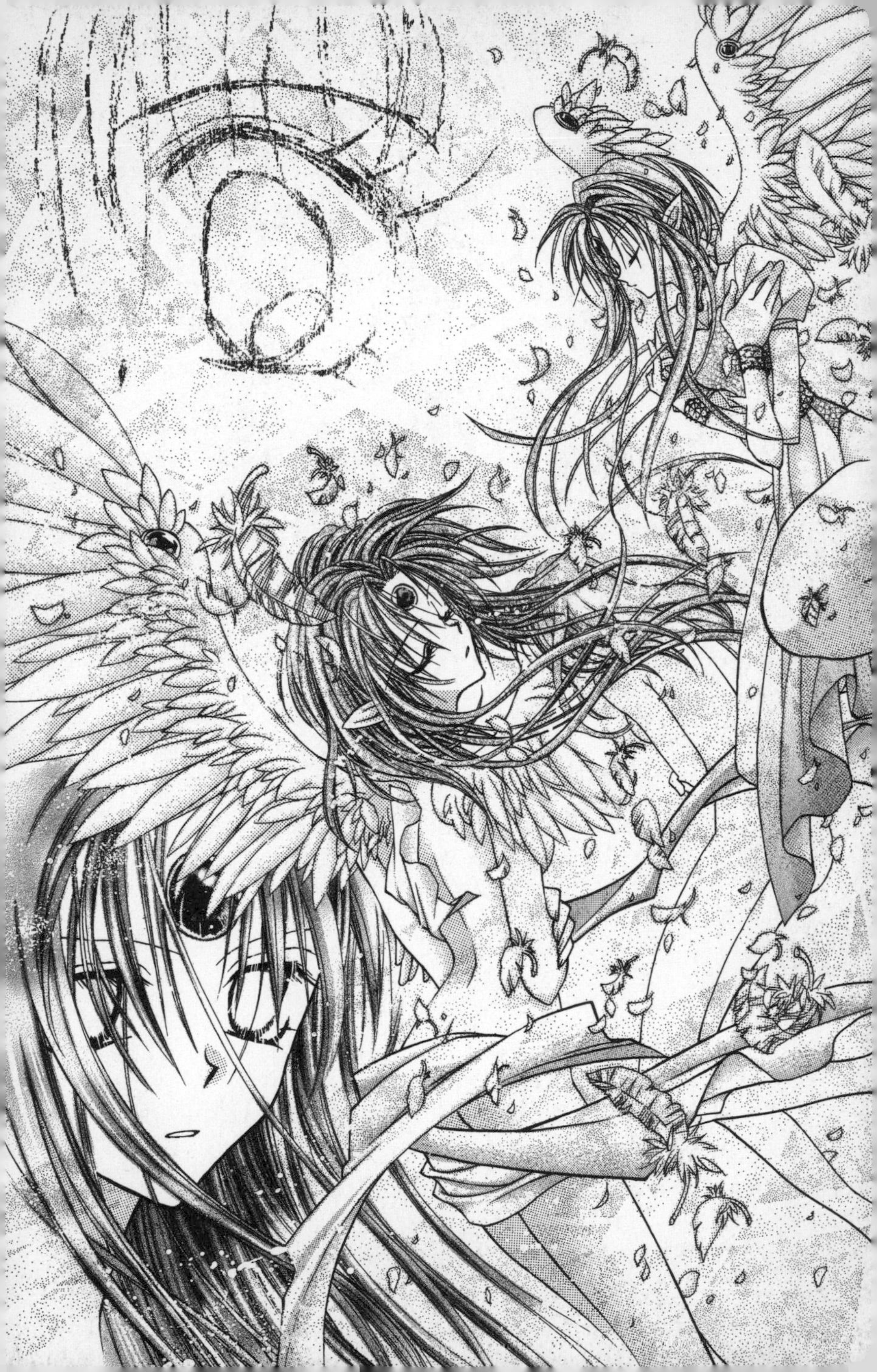

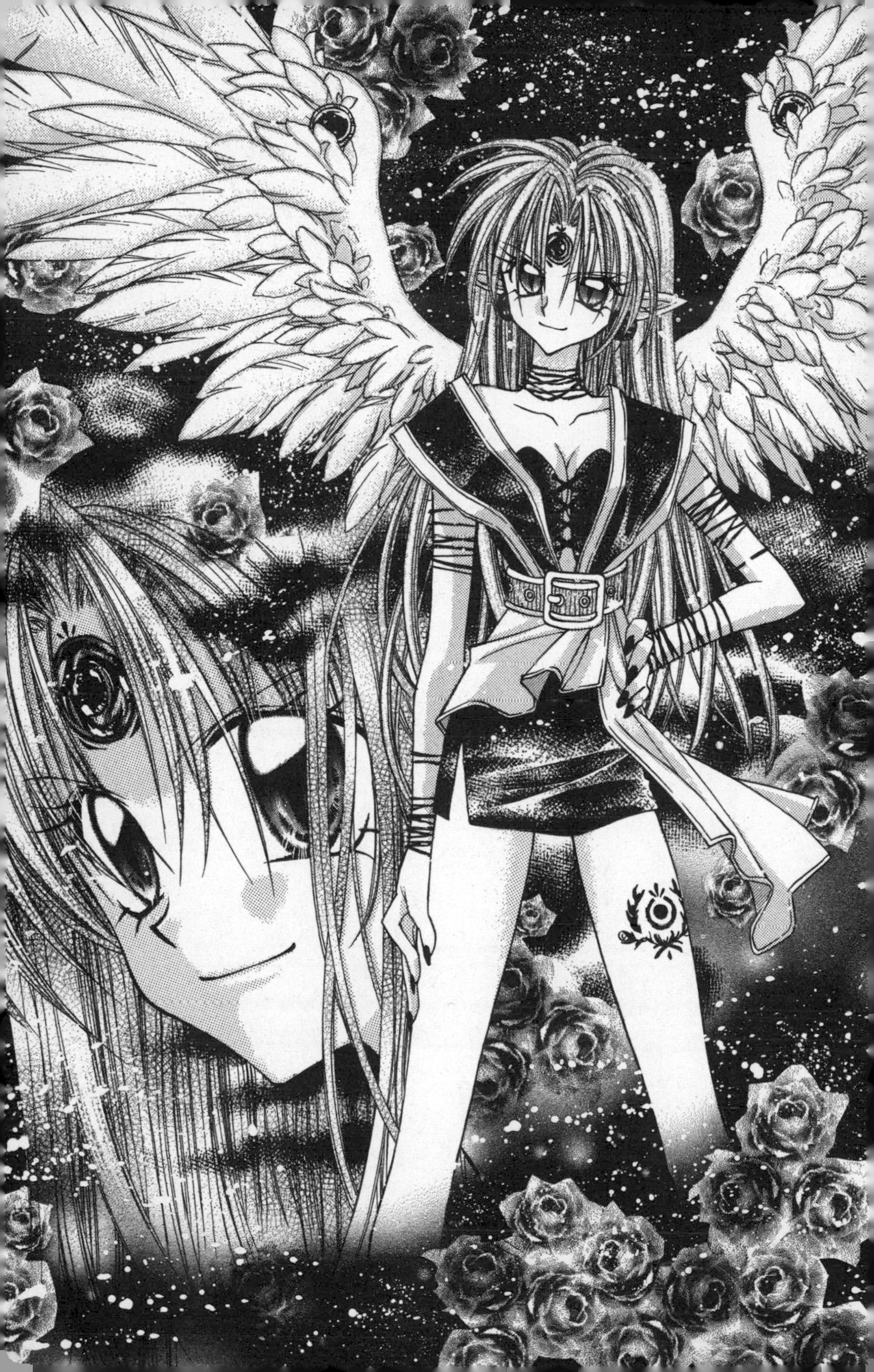

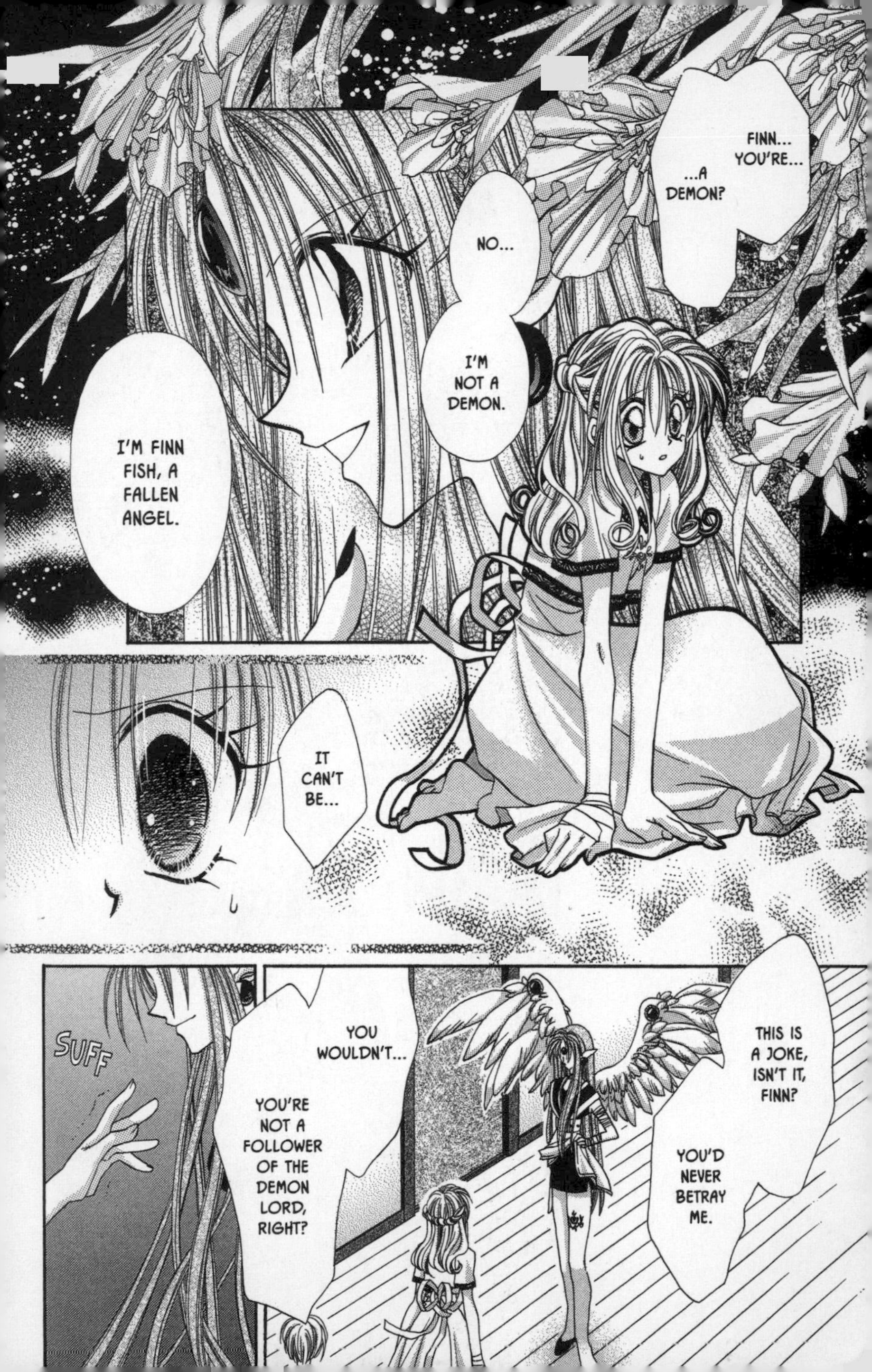
FINN... YOU'RE...
...A DEMON?
NO...
I'M NOT A DEMON.
I'M FINN FISH, A FALLEN ANGEL.
IT CAN'T BE...
THIS IS A JOKE, ISN'T IT, FINN?
YOU'D NEVER BETRAY ME.
YOU WOULDN'T...
YOU'RE NOT A FOLLOWER OF THE DEMON LORD, RIGHT?
SUFF

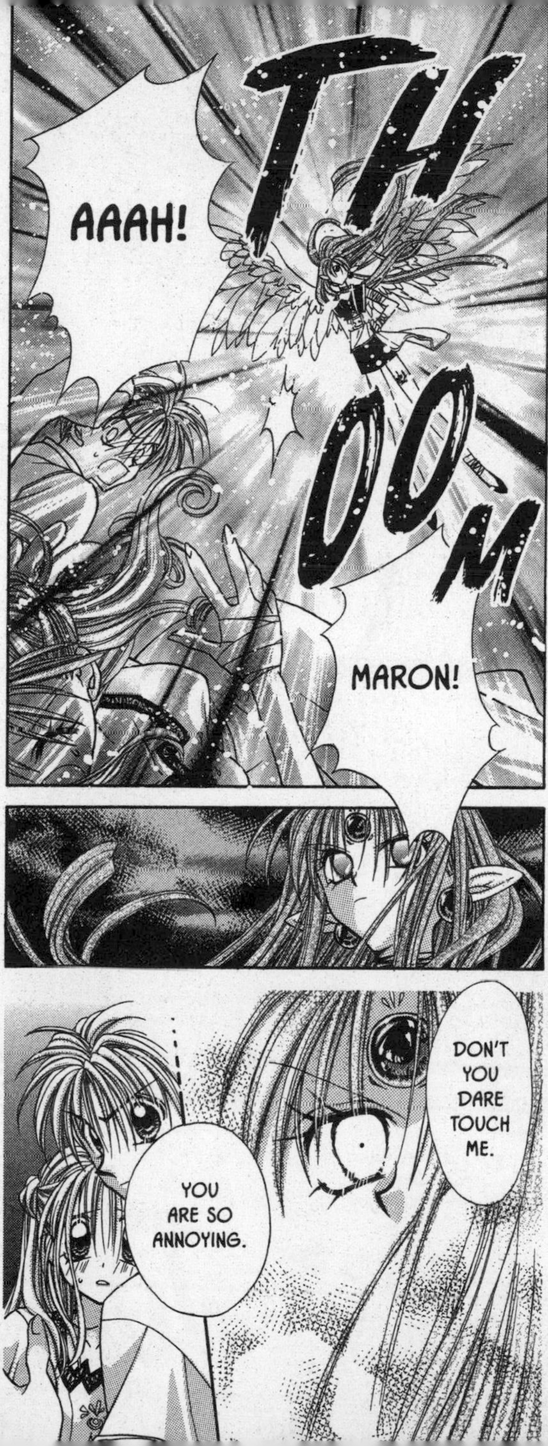
THOOM
AAAH!
MARON!
DON'T YOU DARE TOUCH ME.
YOU ARE SO ANNOYING.

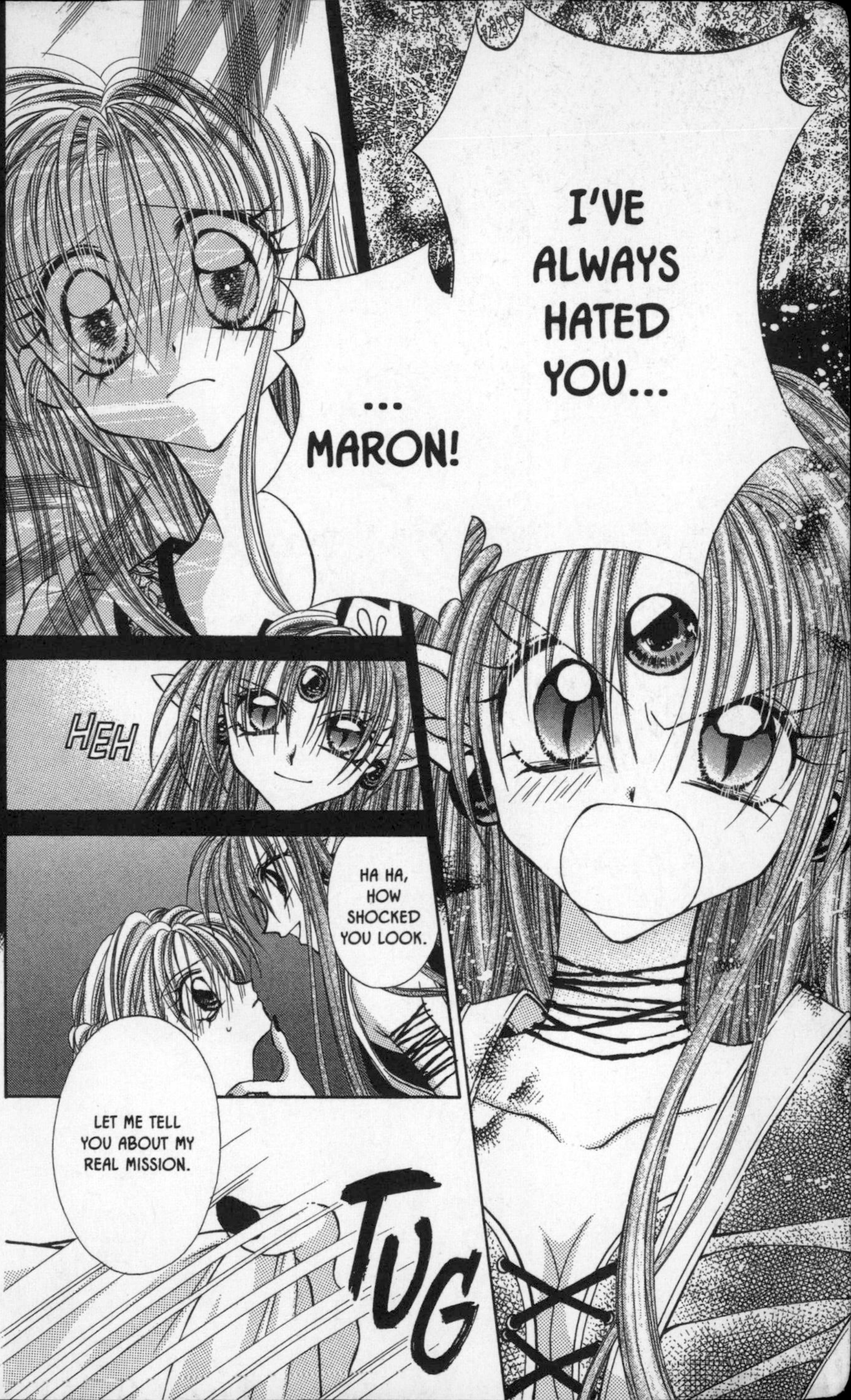
I'VE ALWAYS HATED YOU...
... MARON!
HEH
HA HA, HOW SHOCKED YOU LOOK.
LET ME TELL YOU ABOUT MY REAL MISSION.
TUG

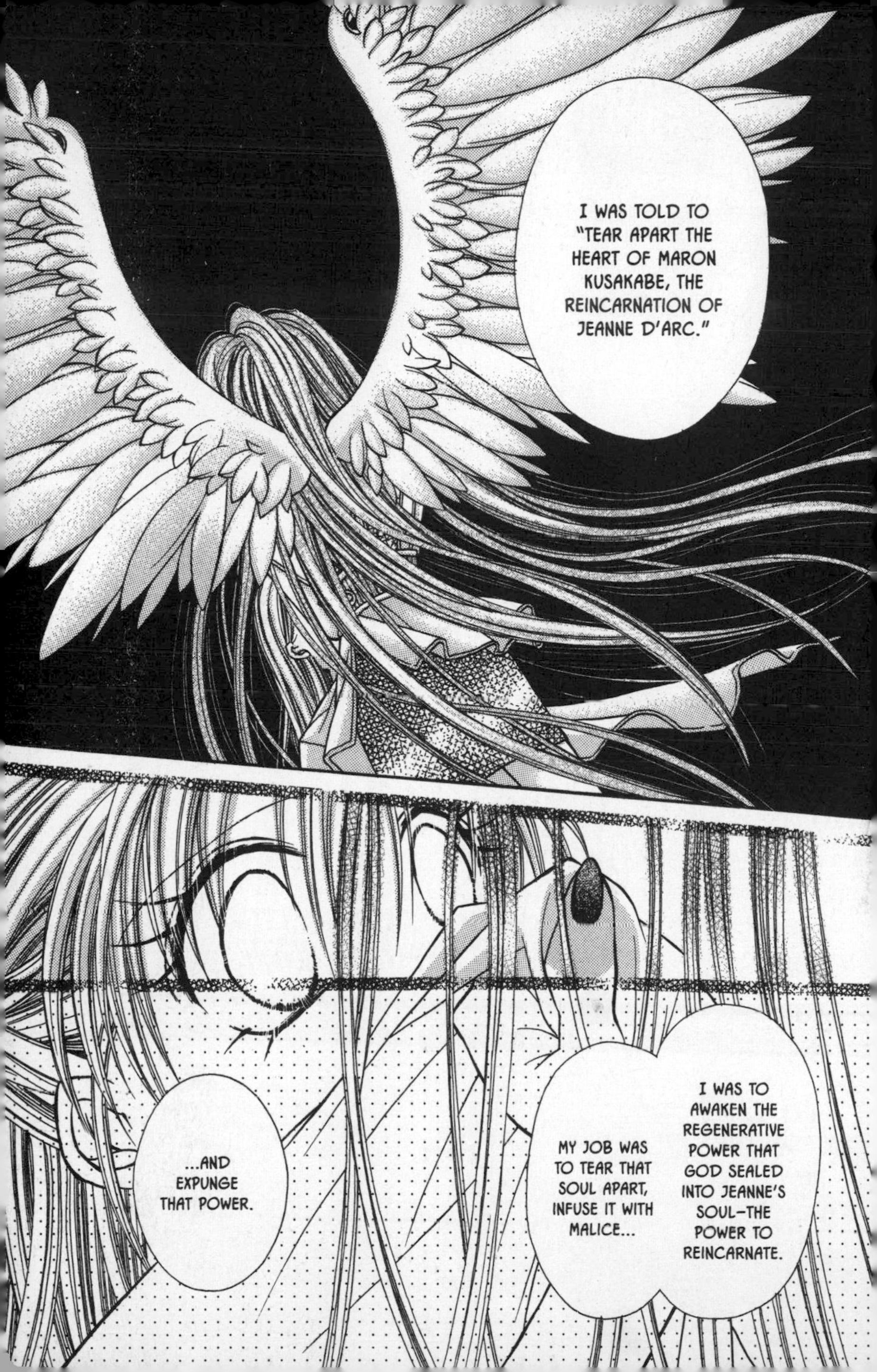
I WAS TOLD TO "TEAR APART THE HEART OF MARON KUSAKABE, THE REINCARNATION OF JEANNE D'ARC."
I WAS TO AWAKEN THE REGENERATIVE POWER THAT GOD SEALED INTO JEANNE'S SOUL—THE POWER TO REINCARNATE.
MY JOB WAS TO TEAR THAT SOUL APART, INFUSE IT WITH MALICE...
...AND EXPUNGE THAT POWER.

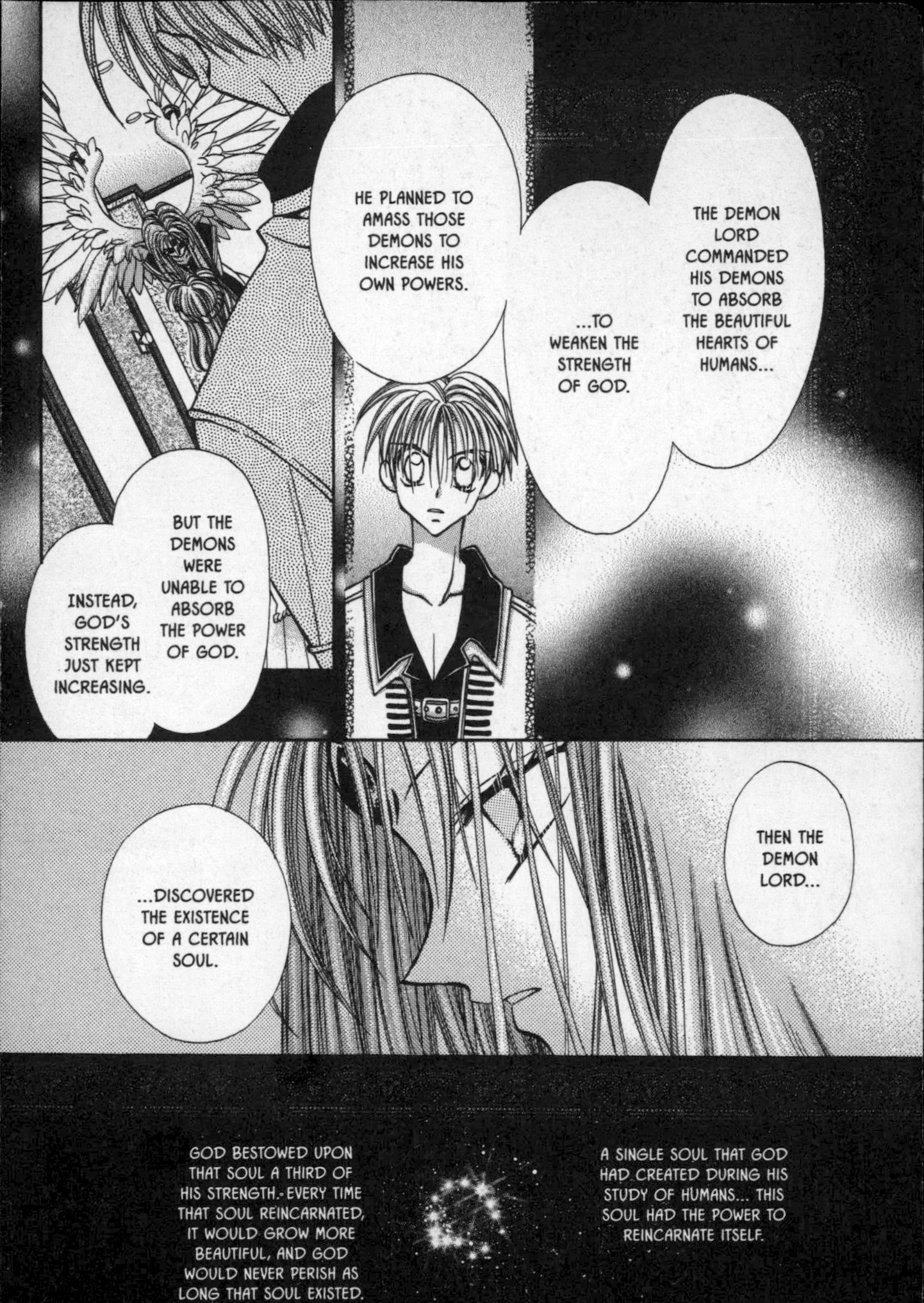
THE DEMON LORD COMMANDED HIS DEMONS TO ABSORB THE BEAUTIFUL HEARTS OF HUMANS...
...TO WEAKEN THE STRENGTH OF GOD.
HE PLANNED TO AMASS THOSE DEMONS TO INCREASE HIS OWN POWERS.
BUT THE DEMONS WERE UNABLE TO ABSORB THE POWER OF GOD.
INSTEAD, GOD'S STRENGTH JUST KEPT INCREASING.
THEN THE DEMON LORD...
...DISCOVERED THE EXISTENCE OF A CERTAIN SOUL.
A SINGLE SOUL THAT GOD HAD CREATED DURING HIS STUDY OF HUMANS... THIS SOUL HAD THE POWER TO REINCARNATE ITSELF.
GOD BESTOWED UPON THAT SOUL A THIRD OF HIS STRENGTH. EVERY TIME THAT SOUL REINCARNATED, IT WOULD GROW MORE BEAUTIFUL, AND GOD WOULD NEVER PERISH AS LONG THAT SOUL EXISTED.

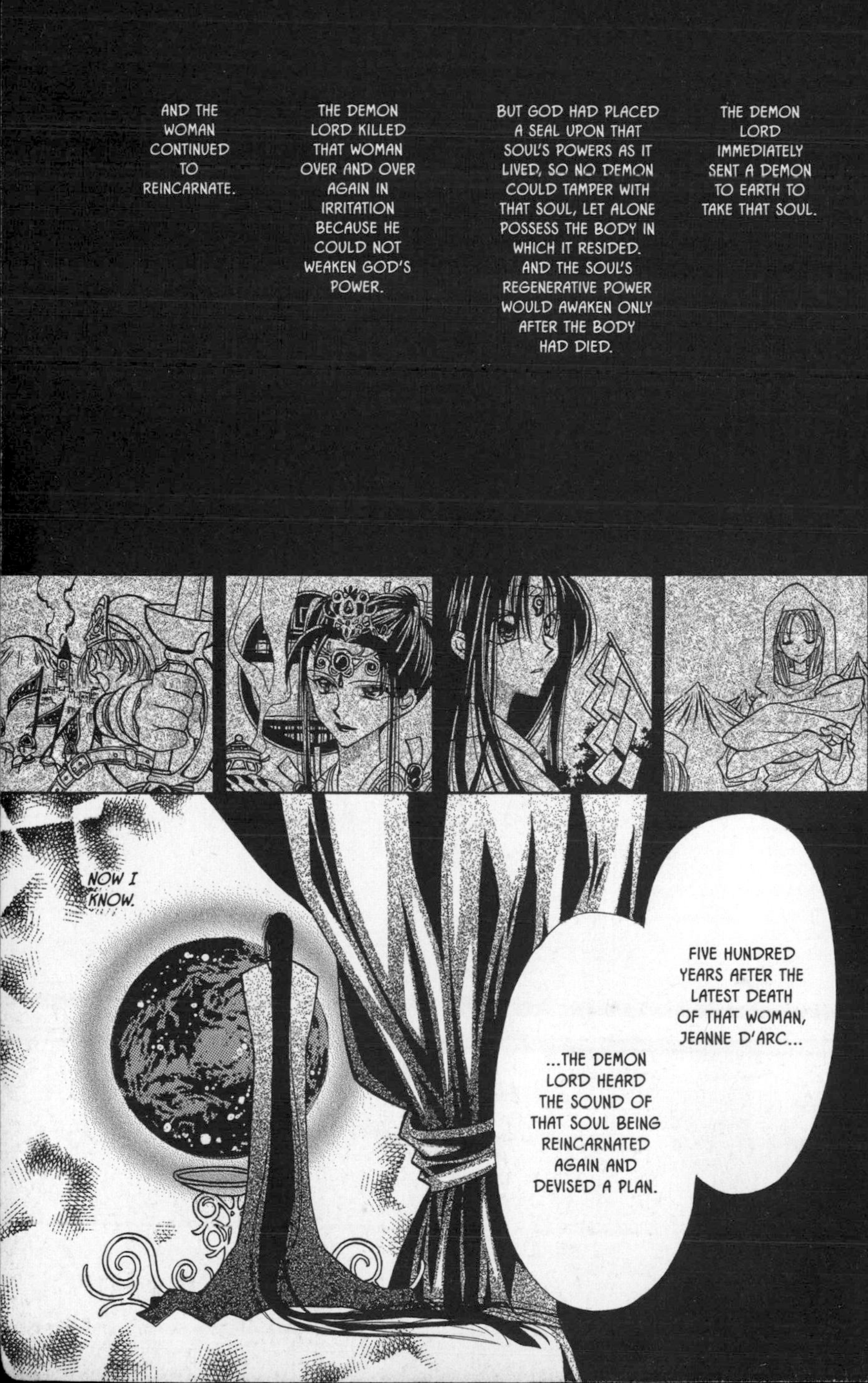
THE DEMON LORD IMMEDIATELY SENT A DEMON TO EARTH TO TAKE THAT SOUL.
BUT GOD HAD PLACED A SEAL UPON THAT SOUL'S POWERS AS IT LIVED, SO NO DEMON COULD TAMPER WITH THAT SOUL, LET ALONE POSSESS THE BODY IN WHICH IT RESIDED. AND THE SOUL'S REGENERATIVE POWER WOULD AWAKEN ONLY AFTER THE BODY HAD DIED.
THE DEMON LORD KILLED THAT WOMAN OVER AND OVER AGAIN IN IRRITATION BECAUSE HE COULD NOT WEAKEN GOD'S POWER.
AND THE WOMAN CONTINUED TO REINCARNATE.
FIVE HUNDRED YEARS AFTER THE LATEST DEATH OF THAT WOMAN, JEANNE D'ARC...
...THE DEMON LORD HEARD THE SOUND OF THAT SOUL BEING REINCARNATED AGAIN AND DEVISED A PLAN.
NOW I KNOW.

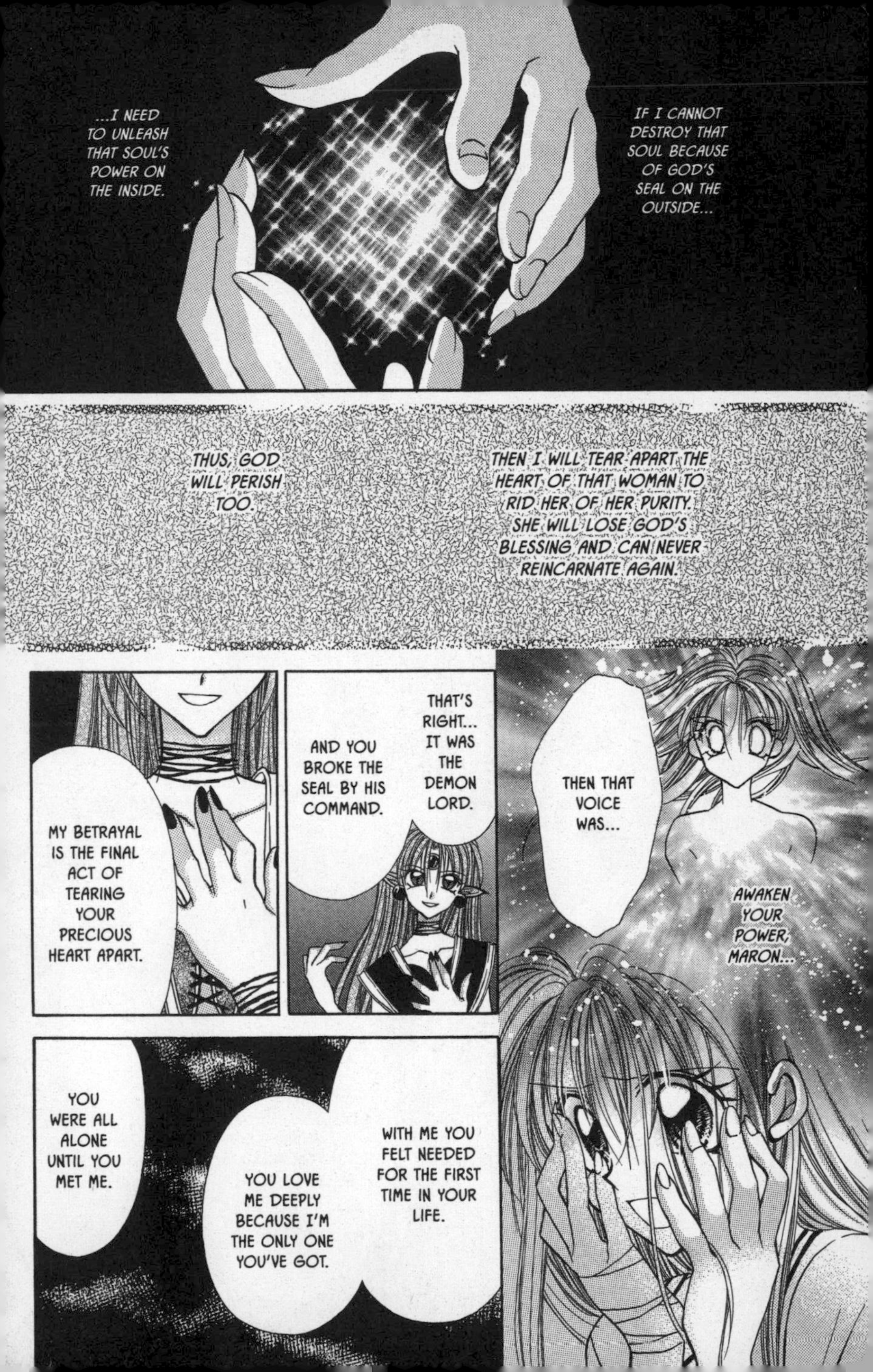
IF I CANNOT DESTROY THAT SOUL BECAUSE OF GOD'S SEAL ON THE OUTSIDE...
...I NEED TO UNLEASH THAT SOUL'S POWER ON THE INSIDE.
THEN I WILL TEAR APART THE HEART OF THAT WOMAN TO RID HER OF HER PURITY. SHE WILL LOSE GOD'S BLESSING AND CAN NEVER REINCARNATE AGAIN.
THUS, GOD WILL PERISH TOO.
THEN THAT VOICE WAS...
AWAKEN YOUR POWER, MARON...
THAT'S RIGHT... IT WAS THE DEMON LORD.
AND YOU BROKE THE SEAL BY HIS COMMAND.
MY BETRAYAL IS THE FINAL ACT OF TEARING YOUR PRECIOUS HEART APART.
WITH ME YOU FELT NEEDED FOR THE FIRST TIME IN YOUR LIFE.
YOU LOVE ME DEEPLY BECAUSE I'M THE ONLY ONE YOU'VE GOT.
YOU WERE ALL ALONE UNTIL YOU MET ME.

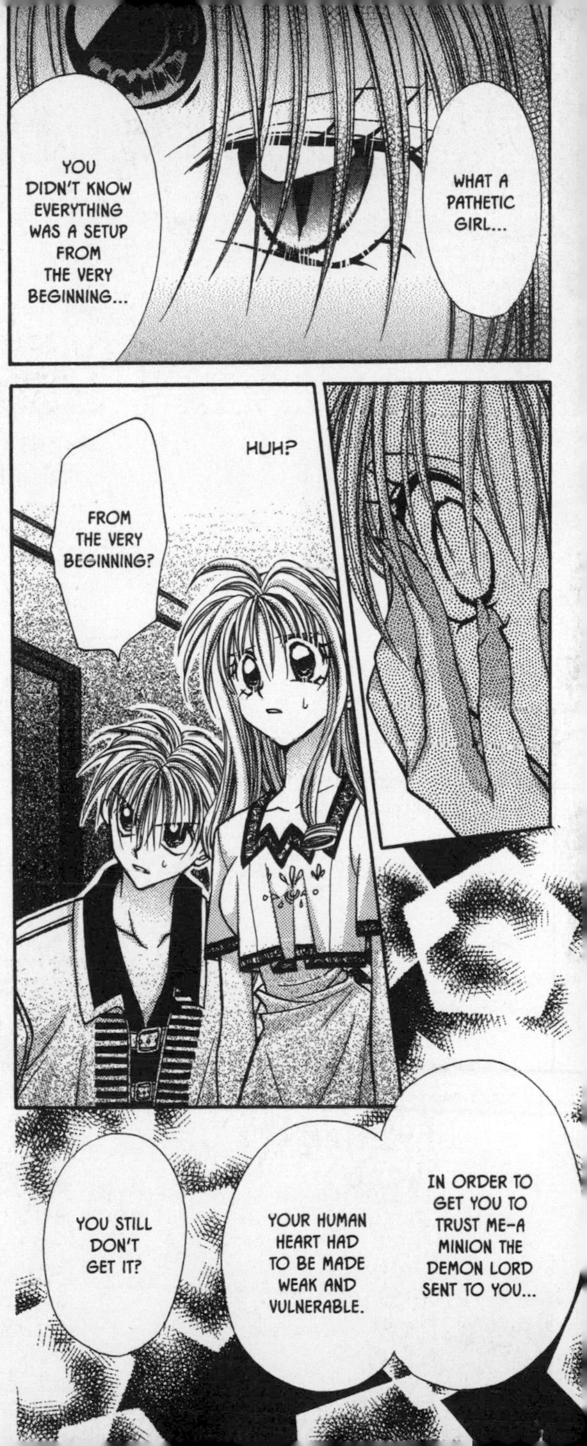
WHAT A PATHETIC GIRL...
YOU DIDN'T KNOW EVERYTHING WAS A SETUP FROM THE VERY BEGINNING...
HUH?
FROM THE VERY BEGINNING?
IN ORDER TO GET YOU TO TRUST ME—A MINION THE DEMON LORD SENT TO YOU...
YOUR HUMAN HEART HAD TO BE MADE WEAK AND VULNERABLE.
YOU STILL DON'T GET IT?

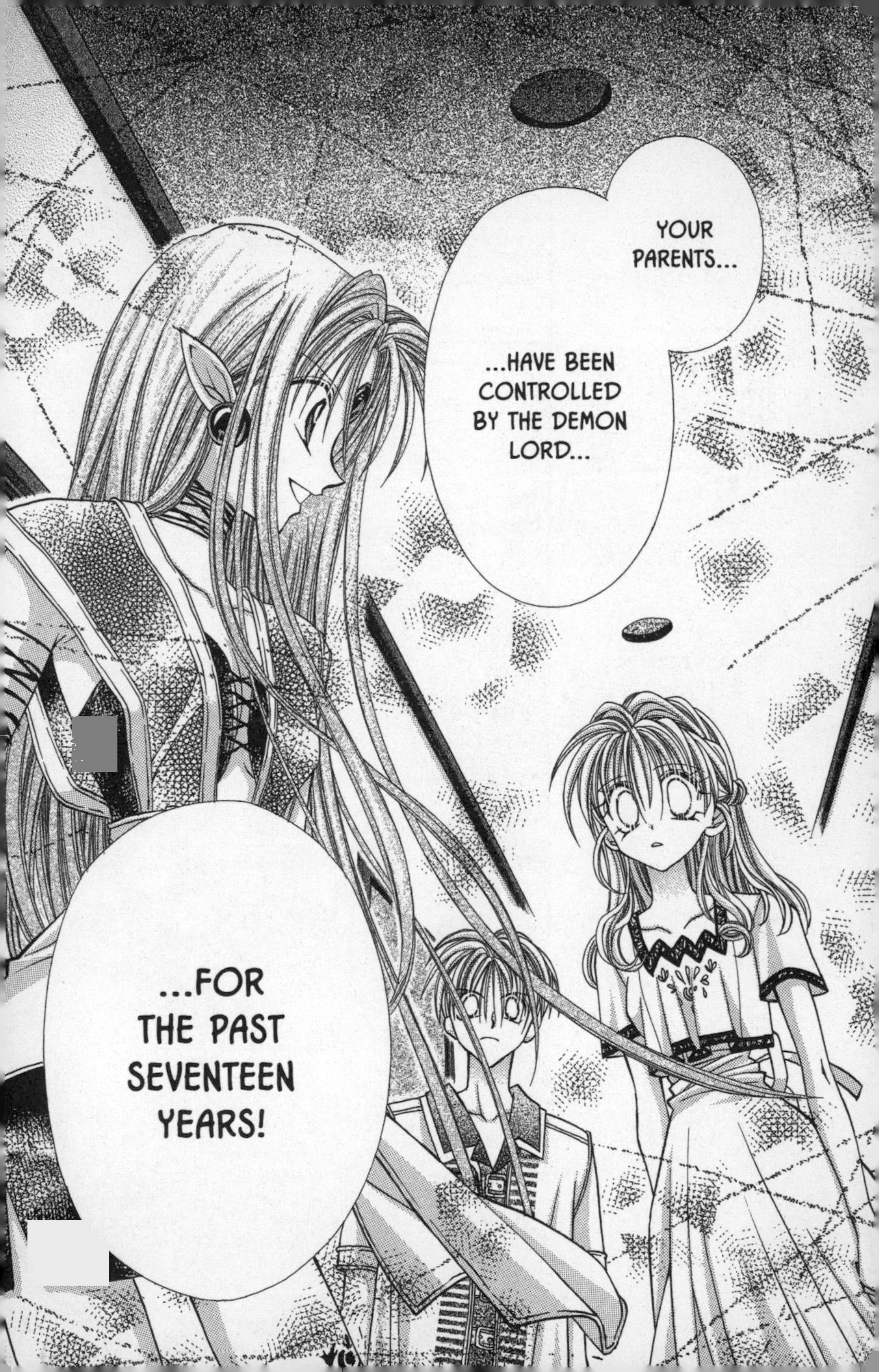
YOUR PARENTS...
...HAVE BEEN CONTROLLED BY THE DEMON LORD...
...FOR THE PAST SEVENTEEN YEARS!

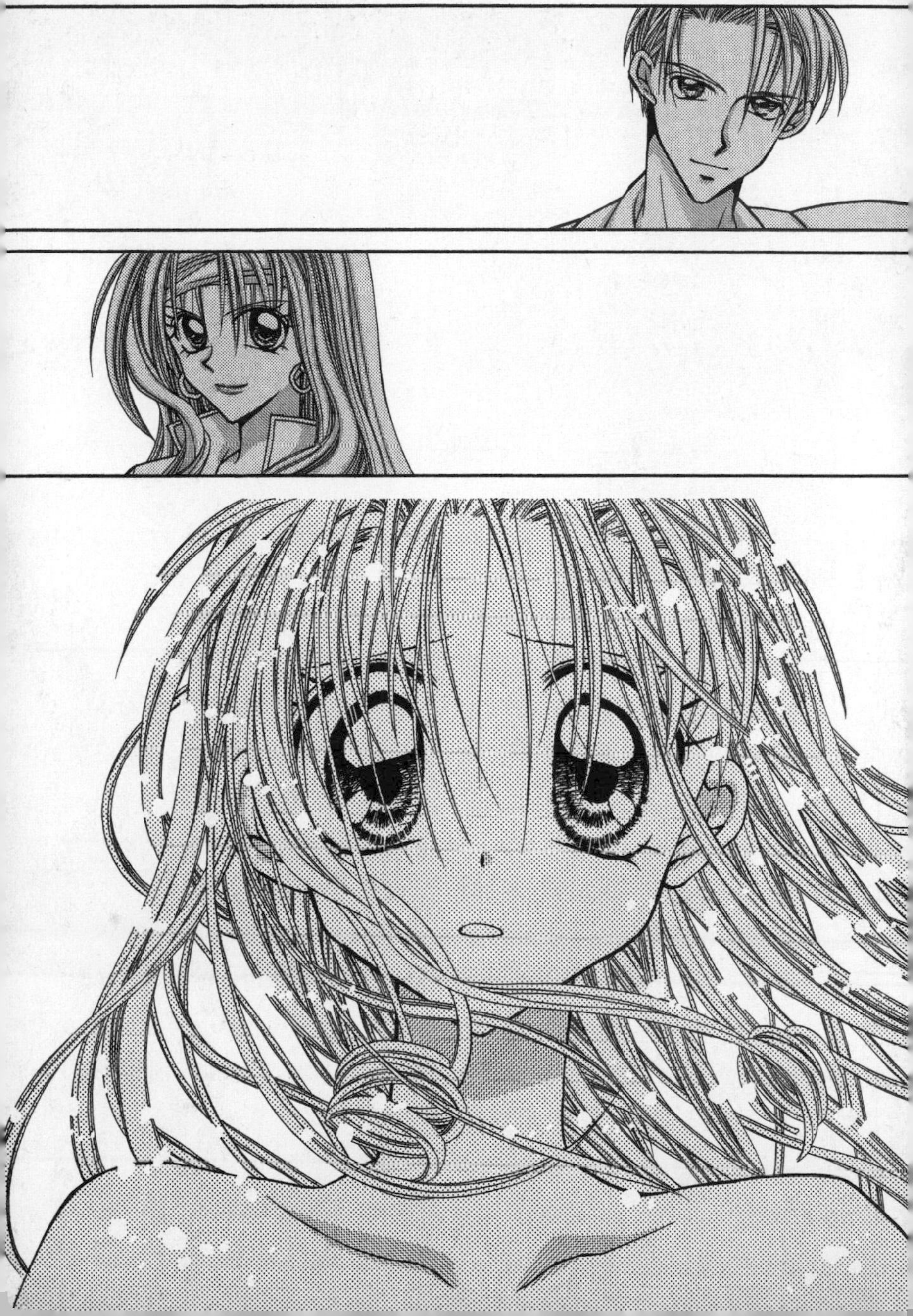

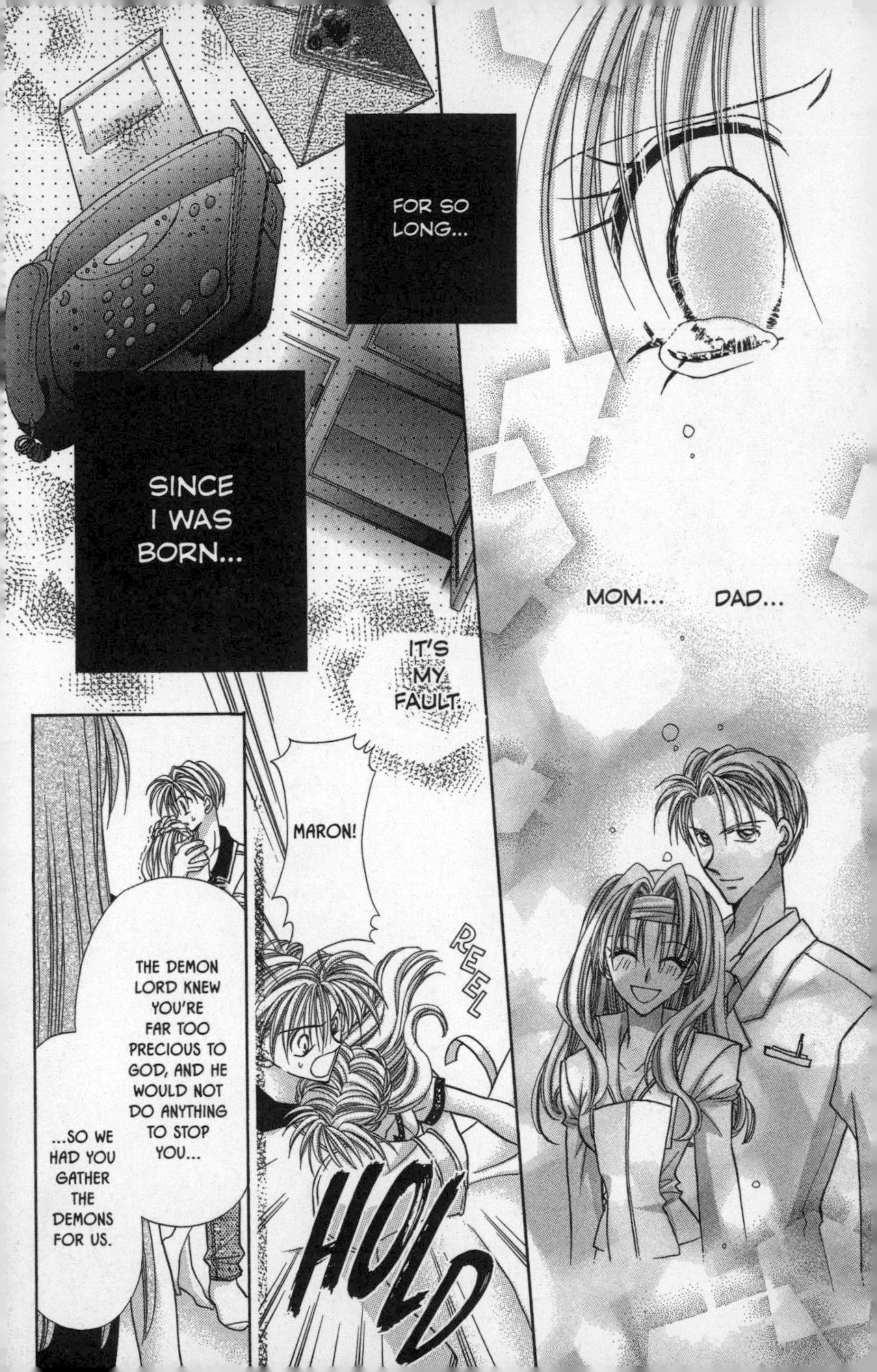
MOM... DAD...
FOR SO LONG...
SINCE I WAS BORN...
IT'S MY FAULT.
MARON!
REEL
HOLD
THE DEMON LORD KNEW YOU'RE FAR TOO PRECIOUS TO GOD, AND HE WOULD NOT DO ANYTHING TO STOP YOU...
...SO WE HAD YOU GATHER THE DEMONS FOR US.

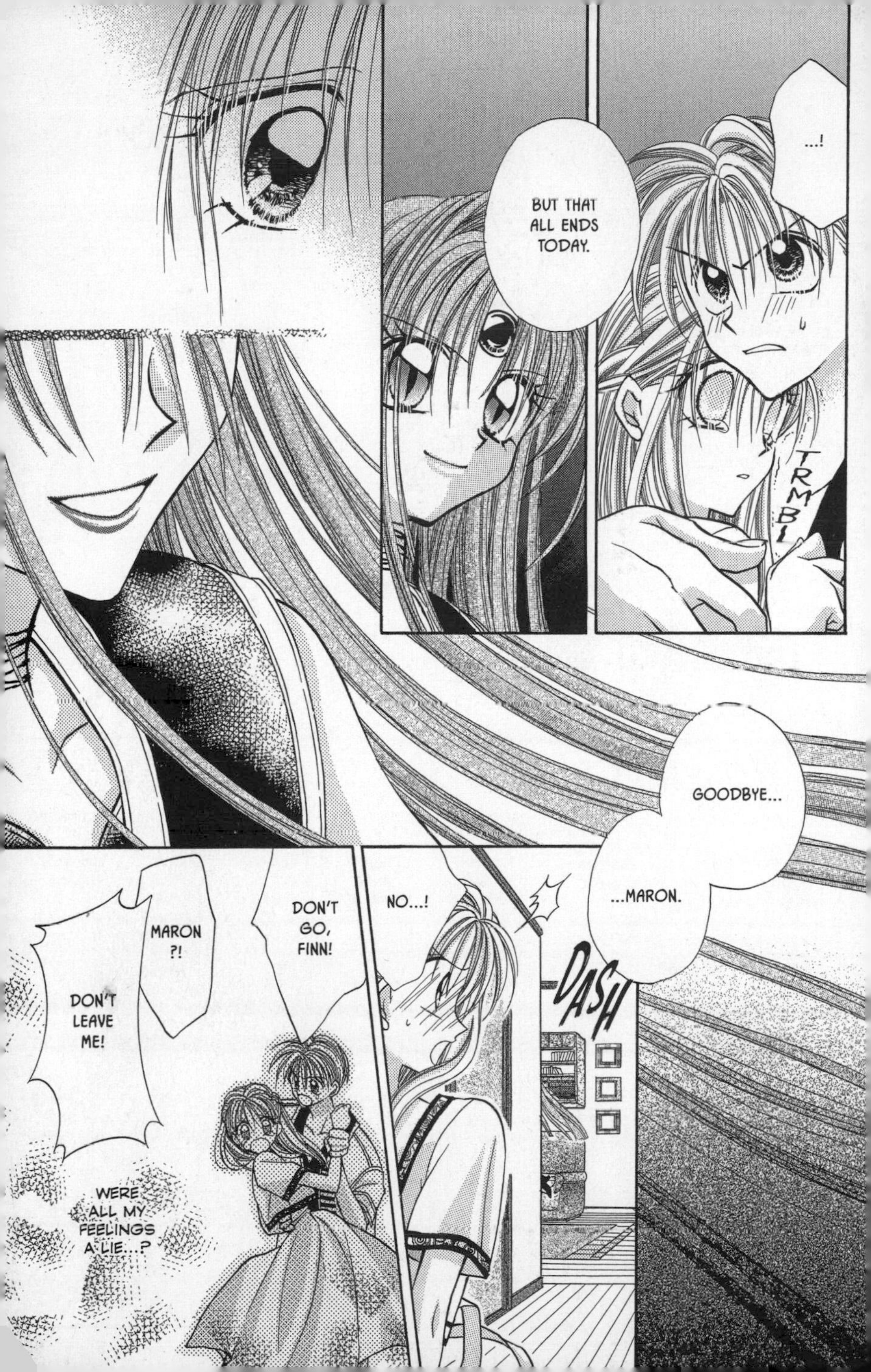
...!
BUT THAT ALL ENDS TODAY.
TRMBL
GOODBYE...
...MARON.
DASH
NO...!
DON'T GO, FINN!
MARON ?!
DON'T LEAVE ME!
WERE ALL MY FEELINGS A LIE...?

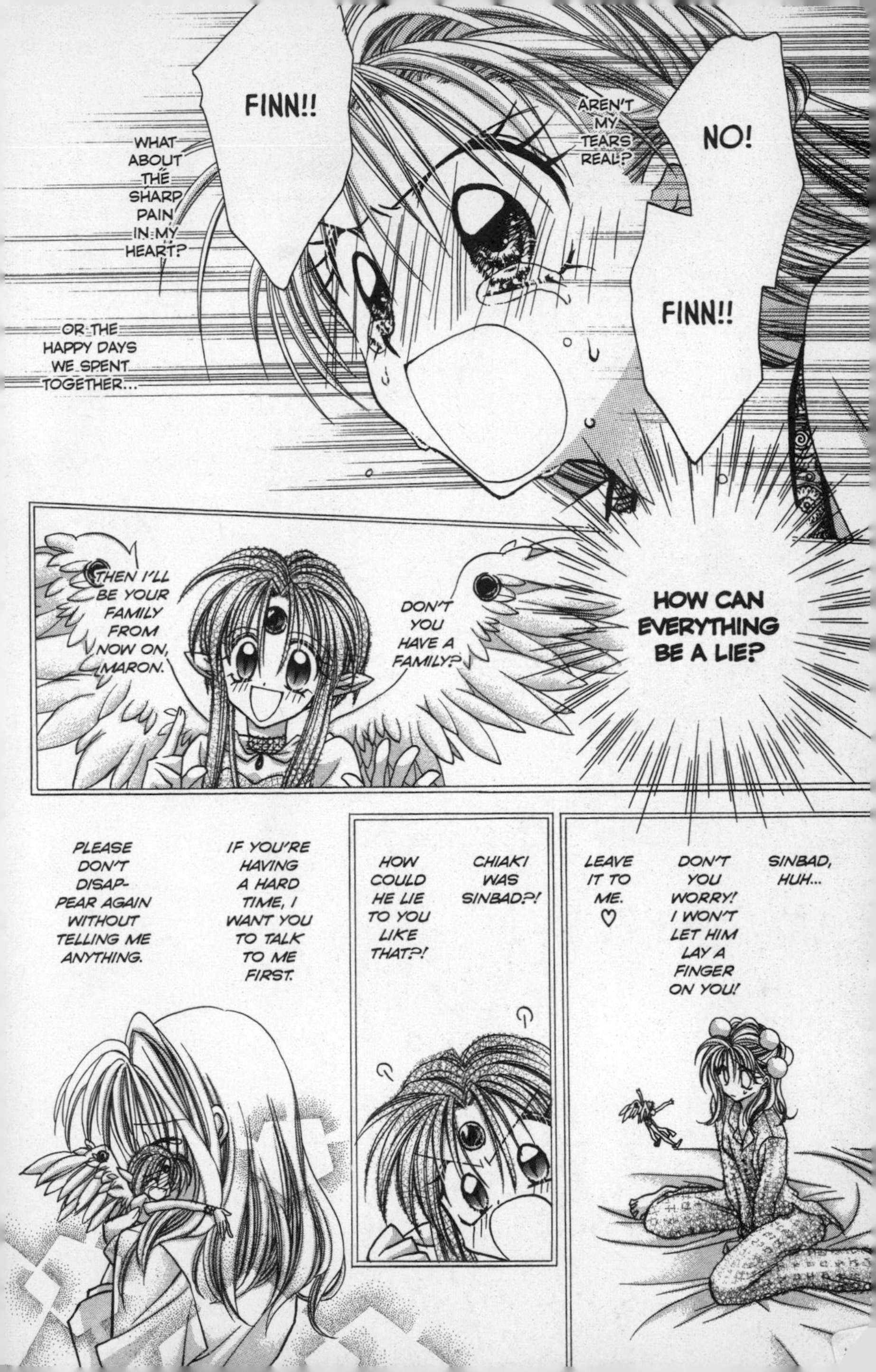
NO!
FINN!!
AREN'T MY TEARS REAL?
FINN!!
WHAT ABOUT THE SHARP PAIN IN MY HEART?
OR THE HAPPY DAYS WE SPENT TOGETHER...
HOW CAN EVERYTHING BE A LIE?
DON'T YOU HAVE A FAMILY?
THEN I'LL BE YOUR FAMILY FROM NOW ON, MARON.
SINBAD, HUH...
DON'T YOU WORRY! I WON'T LET HIM LAY A FINGER ON YOU!
LEAVE IT TO ME. ♡
CHIAKI WAS SINBAD?!
HOW COULD HE LIE TO YOU LIKE THAT?!
IF YOU'RE HAVING A HARD TIME, I WANT YOU TO TALK TO ME FIRST.
PLEASE DON'T DISAP-PEAR AGAIN WITHOUT TELLING ME ANYTHING.

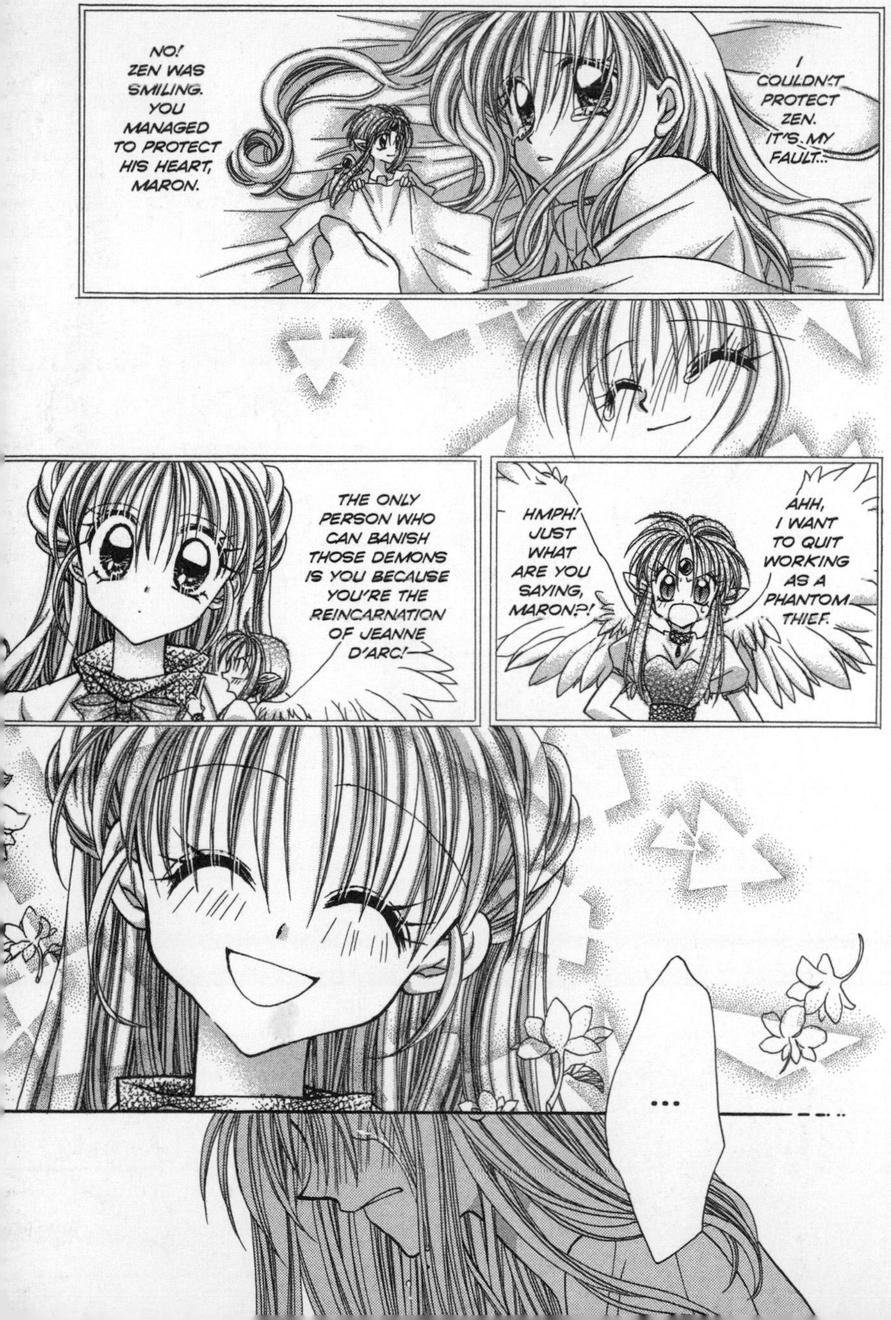
I COULDN'T PROTECT ZEN. IT'S MY FAULT...
NO! ZEN WAS SMILING. YOU MANAGED TO PROTECT HIS HEART, MARON.
AHH, I WANT TO QUIT WORKING AS A PHANTOM THIEF.
HMPH! JUST WHAT ARE YOU SAYING, MARON?!
THE ONLY PERSON WHO CAN BANISH THOSE DEMONS IS YOU BECAUSE YOU'RE THE REINCARNATION OF JEANNE D'ARC!
...

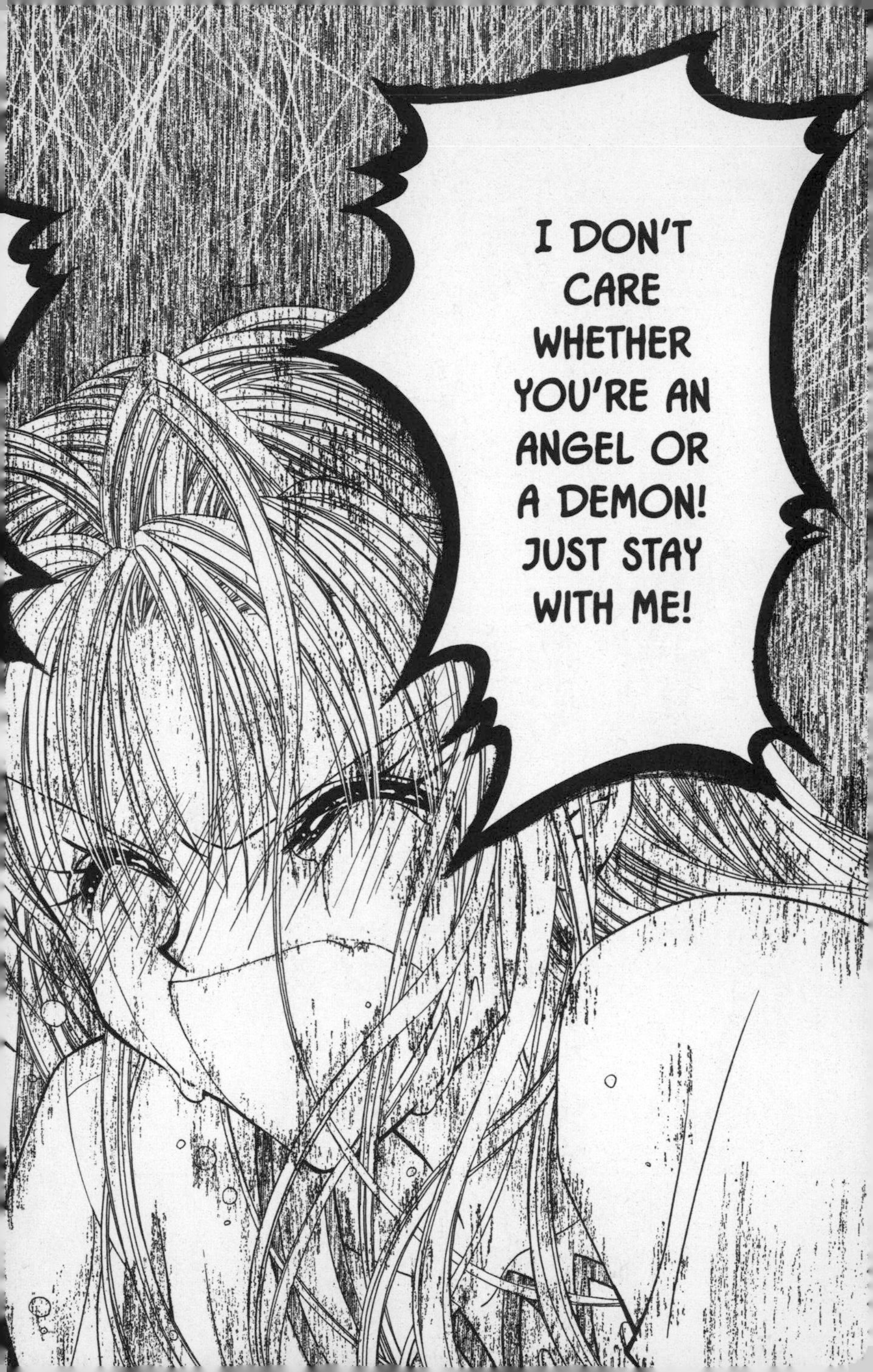
I DON'T CARE WHETHER YOU'RE AN ANGEL OR A DEMON! JUST STAY WITH ME!

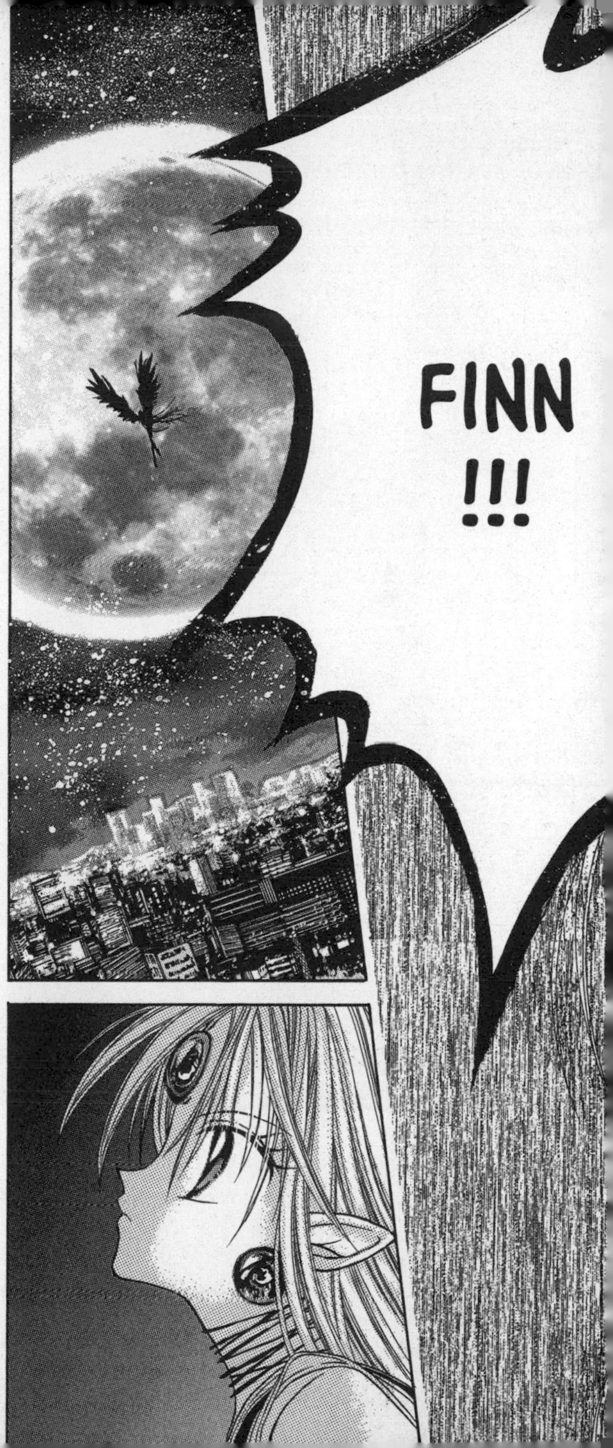
FINN !!!

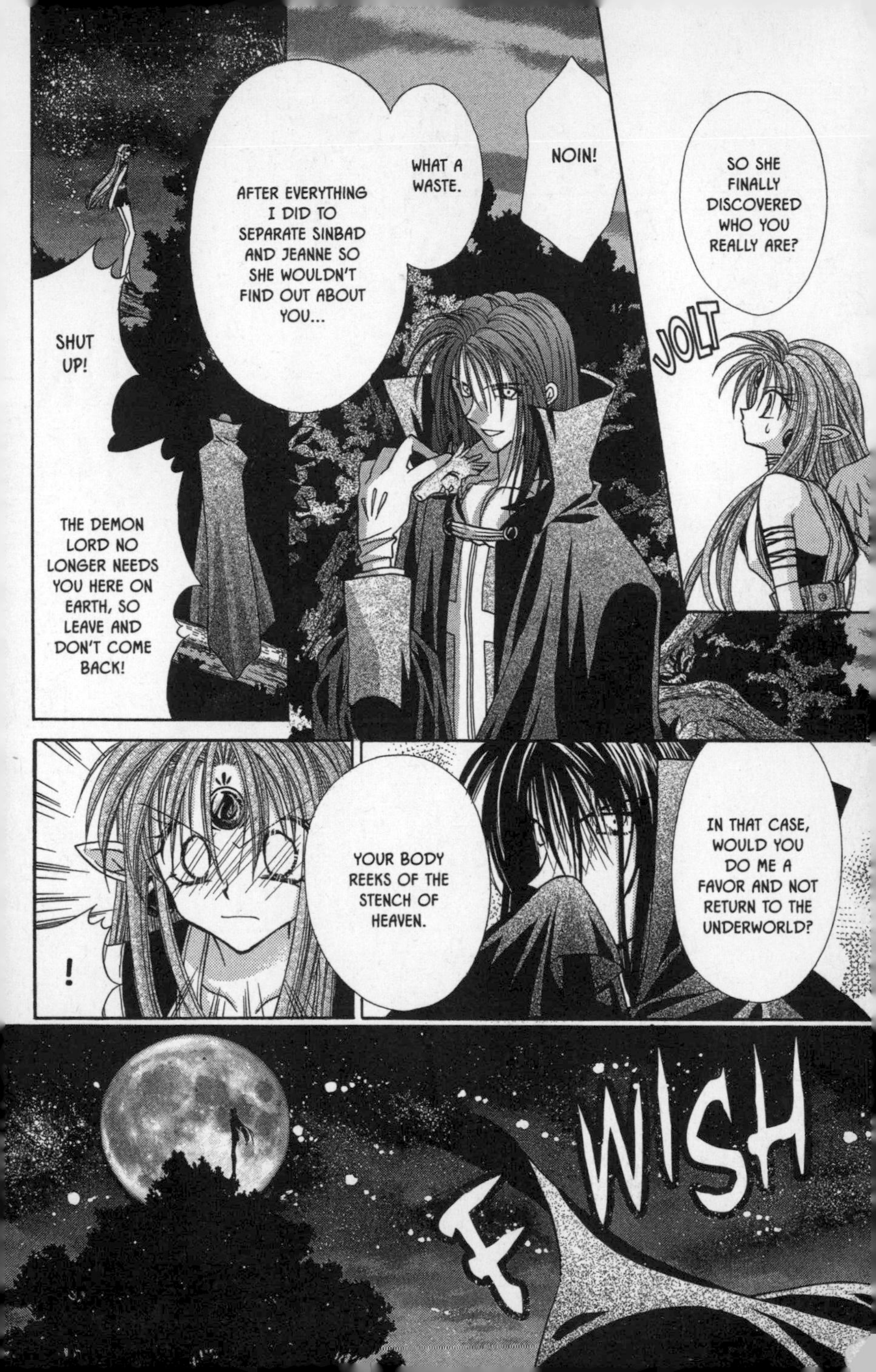
SO SHE FINALLY DISCOVERED WHO YOU REALLY ARE?
JOLT
NOIN!
WHAT A WASTE.
AFTER EVERYTHING I DID TO SEPARATE SINBAD AND JEANNE SO SHE WOULDN'T FIND OUT ABOUT YOU...
SHUT UP!
THE DEMON LORD NO LONGER NEEDS YOU HERE ON EARTH, SO LEAVE AND DON'T COME BACK!
IN THAT CASE, WOULD YOU DO ME A FAVOR AND NOT RETURN TO THE UNDERWORLD?
YOUR BODY REEKS OF THE STENCH OF HEAVEN.
!
I WISH

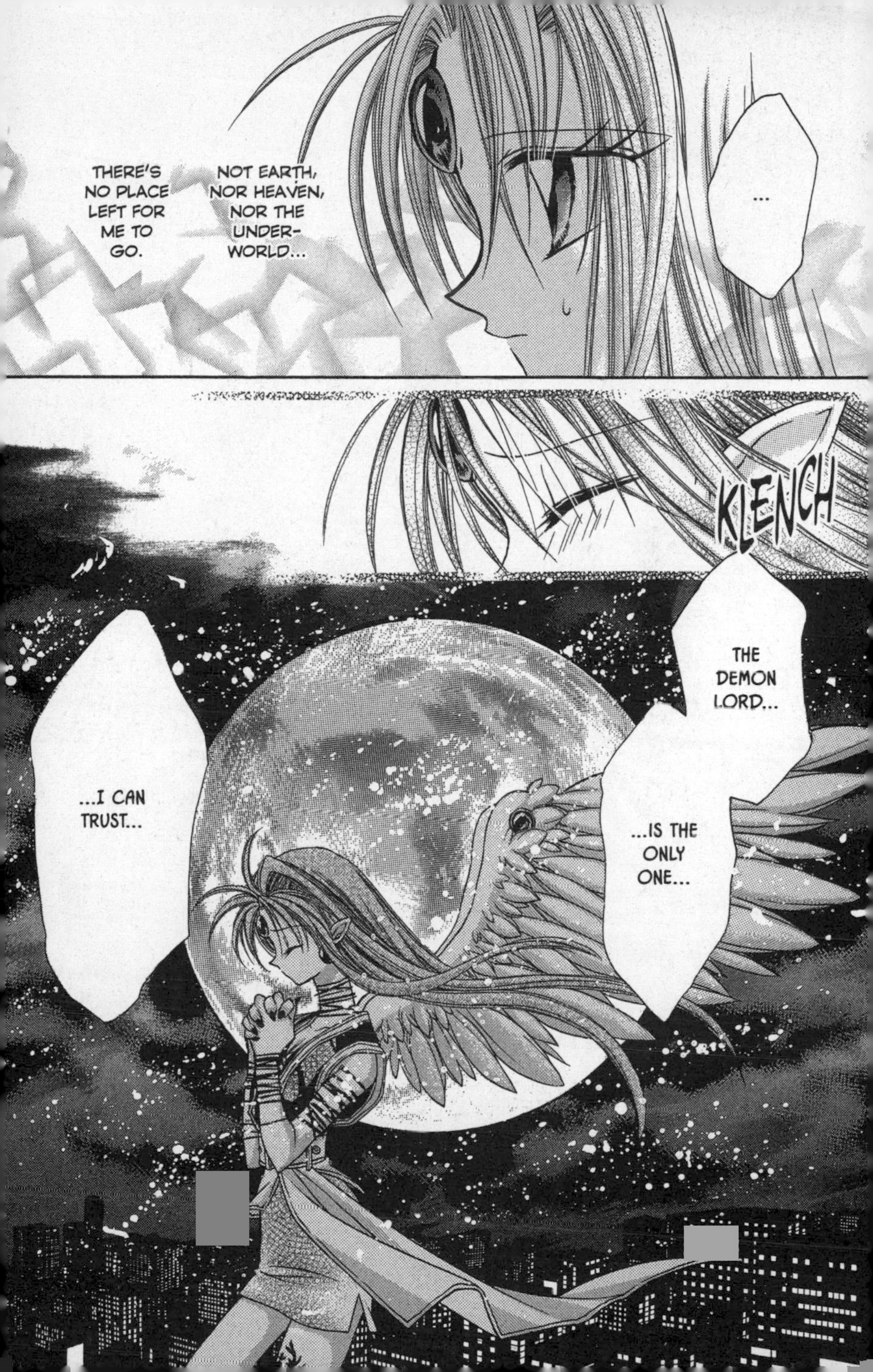
...
NOT EARTH, NOR HEAVEN, NOR THE UNDER-WORLD...
THERE'S NO PLACE LEFT FOR ME TO GO.
KLENCH
THE DEMON LORD...
...IS THE ONLY ONE...
...I CAN TRUST...

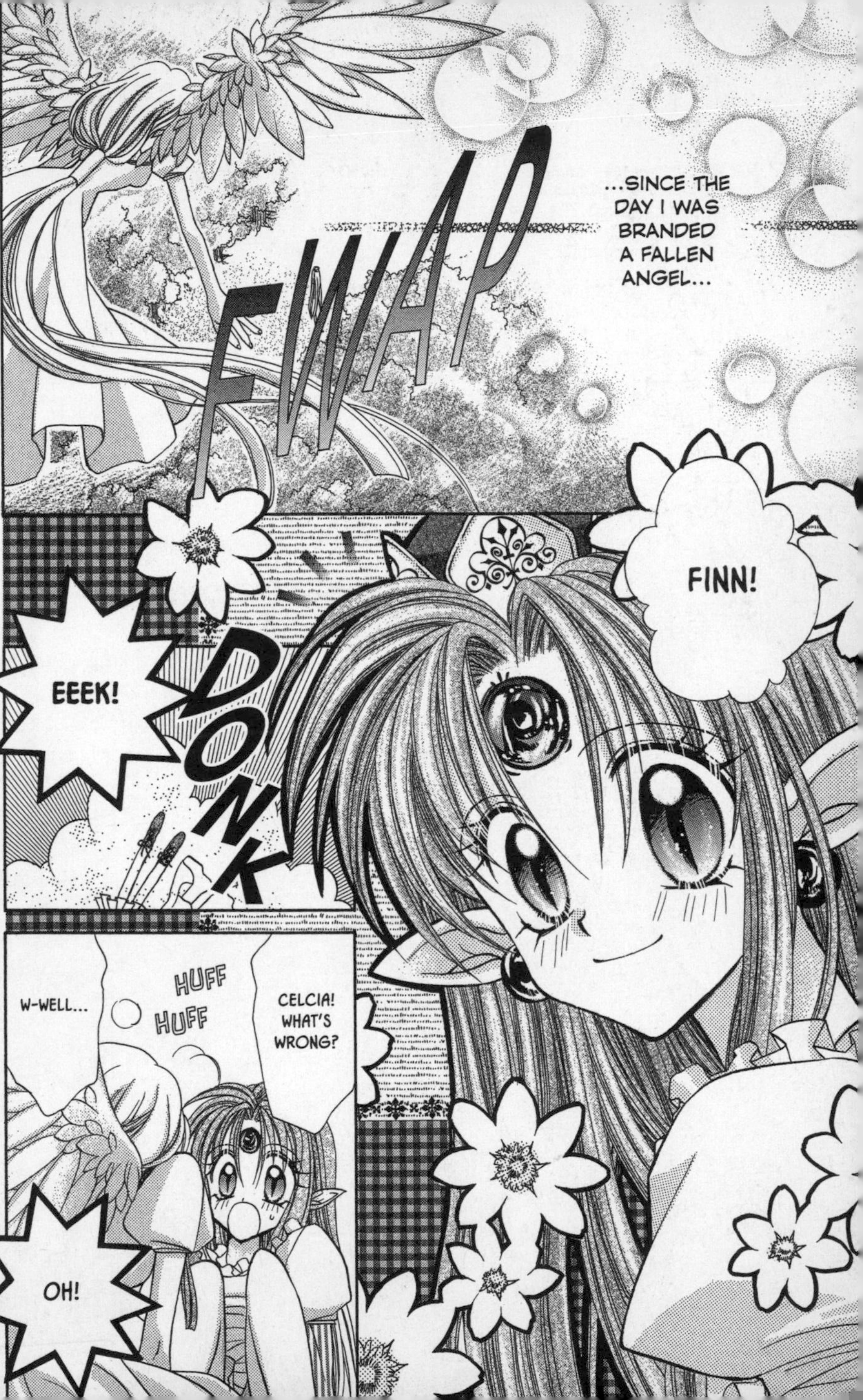
...SINCE THE DAY I WAS BRANDED A FALLEN ANGEL...
FWAP
FINN!
DONK
EEEK!
CELCIA! WHAT'S WRONG?
HUFF HUFF
W-WELL...
OH!

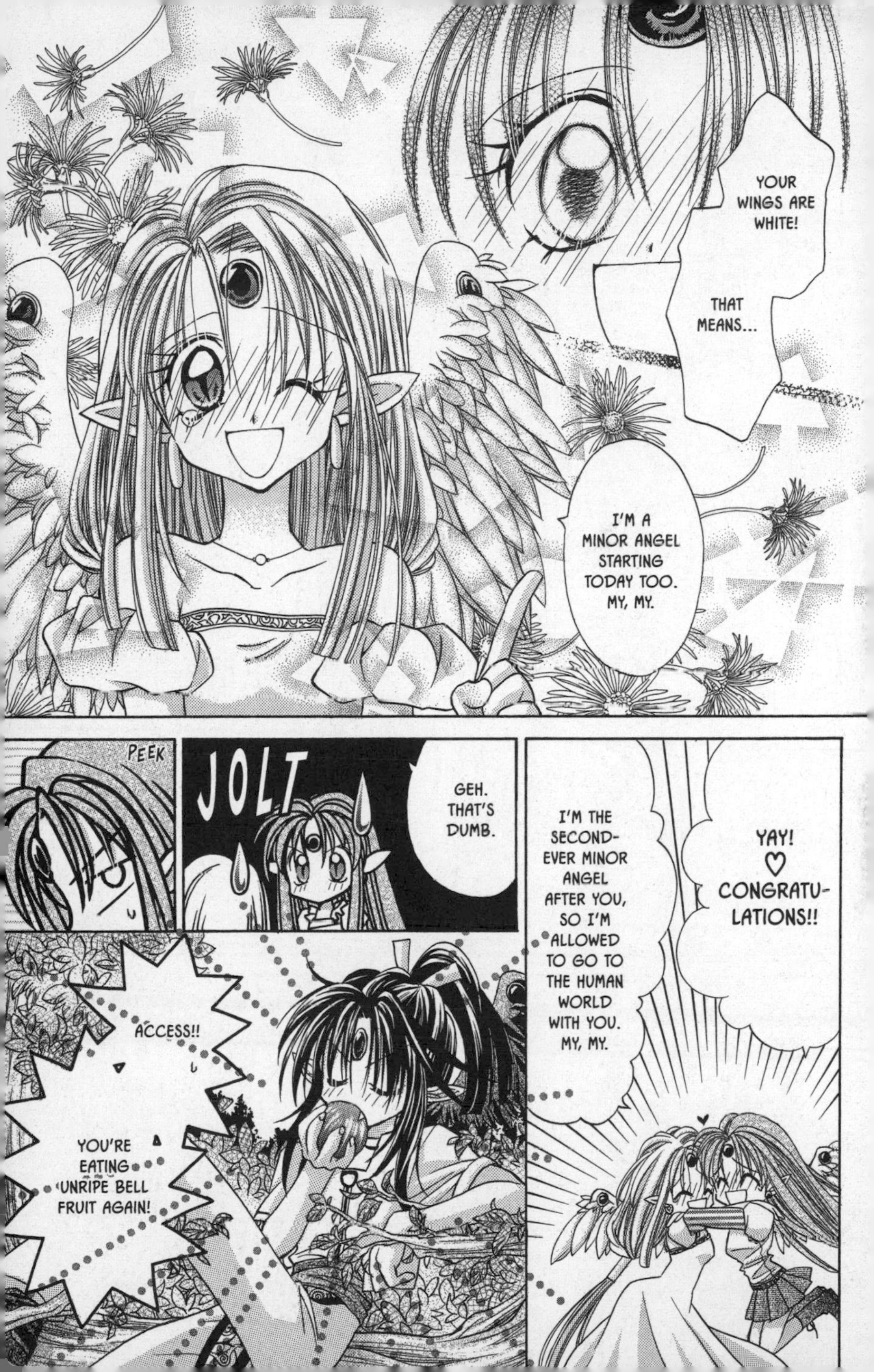
YOUR WINGS ARE WHITE!
THAT MEANS...
I'M A MINOR ANGEL STARTING TODAY TOO. MY, MY.
YAY! ♡ CONGRATULATIONS!!
I'M THE SECOND-EVER MINOR ANGEL AFTER YOU, SO I'M ALLOWED TO GO TO THE HUMAN WORLD WITH YOU. MY, MY.
GEH. THAT'S DUMB.
JOLT
PEEK
ACCESS!!
YOU'RE EATING UNRIPE BELL FRUIT AGAIN!

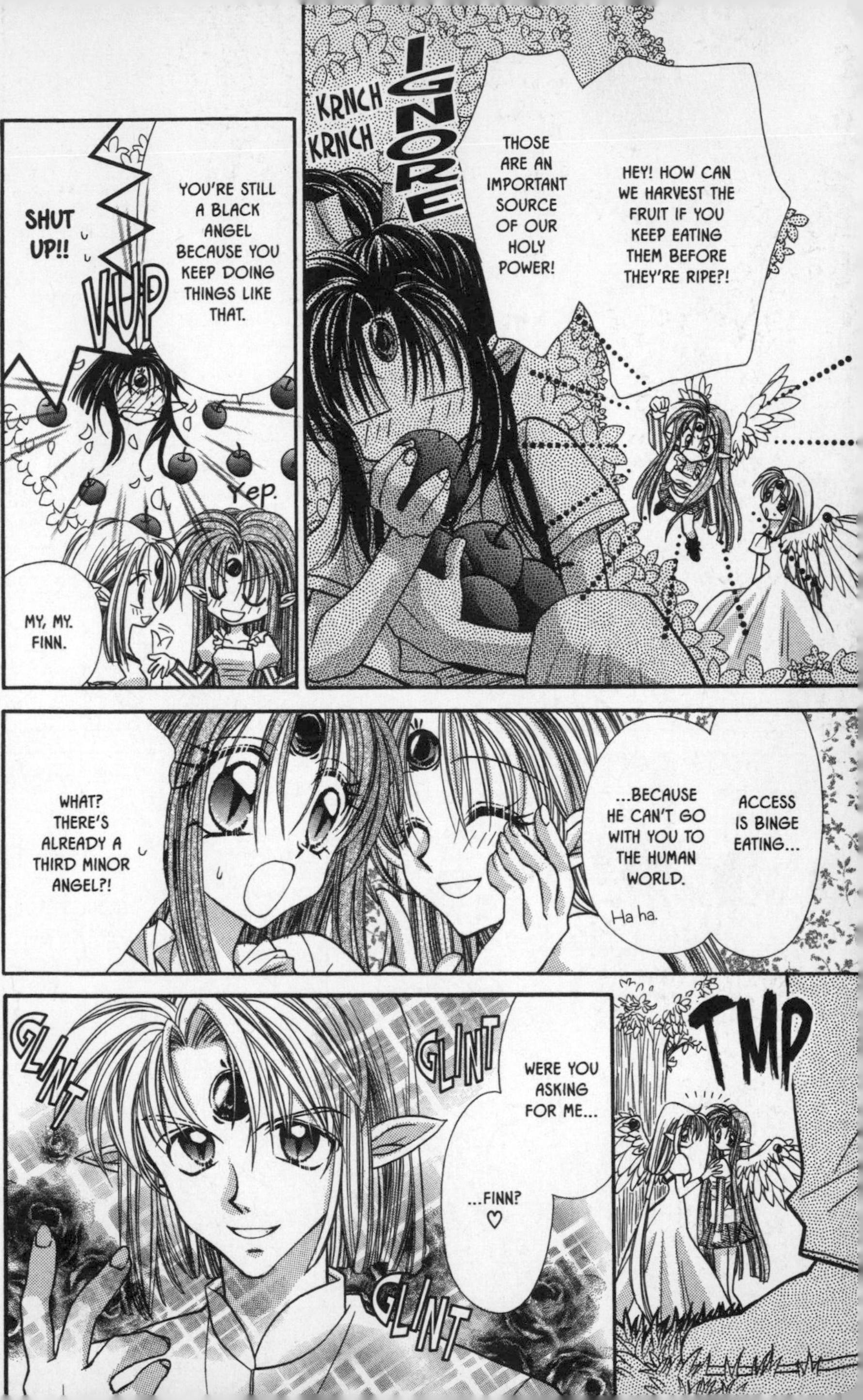
HEY! HOW CAN WE HARVEST THE FRUIT IF YOU KEEP EATING THEM BEFORE THEY'RE RIPE?!
THOSE ARE AN IMPORTANT SOURCE OF OUR HOLY POWER!
IGNORE
KRNCH KRNCH
YOU'RE STILL A BLACK ANGEL BECAUSE YOU KEEP DOING THINGS LIKE THAT.
SHUT UP!!
VWIP
Yep.
MY, MY. FINN.
ACCESS IS BINGE EATING...
...BECAUSE HE CAN'T GO WITH YOU TO THE HUMAN WORLD.
Ha ha.
WHAT? THERE'S ALREADY A THIRD MINOR ANGEL?!
TMP
WERE YOU ASKING FOR ME...
...FINN? ♡
GLINT
GLINT
GLINT

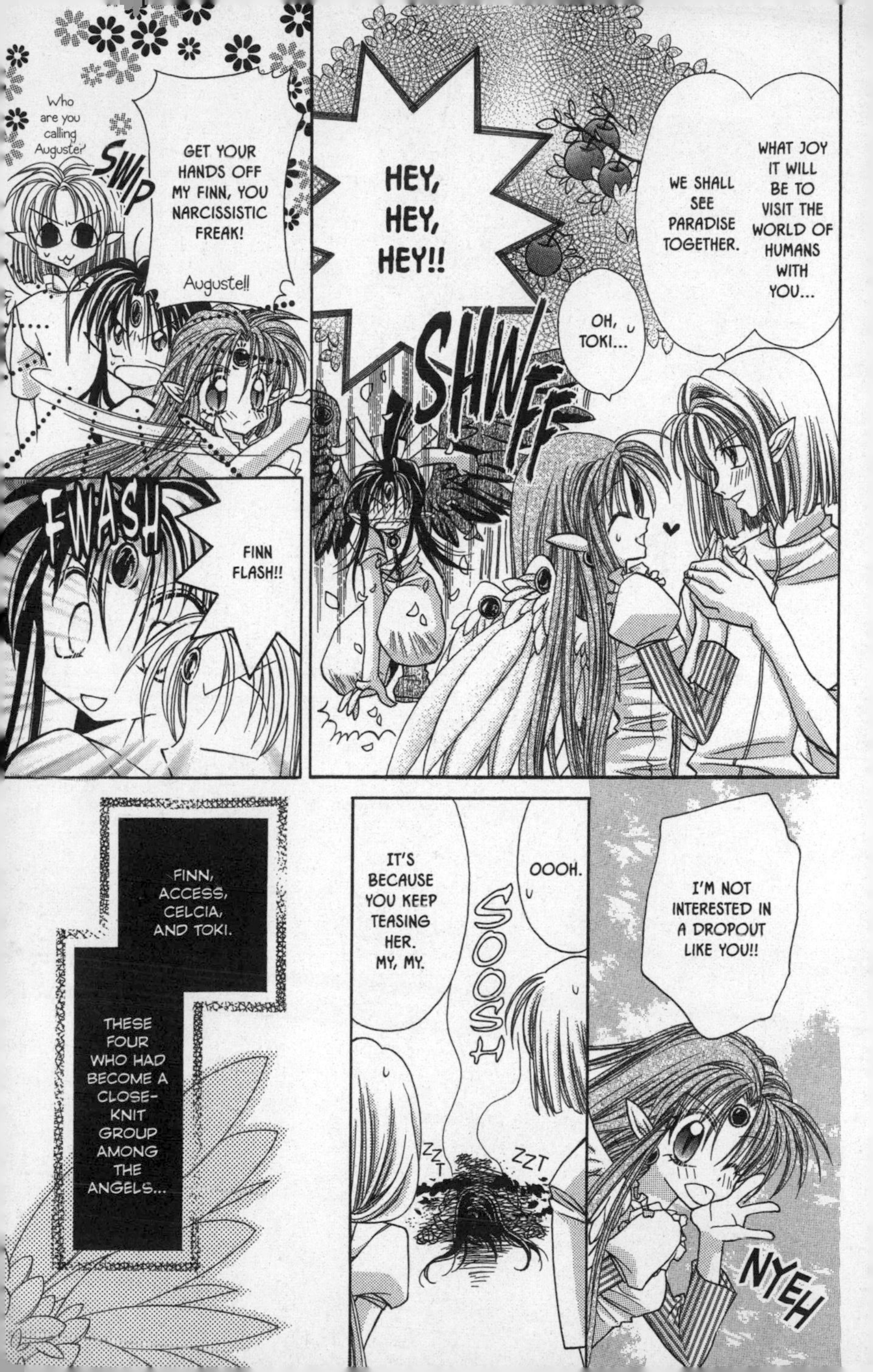
WHAT JOY IT WILL BE TO VISIT THE WORLD OF HUMANS WITH YOU...
WE SHALL SEE PARADISE TOGETHER.
OH, TOKI...
HEY, HEY, HEY!!
SHWFF
GET YOUR HANDS OFF MY FINN, YOU NARCISSISTIC FREAK!
Augustel!
Who are you calling Auguste?
SWIP
FWASH
FINN FLASH!!
I'M NOT INTERESTED IN A DROPOUT LIKE YOU!!
NYEH
OOOH.
SOOOSH
IT'S BECAUSE YOU KEEP TEASING HER. MY, MY.
ZZT
ZZT
FINN, ACCESS, CELCIA, AND TOKI.
THESE FOUR WHO HAD BECOME A CLOSE-KNIT GROUP AMONG THE ANGELS...

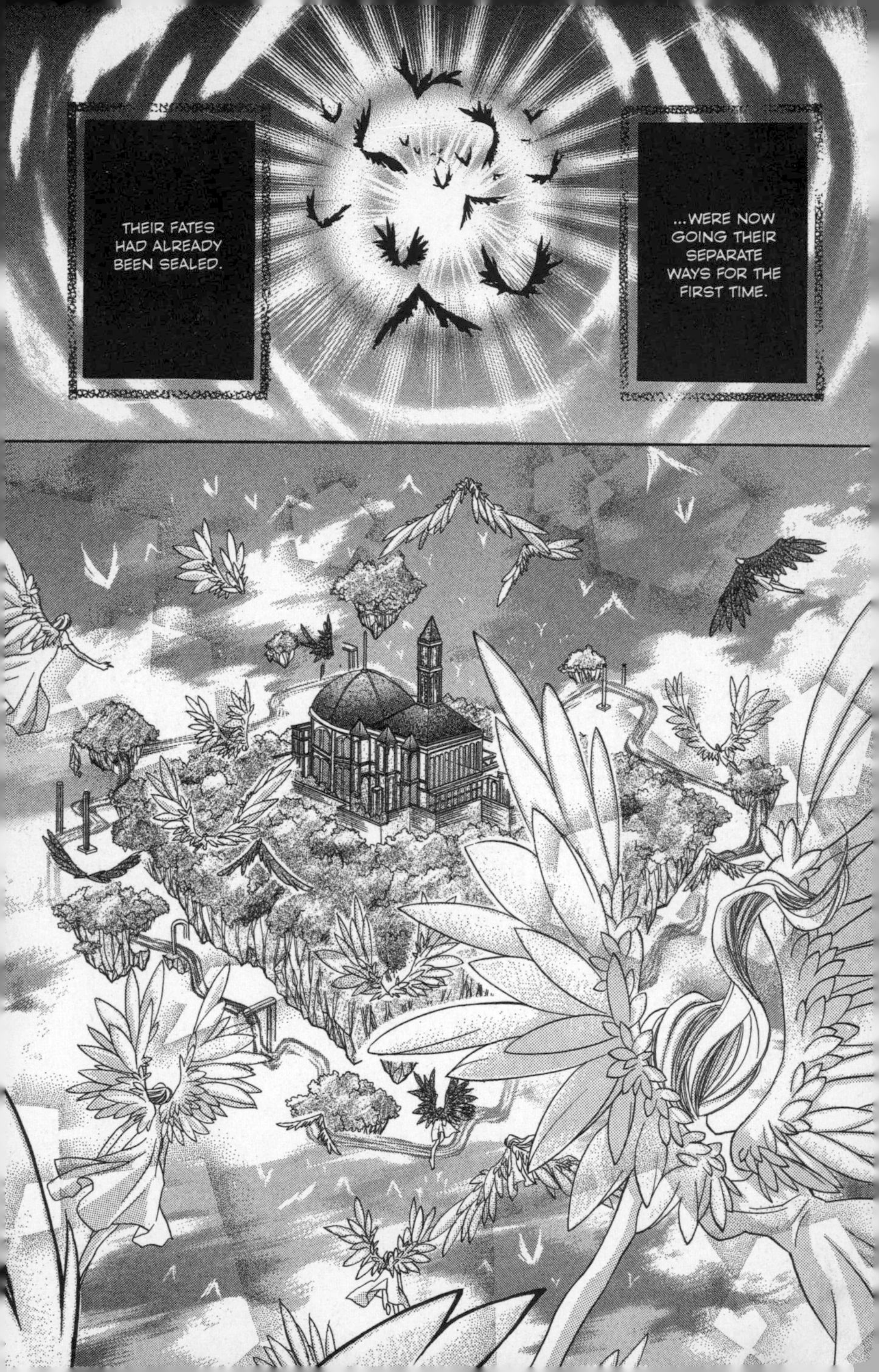
...WERE NOW GOING THEIR SEPARATE WAYS FOR THE FIRST TIME.
THEIR FATES HAD ALREADY BEEN SEALED.

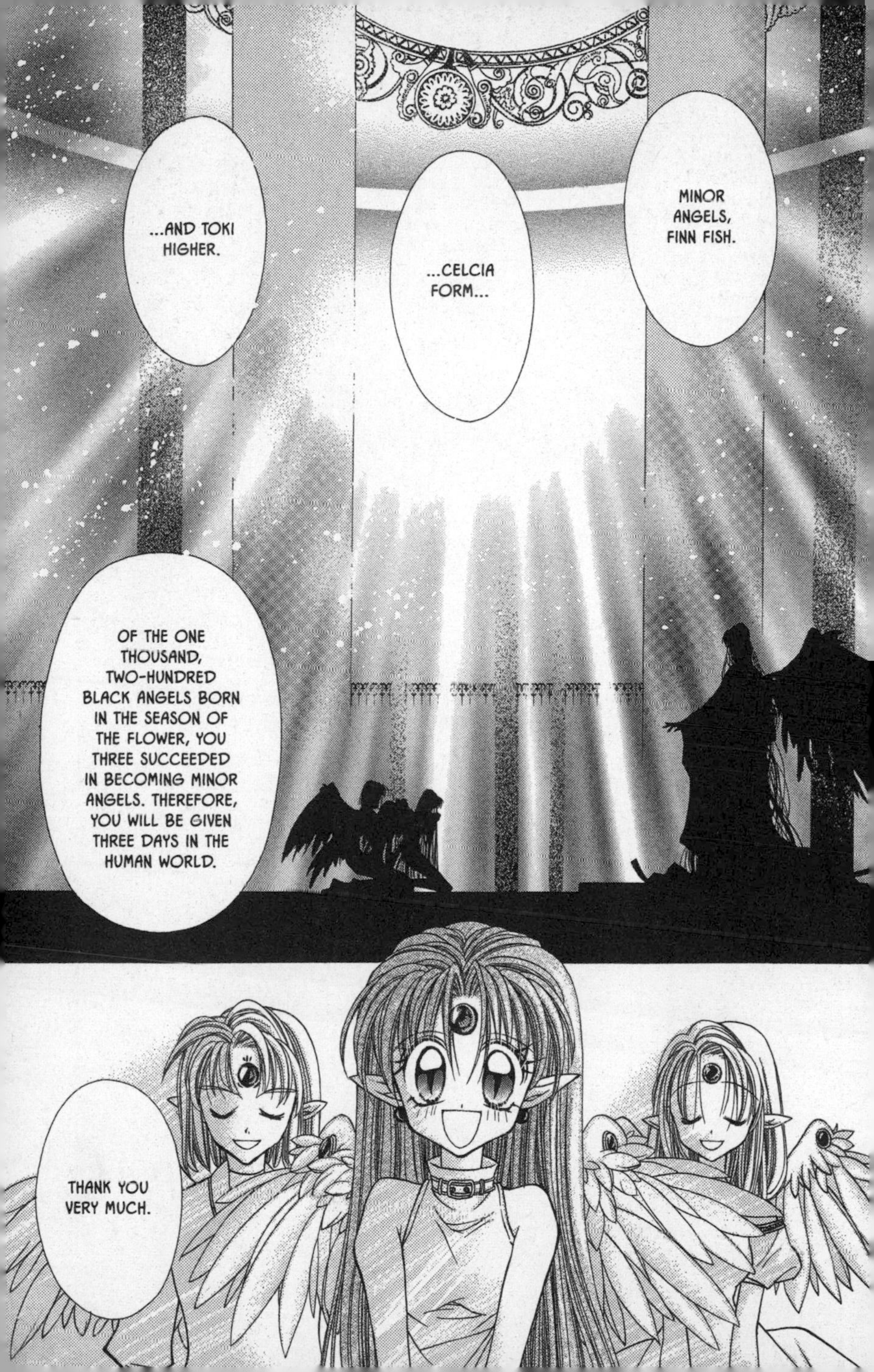

MINOR ANGELS, FINN FISH.
...CELCIA FORM...
...AND TOKI HIGHER.
OF THE ONE THOUSAND, TWO-HUNDRED BLACK ANGELS BORN IN THE SEASON OF THE FLOWER, YOU THREE SUCCEEDED IN BECOMING MINOR ANGELS. THEREFORE, YOU WILL BE GIVEN THREE DAYS IN THE HUMAN WORLD.
THANK YOU VERY MUCH.

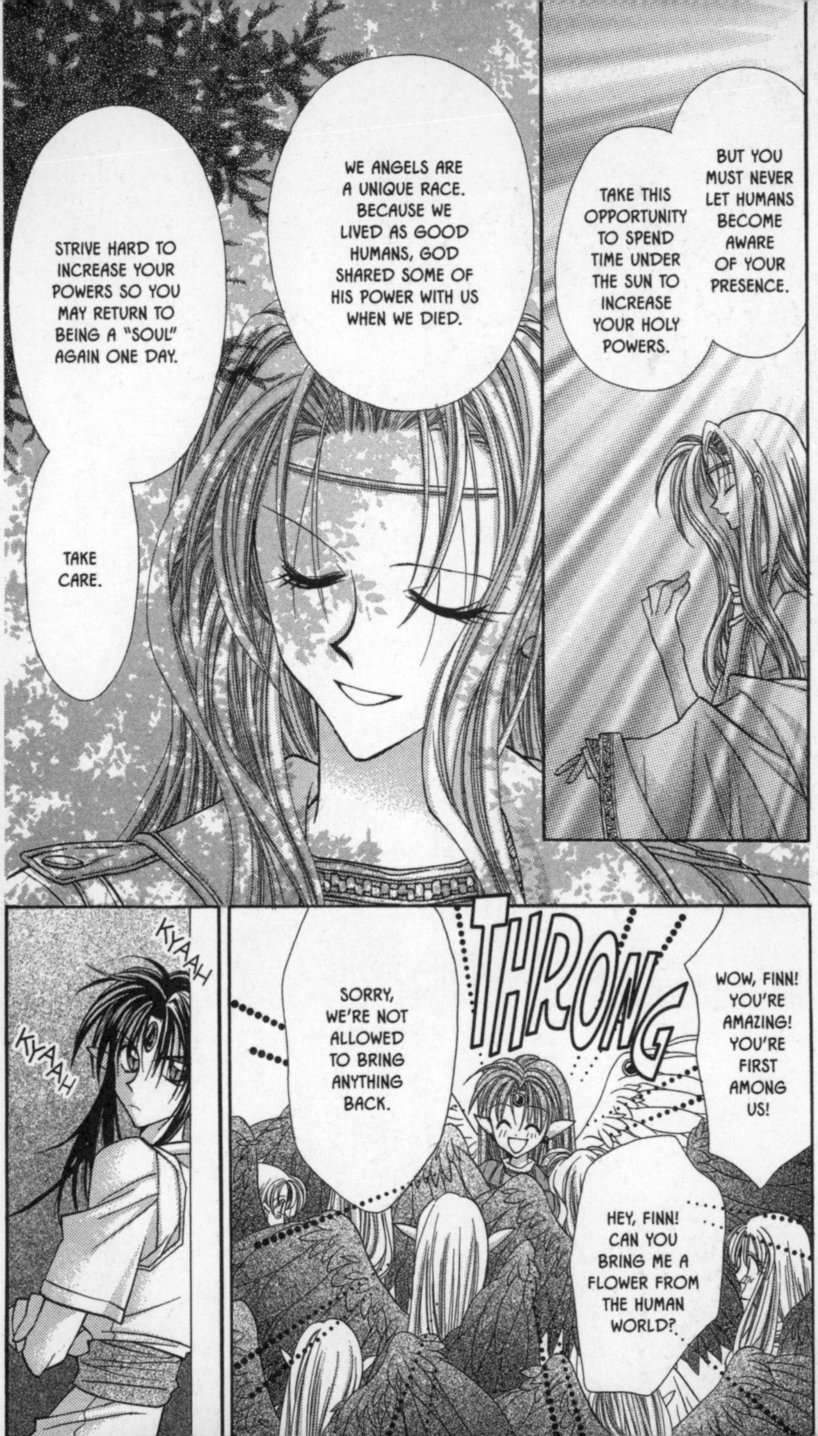
TAKE THIS OPPORTUNITY TO SPEND TIME UNDER THE SUN TO INCREASE YOUR HOLY POWERS.
BUT YOU MUST NEVER LET HUMANS BECOME AWARE OF YOUR PRESENCE.
WE ANGELS ARE A UNIQUE RACE. BECAUSE WE LIVED AS GOOD HUMANS, GOD SHARED SOME OF HIS POWER WITH US WHEN WE DIED.
STRIVE HARD TO INCREASE YOUR POWERS SO YOU MAY RETURN TO BEING A "SOUL" AGAIN ONE DAY.
TAKE CARE.
WOW, FINN! YOU'RE AMAZING! YOU'RE FIRST AMONG US!
THRONG
HEY, FINN! CAN YOU BRING ME A FLOWER FROM THE HUMAN WORLD?
SORRY, WE'RE NOT ALLOWED TO BRING ANYTHING BACK.
KYAAH
KYAAH

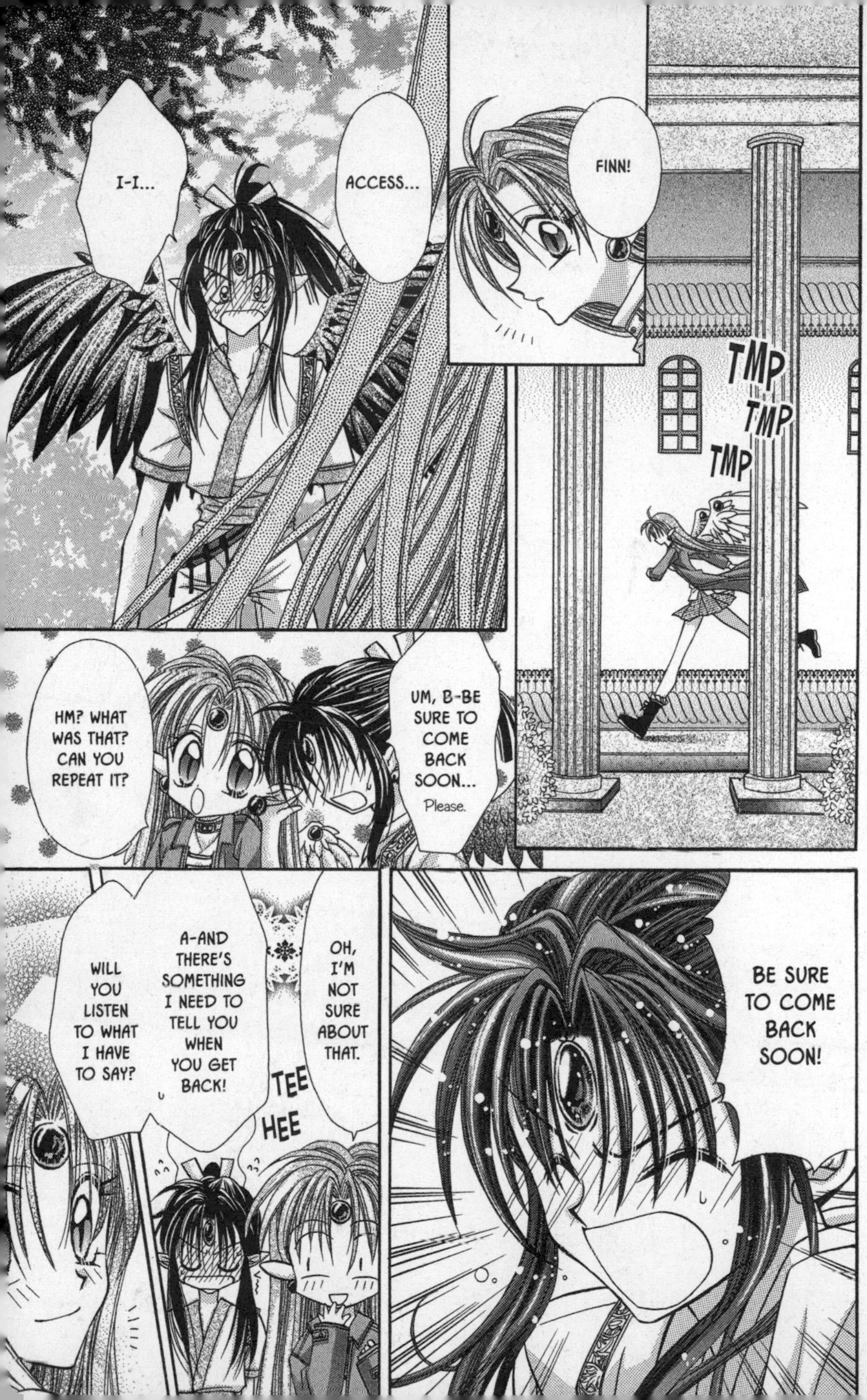
TMP TMP TMP
FINN!
ACCESS...
I-I...
UM, B-BE SURE TO COME BACK SOON... Please.
HM? WHAT WAS THAT? CAN YOU REPEAT IT?
BE SURE TO COME BACK SOON!
OH, I'M NOT SURE ABOUT THAT.
A-AND THERE'S SOMETHING I NEED TO TELL YOU WHEN YOU GET BACK!
WILL YOU LISTEN TO WHAT I HAVE TO SAY?
TEE HEE

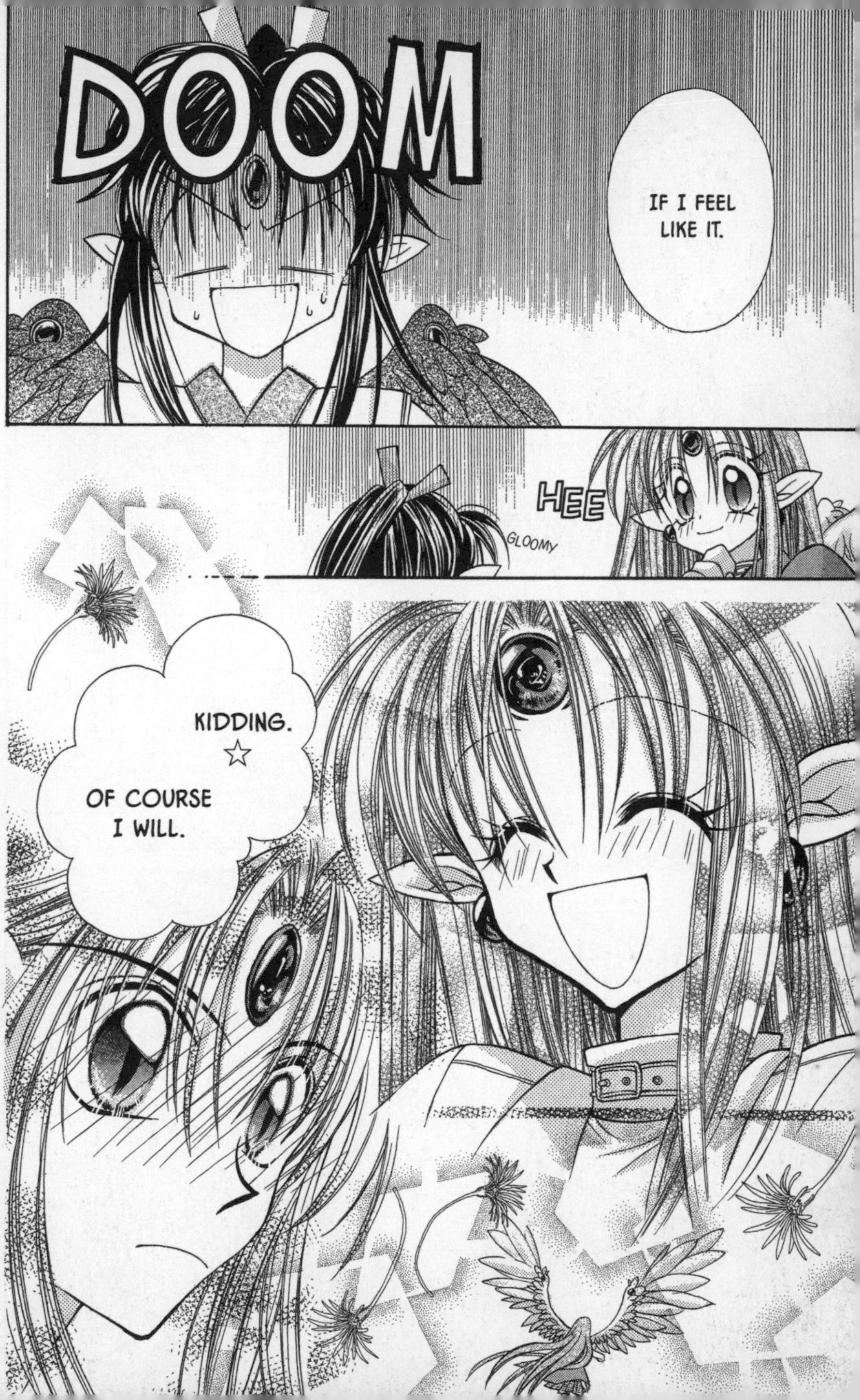
IF I FEEL LIKE IT.
DOOM
HEE
GLOOMY
KIDDING. ☆
OF COURSE I WILL.

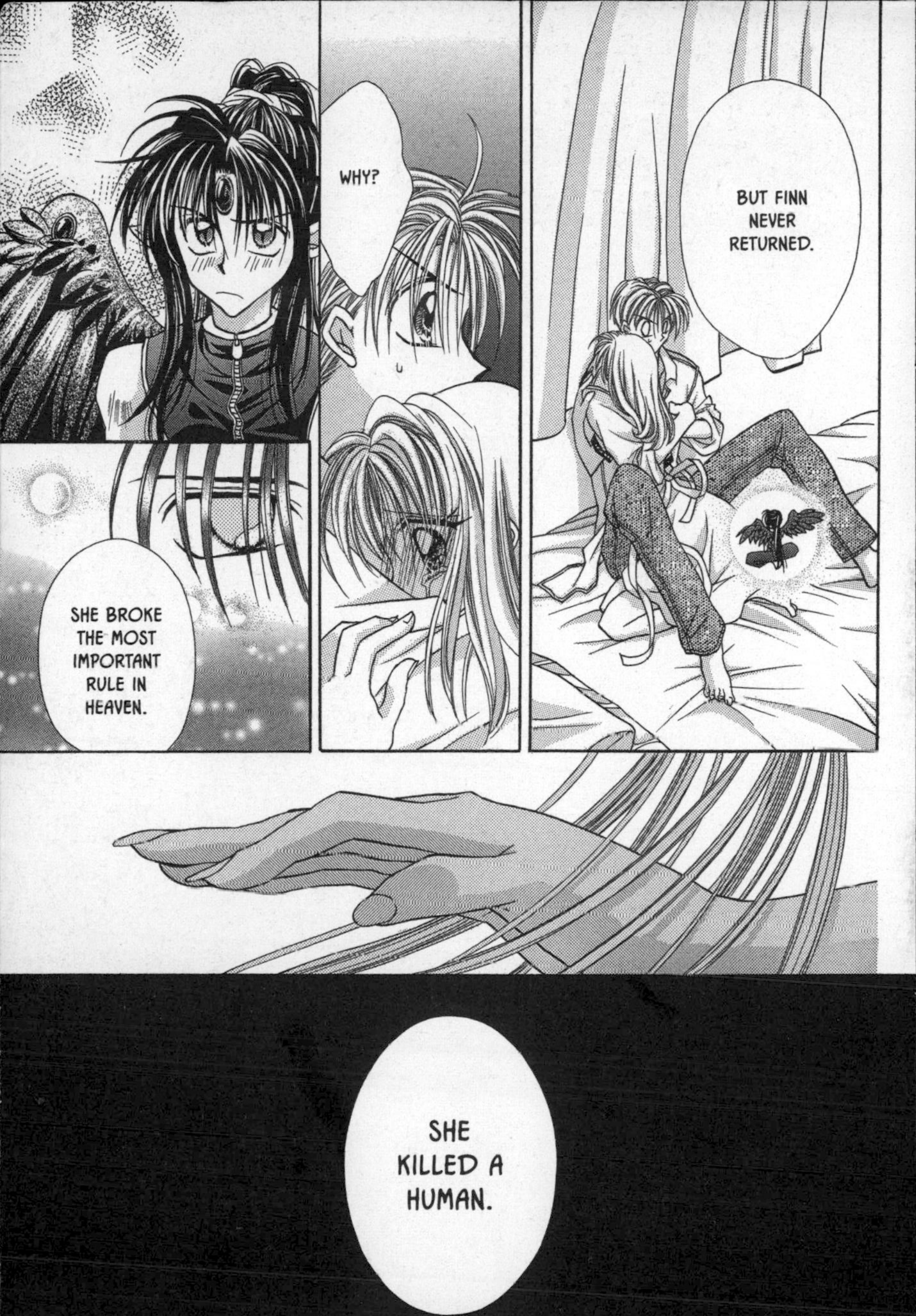
BUT FINN NEVER RETURNED.
WHY?
SHE BROKE THE MOST IMPORTANT RULE IN HEAVEN.
SHE KILLED A HUMAN.

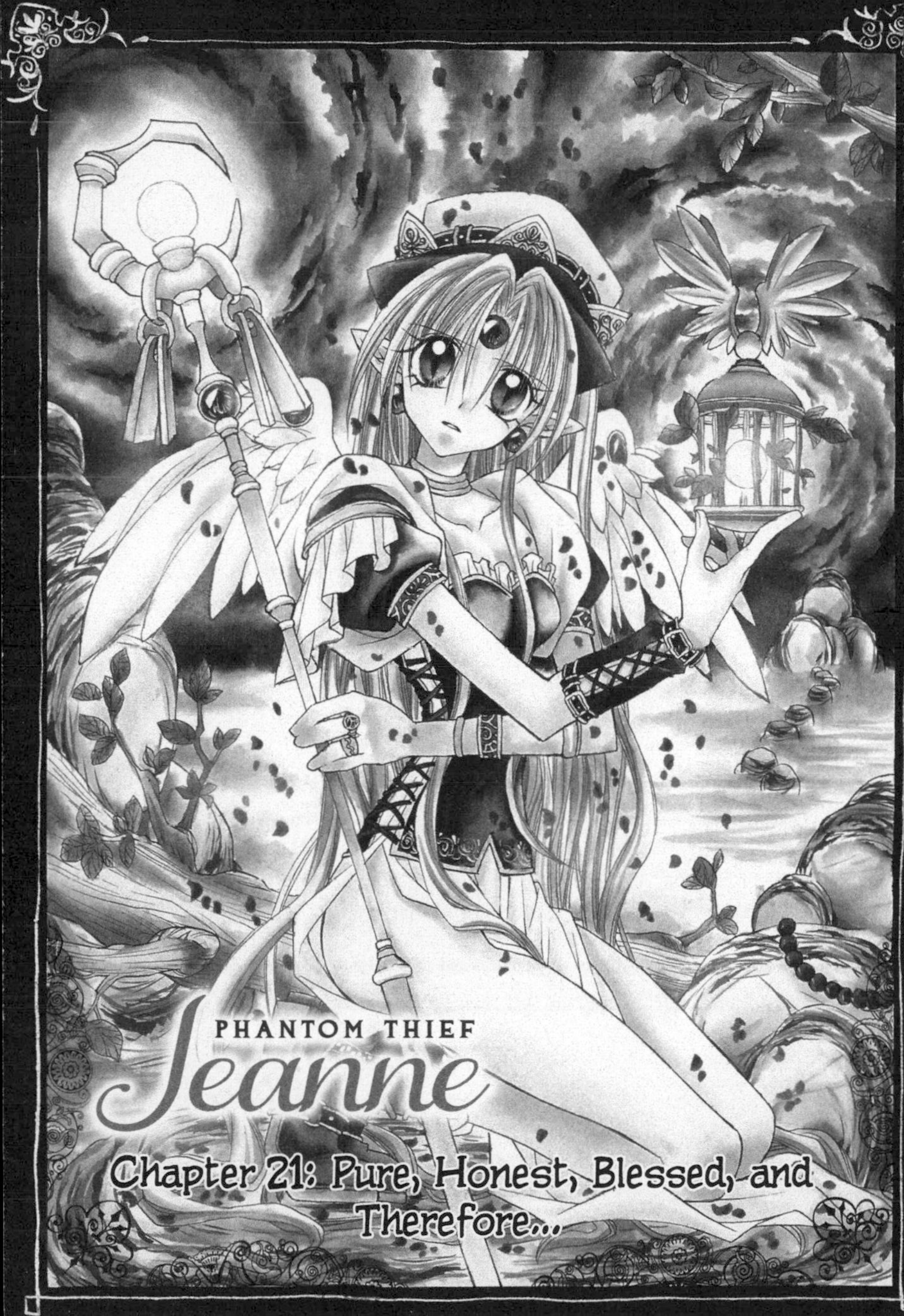
PHANTOM THIEF
Jeanne
Chapter 21: Pure, Honest, Blessed, and
Therefore...

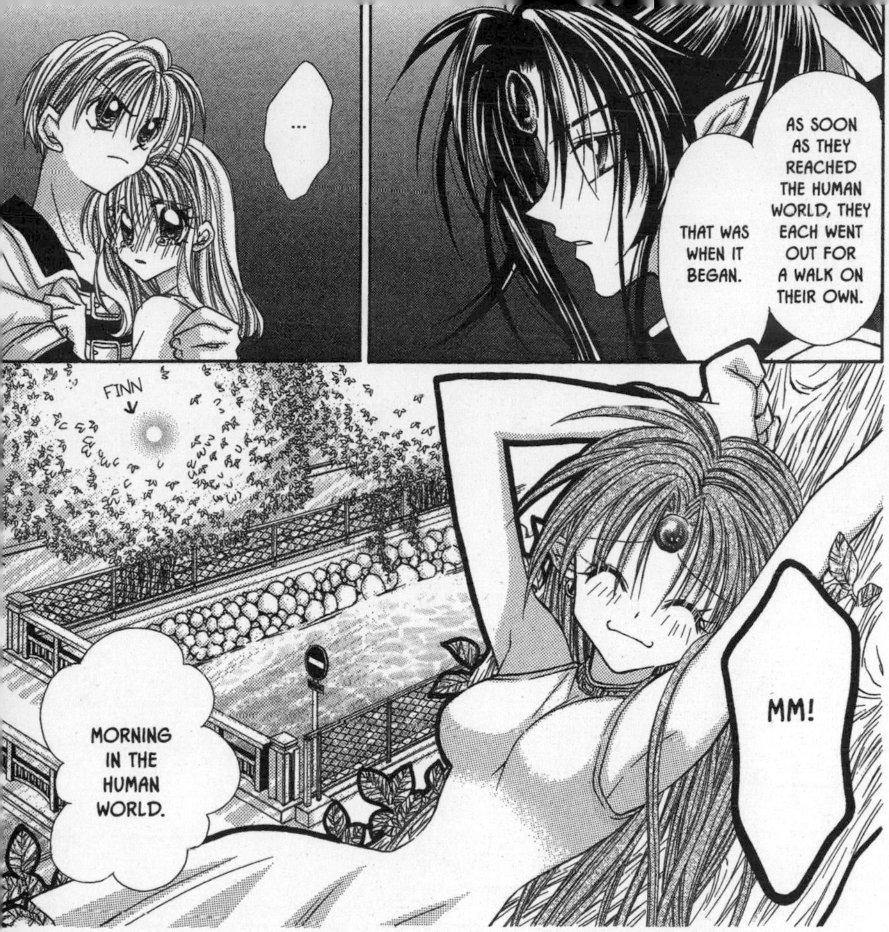
AS SOON AS THEY REACHED THE HUMAN WORLD, THEY EACH WENT OUT FOR A WALK ON THEIR OWN.
THAT WAS WHEN IT BEGAN.
...
MM!
FINN
MORNING IN THE HUMAN WORLD.

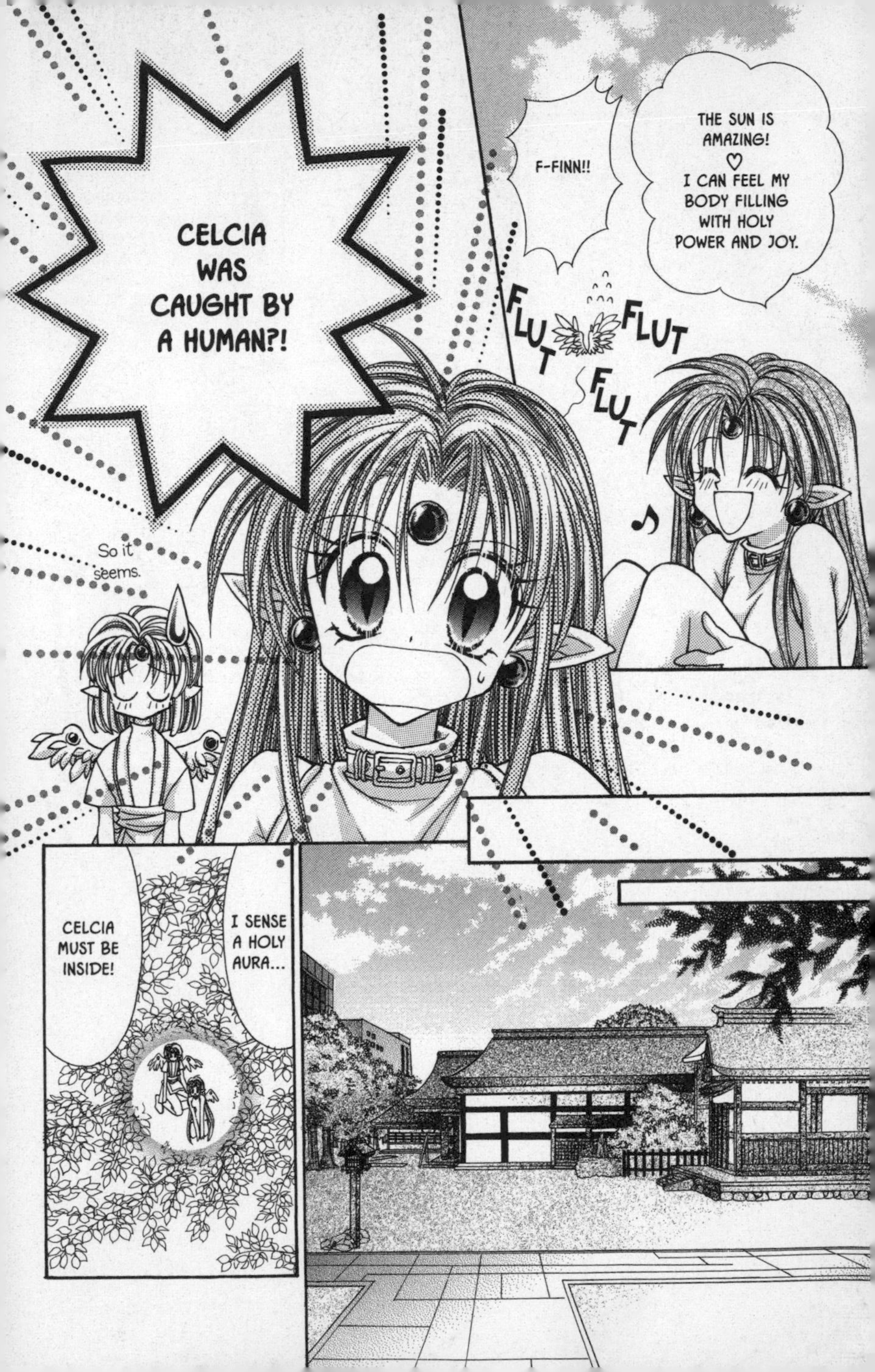
THE SUN IS AMAZING! ♡ I CAN FEEL MY BODY FILLING WITH HOLY POWER AND JOY.
F-FINN!!
FLUT FLUT FLUT
CELCIA WAS CAUGHT BY A HUMAN?!
So it seems.
I SENSE A HOLY AURA...
CELCIA MUST BE INSIDE!

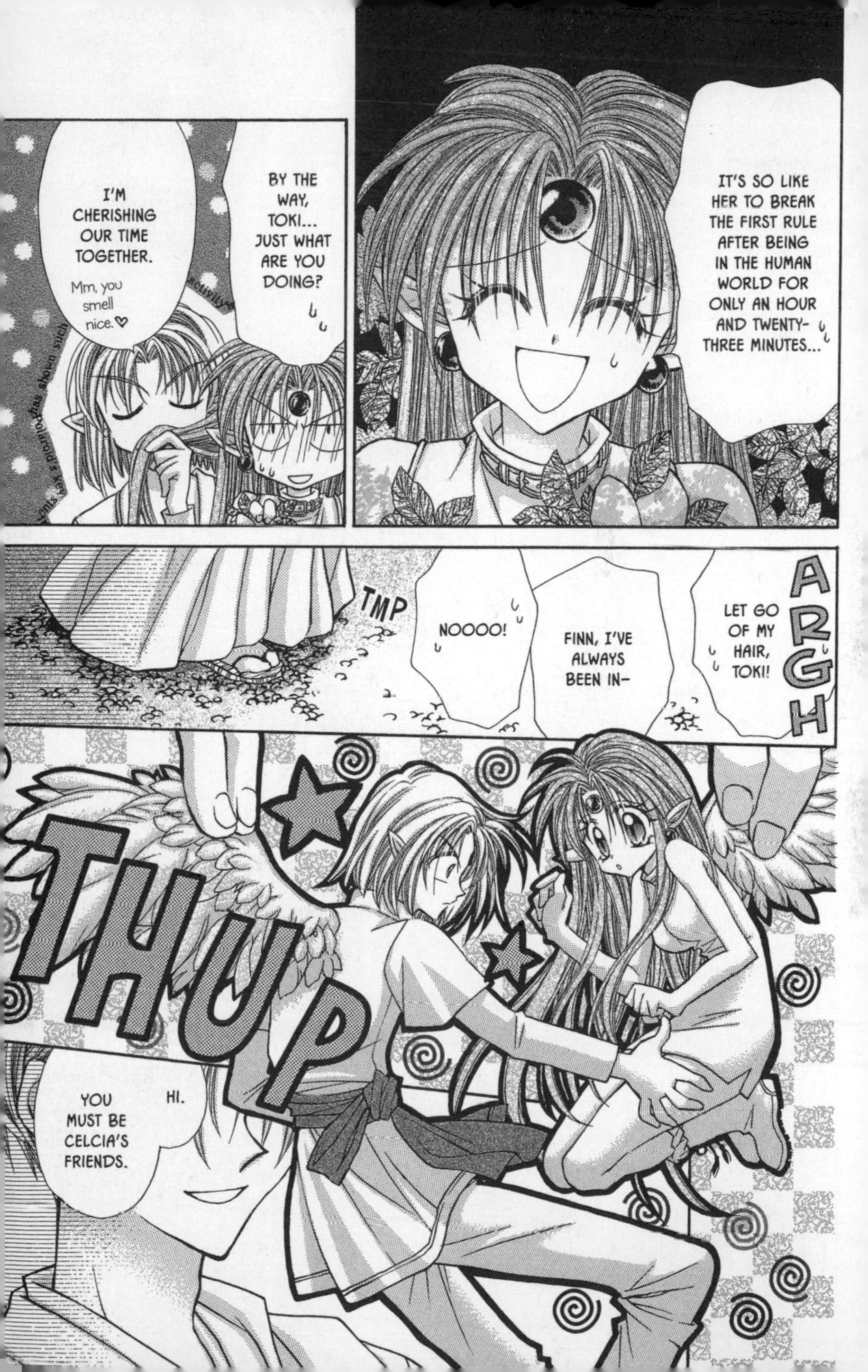
IT'S SO LIKE HER TO BREAK THE FIRST RULE AFTER BEING IN THE HUMAN WORLD FOR ONLY AN HOUR AND TWENTY-THREE MINUTES...
BY THE WAY, TOKI... JUST WHAT ARE YOU DOING?
I'M CHERISHING OUR TIME TOGETHER.
Mm, you smell nice.♥
ARGH
LET GO OF MY HAIR, TOKI!
FINN, I'VE ALWAYS BEEN IN-
NOOOO!
TMP
THUP
HI.
YOU MUST BE CELCIA'S FRIENDS.

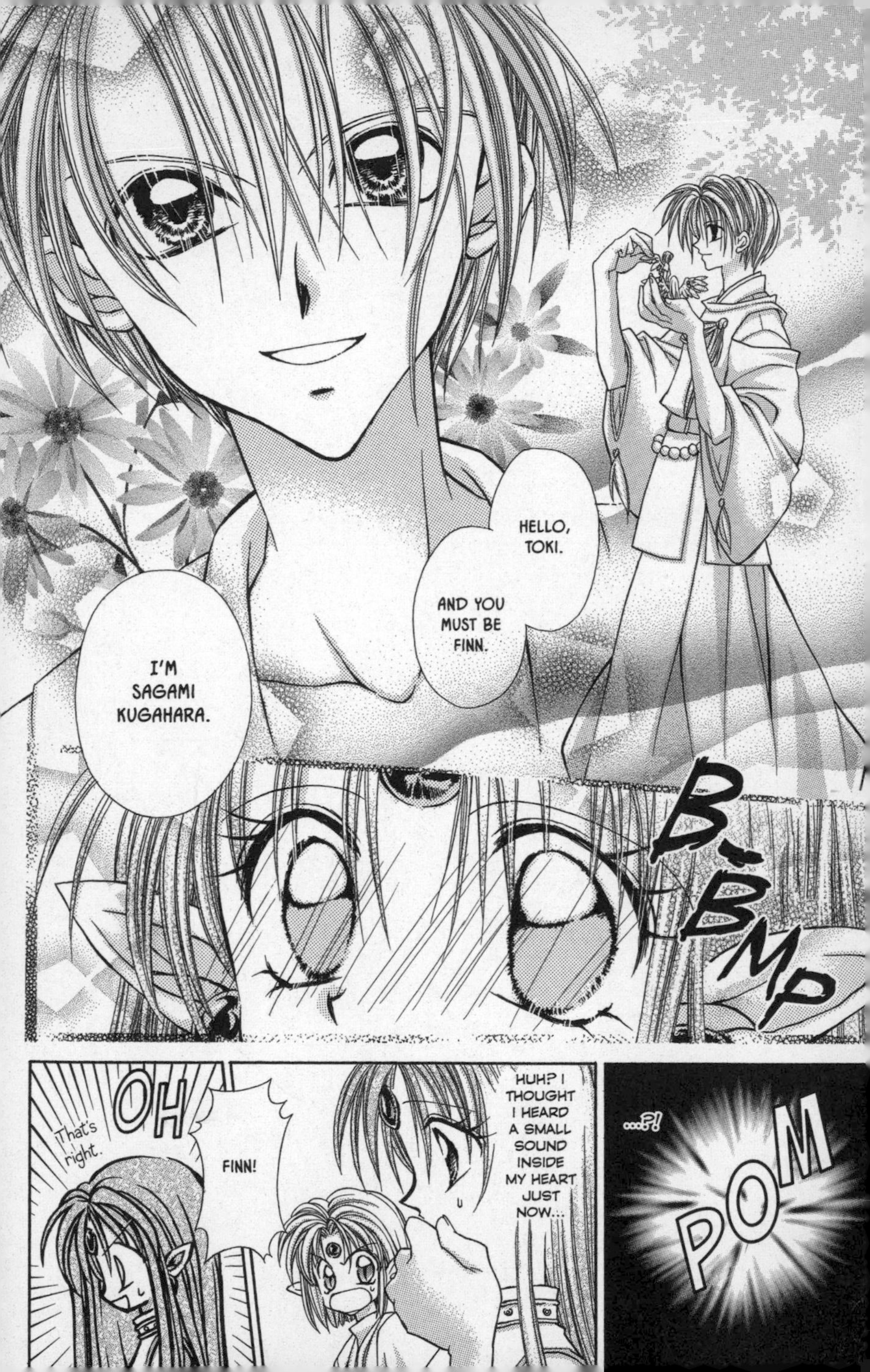
HELLO, TOKI.
AND YOU MUST BE FINN.
I'M SAGAMI KUGAHARA.
B-BMP
...?!
POM
HUH? I THOUGHT I HEARD A SMALL SOUND INSIDE MY HEART JUST NOW...
FINN!
OH
That's right.

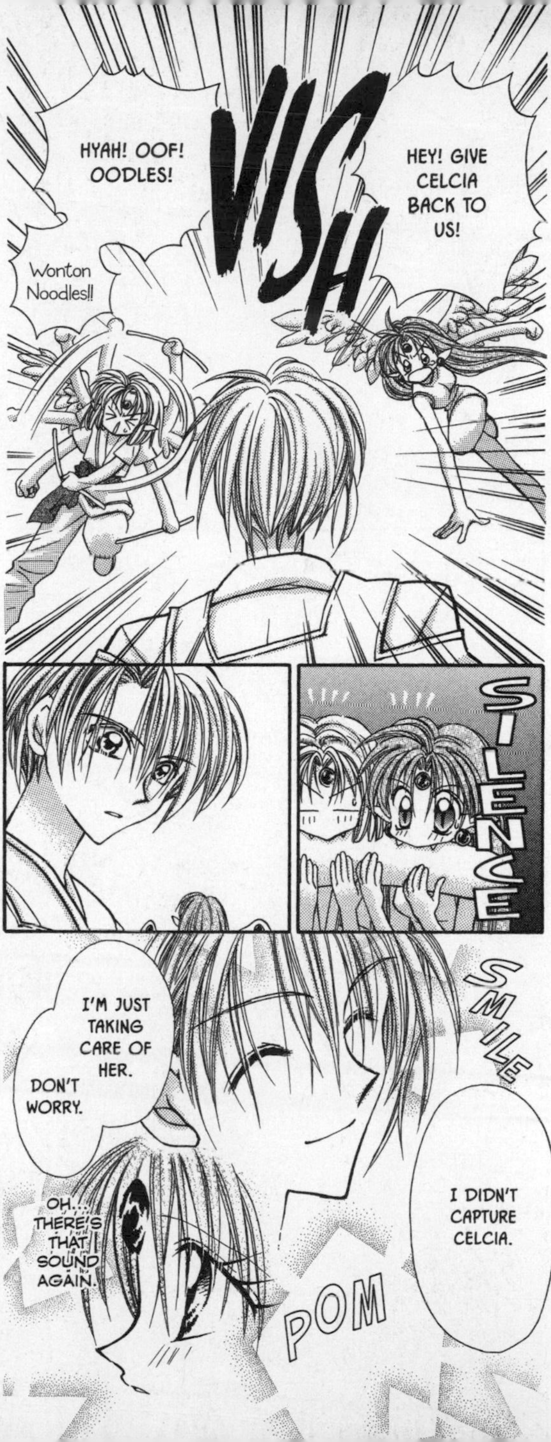
HEY! GIVE CELCIA BACK TO US!
VISH
HYAH! OOF! OODLES!
Wonton Noodles!!
SILENCE
SMILE
I DIDN'T CAPTURE CELCIA.
I'M JUST TAKING CARE OF HER.
DON'T WORRY.
POM
OH... THERE'S THAT SOUND AGAIN.

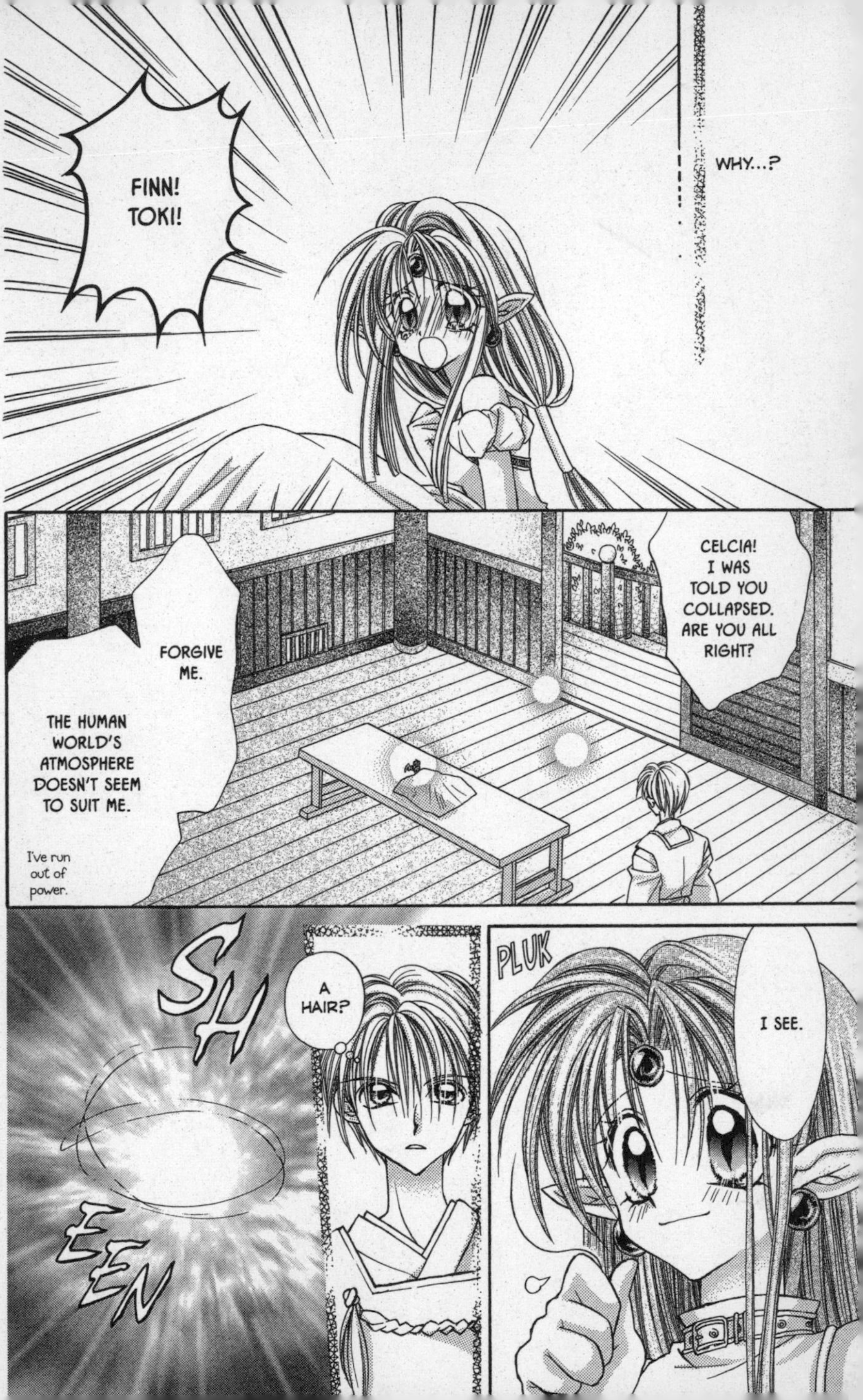
WHY...?
FINN! TOKI!
CELCIA! I WAS TOLD YOU COLLAPSED. ARE YOU ALL RIGHT?
FORGIVE ME.
THE HUMAN WORLD'S ATMOSPHERE DOESN'T SEEM TO SUIT ME.
I've run out of power.
PLUK
I SEE.
A HAIR?
SHEEN

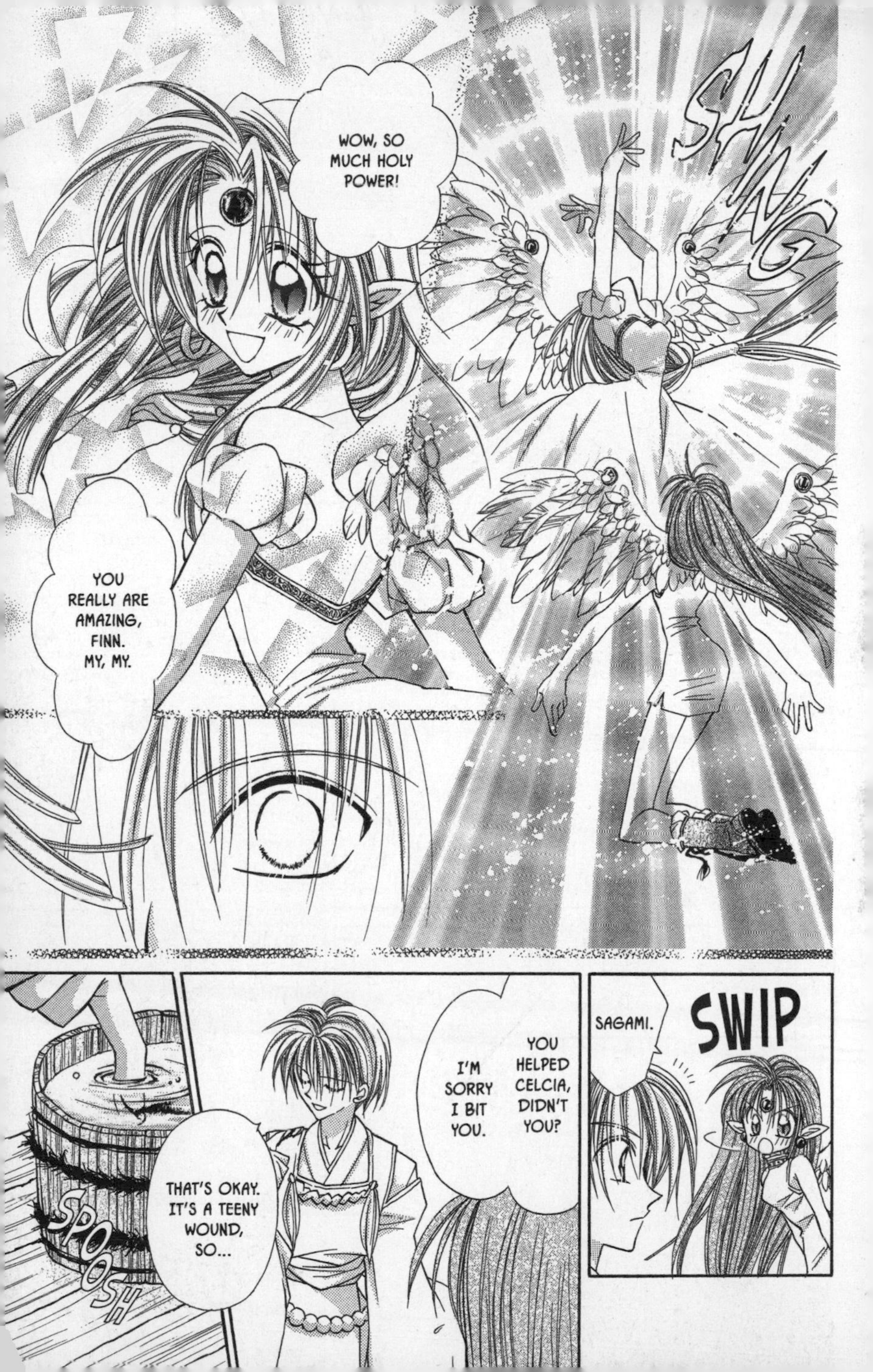
SHING
WOW, SO MUCH HOLY POWER!
YOU REALLY ARE AMAZING, FINN. MY, MY.
SWIP
SAGAMI.
YOU HELPED CELCIA, DIDN'T YOU?
I'M SORRY I BIT YOU.
THAT'S OKAY. IT'S A TEENY WOUND, SO...
SPOOSH

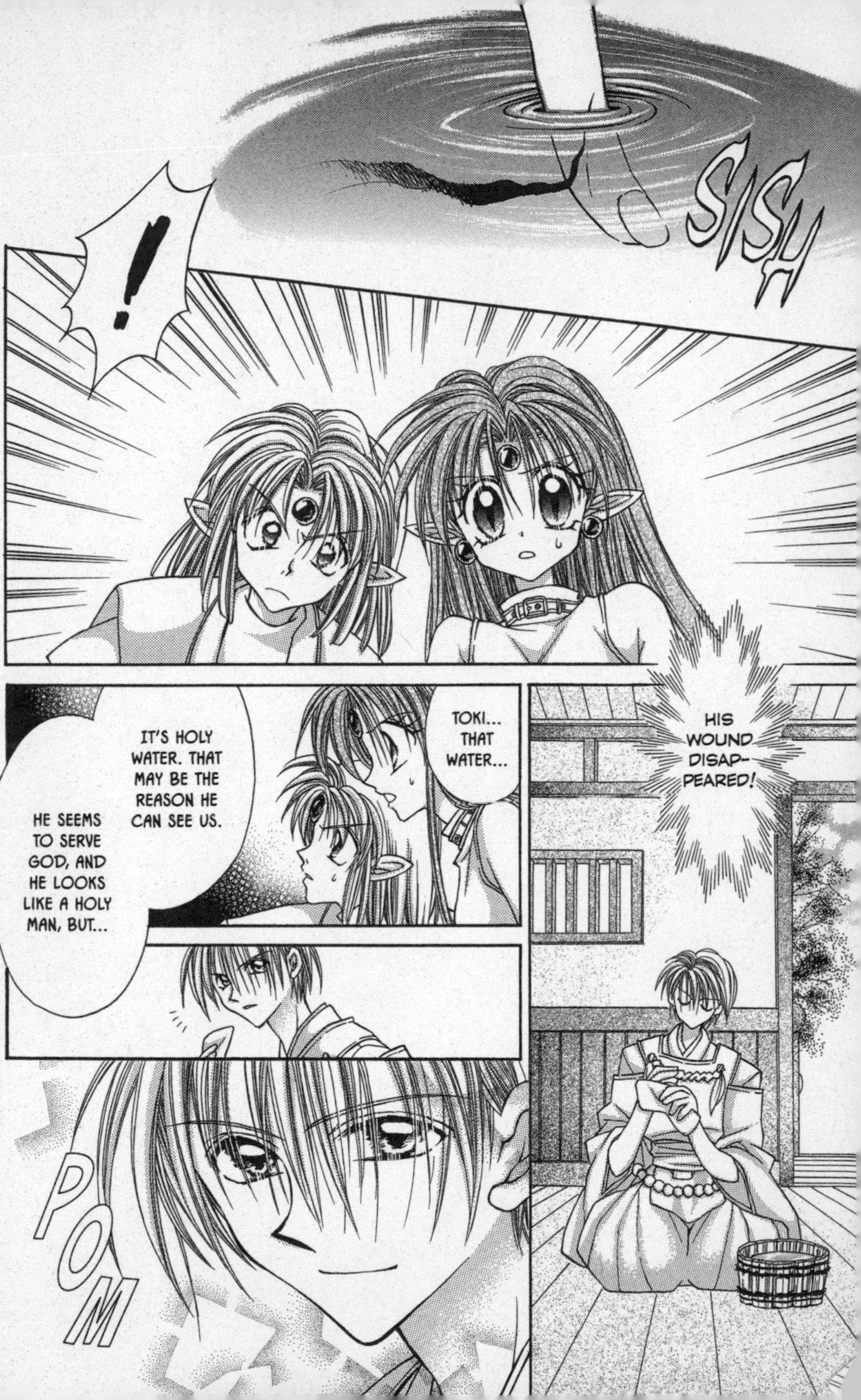
SISH
!
HIS WOUND DISAP-PEARED!
TOKI... THAT WATER...
IT'S HOLY WATER. THAT MAY BE THE REASON HE CAN SEE US.
HE SEEMS TO SERVE GOD, AND HE LOOKS LIKE A HOLY MAN, BUT...
POM

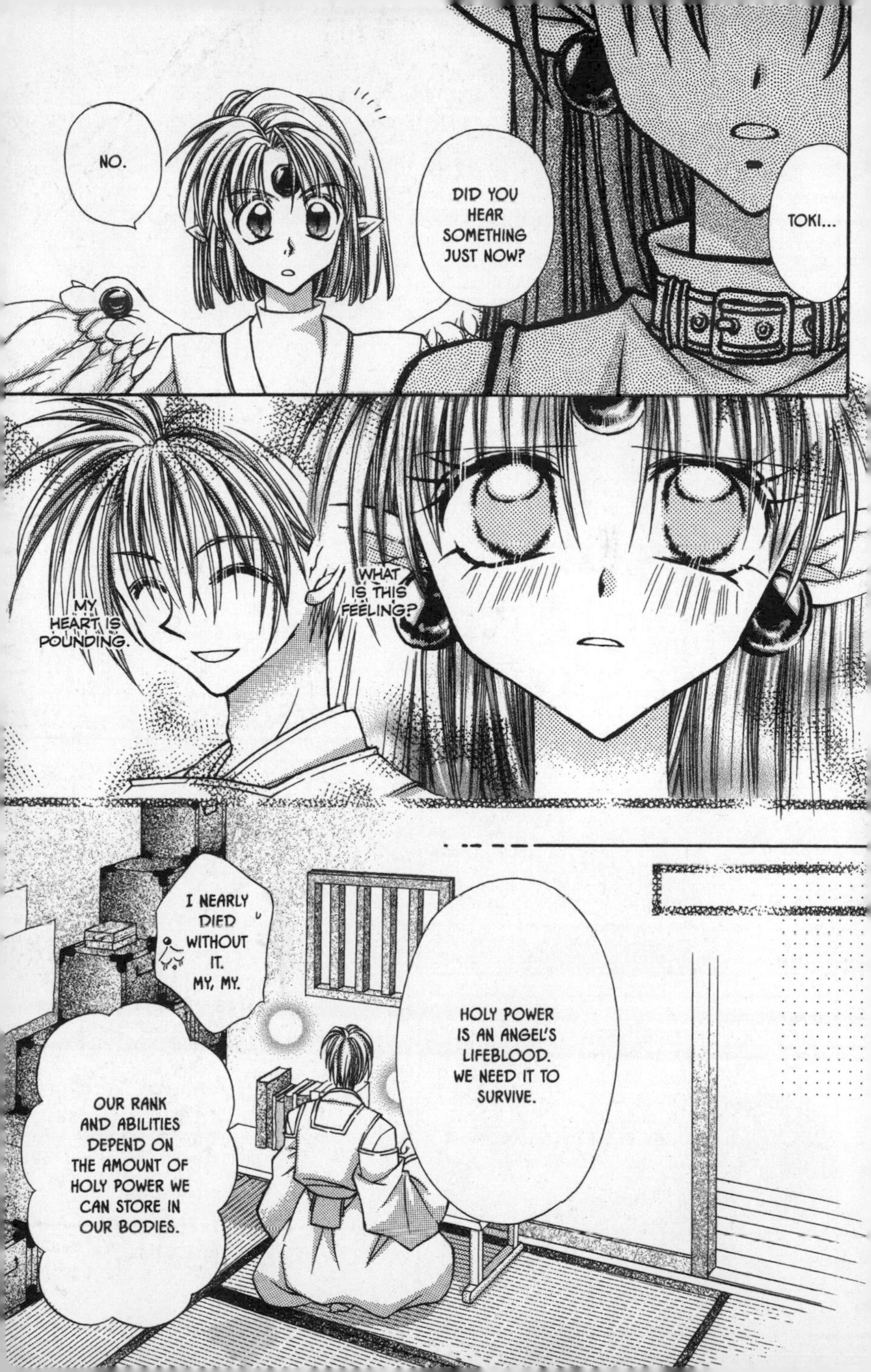
TOKI...
DID YOU HEAR SOMETHING JUST NOW?
NO.
WHAT IS THIS FEELING?
MY HEART IS POUNDING.
HOLY POWER IS AN ANGEL'S LIFEBLOOD. WE NEED IT TO SURVIVE.
I NEARLY DIED WITHOUT IT. MY, MY.
OUR RANK AND ABILITIES DEPEND ON THE AMOUNT OF HOLY POWER WE CAN STORE IN OUR BODIES.

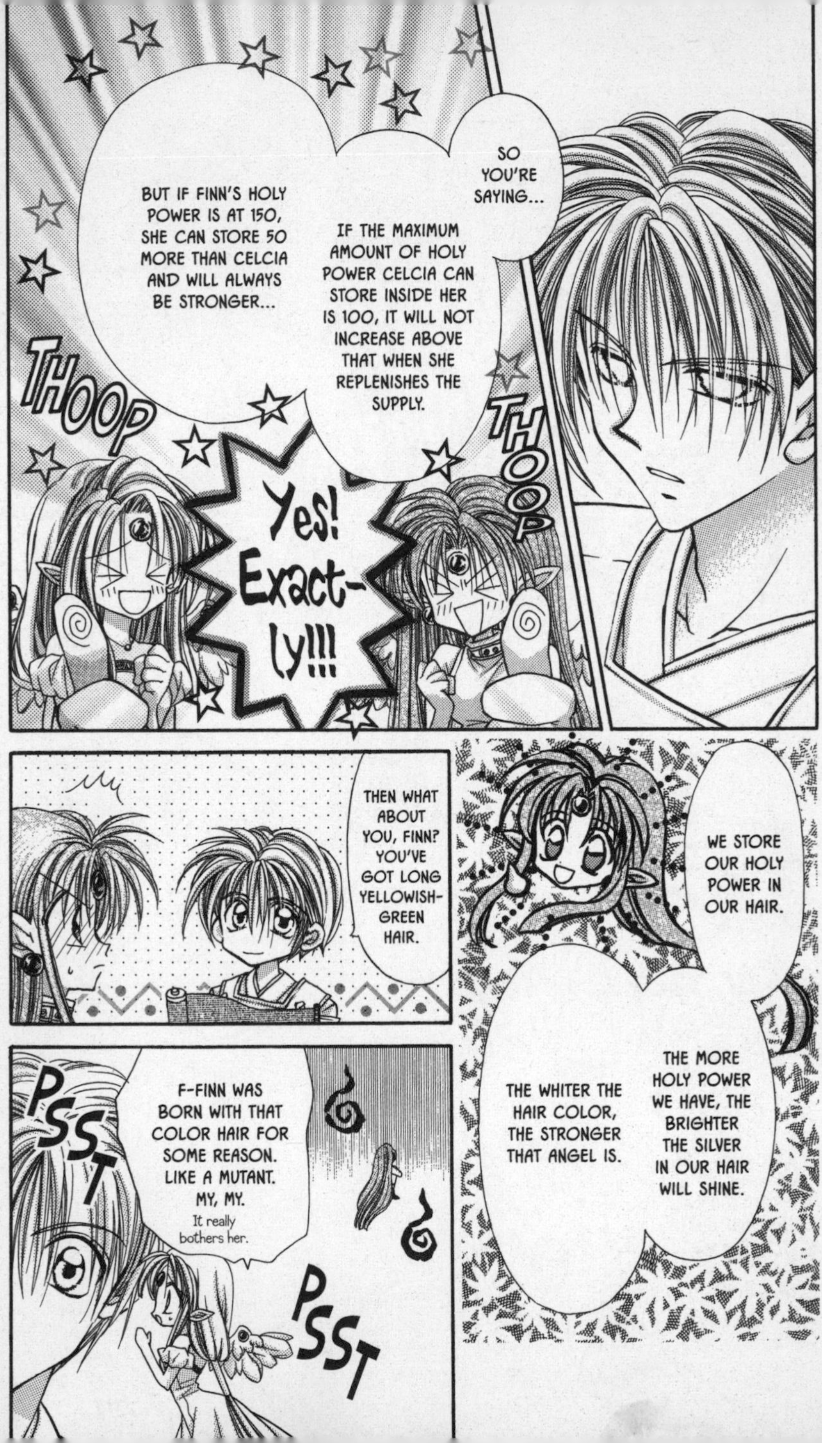
SO YOU'RE SAYING...
IF THE MAXIMUM AMOUNT OF HOLY POWER CELCIA CAN STORE INSIDE HER IS 100, IT WILL NOT INCREASE ABOVE THAT WHEN SHE REPLENISHES THE SUPPLY.
BUT IF FINN'S HOLY POWER IS AT 150, SHE CAN STORE 50 MORE THAN CELCIA AND WILL ALWAYS BE STRONGER...
THOOP
Yes! Exact-ly!!!
THOOP
WE STORE OUR HOLY POWER IN OUR HAIR.
THE MORE HOLY POWER WE HAVE, THE BRIGHTER THE SILVER IN OUR HAIR WILL SHINE.
THE WHITER THE HAIR COLOR, THE STRONGER THAT ANGEL IS.
THEN WHAT ABOUT YOU, FINN? YOU'VE GOT LONG YELLOWISH-GREEN HAIR.
F-FINN WAS BORN WITH THAT COLOR HAIR FOR SOME REASON. LIKE A MUTANT. MY, MY.
It really bothers her.
PSST
PSST

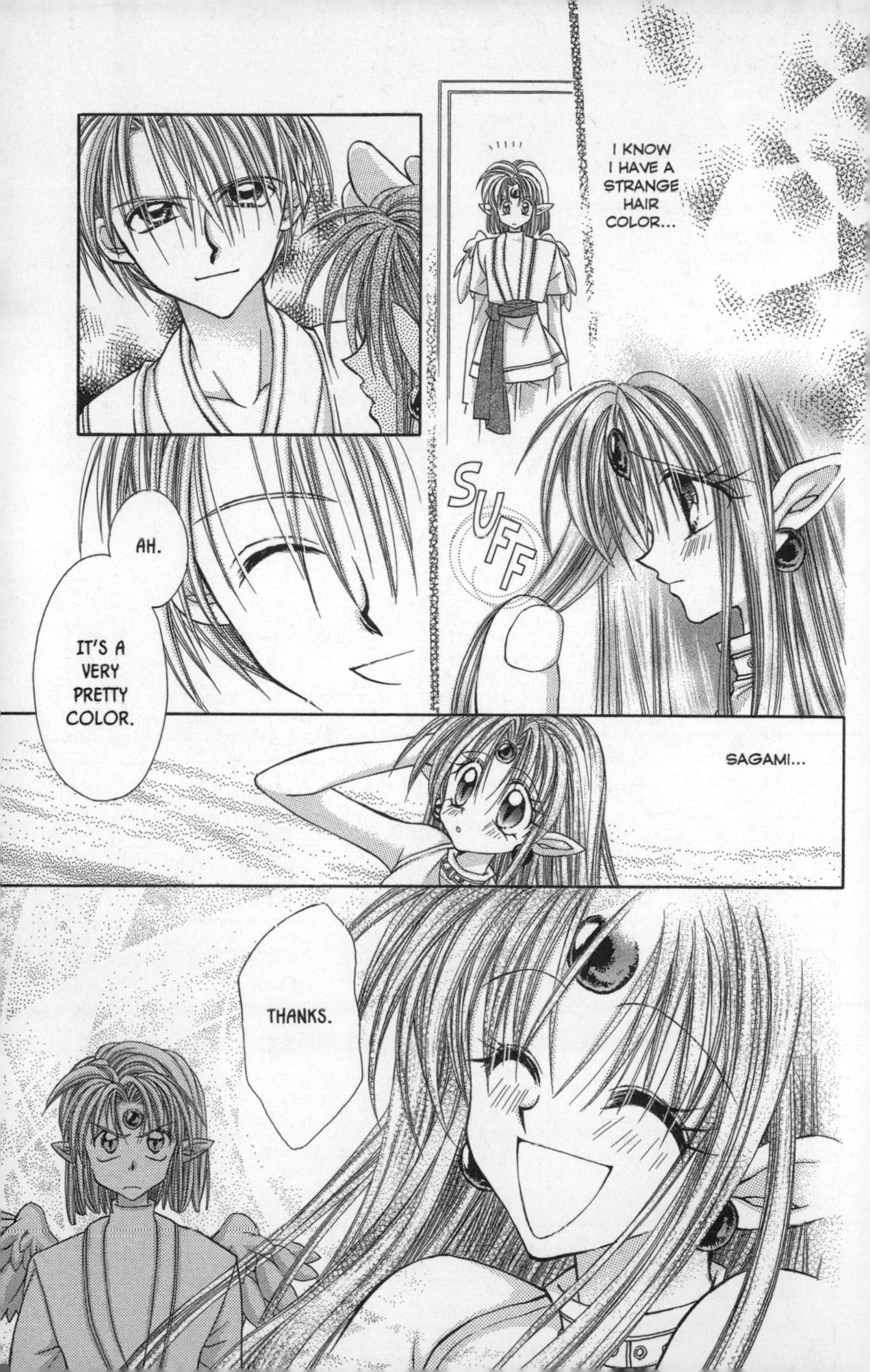
I KNOW I HAVE A STRANGE HAIR COLOR...
SUFF
AH.
IT'S A VERY PRETTY COLOR.
SAGAMI...
THANKS.

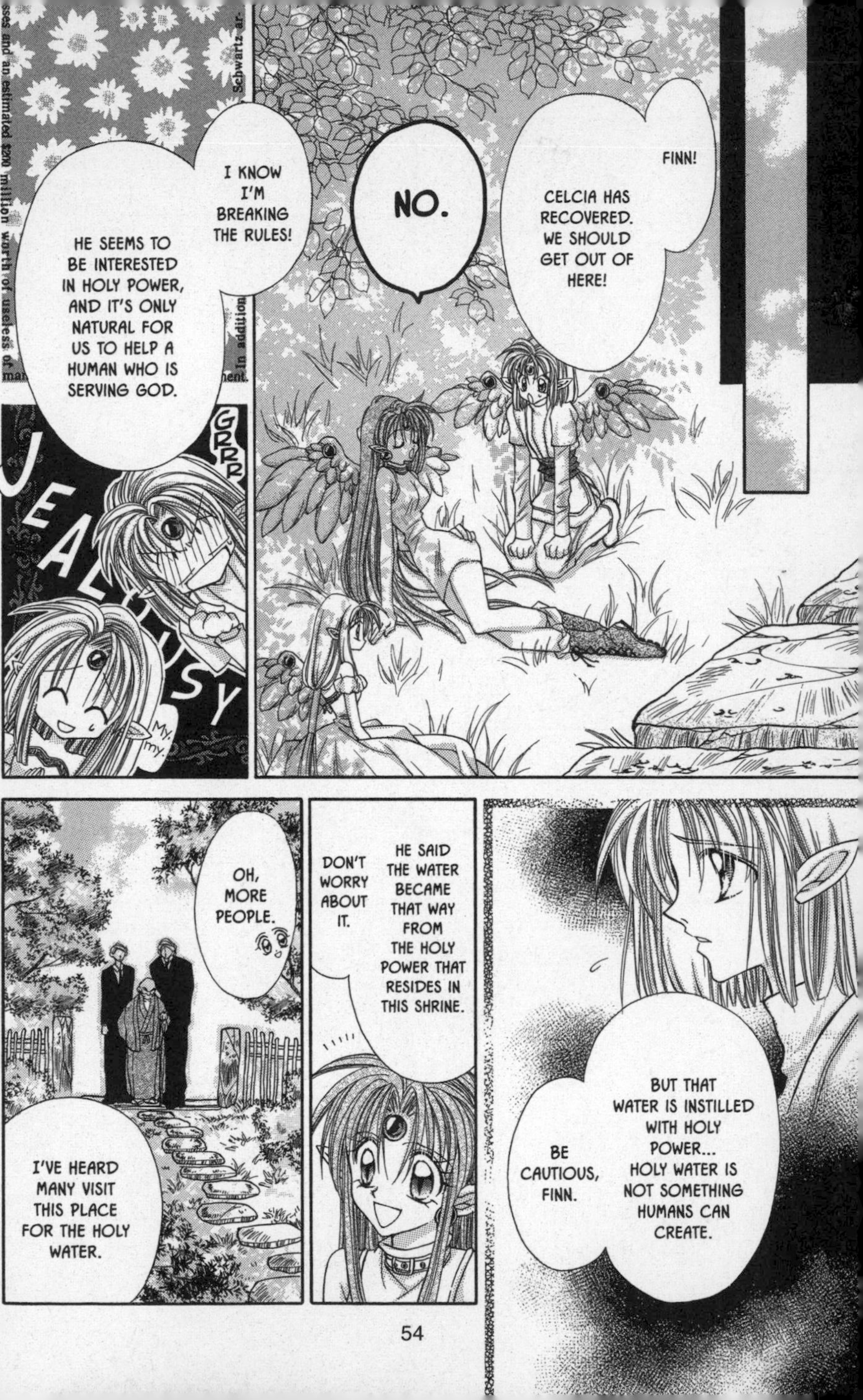
FINN!
CELCIA HAS RECOVERED. WE SHOULD GET OUT OF HERE!
NO.
I KNOW I'M BREAKING THE RULES!
HE SEEMS TO BE INTERESTED IN HOLY POWER, AND IT'S ONLY NATURAL FOR US TO HELP A HUMAN WHO IS SERVING GOD.
GRRR
JEALOUSY
My, my.
BUT THAT WATER IS INSTILLED WITH HOLY POWER... HOLY WATER IS NOT SOMETHING HUMANS CAN CREATE.
BE CAUTIOUS, FINN.
HE SAID THE WATER BECAME THAT WAY FROM THE HOLY POWER THAT RESIDES IN THIS SHRINE.
DON'T WORRY ABOUT IT.
OH, MORE PEOPLE.
I'VE HEARD MANY VISIT THIS PLACE FOR THE HOLY WATER.

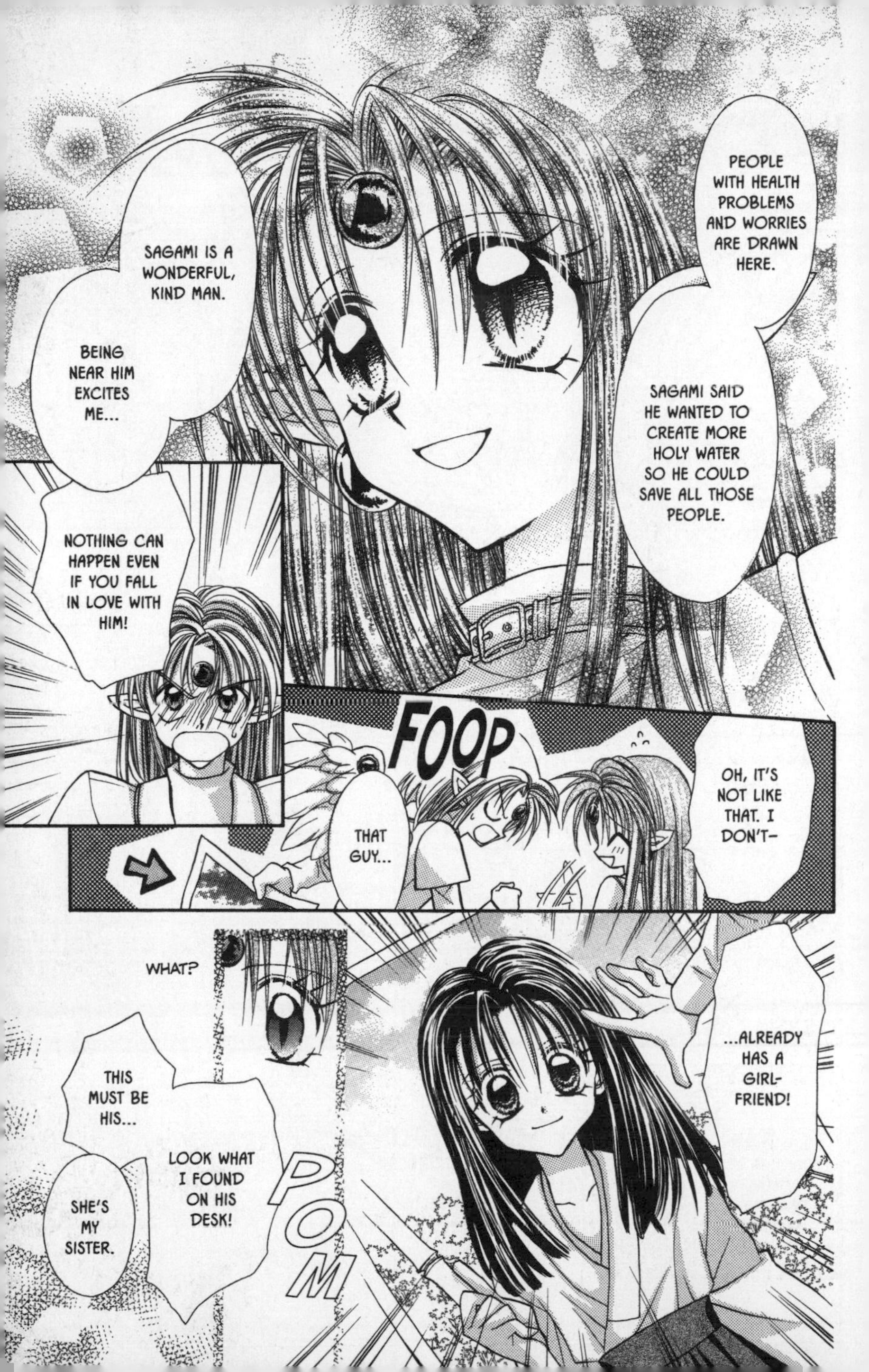
PEOPLE WITH HEALTH PROBLEMS AND WORRIES ARE DRAWN HERE.
SAGAMI SAID HE WANTED TO CREATE MORE HOLY WATER SO HE COULD SAVE ALL THOSE PEOPLE.
SAGAMI IS A WONDERFUL, KIND MAN.
BEING NEAR HIM EXCITES ME...
NOTHING CAN HAPPEN EVEN IF YOU FALL IN LOVE WITH HIM!
OH, IT'S NOT LIKE THAT. I DON'T—
FOOP
THAT GUY...
...ALREADY HAS A GIRL-FRIEND!
POM
LOOK WHAT I FOUND ON HIS DESK!
THIS MUST BE HIS...
WHAT?
SHE'S MY SISTER.

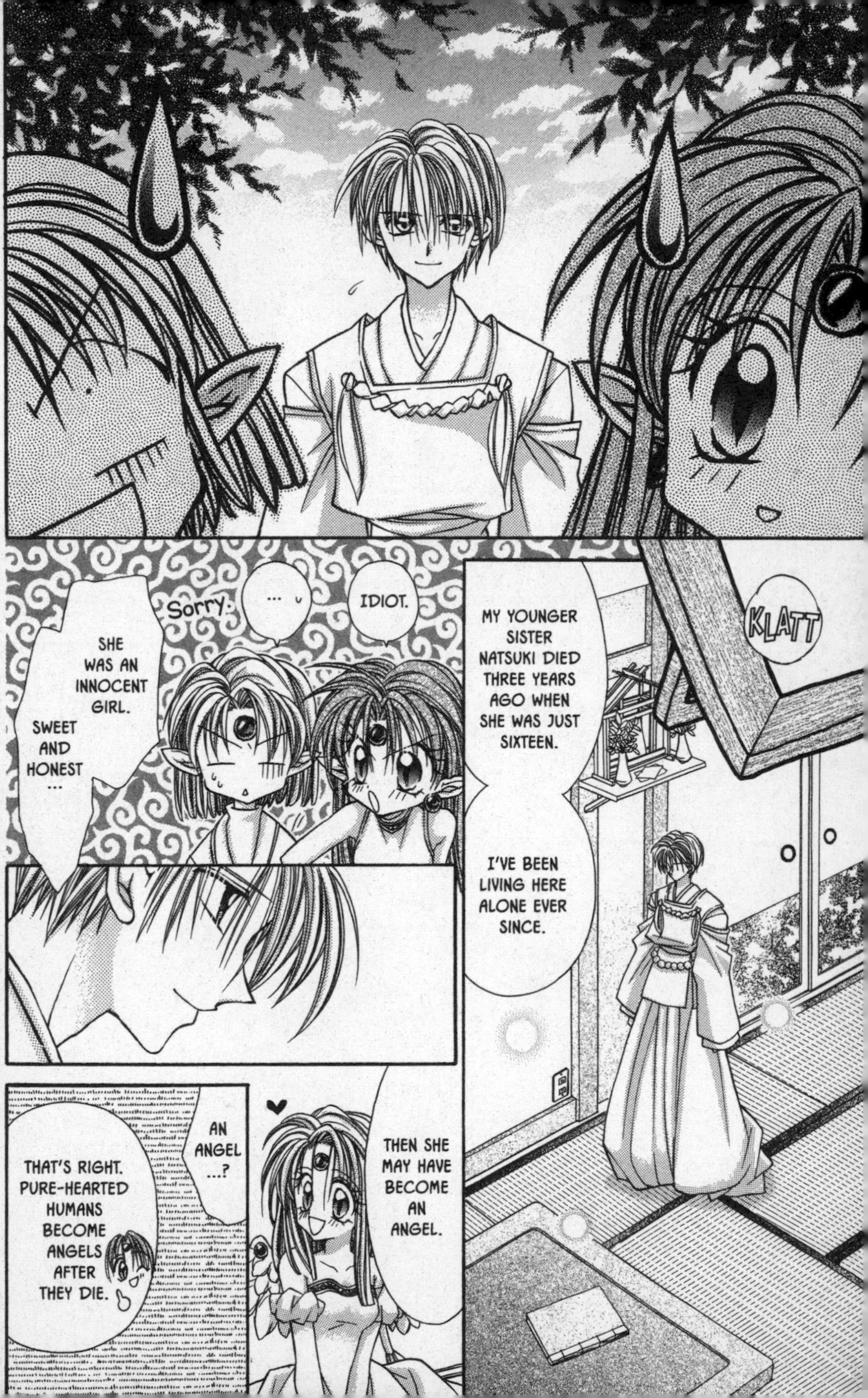
KLATT
MY YOUNGER SISTER NATSUKI DIED THREE YEARS AGO WHEN SHE WAS JUST SIXTEEN.
I'VE BEEN LIVING HERE ALONE EVER SINCE.
IDIOT.
...
Sorry.
SHE WAS AN INNOCENT GIRL.
SWEET AND HONEST ...
THEN SHE MAY HAVE BECOME AN ANGEL.
AN ANGEL ...?
THAT'S RIGHT. PURE-HEARTED HUMANS BECOME ANGELS AFTER THEY DIE.

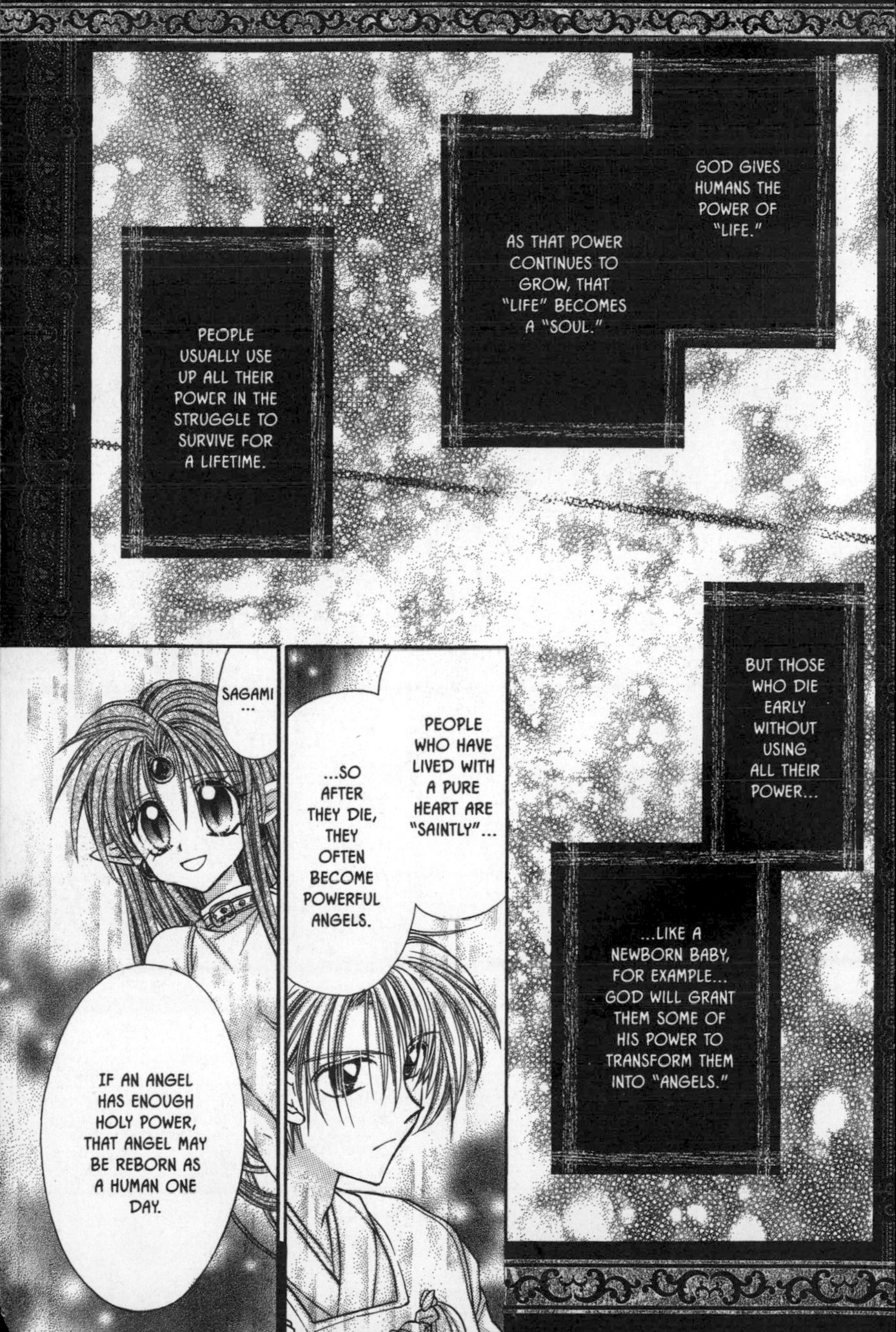
GOD GIVES HUMANS THE POWER OF "LIFE."
AS THAT POWER CONTINUES TO GROW, THAT "LIFE" BECOMES A "SOUL."
PEOPLE USUALLY USE UP ALL THEIR POWER IN THE STRUGGLE TO SURVIVE FOR A LIFETIME.
BUT THOSE WHO DIE EARLY WITHOUT USING ALL THEIR POWER...
...LIKE A NEWBORN BABY, FOR EXAMPLE... GOD WILL GRANT THEM SOME OF HIS POWER TO TRANSFORM THEM INTO "ANGELS."
PEOPLE WHO HAVE LIVED WITH A PURE HEART ARE "SAINTLY"...
...SO AFTER THEY DIE, THEY OFTEN BECOME POWERFUL ANGELS.
SAGAMI ...
IF AN ANGEL HAS ENOUGH HOLY POWER, THAT ANGEL MAY BE REBORN AS A HUMAN ONE DAY.

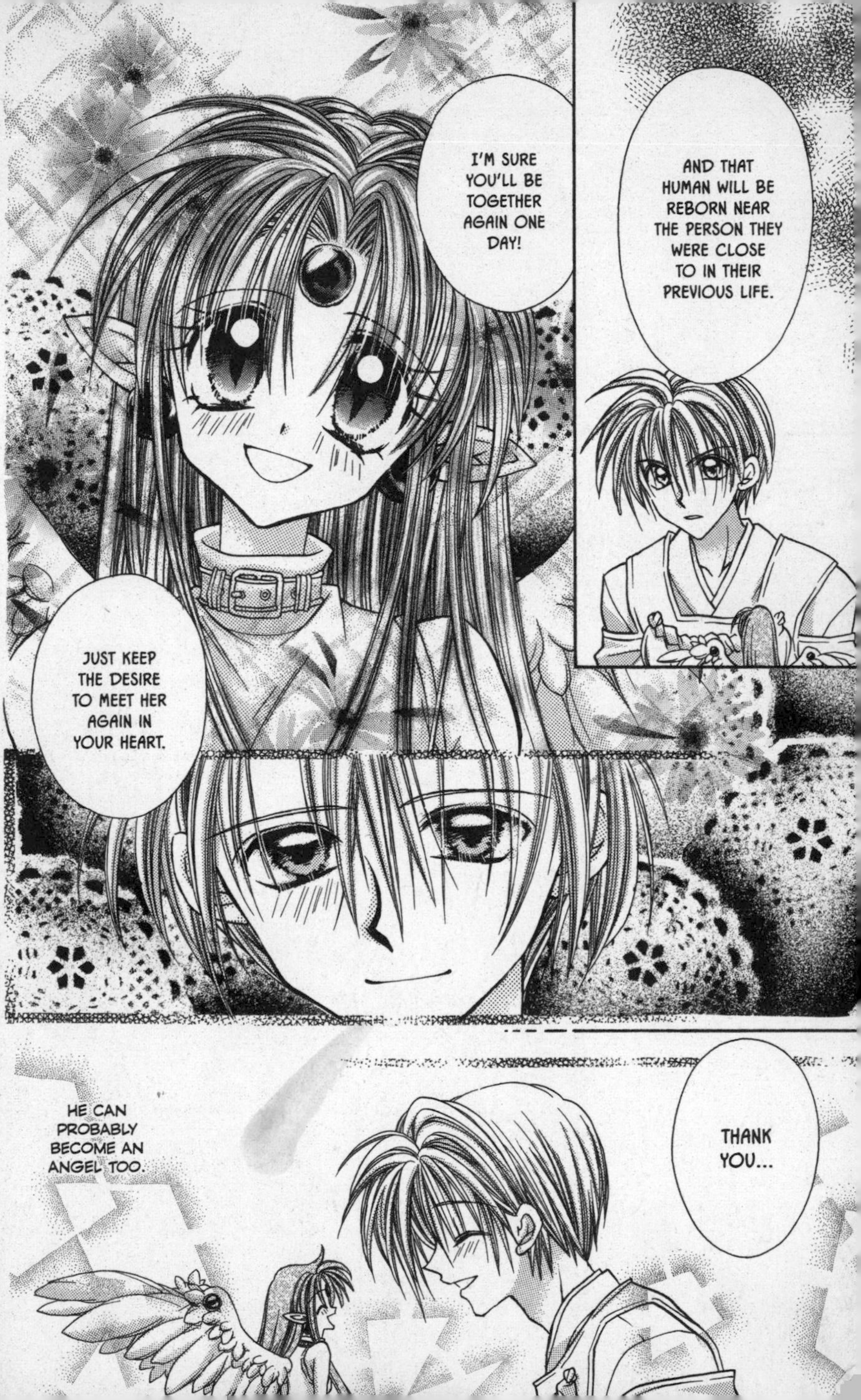
AND THAT HUMAN WILL BE REBORN NEAR THE PERSON THEY WERE CLOSE TO IN THEIR PREVIOUS LIFE.
I'M SURE YOU'LL BE TOGETHER AGAIN ONE DAY!
JUST KEEP THE DESIRE TO MEET HER AGAIN IN YOUR HEART.
THANK YOU...
HE CAN PROBABLY BECOME AN ANGEL TOO.

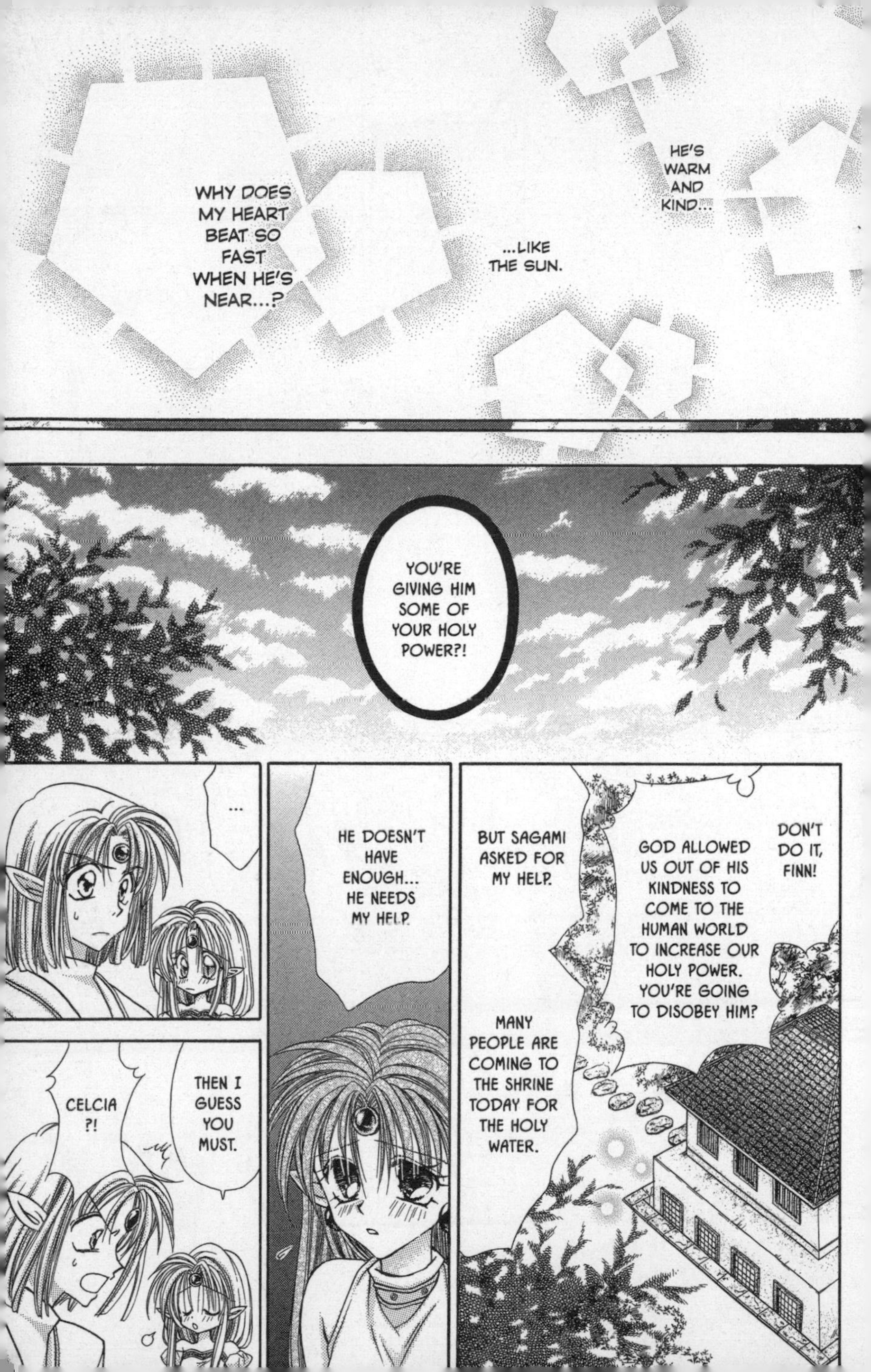
HE'S WARM AND KIND...
...LIKE THE SUN.
WHY DOES MY HEART BEAT SO FAST WHEN HE'S NEAR...?
YOU'RE GIVING HIM SOME OF YOUR HOLY POWER?!
DON'T DO IT, FINN!
GOD ALLOWED US OUT OF HIS KINDNESS TO COME TO THE HUMAN WORLD TO INCREASE OUR HOLY POWER. YOU'RE GOING TO DISOBEY HIM?
BUT SAGAMI ASKED FOR MY HELP.
MANY PEOPLE ARE COMING TO THE SHRINE TODAY FOR THE HOLY WATER.
HE DOESN'T HAVE ENOUGH... HE NEEDS MY HELP.
...
THEN I GUESS YOU MUST.
CELCIA?!

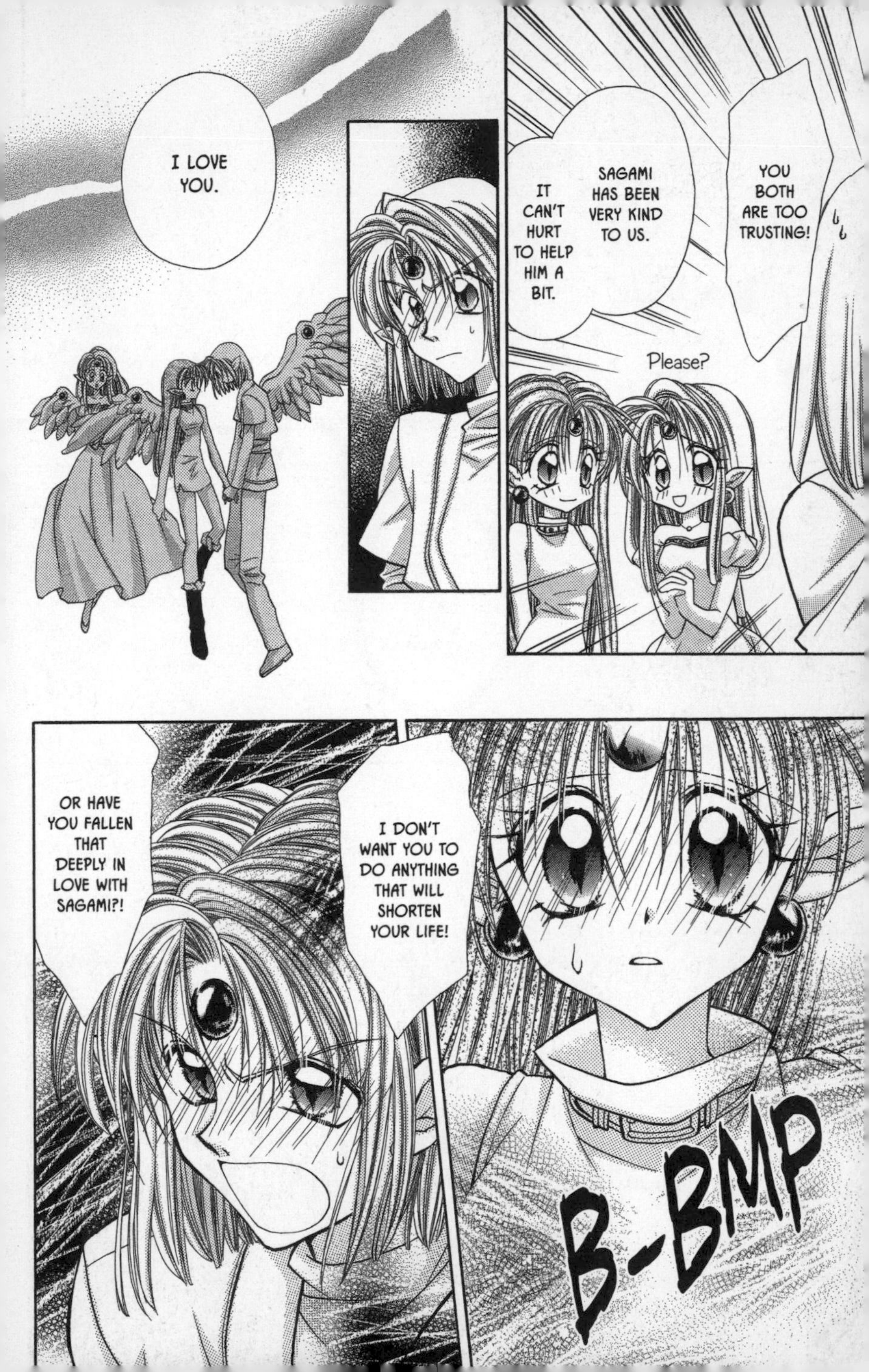
YOU BOTH ARE TOO TRUSTING!
SAGAMI HAS BEEN VERY KIND TO US.
IT CAN'T HURT TO HELP HIM A BIT.
Please?
I LOVE YOU.
I DON'T WANT YOU TO DO ANYTHING THAT WILL SHORTEN YOUR LIFE!
OR HAVE YOU FALLEN THAT DEEPLY IN LOVE WITH SAGAMI?!
B-BMP

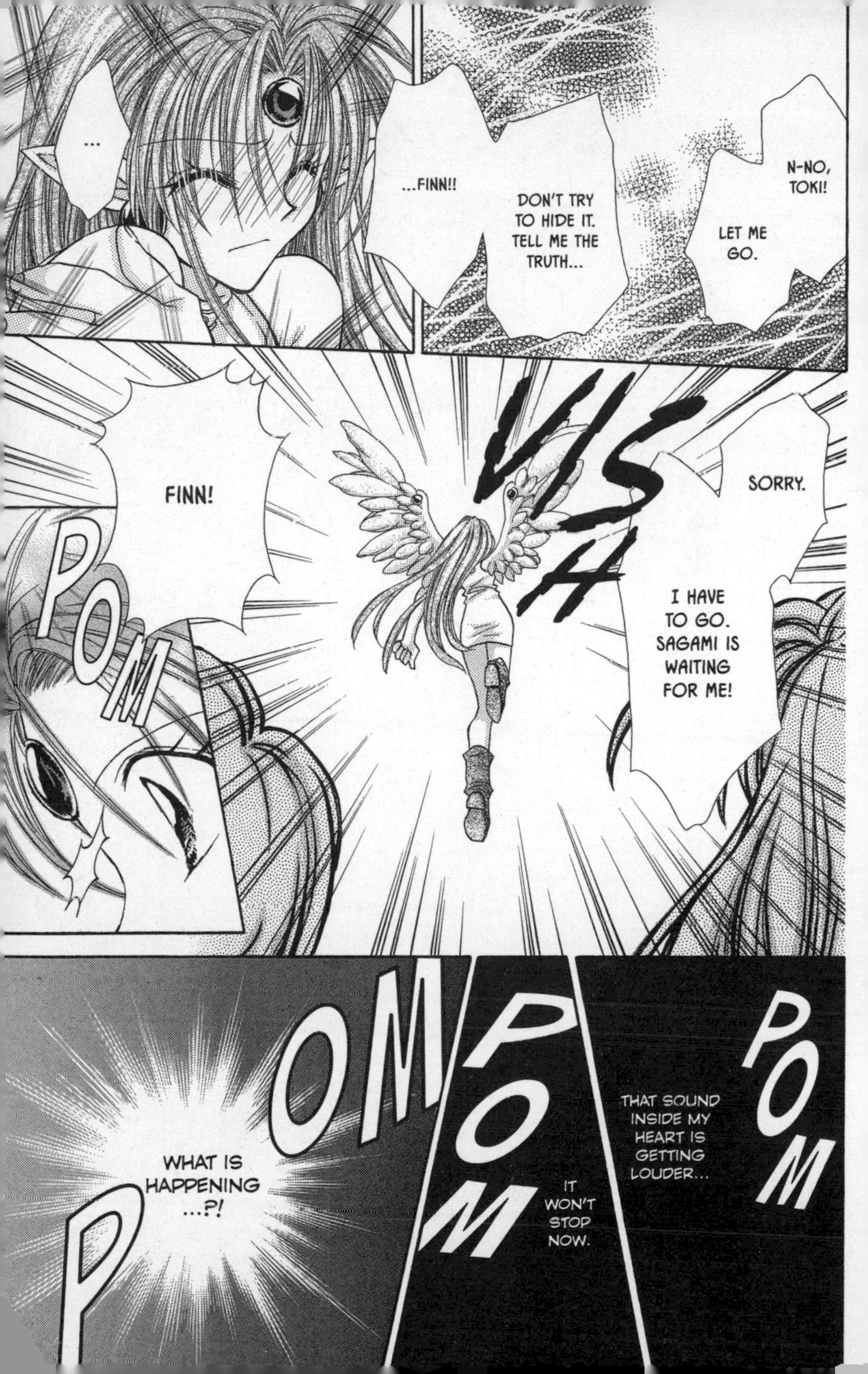
N-NO, TOKI!
LET ME GO.
DON'T TRY TO HIDE IT. TELL ME THE TRUTH...
...FINN!!
...
SORRY.
VISH
I HAVE TO GO. SAGAMI IS WAITING FOR ME!
FINN!
POM
POM
THAT SOUND INSIDE MY HEART IS GETTING LOUDER...
POM
IT WON'T STOP NOW.
OM
WHAT IS HAPPENING ...?!
P

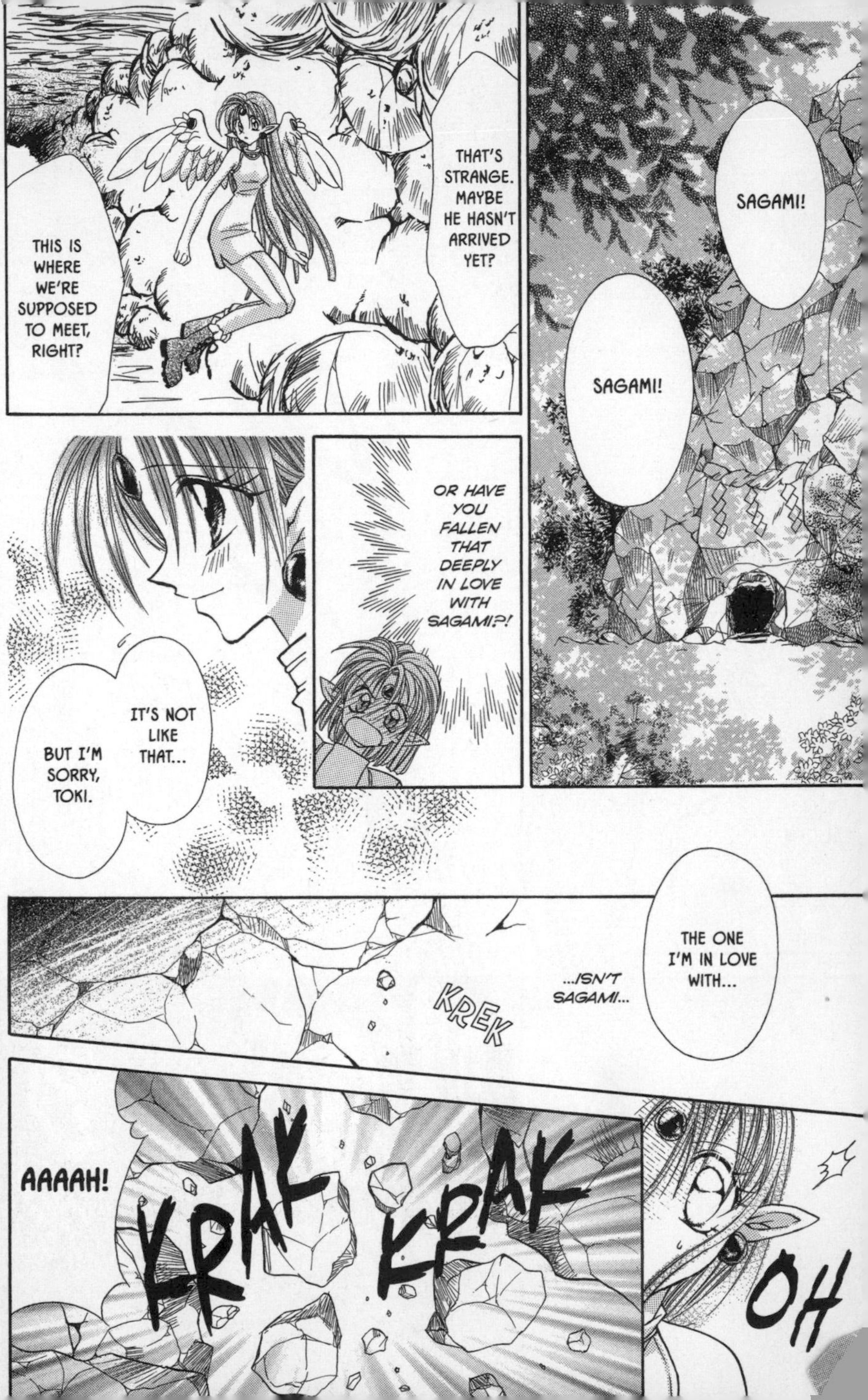
SAGAMI!
SAGAMI!
THAT'S STRANGE. MAYBE HE HASN'T ARRIVED YET?
THIS IS WHERE WE'RE SUPPOSED TO MEET, RIGHT?
OR HAVE YOU FALLEN THAT DEEPLY IN LOVE WITH SAGAMI?!
IT'S NOT LIKE THAT...
BUT I'M SORRY, TOKI.
THE ONE I'M IN LOVE WITH...
...ISN'T SAGAMI...
KREK
OH
KRAK KRAK
AAAAH!

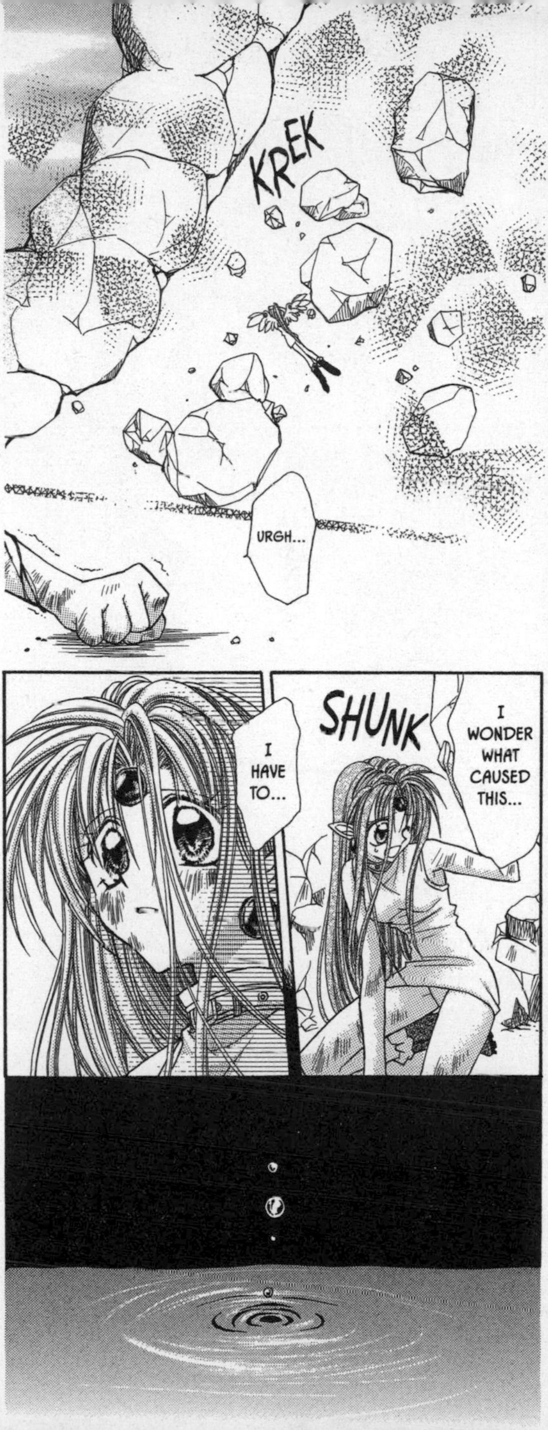
KREK
URGH...
SHUNK
I WONDER WHAT CAUSED THIS...
I HAVE TO...

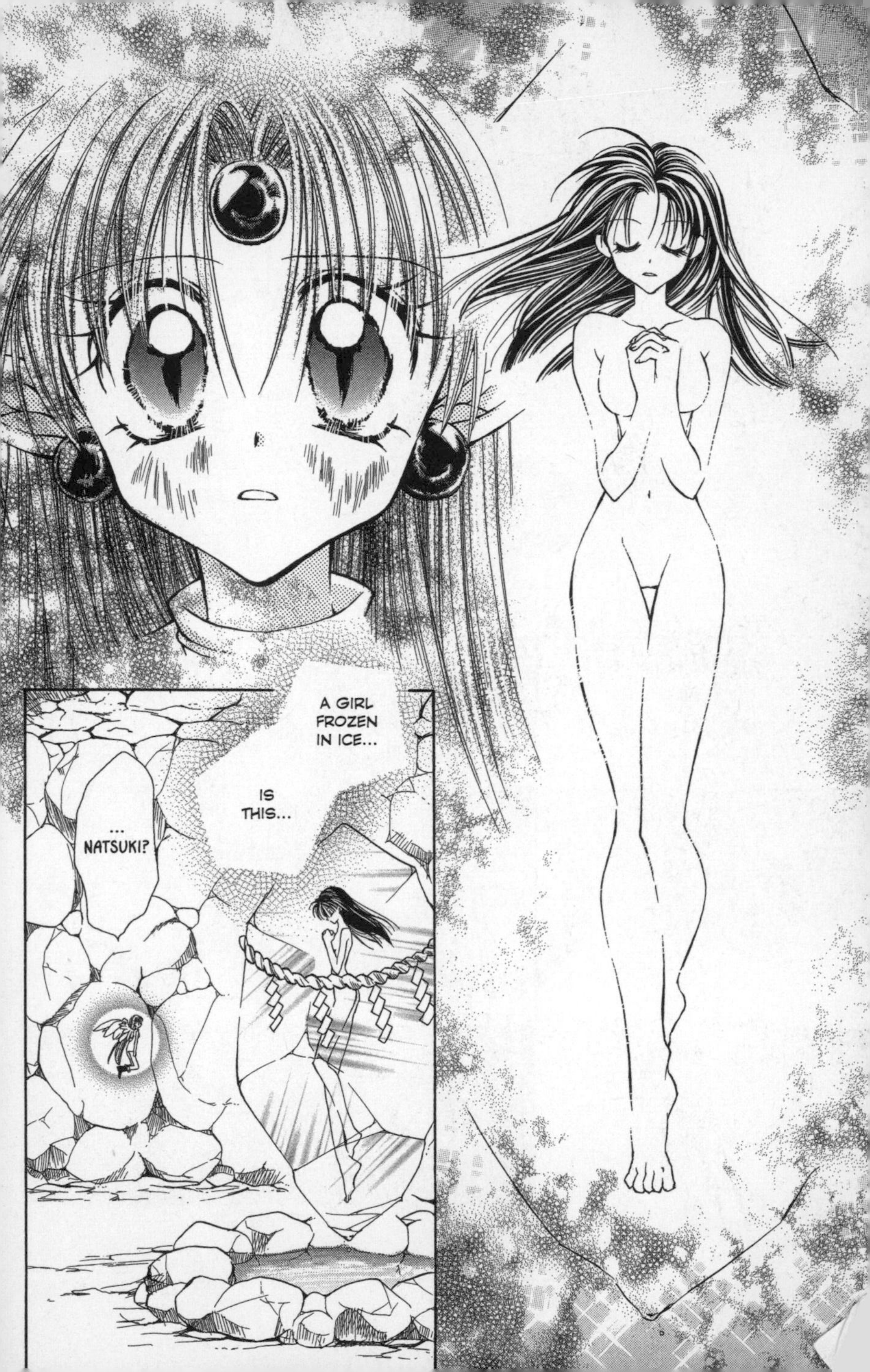
A GIRL FROZEN IN ICE...
IS THIS...
...NATSUKI?

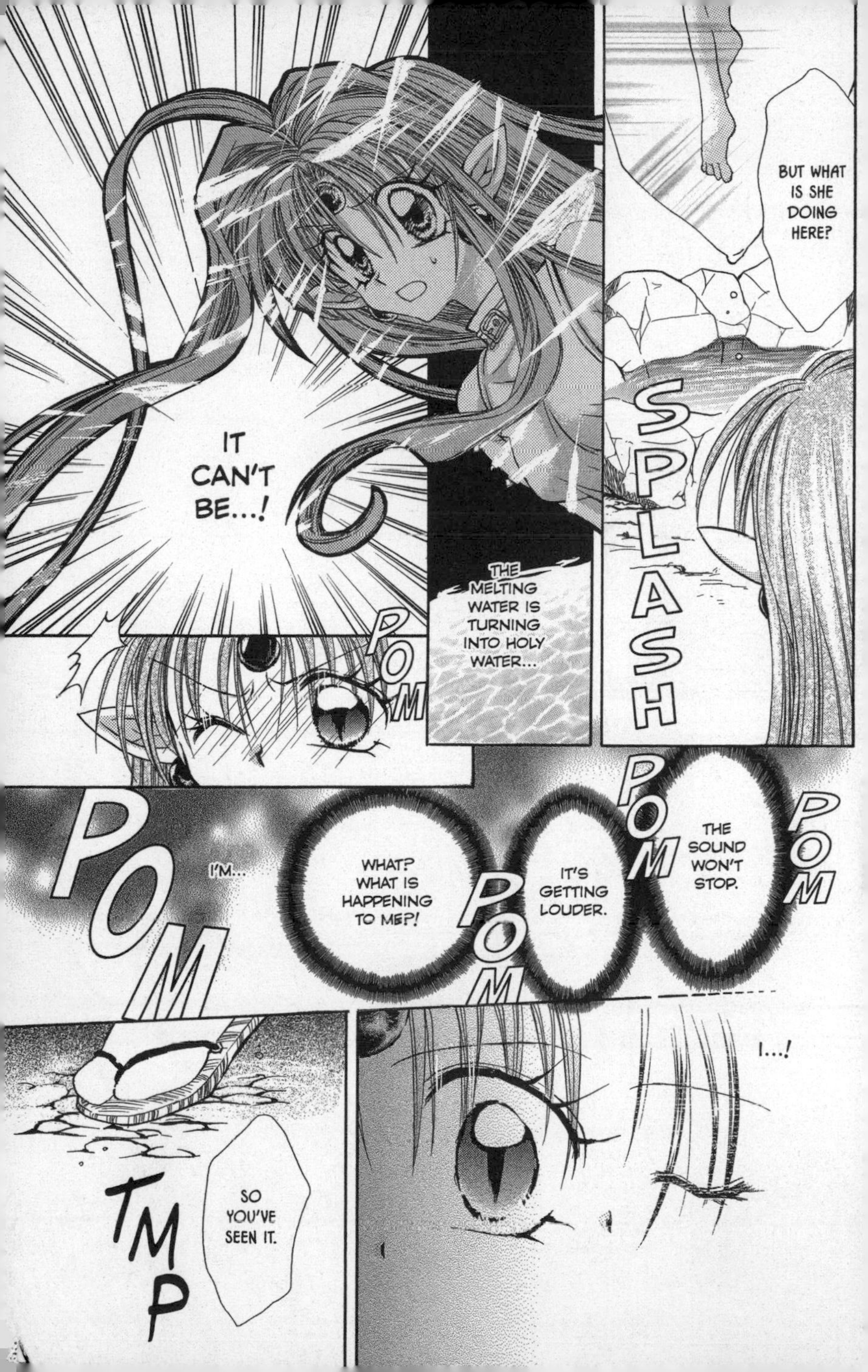
BUT WHAT IS SHE DOING HERE?
SPLASH
THE MELTING WATER IS TURNING INTO HOLY WATER...
IT CAN'T BE...!
POM
POM
POM
THE SOUND WON'T STOP.
POM
IT'S GETTING LOUDER.
POM
WHAT? WHAT IS HAPPENING TO ME?!
I'M...
POM
I...!
SO YOU'VE SEEN IT.
TMP

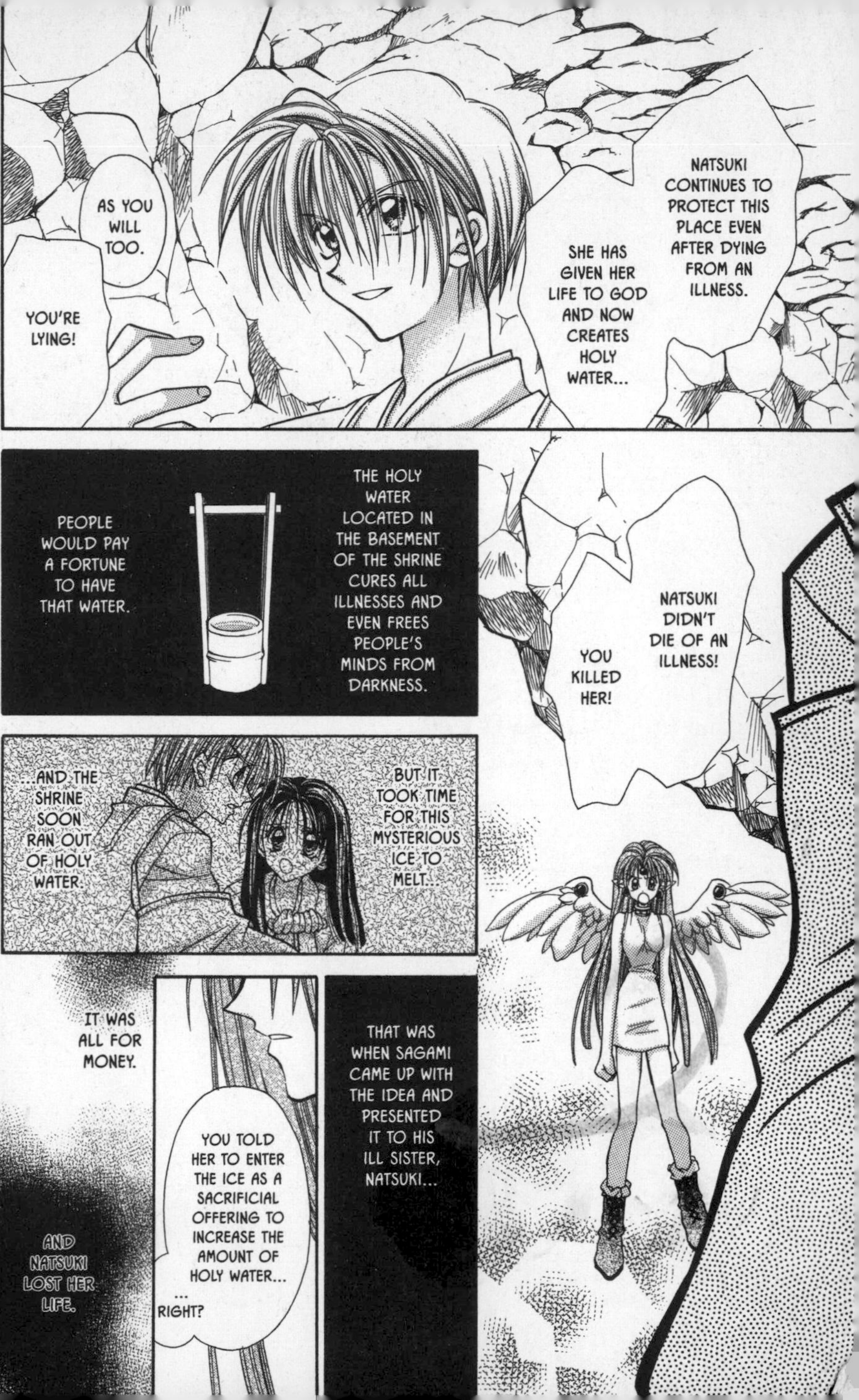
NATSUKI CONTINUES TO PROTECT THIS PLACE EVEN AFTER DYING FROM AN ILLNESS.
SHE HAS GIVEN HER LIFE TO GOD AND NOW CREATES HOLY WATER...
AS YOU WILL TOO.
YOU'RE LYING!
NATSUKI DIDN'T DIE OF AN ILLNESS!
YOU KILLED HER!
THE HOLY WATER LOCATED IN THE BASEMENT OF THE SHRINE CURES ALL ILLNESSES AND EVEN FREES PEOPLE'S MINDS FROM DARKNESS.
PEOPLE WOULD PAY A FORTUNE TO HAVE THAT WATER.
BUT IT TOOK TIME FOR THIS MYSTERIOUS ICE TO MELT...
...AND THE SHRINE SOON RAN OUT OF HOLY WATER.
THAT WAS WHEN SAGAMI CAME UP WITH THE IDEA AND PRESENTED IT TO HIS ILL SISTER, NATSUKI...
IT WAS ALL FOR MONEY.
YOU TOLD HER TO ENTER THE ICE AS A SACRIFICIAL OFFERING TO INCREASE THE AMOUNT OF HOLY WATER...
...RIGHT?
AND NATSUKI LOST HER LIFE.

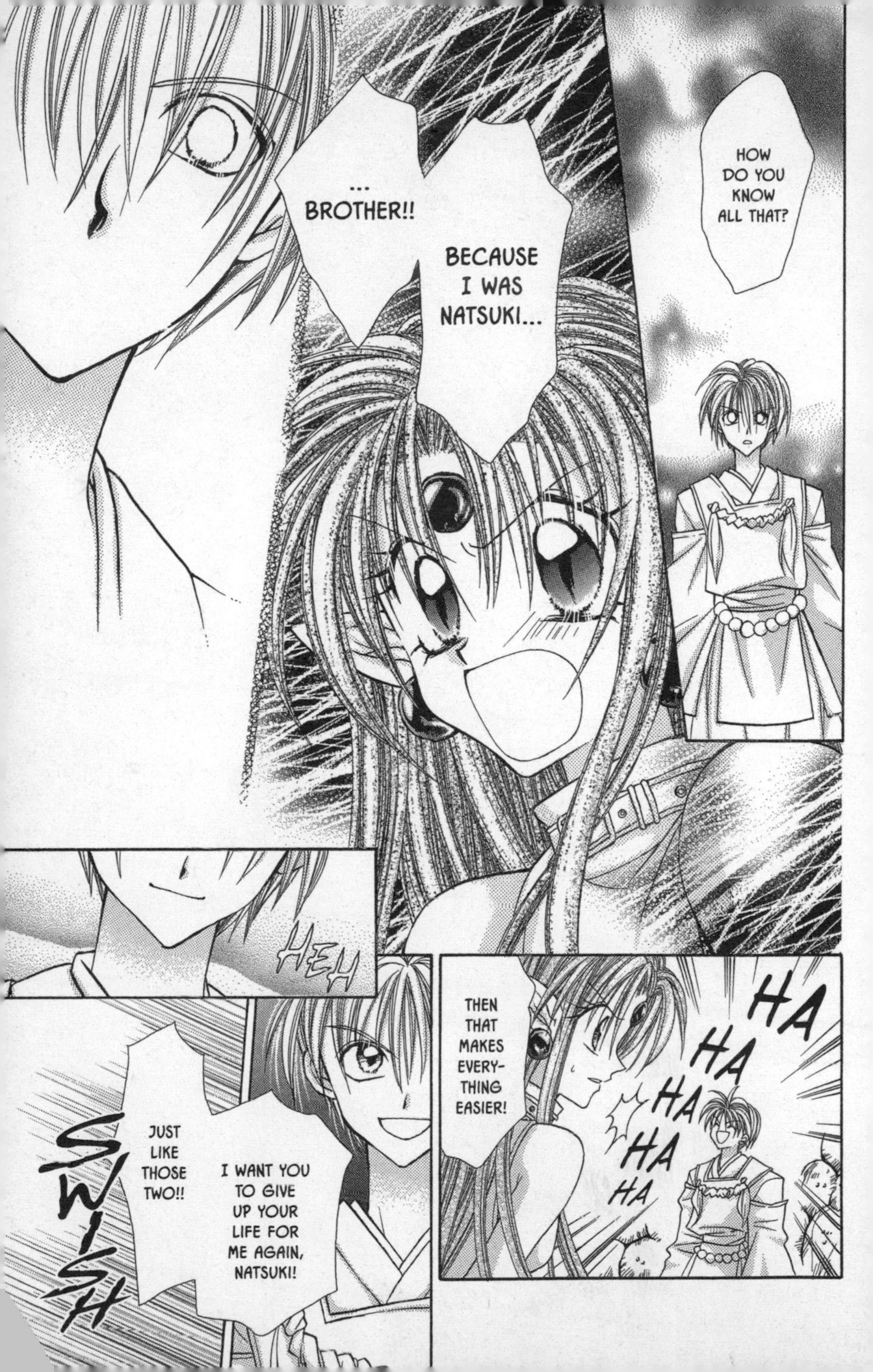
HOW DO YOU KNOW ALL THAT?
BECAUSE I WAS NATSUKI...
...BROTHER!!
HEH
HA HA HA HA HA
THEN THAT MAKES EVERY-THING EASIER!
I WANT YOU TO GIVE UP YOUR LIFE FOR ME AGAIN, NATSUKI!
JUST LIKE THOSE TWO!!
SWISH

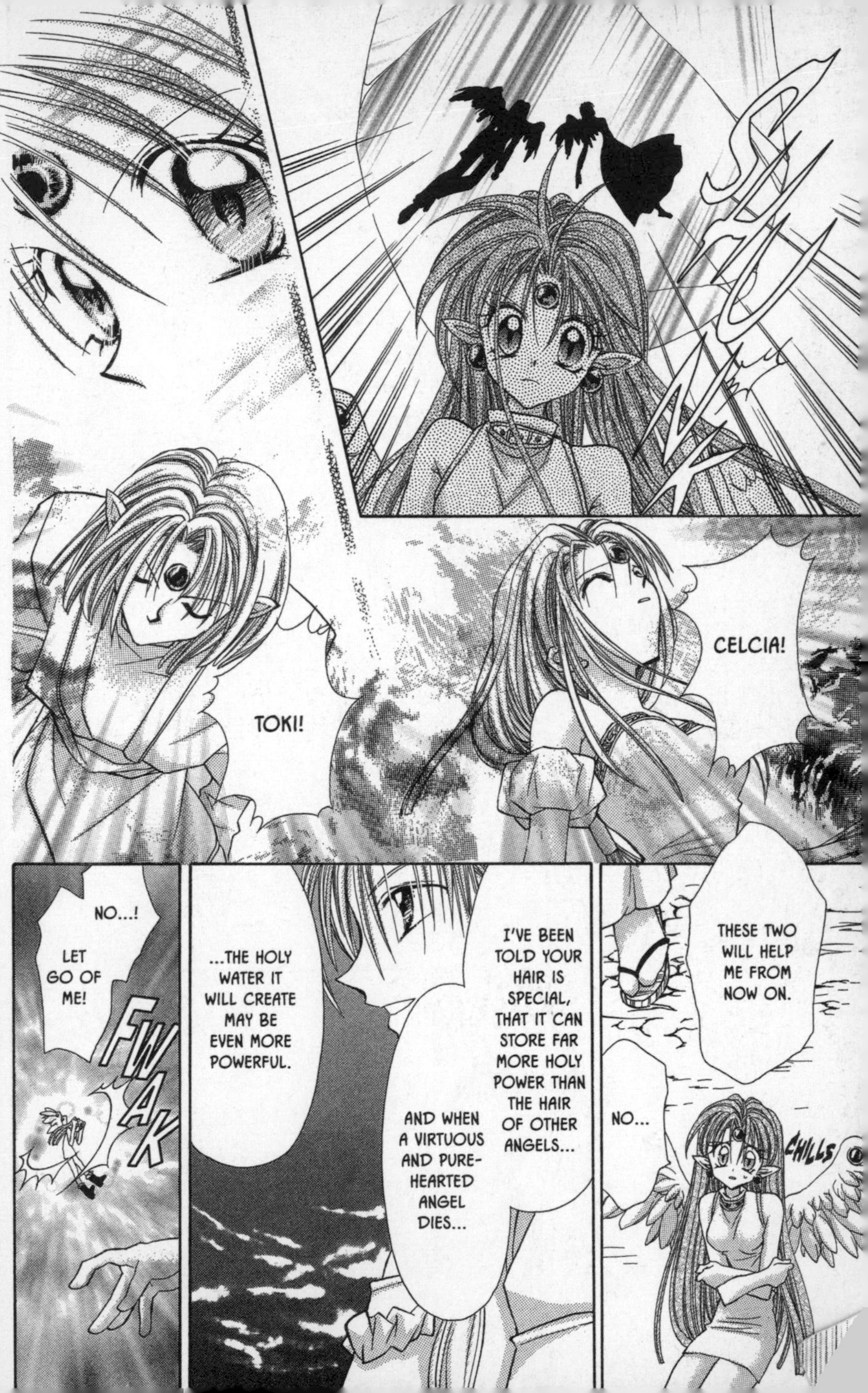
CELCIA!
TOKI!
THESE TWO WILL HELP ME FROM NOW ON.
NO...
CHILLS
I'VE BEEN TOLD YOUR HAIR IS SPECIAL, THAT IT CAN STORE FAR MORE HOLY POWER THAN THE HAIR OF OTHER ANGELS...
AND WHEN A VIRTUOUS AND PURE-HEARTED ANGEL DIES...
...THE HOLY WATER IT WILL CREATE MAY BE EVEN MORE POWERFUL.
NO...!
LET GO OF ME!
FWAK

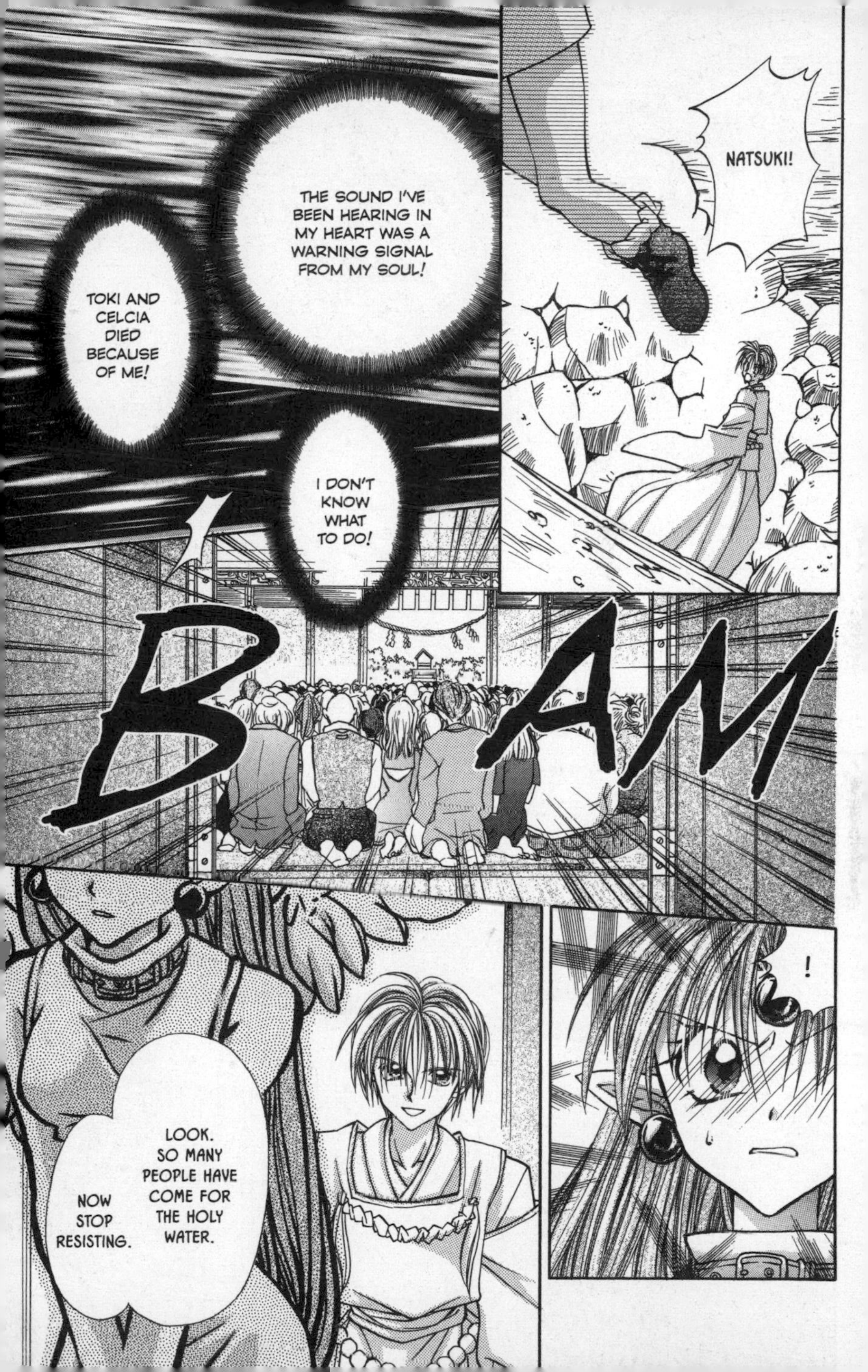
NATSUKI!
THE SOUND I'VE BEEN HEARING IN MY HEART WAS A WARNING SIGNAL FROM MY SOUL!
TOKI AND CELCIA DIED BECAUSE OF ME!
I DON'T KNOW WHAT TO DO!
BAM
!
LOOK. SO MANY PEOPLE HAVE COME FOR THE HOLY WATER.
NOW STOP RESISTING.

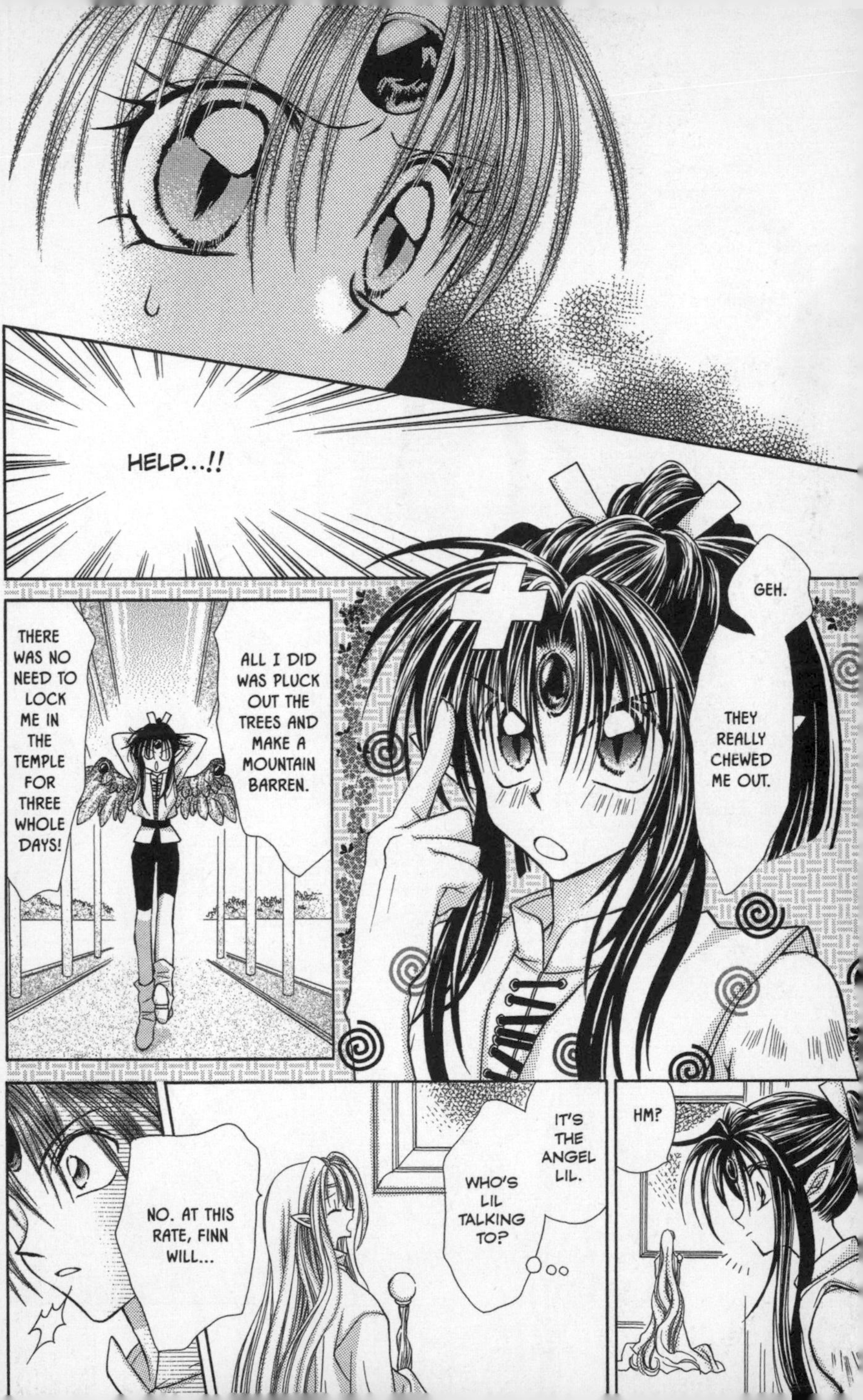
HELP...!!
GEH.
THEY REALLY CHEWED ME OUT.
ALL I DID WAS PLUCK OUT THE TREES AND MAKE A MOUNTAIN BARREN.
THERE WAS NO NEED TO LOCK ME IN THE TEMPLE FOR THREE WHOLE DAYS!
HM?
IT'S THE ANGEL LIL.
WHO'S LIL TALKING TO?
NO. AT THIS RATE, FINN WILL...

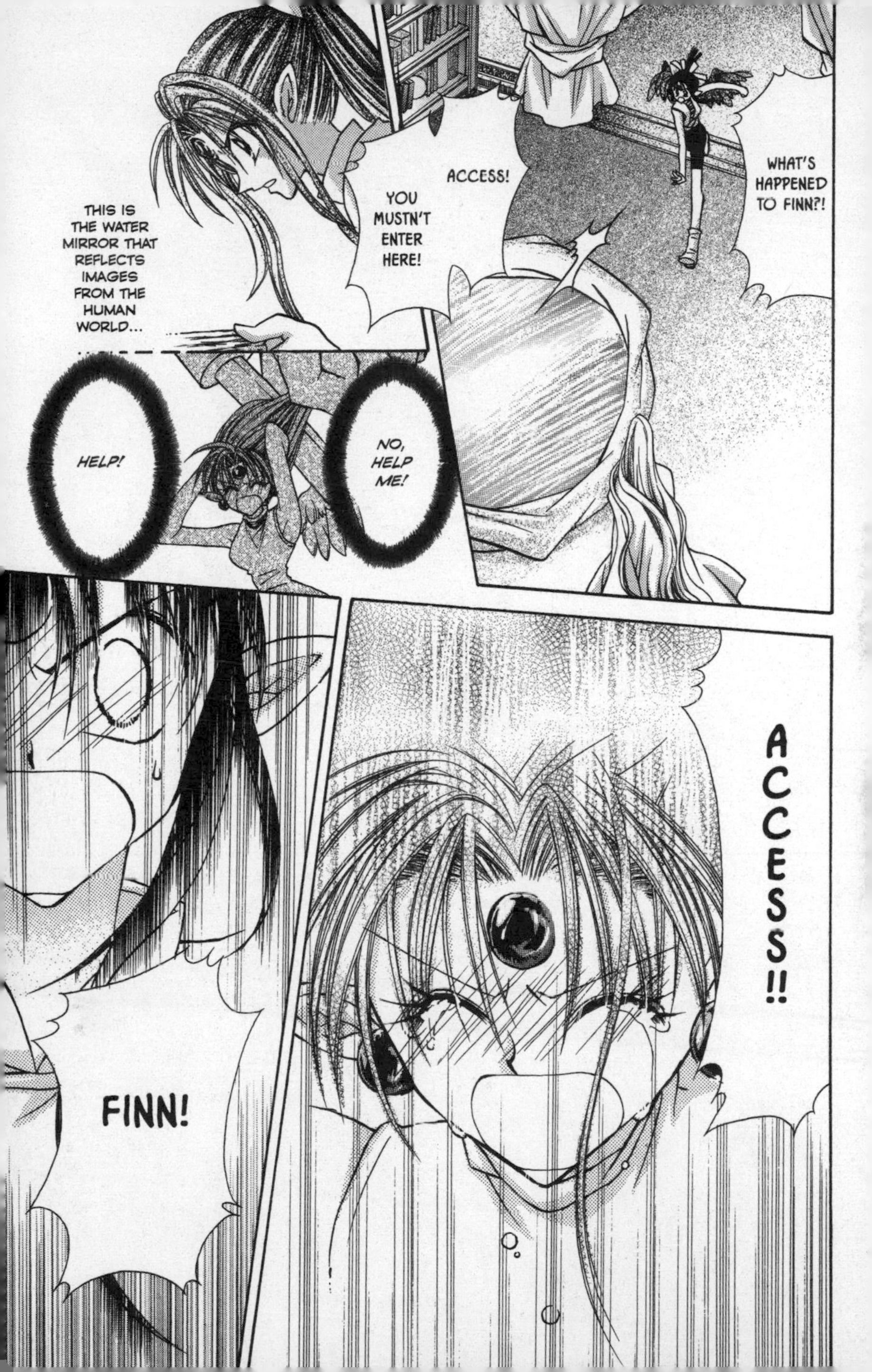
WHAT'S HAPPENED TO FINN?!
ACCESS!
YOU MUSTN'T ENTER HERE!
THIS IS THE WATER MIRROR THAT REFLECTS IMAGES FROM THE HUMAN WORLD...
NO, HELP ME!
HELP!
ACCESS!!
FINN!

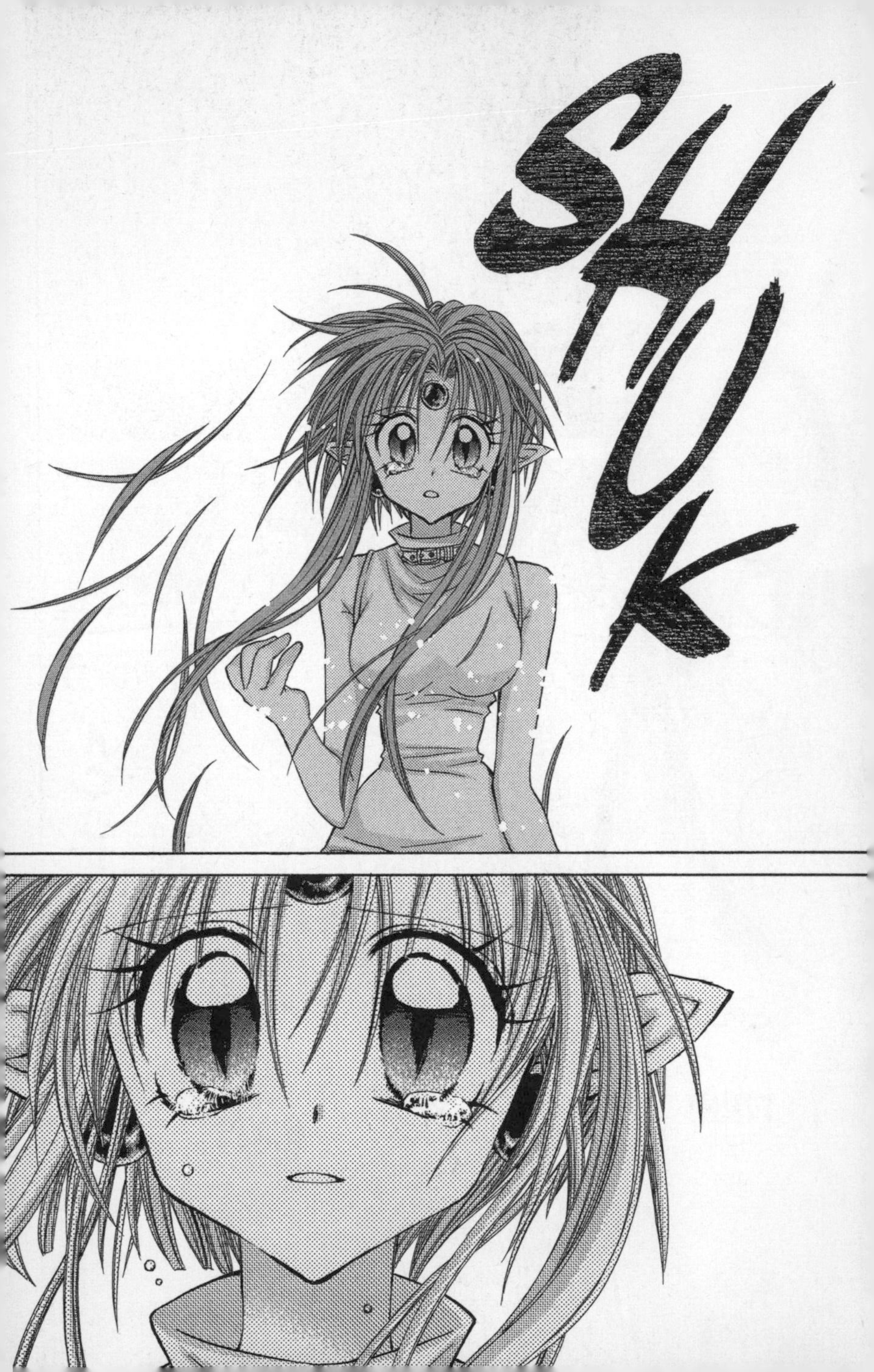
SHUK

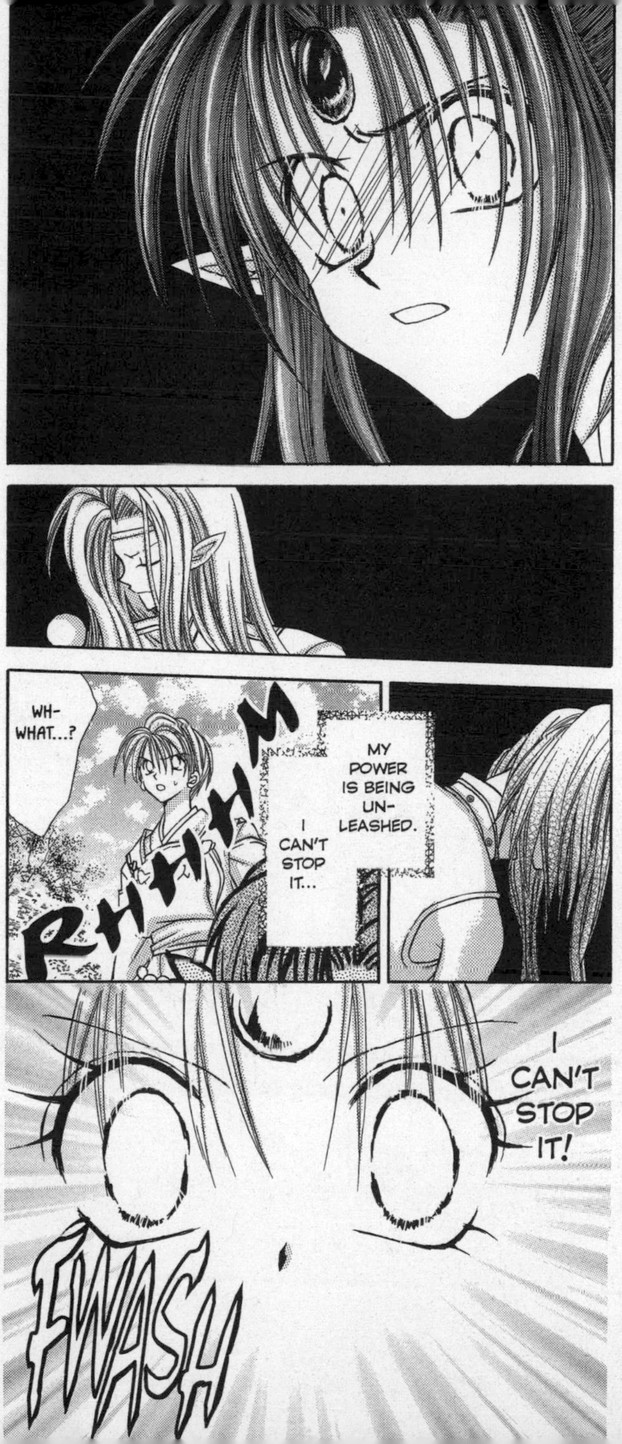
MY POWER IS BEING UN-LEASHED.
I CAN'T STOP IT...
WH-WHAT...?
RHHHM
I CAN'T STOP IT!
FWASH

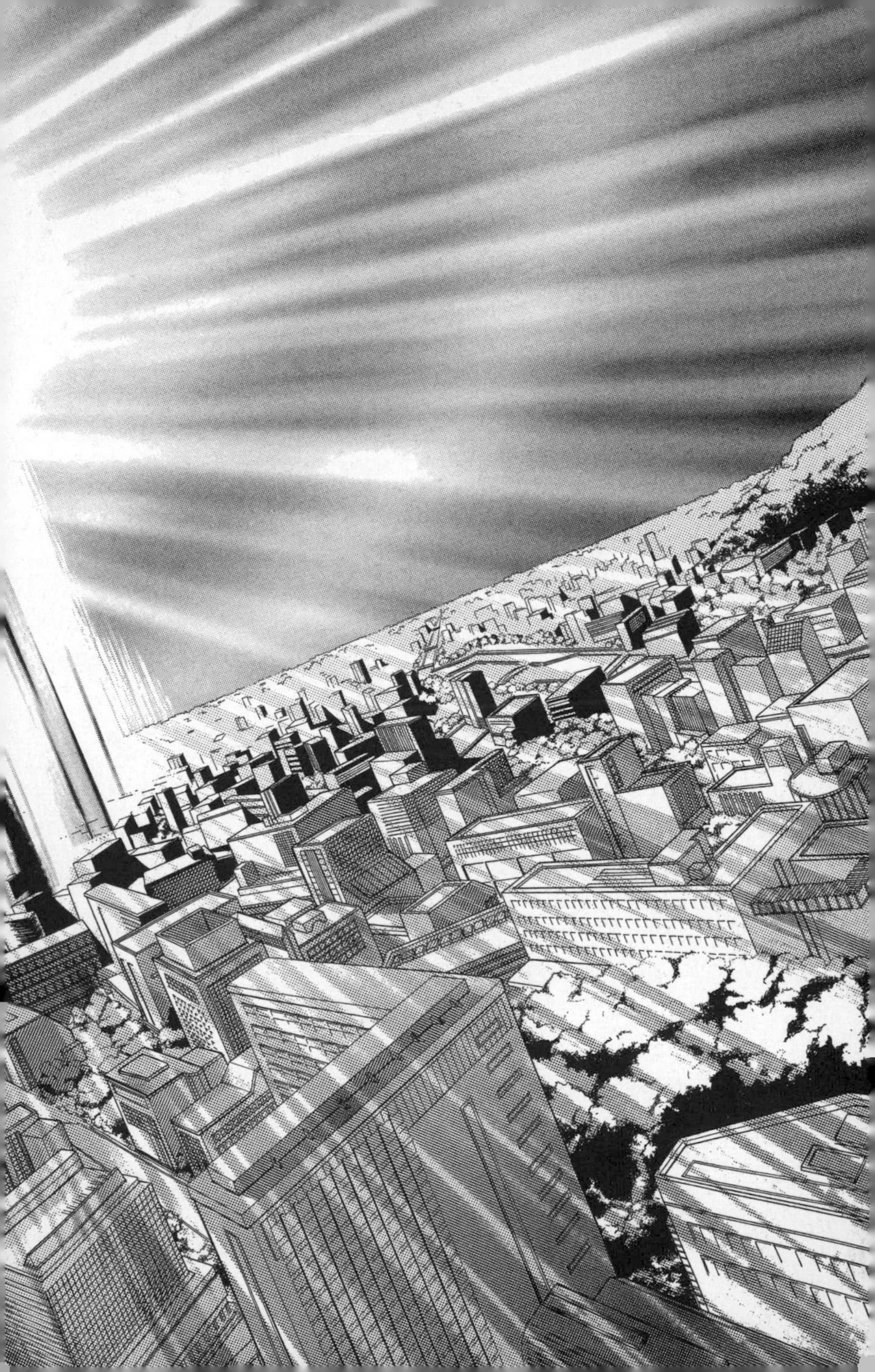

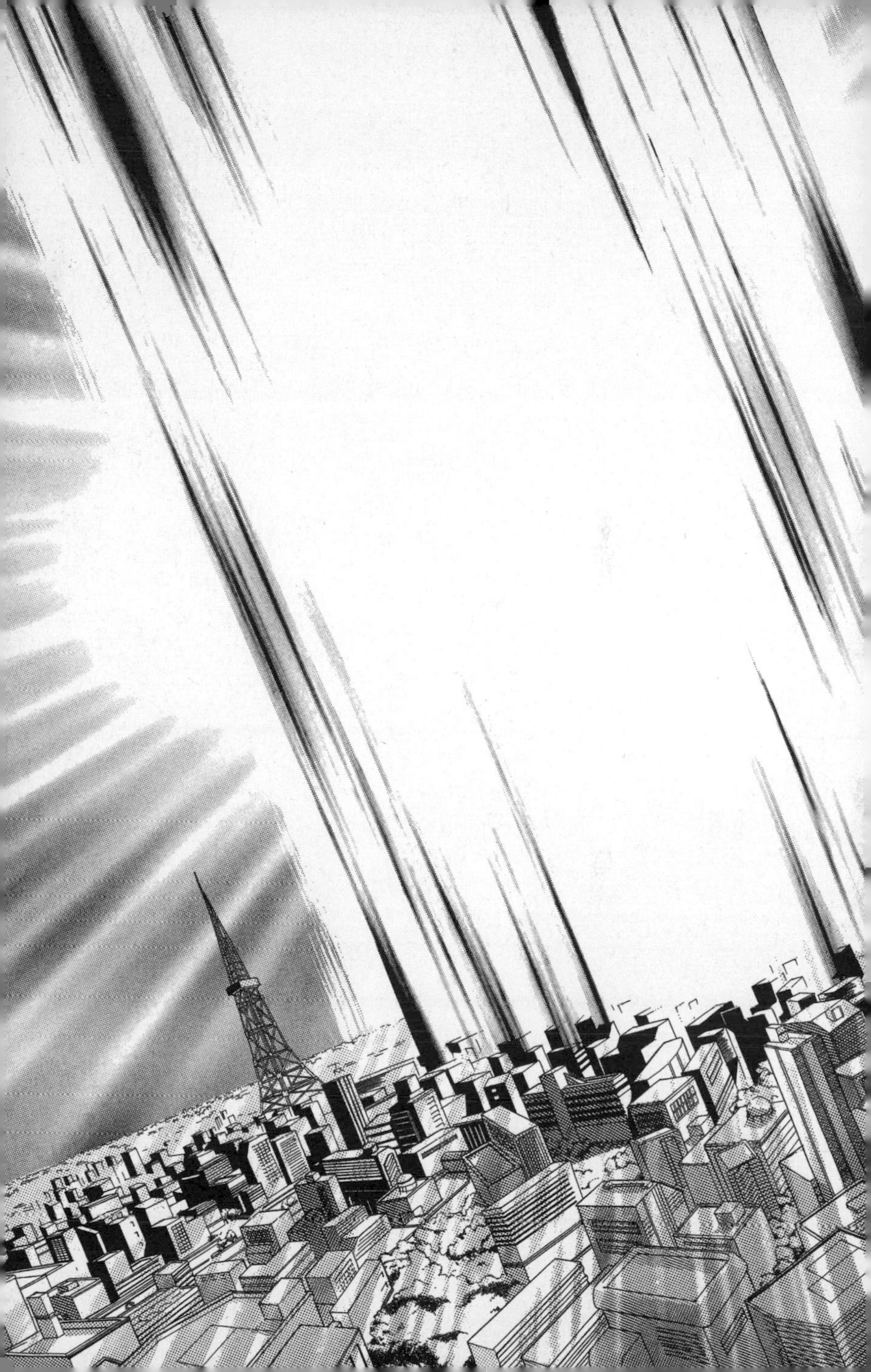

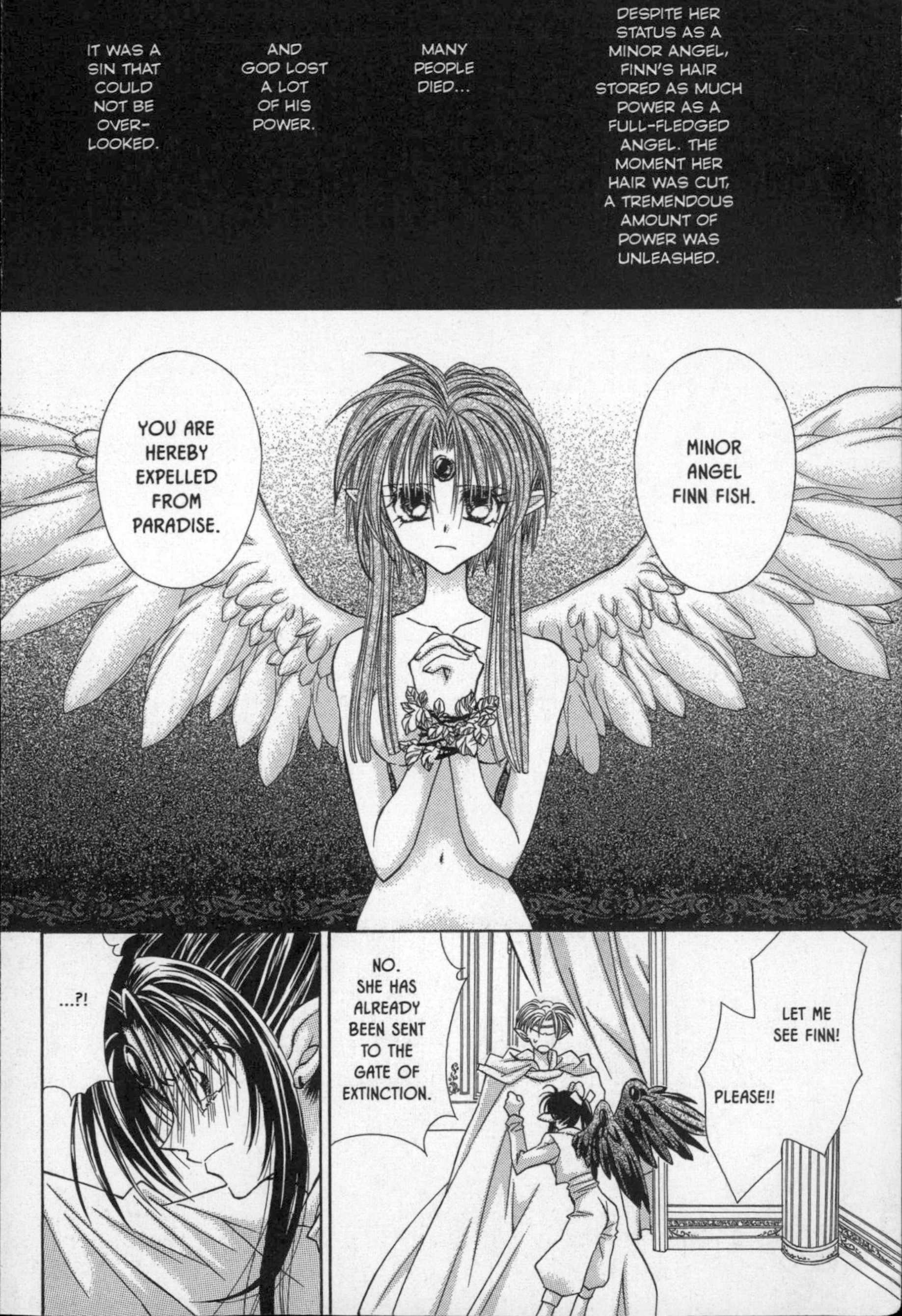
DESPITE HER STATUS AS A MINOR ANGEL, FINN'S HAIR STORED AS MUCH POWER AS A FULL-FLEDGED ANGEL. THE MOMENT HER HAIR WAS CUT, A TREMENDOUS AMOUNT OF POWER WAS UNLEASHED.
MANY PEOPLE DIED...
AND GOD LOST A LOT OF HIS POWER.
IT WAS A SIN THAT COULD NOT BE OVER-LOOKED.
MINOR ANGEL FINN FISH.
YOU ARE HEREBY EXPELLED FROM PARADISE.
LET ME SEE FINN!
PLEASE!!
NO. SHE HAS ALREADY BEEN SENT TO THE GATE OF EXTINCTION.
...?!

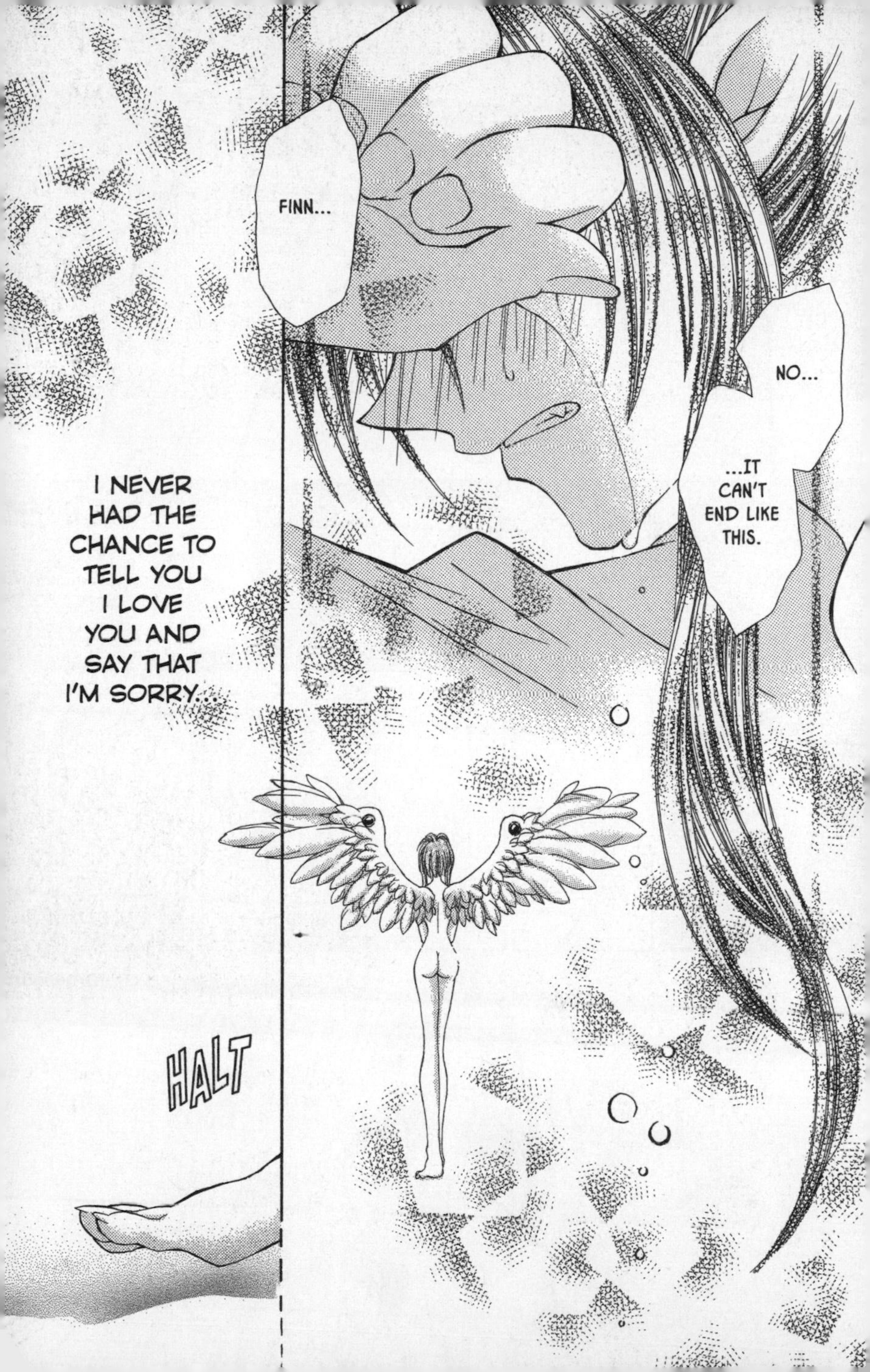
FINN...
NO...
...IT CAN'T END LIKE THIS.
I NEVER HAD THE CHANCE TO TELL YOU I LOVE YOU AND SAY THAT I'M SORRY...
HALT

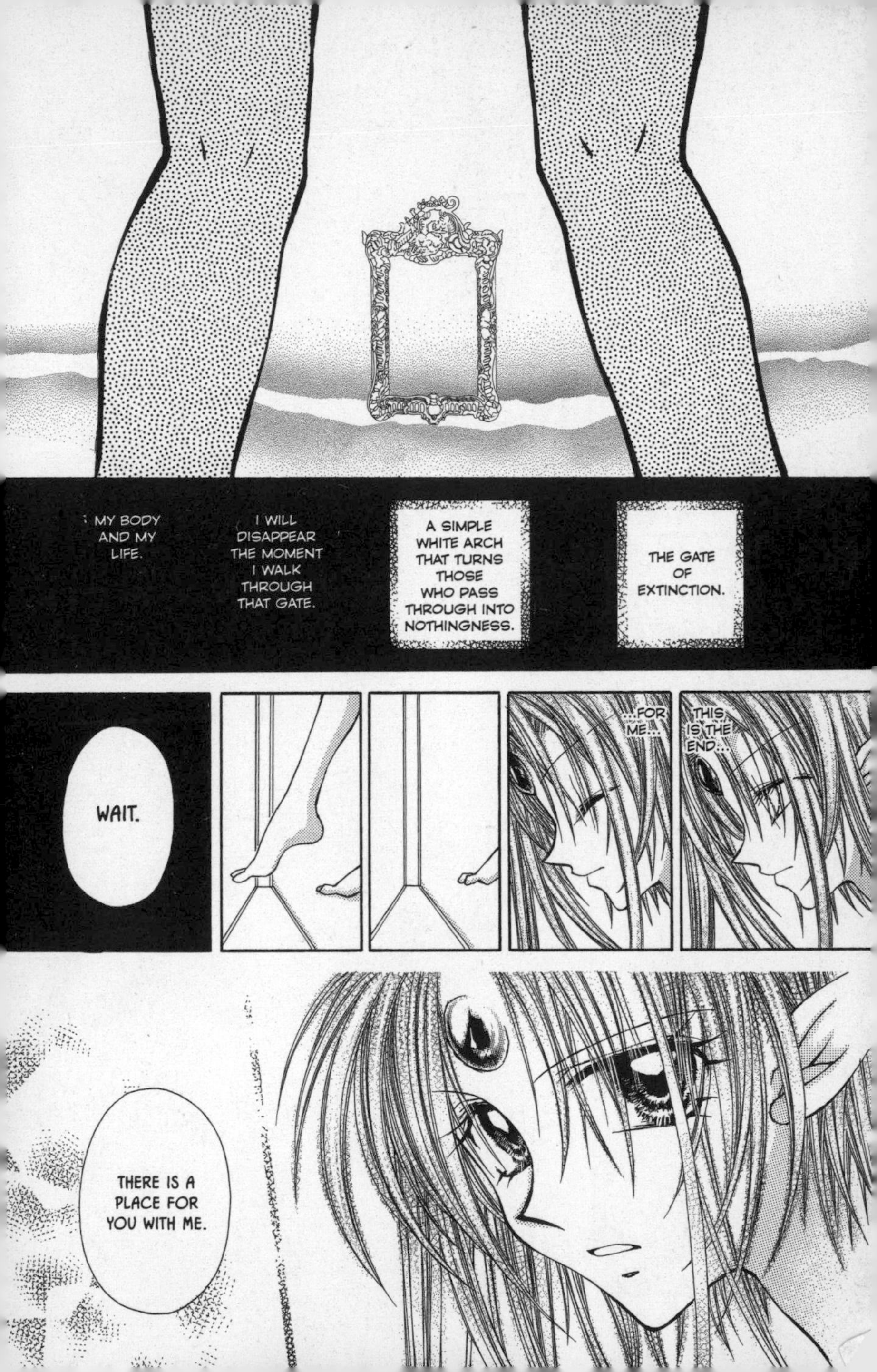
THE GATE OF EXTINCTION.
A SIMPLE WHITE ARCH THAT TURNS THOSE WHO PASS THROUGH INTO NOTHINGNESS.
I WILL DISAPPEAR THE MOMENT I WALK THROUGH THAT GATE.
MY BODY AND MY LIFE.
THIS IS THE END...
...FOR ME...
WAIT.
THERE IS A PLACE FOR YOU WITH ME.

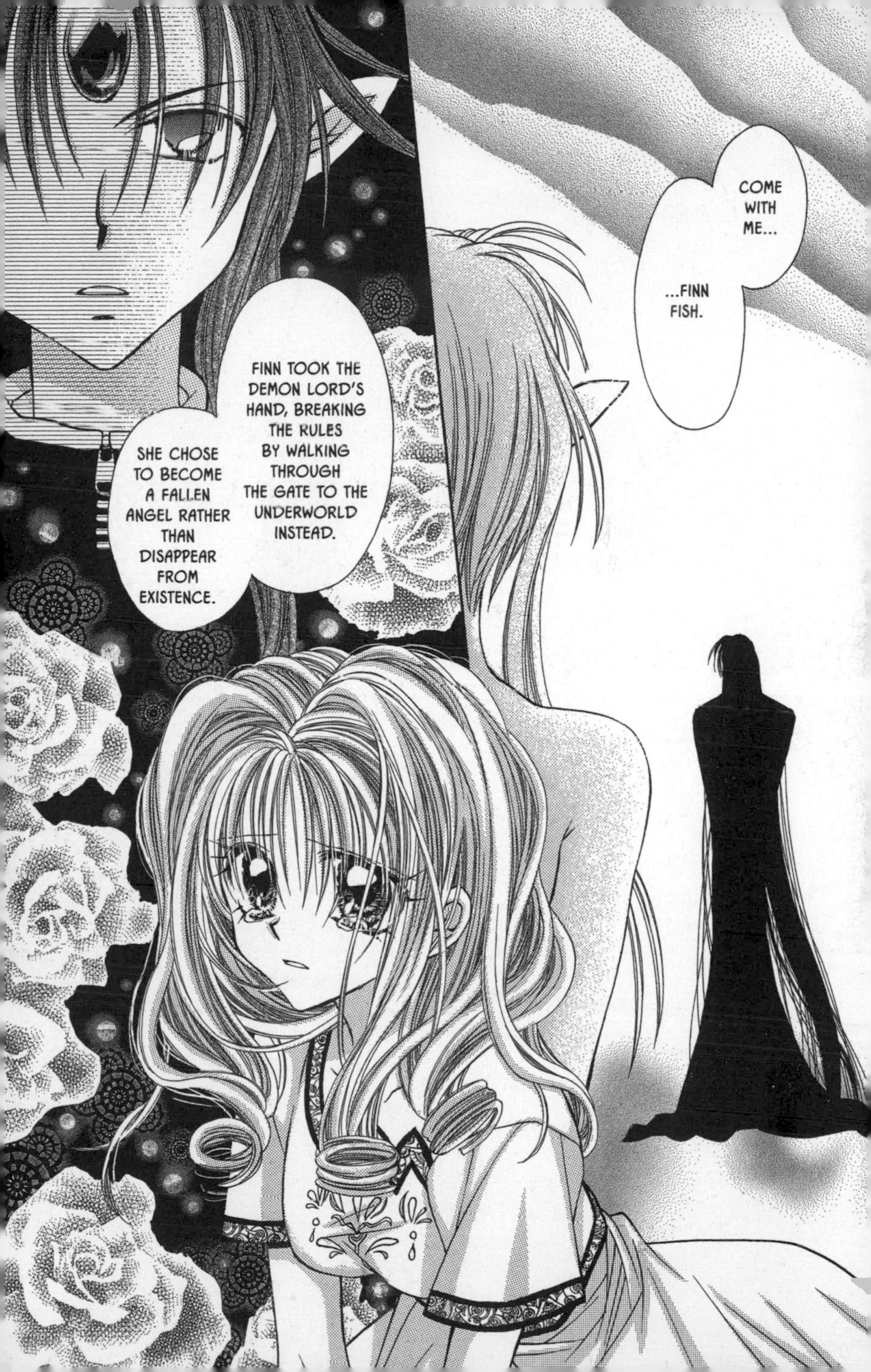
COME WITH ME...
...FINN FISH.
FINN TOOK THE DEMON LORD'S HAND, BREAKING THE RULES BY WALKING THROUGH THE GATE TO THE UNDERWORLD INSTEAD.
SHE CHOSE TO BECOME A FALLEN ANGEL RATHER THAN DISAPPEAR FROM EXISTENCE.

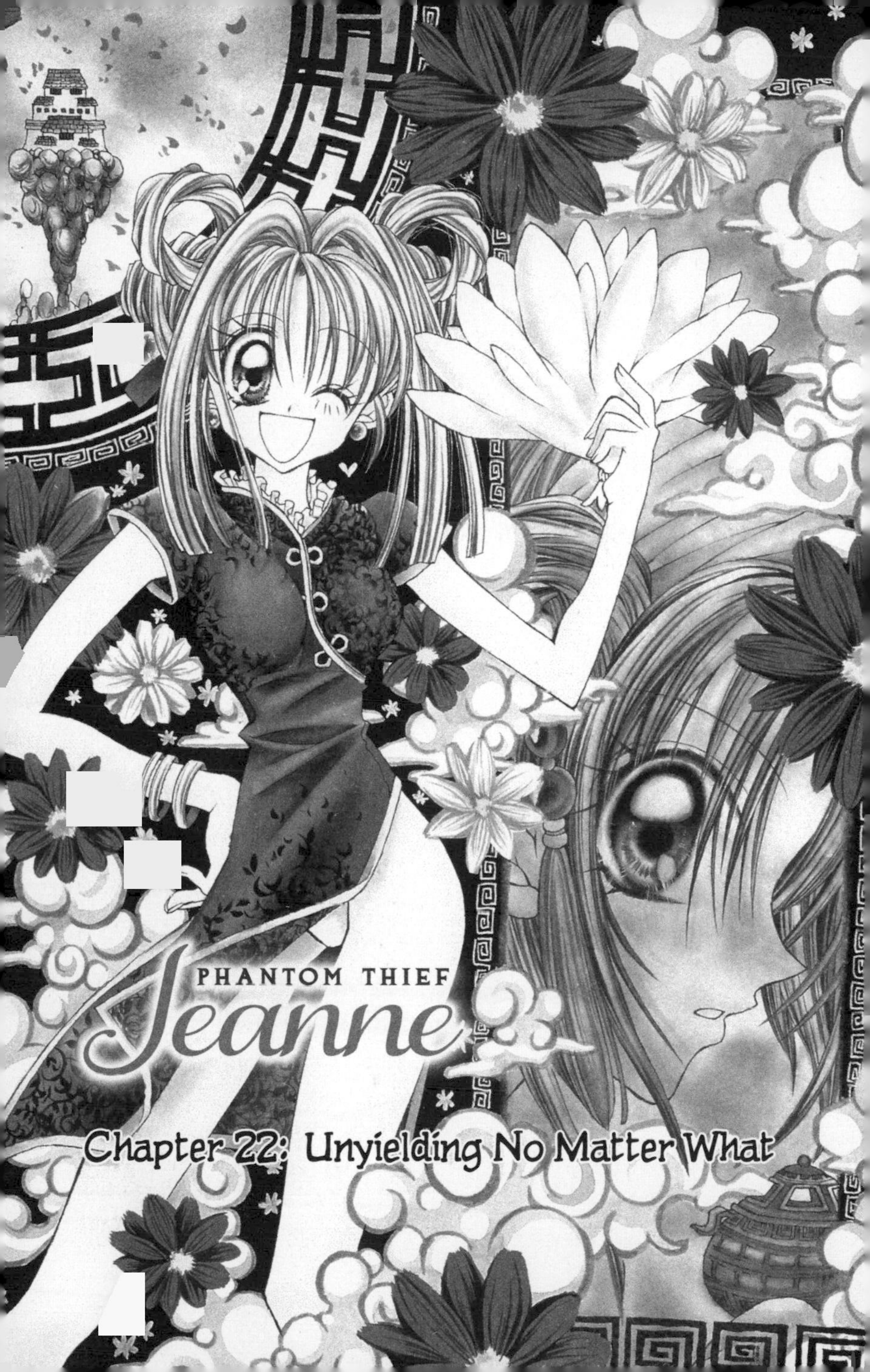
PHANTOM THIEF
Jeanne
Chapter 22: Unyielding No Matter What

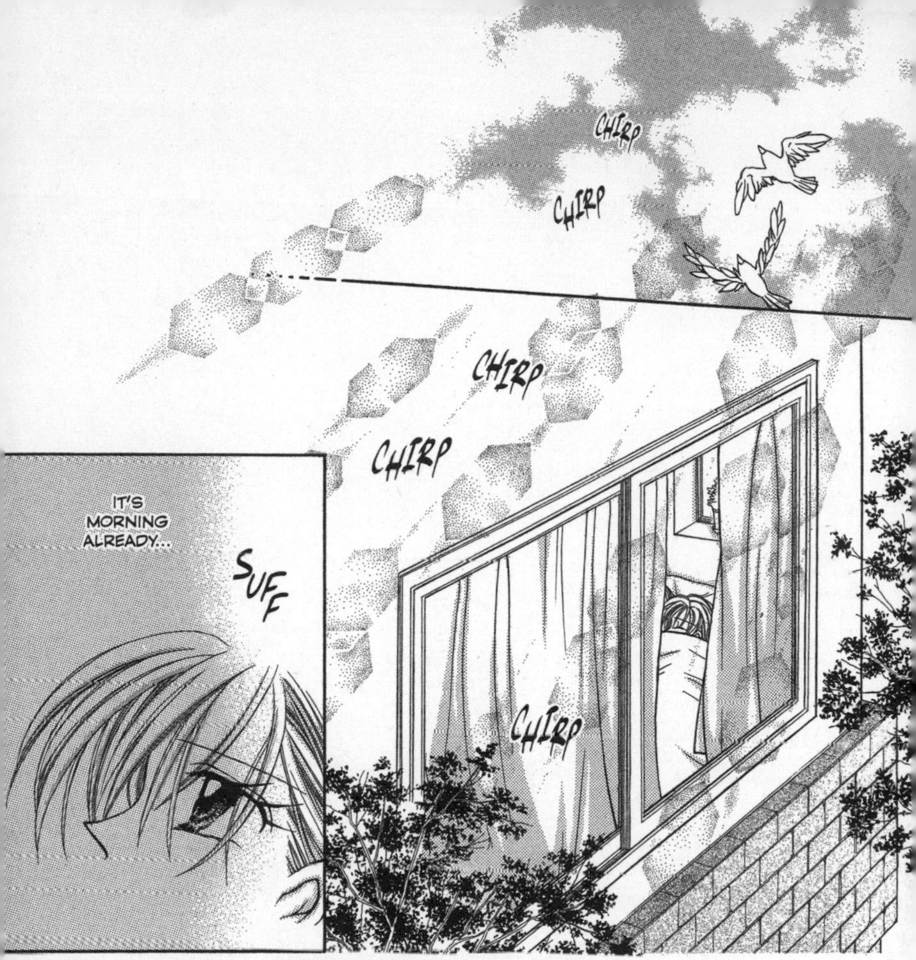
CHIRP
CHIRP
CHIRP
CHIRP
CHIRP
IT'S MORNING ALREADY...
SUFF

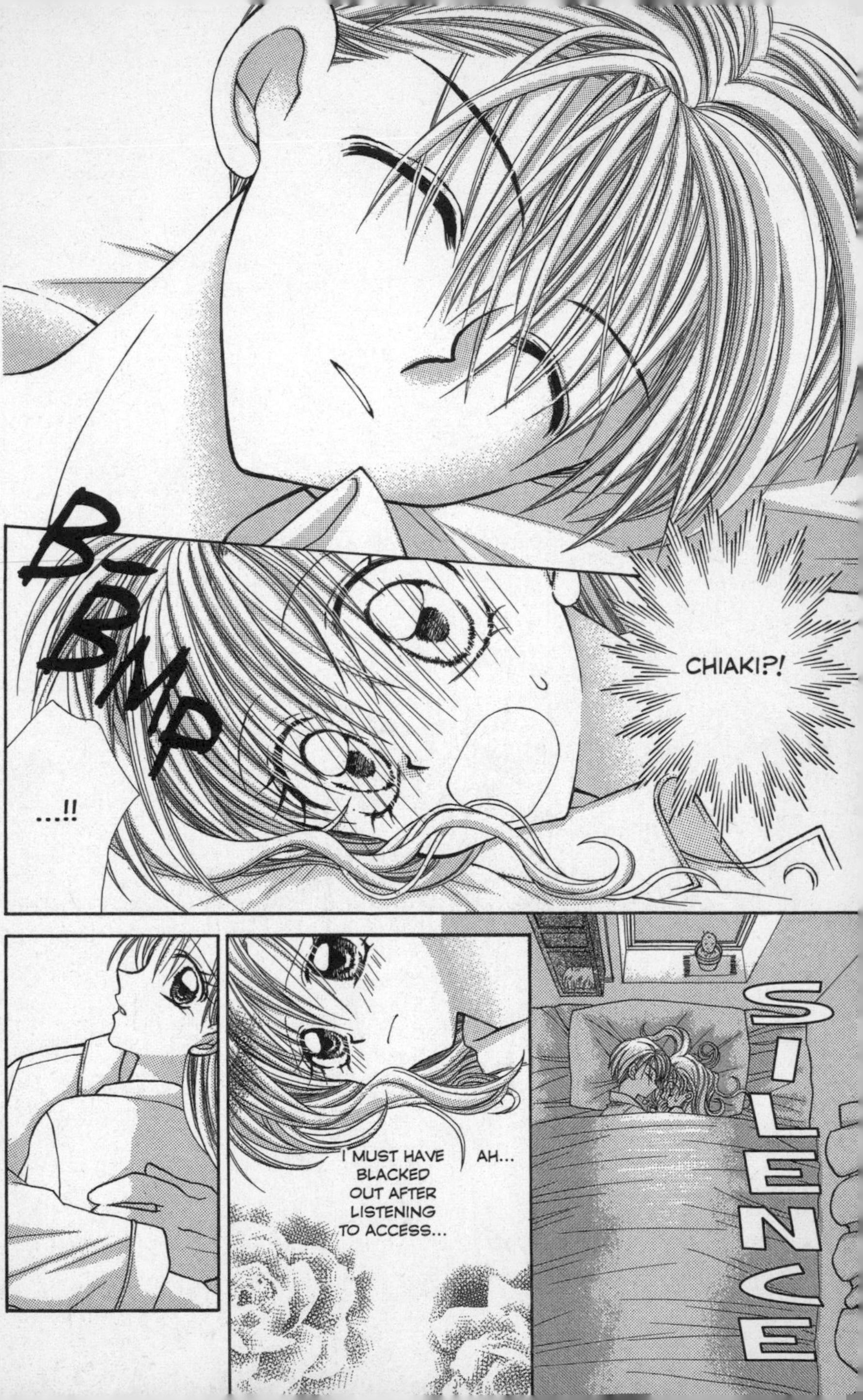
CHIAKI?!
B-BMP
...!!
SILENCE
AH...
I MUST HAVE BLACKED OUT AFTER LISTENING TO ACCESS...

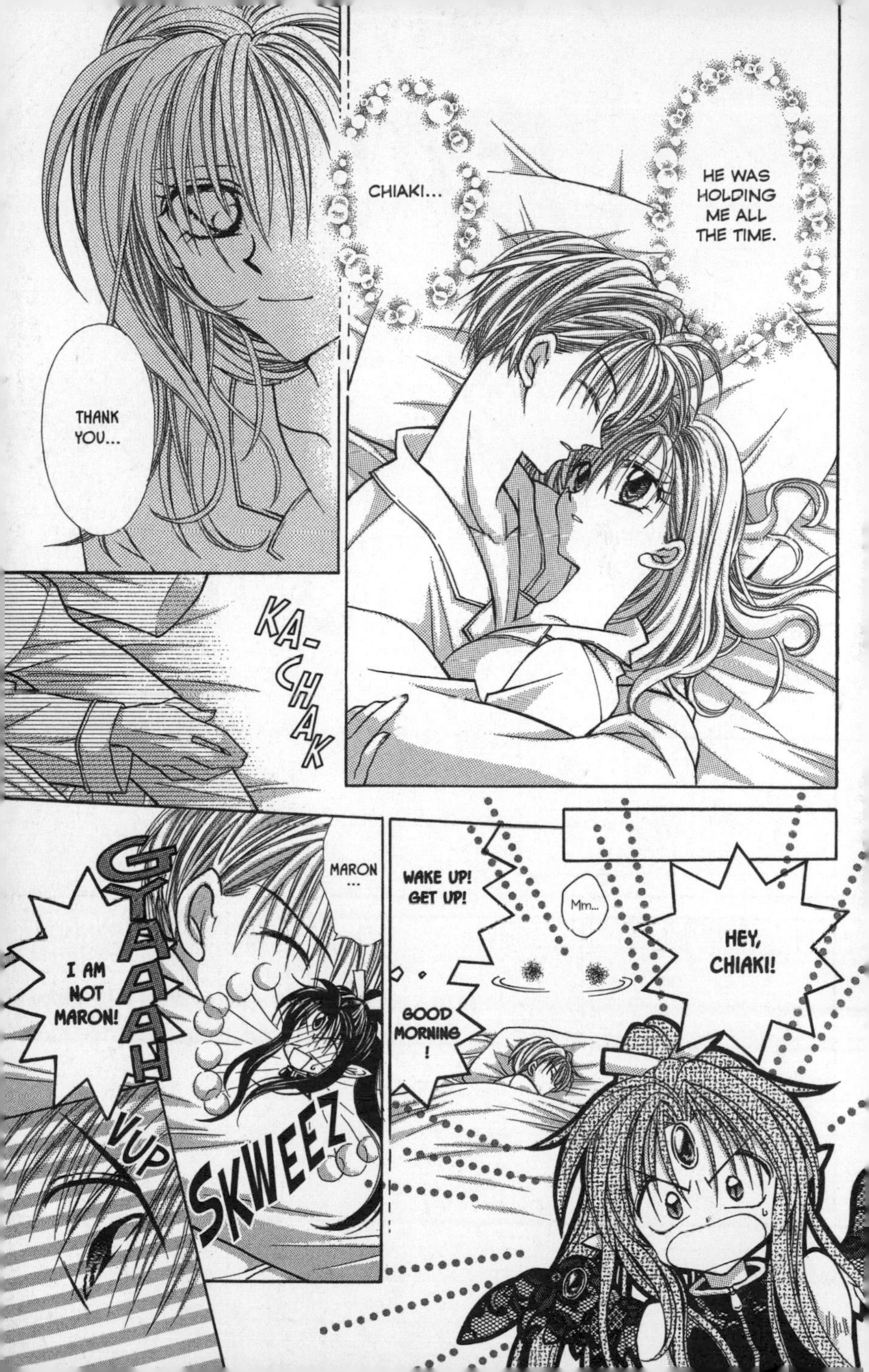
HE WAS HOLDING ME ALL THE TIME.
CHIAKI...
THANK YOU...
KA-CHAK
HEY, CHIAKI!
Mm...
WAKE UP! GET UP!
GOOD MORNING!
MARON ...
GYAAAAH
I AM NOT MARON!
SKWEEZ
VUP

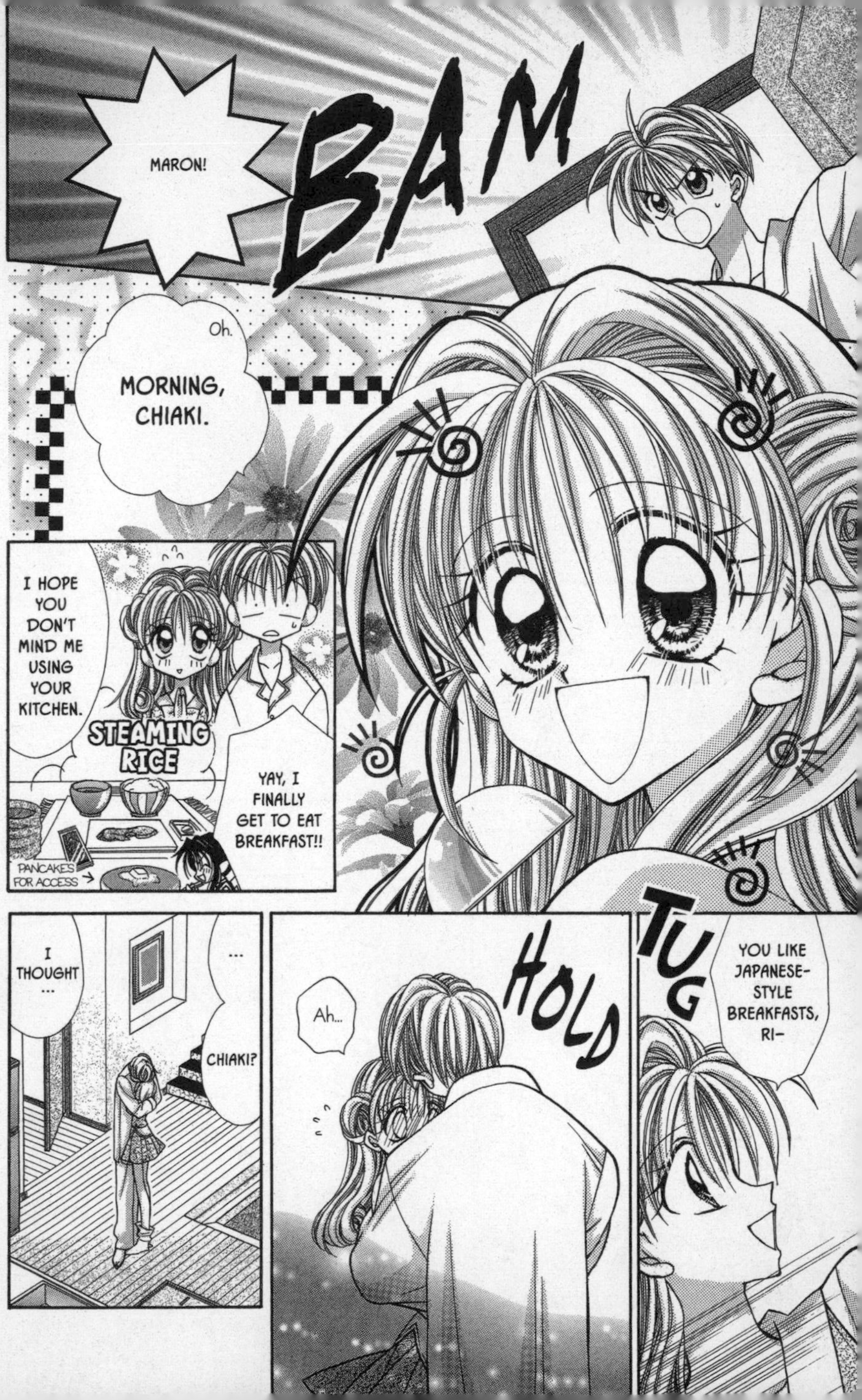
BAM
MARON!
Oh.
MORNING, CHIAKI.
I HOPE YOU DON'T MIND ME USING YOUR KITCHEN.
STEAMING RICE
YAY, I FINALLY GET TO EAT BREAKFAST!!
PANCAKES FOR ACCESS
YOU LIKE JAPANESE-STYLE BREAKFASTS, RI–
TUG
HOLD
Ah...
...
CHIAKI?
I THOUGHT ...

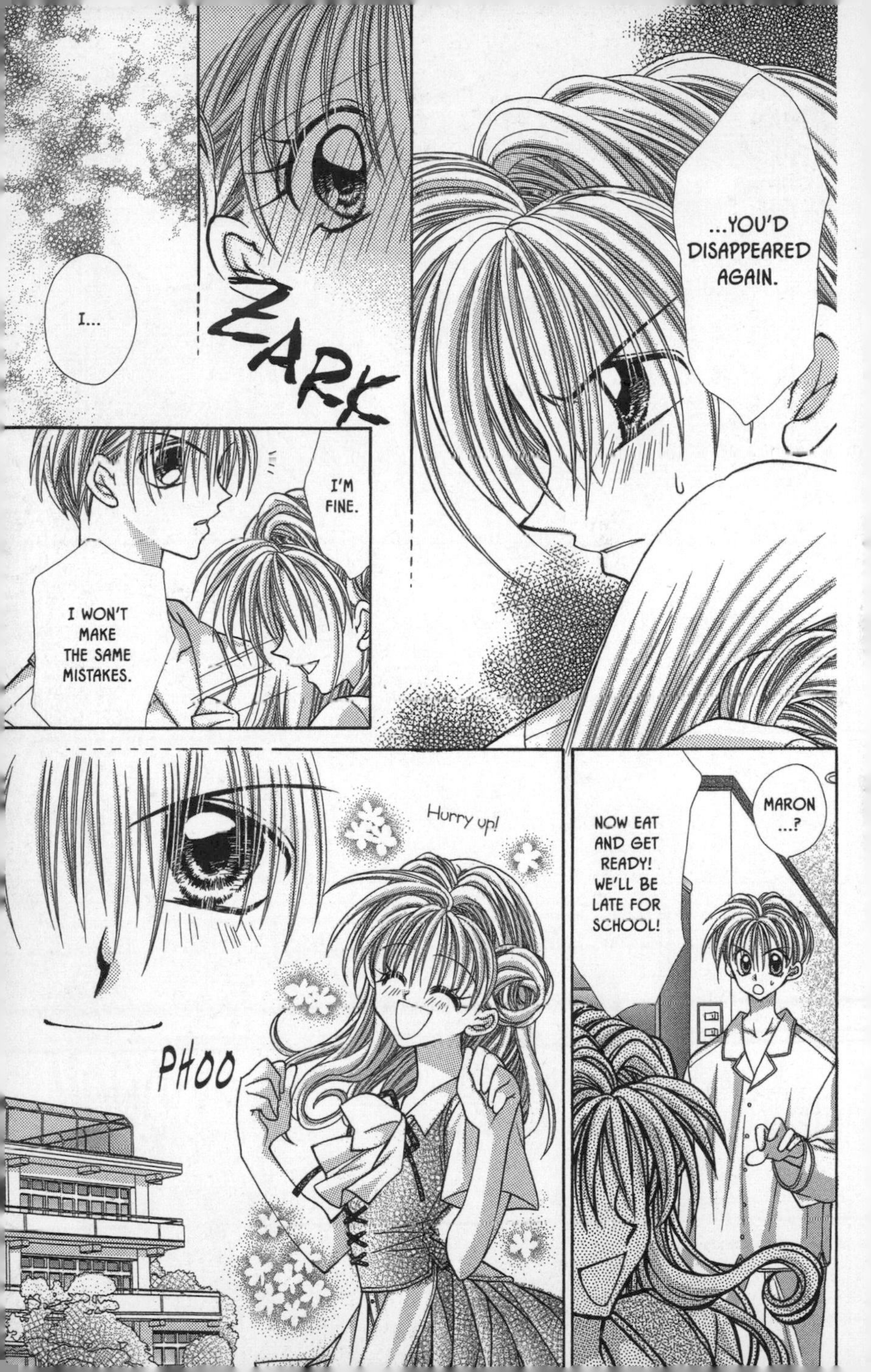
...YOU'D DISAPPEARED AGAIN.
ZARK
I...
I'M FINE.
I WON'T MAKE THE SAME MISTAKES.
MARON ...?
NOW EAT AND GET READY! WE'LL BE LATE FOR SCHOOL!
Hurry up!
PHOO

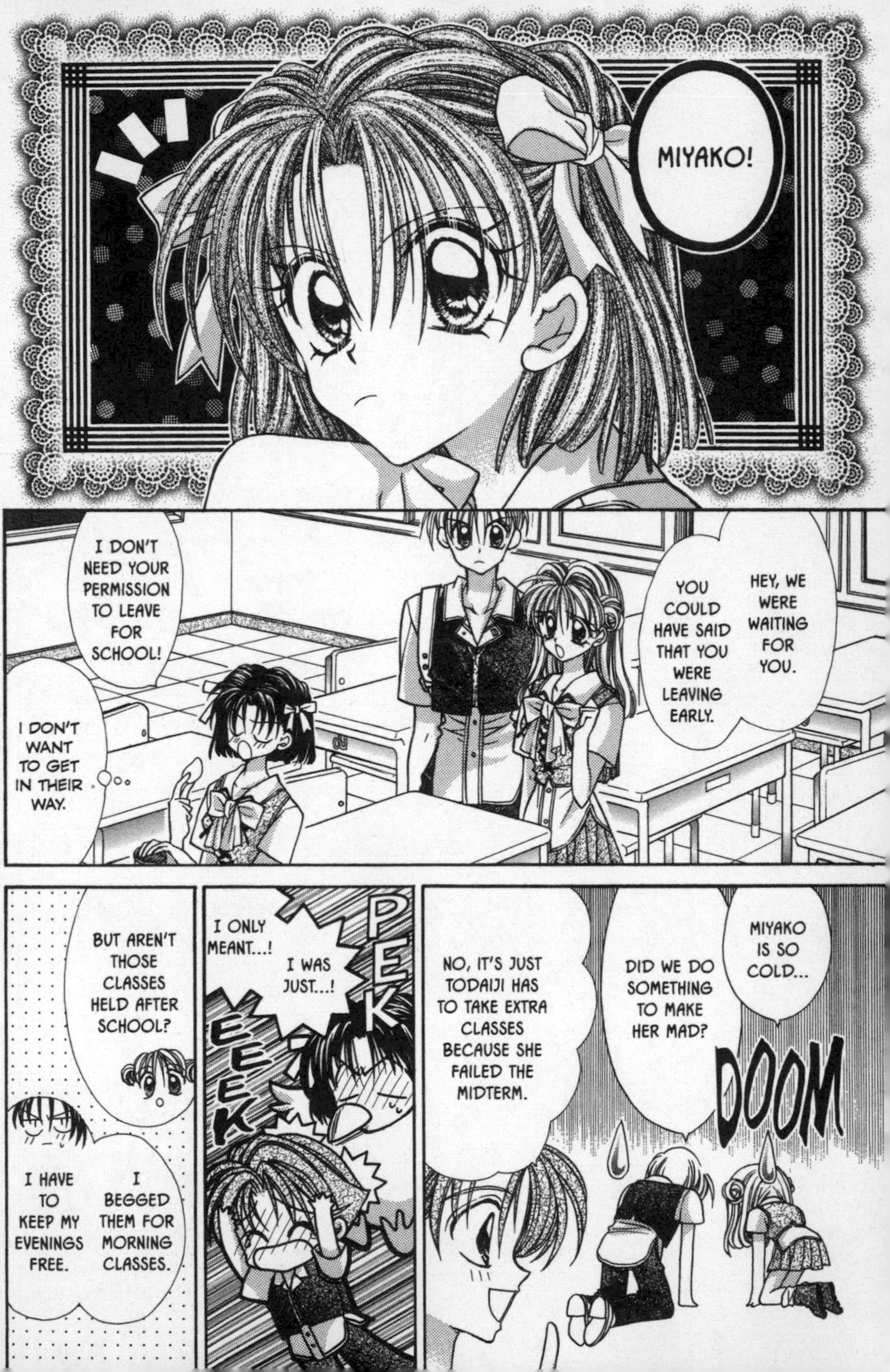
MIYAKO!
HEY, WE WERE WAITING FOR YOU.
YOU COULD HAVE SAID THAT YOU WERE LEAVING EARLY.
I DON'T NEED YOUR PERMISSION TO LEAVE FOR SCHOOL!
I DON'T WANT TO GET IN THEIR WAY.
MIYAKO IS SO COLD...
DID WE DO SOMETHING TO MAKE HER MAD?
DOOM
NO, IT'S JUST TODAIJI HAS TO TAKE EXTRA CLASSES BECAUSE SHE FAILED THE MIDTERM.
PEK
I WAS JUST...!
I ONLY MEANT...!
EEEEK
BUT AREN'T THOSE CLASSES HELD AFTER SCHOOL?
I BEGGED THEM FOR MORNING CLASSES.
I HAVE TO KEEP MY EVENINGS FREE.

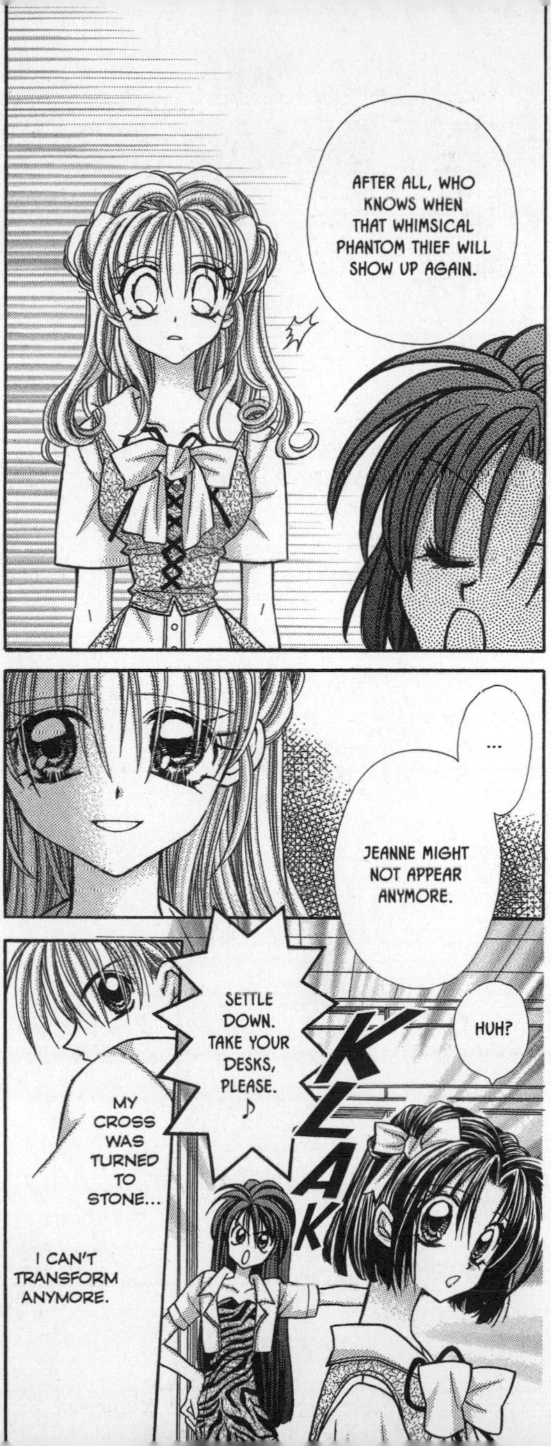
AFTER ALL, WHO KNOWS WHEN THAT WHIMSICAL PHANTOM THIEF WILL SHOW UP AGAIN.
...
JEANNE MIGHT NOT APPEAR ANYMORE.
HUH?
KLAK
SETTLE DOWN. TAKE YOUR DESKS, PLEASE. ♪
MY CROSS WAS TURNED TO STONE...
I CAN'T TRANSFORM ANYMORE.

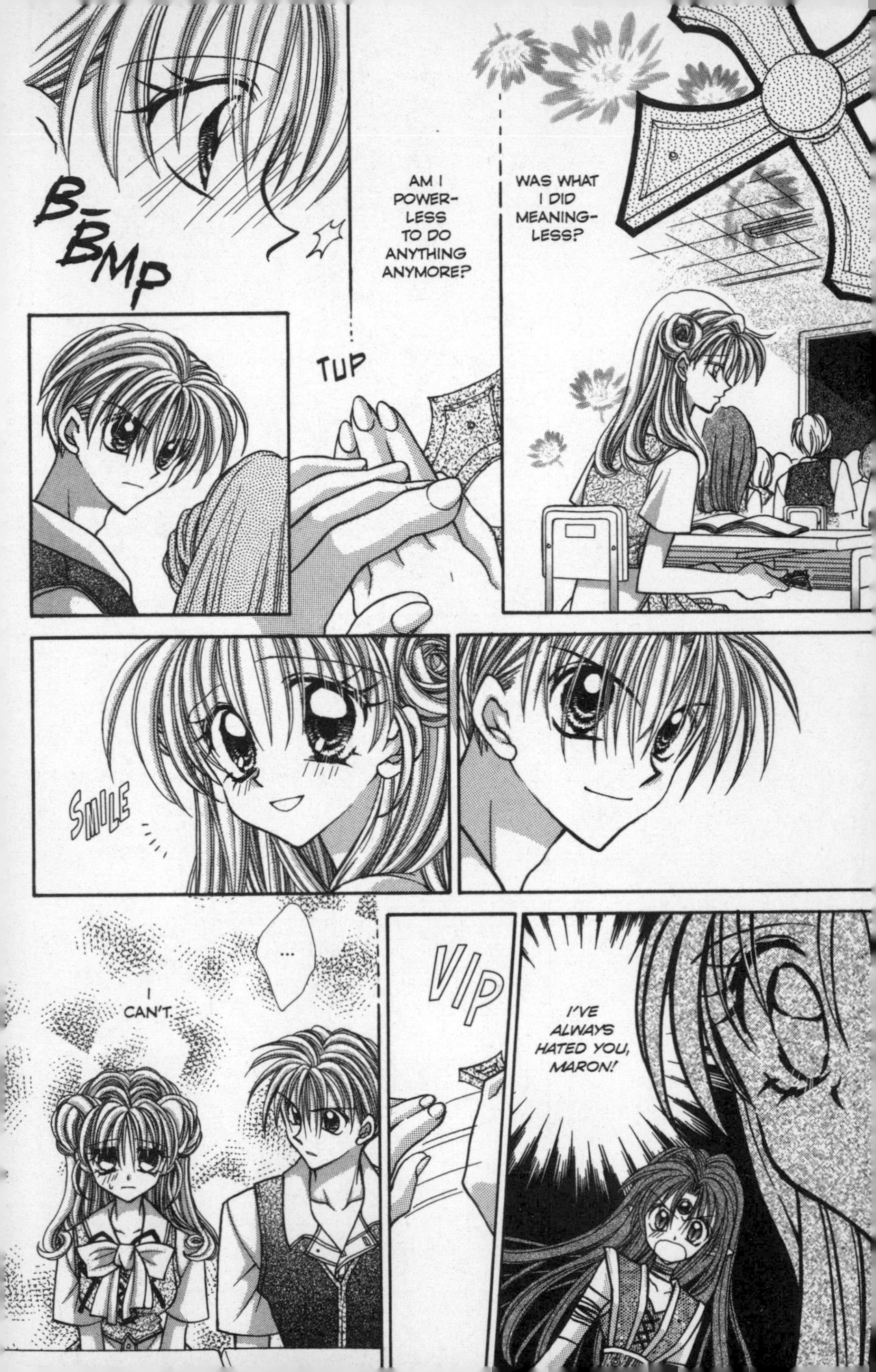
WAS WHAT I DID MEANING-LESS?
AM I POWER-LESS TO DO ANYTHING ANYMORE?
TUP
B-BMP
SMILE
I'VE ALWAYS HATED YOU, MARON!
VIP
...
I CAN'T.

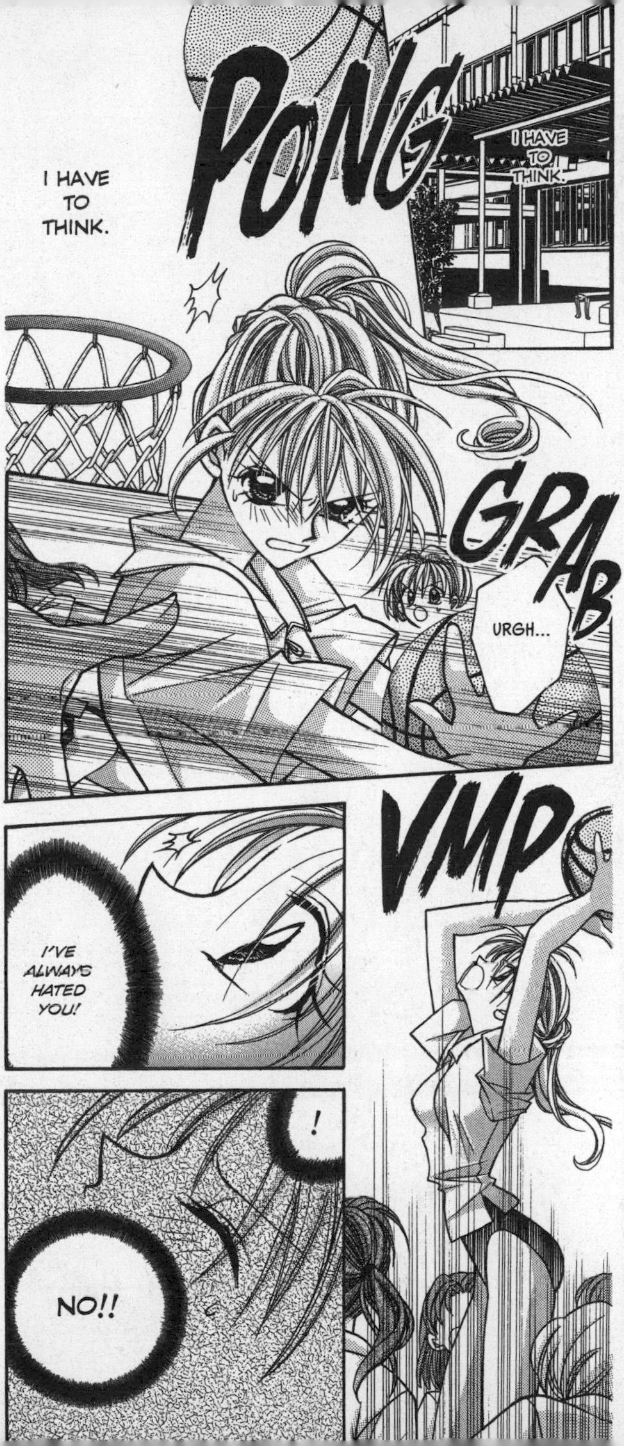
I HAVE TO THINK.
PONG
I HAVE TO THINK.
GRAB
URGH...
VMP
I'VE ALWAYS HATED YOU!
!
NO!!

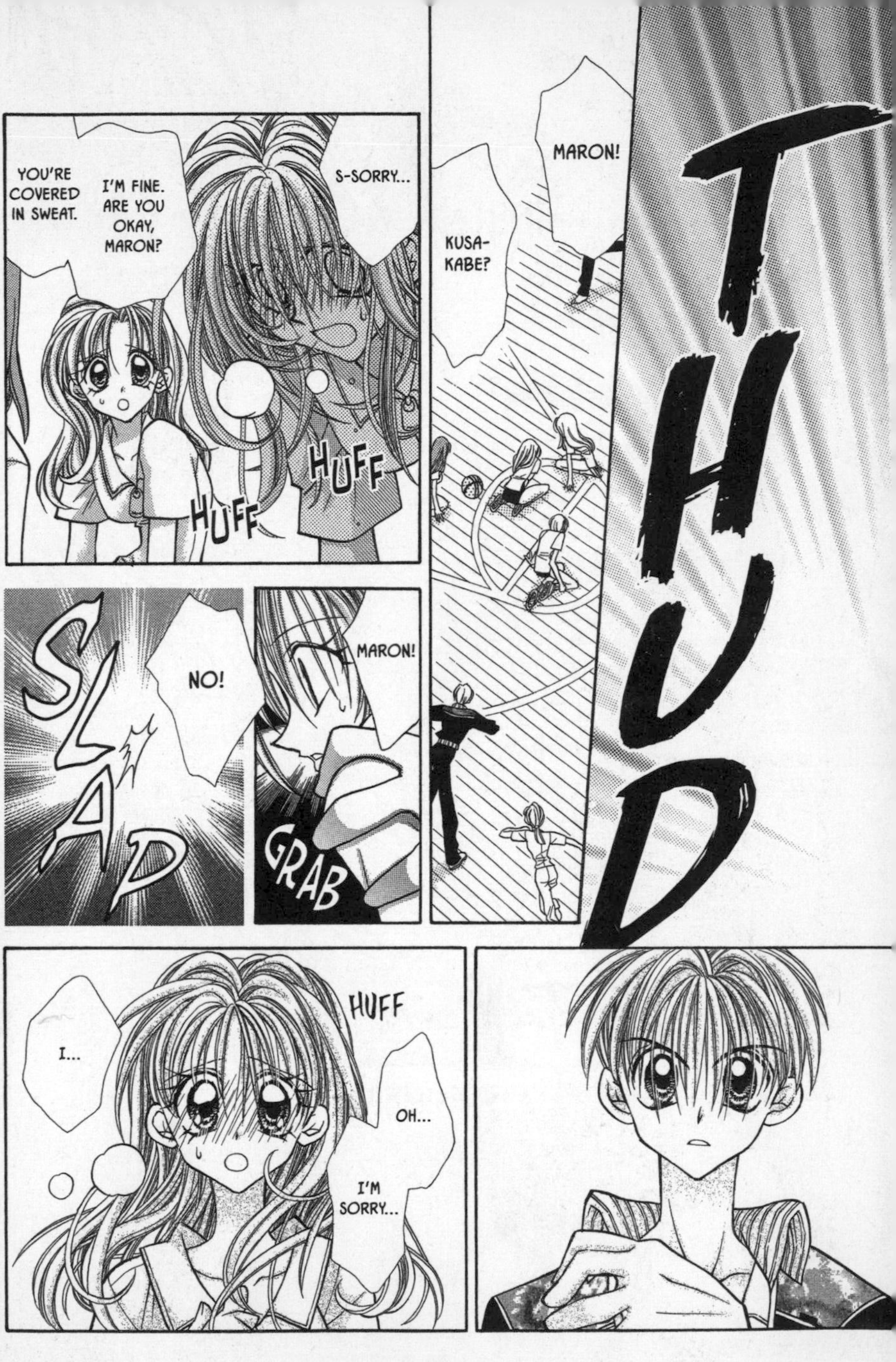
THUD
MARON!
KUSA-KABE?
S-SORRY...
I'M FINE. ARE YOU OKAY, MARON?
YOU'RE COVERED IN SWEAT.
HUFF
HUFF
MARON!
GRAB
NO!
SLAP
HUFF
OH...
I'M SORRY...
I...

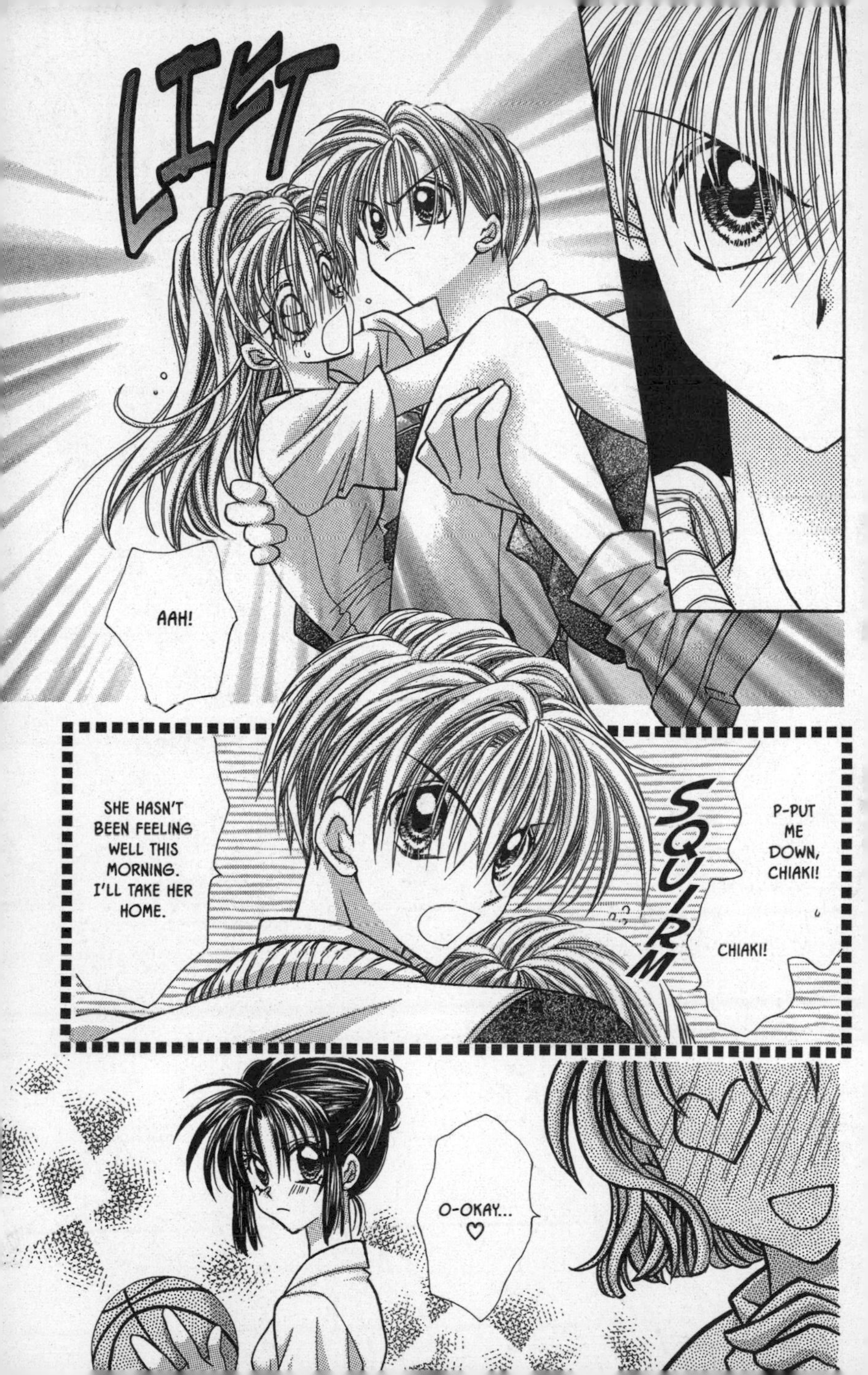
LIFT
AAH!
P-PUT ME DOWN, CHIAKI!
CHIAKI!
SQUIRM
SHE HASN'T BEEN FEELING WELL THIS MORNING. I'LL TAKE HER HOME.
O-OKAY... ♡

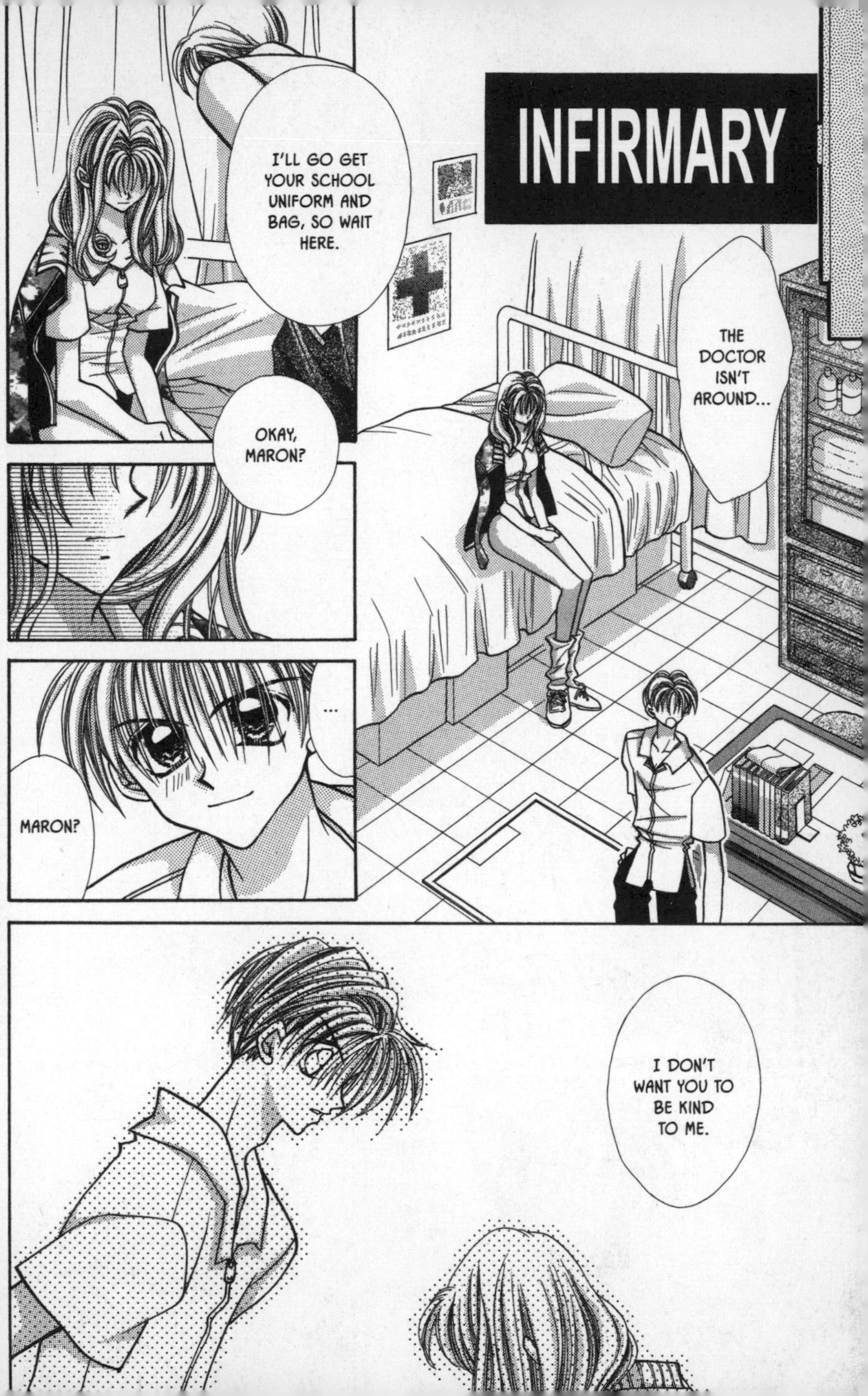
INFIRMARY
THE DOCTOR ISN'T AROUND...
I'LL GO GET YOUR SCHOOL UNIFORM AND BAG, SO WAIT HERE.
OKAY, MARON?
...
MARON?
I DON'T WANT YOU TO BE KIND TO ME.

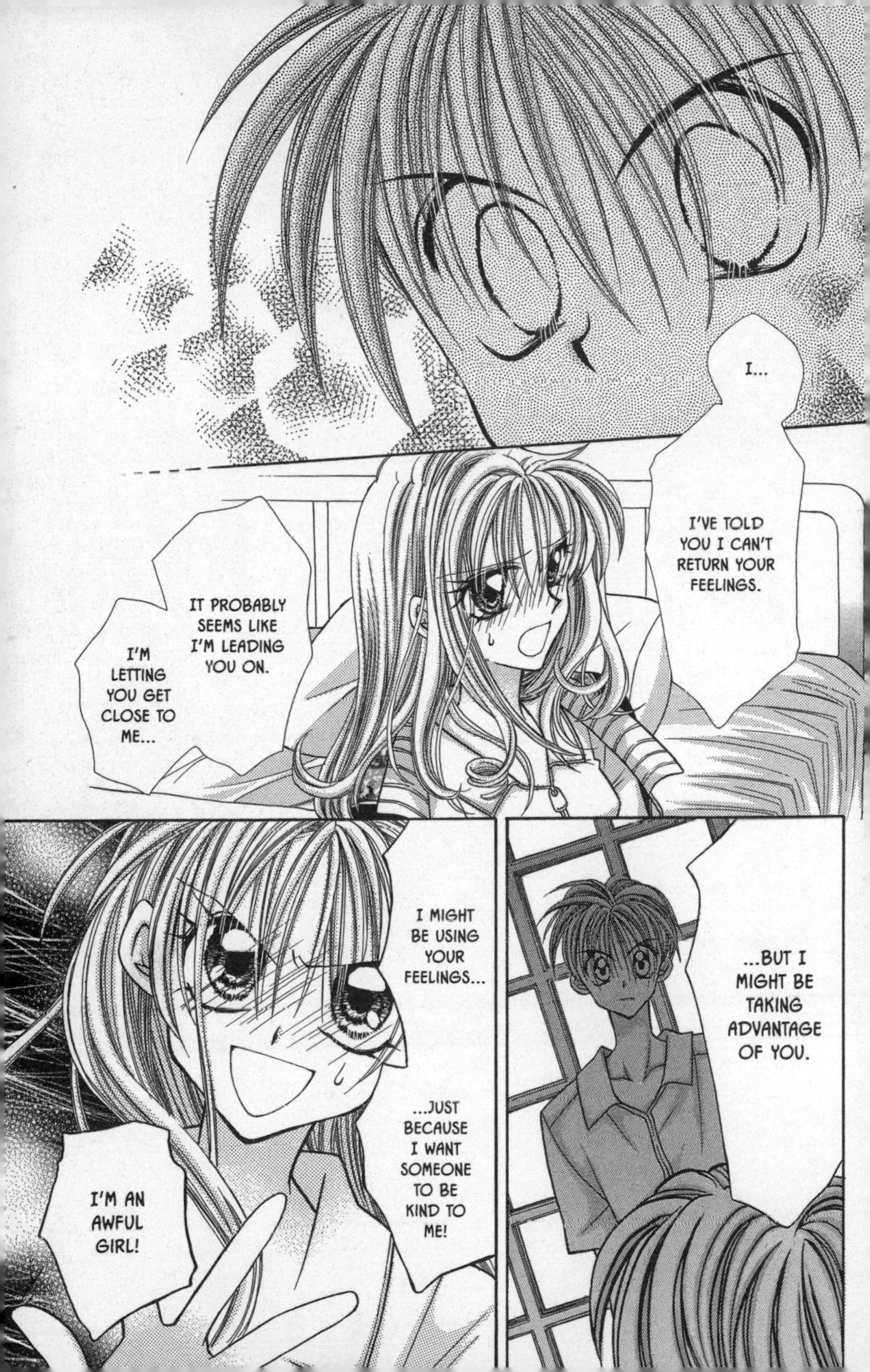
I...
I'VE TOLD YOU I CAN'T RETURN YOUR FEELINGS.
IT PROBABLY SEEMS LIKE I'M LEADING YOU ON.
I'M LETTING YOU GET CLOSE TO ME...
...BUT I MIGHT BE TAKING ADVANTAGE OF YOU.
I MIGHT BE USING YOUR FEELINGS...
...JUST BECAUSE I WANT SOMEONE TO BE KIND TO ME!
I'M AN AWFUL GIRL!

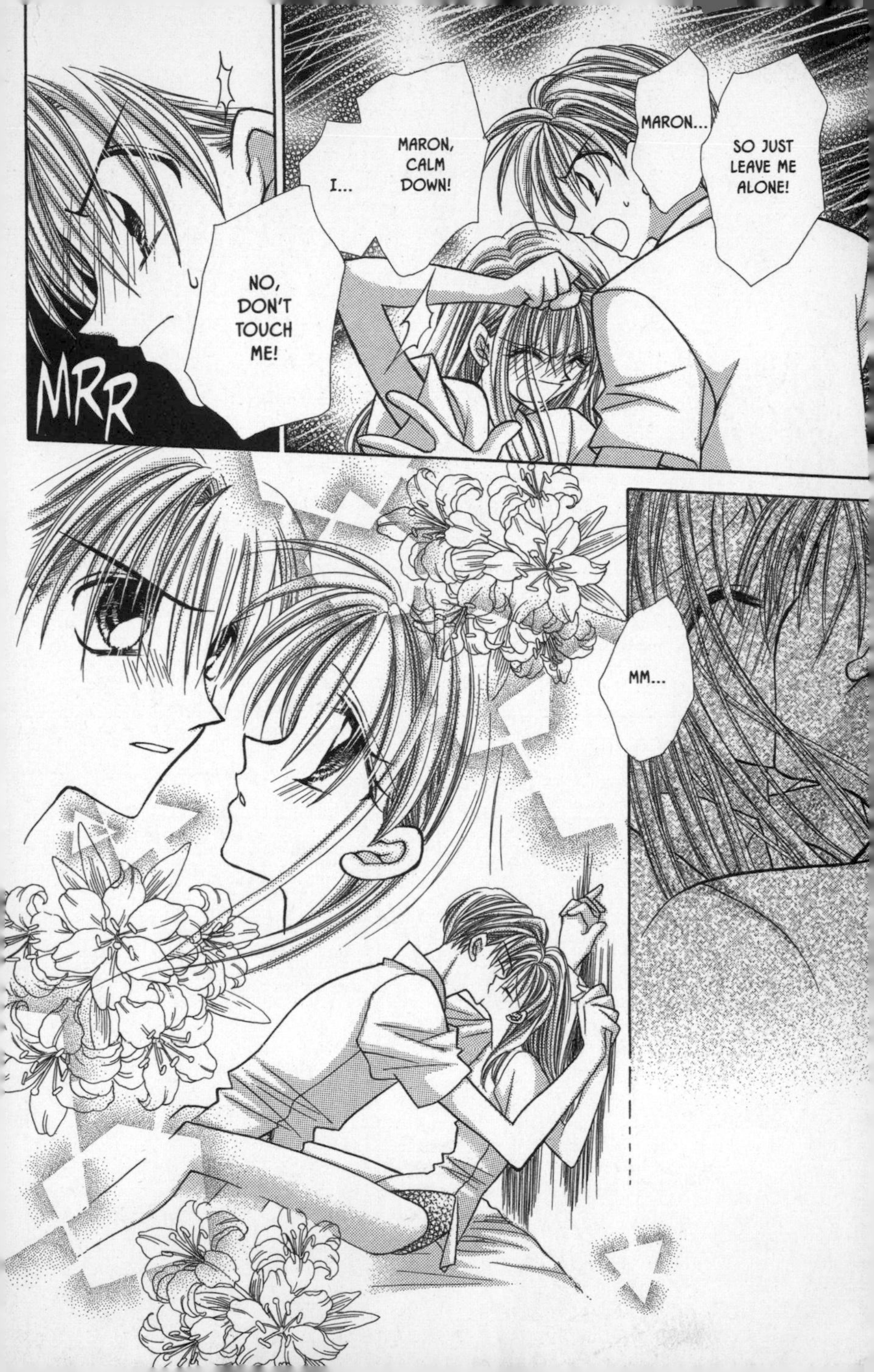
SO JUST LEAVE ME ALONE!
MARON...
MARON, CALM DOWN!
I...
NO, DON'T TOUCH ME!
MRR
MM...

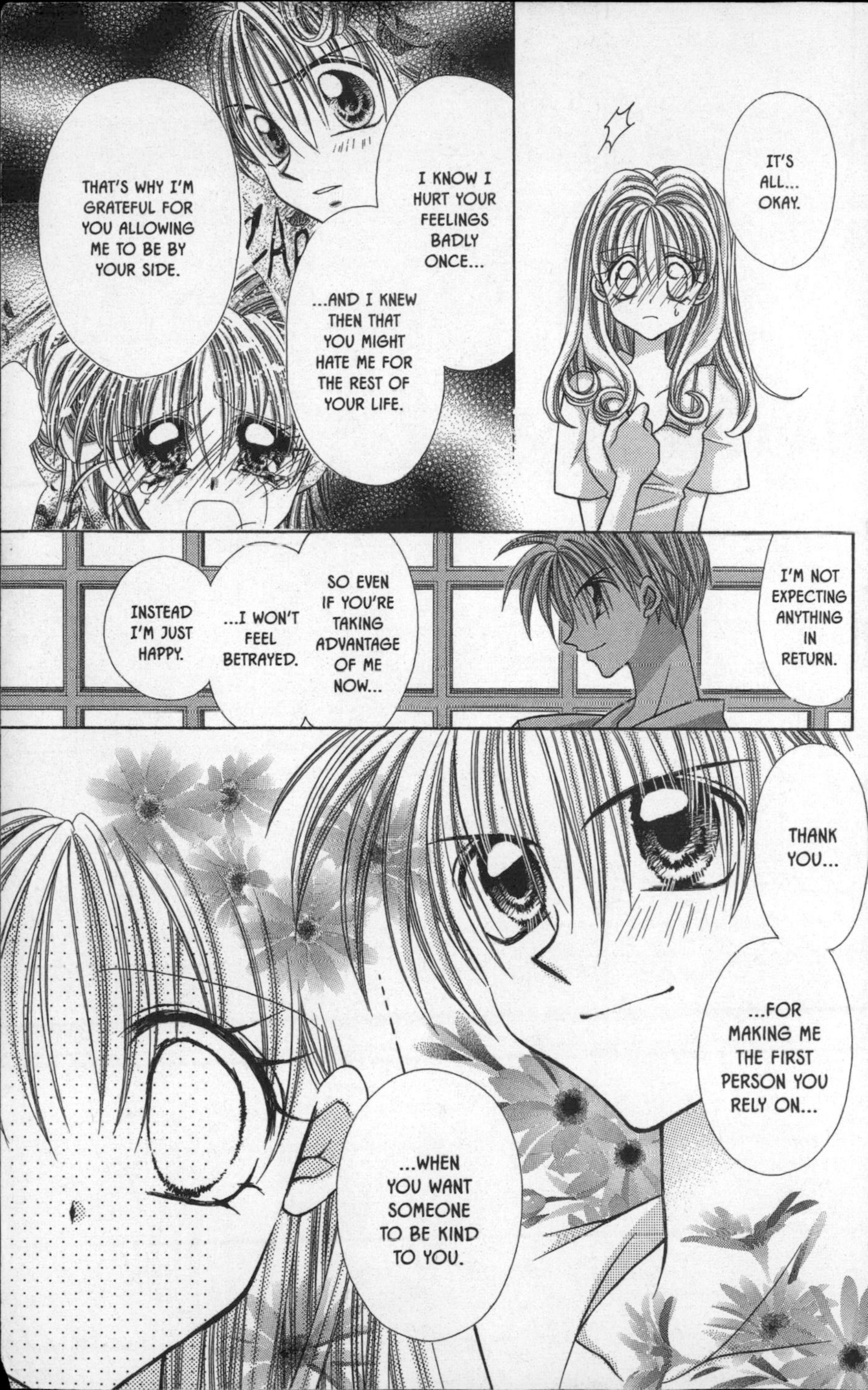
IT'S ALL... OKAY.
I KNOW I HURT YOUR FEELINGS BADLY ONCE...
...AND I KNEW THEN THAT YOU MIGHT HATE ME FOR THE REST OF YOUR LIFE.
THAT'S WHY I'M GRATEFUL FOR YOU ALLOWING ME TO BE BY YOUR SIDE.
I'M NOT EXPECTING ANYTHING IN RETURN.
SO EVEN IF YOU'RE TAKING ADVANTAGE OF ME NOW...
...I WON'T FEEL BETRAYED.
INSTEAD I'M JUST HAPPY.
THANK YOU...
...FOR MAKING ME THE FIRST PERSON YOU RELY ON...
...WHEN YOU WANT SOMEONE TO BE KIND TO YOU.

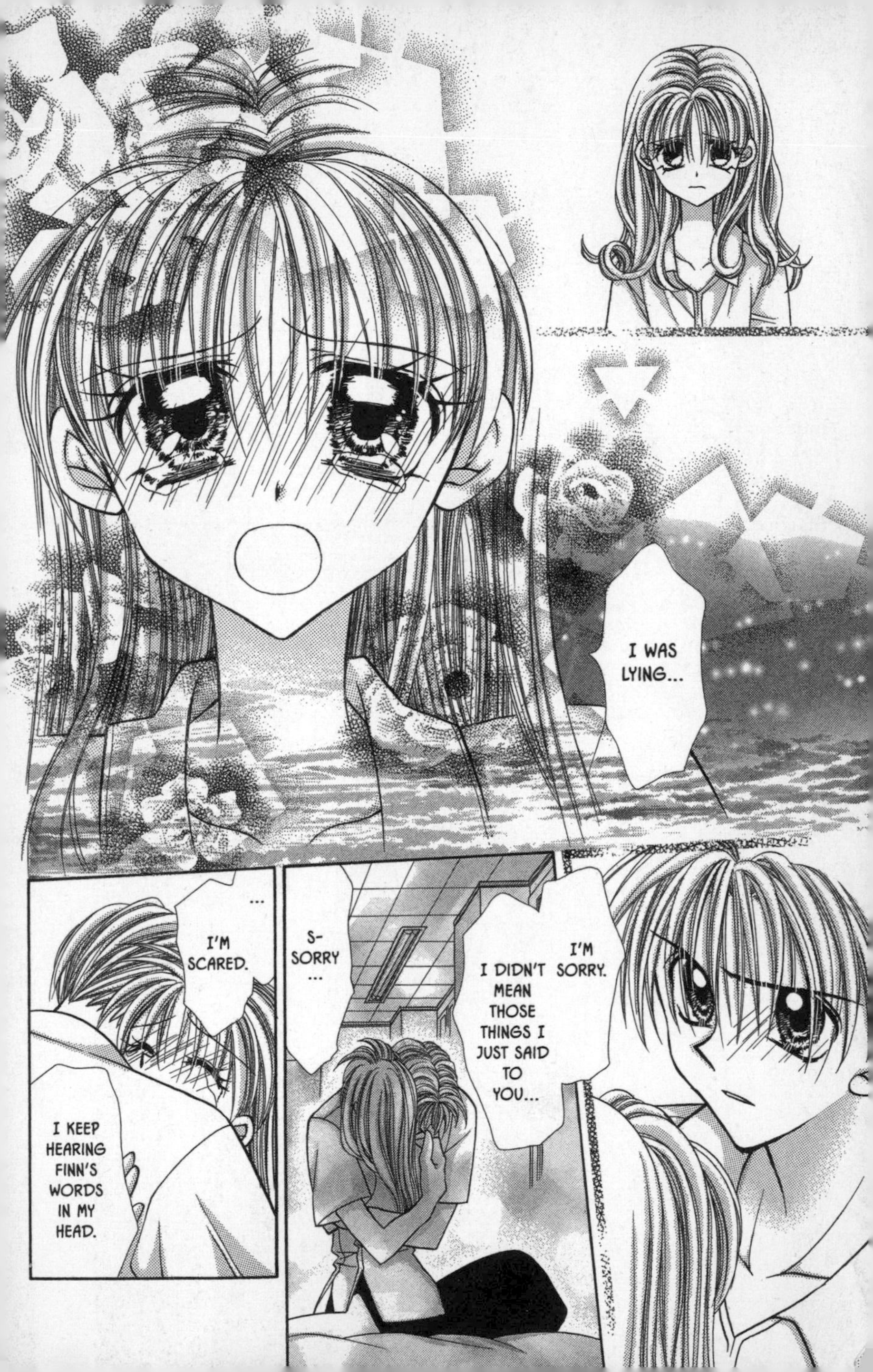
I WAS LYING...
I'M SORRY.
I DIDN'T MEAN THOSE THINGS I JUST SAID TO YOU...
S- SORRY ...
... I'M SCARED.
I KEEP HEARING FINN'S WORDS IN MY HEAD.

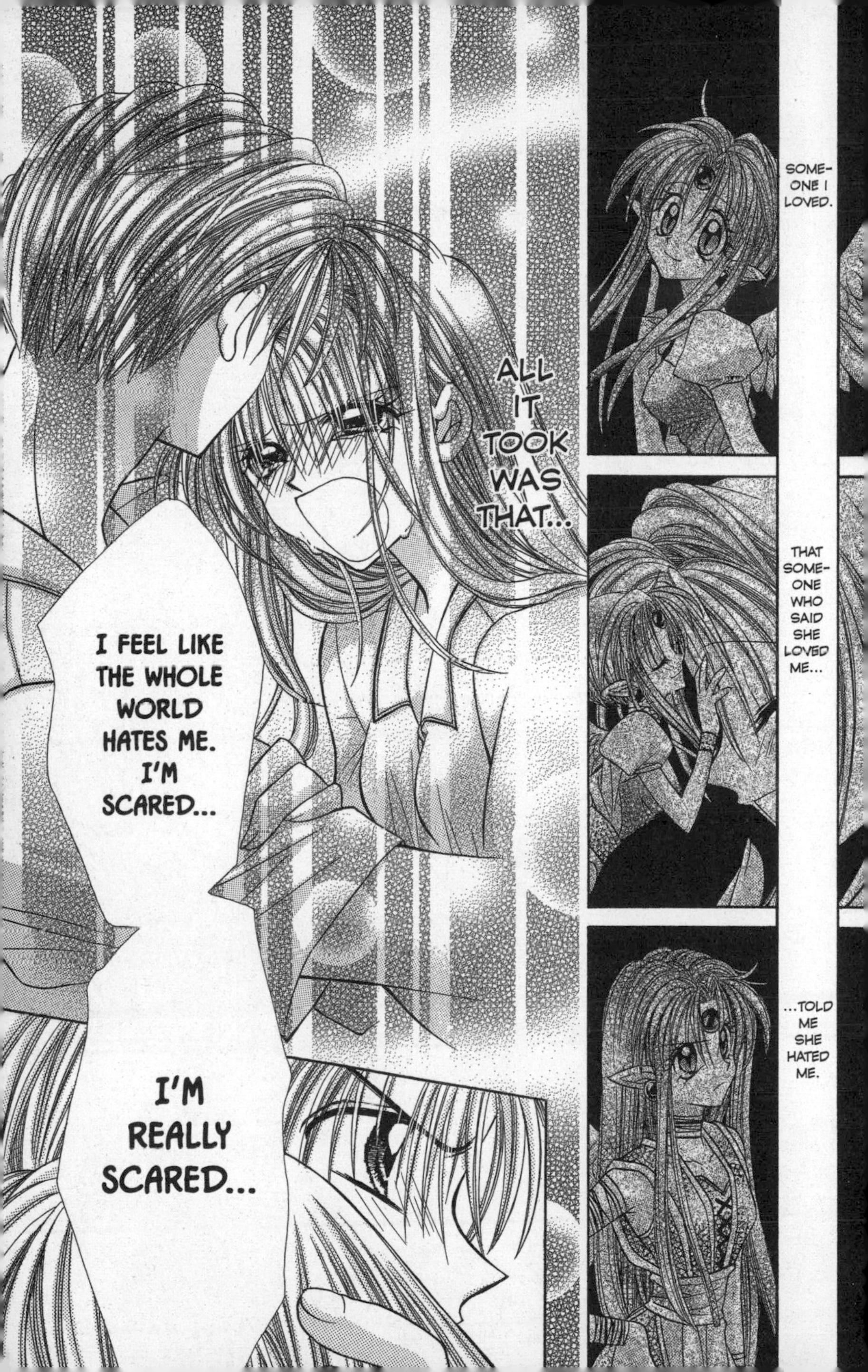
SOME-ONE I LOVED.
THAT SOME-ONE WHO SAID SHE LOVED ME...
...TOLD ME SHE HATED ME.
ALL IT TOOK WAS THAT...
I FEEL LIKE THE WHOLE WORLD HATES ME. I'M SCARED...
I'M REALLY SCARED...

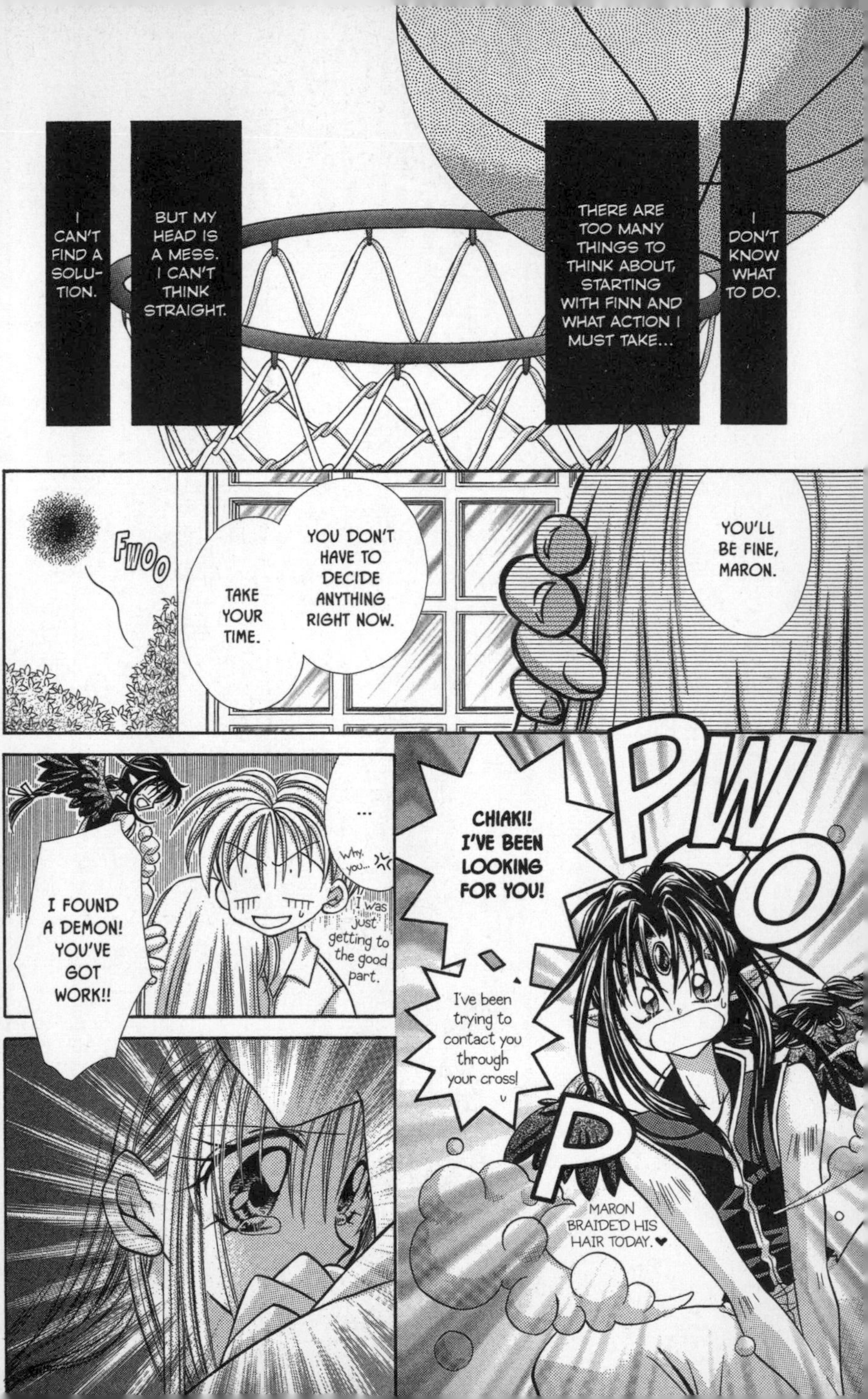
I DON'T KNOW WHAT TO DO.
THERE ARE TOO MANY THINGS TO THINK ABOUT, STARTING WITH FINN AND WHAT ACTION I MUST TAKE...
BUT MY HEAD IS A MESS. I CAN'T THINK STRAIGHT.
I CAN'T FIND A SOLUTION.
YOU'LL BE FINE, MARON.
YOU DON'T HAVE TO DECIDE ANYTHING RIGHT NOW.
TAKE YOUR TIME.
FWOO
PWOP
CHIAKI! I'VE BEEN LOOKING FOR YOU!
I've been trying to contact you through your cross!
MARON BRAIDED HIS HAIR TODAY.❤
...
Why, you...
I was just getting to the good part.
I FOUND A DEMON! YOU'VE GOT WORK!!

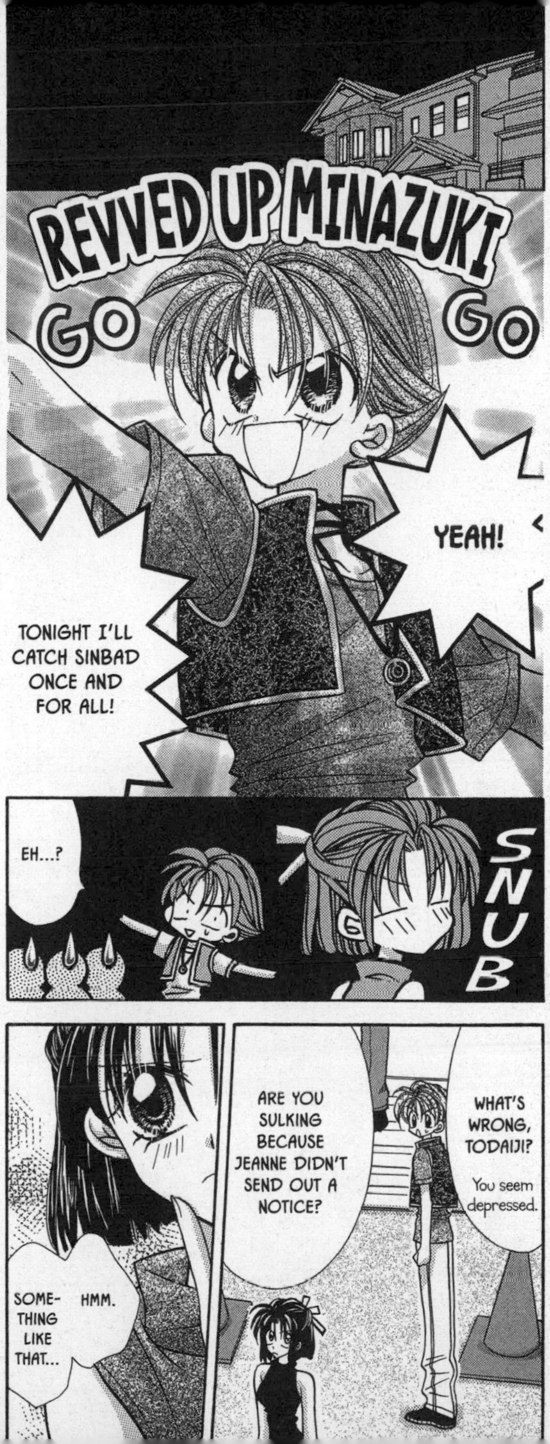
REVVED UP MINAZUKI
GO GO
YEAH!
TONIGHT I'LL CATCH SINBAD ONCE AND FOR ALL!
SNUB
EH...?
WHAT'S WRONG, TODAIJI?
You seem depressed.
ARE YOU SULKING BECAUSE JEANNE DIDN'T SEND OUT A NOTICE?
HMM.
SOME-THING LIKE THAT...

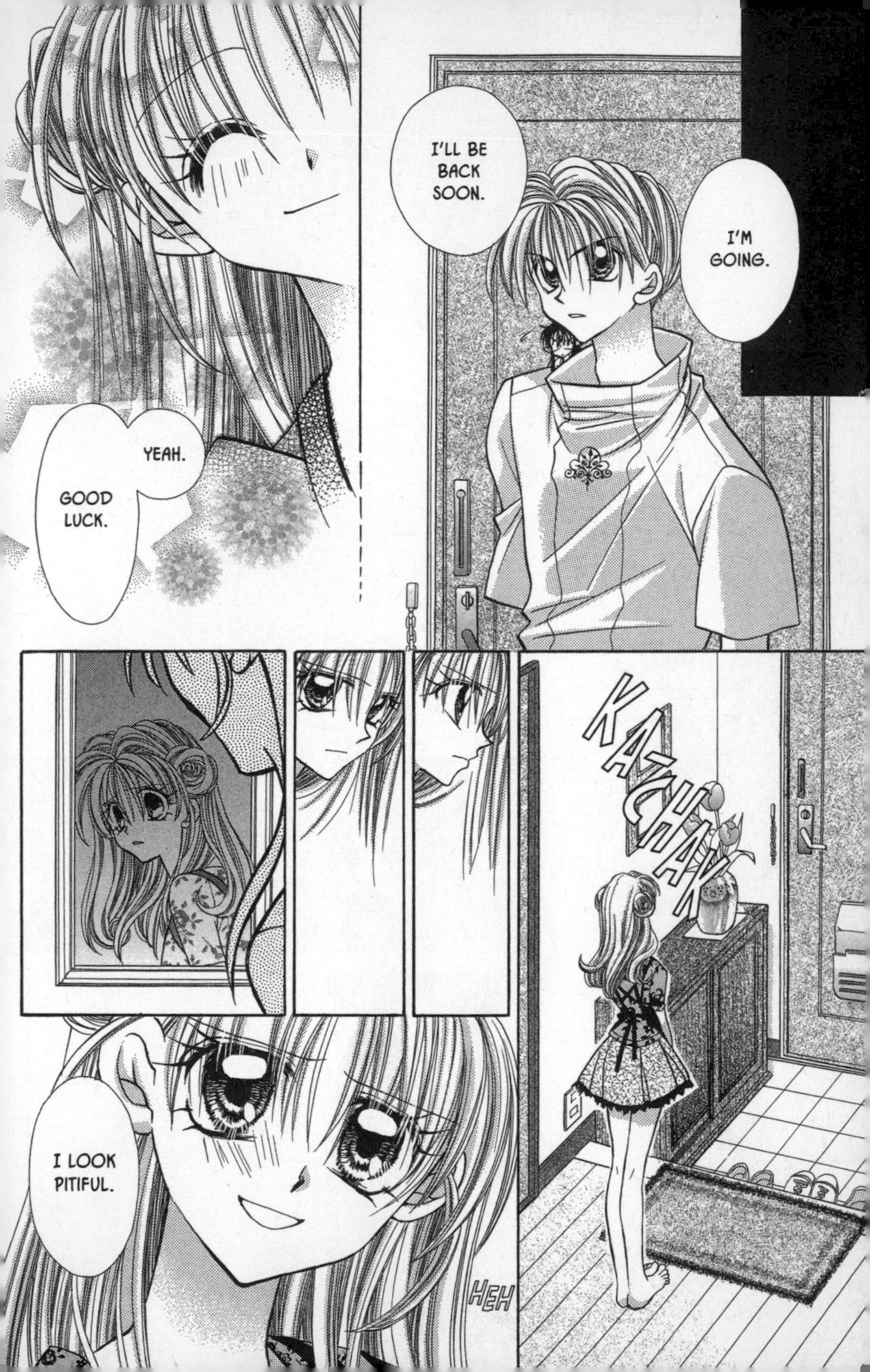
I'M GOING.
I'LL BE BACK SOON.
YEAH.
GOOD LUCK.
KA-CHAK
I LOOK PITIFUL.
HEH

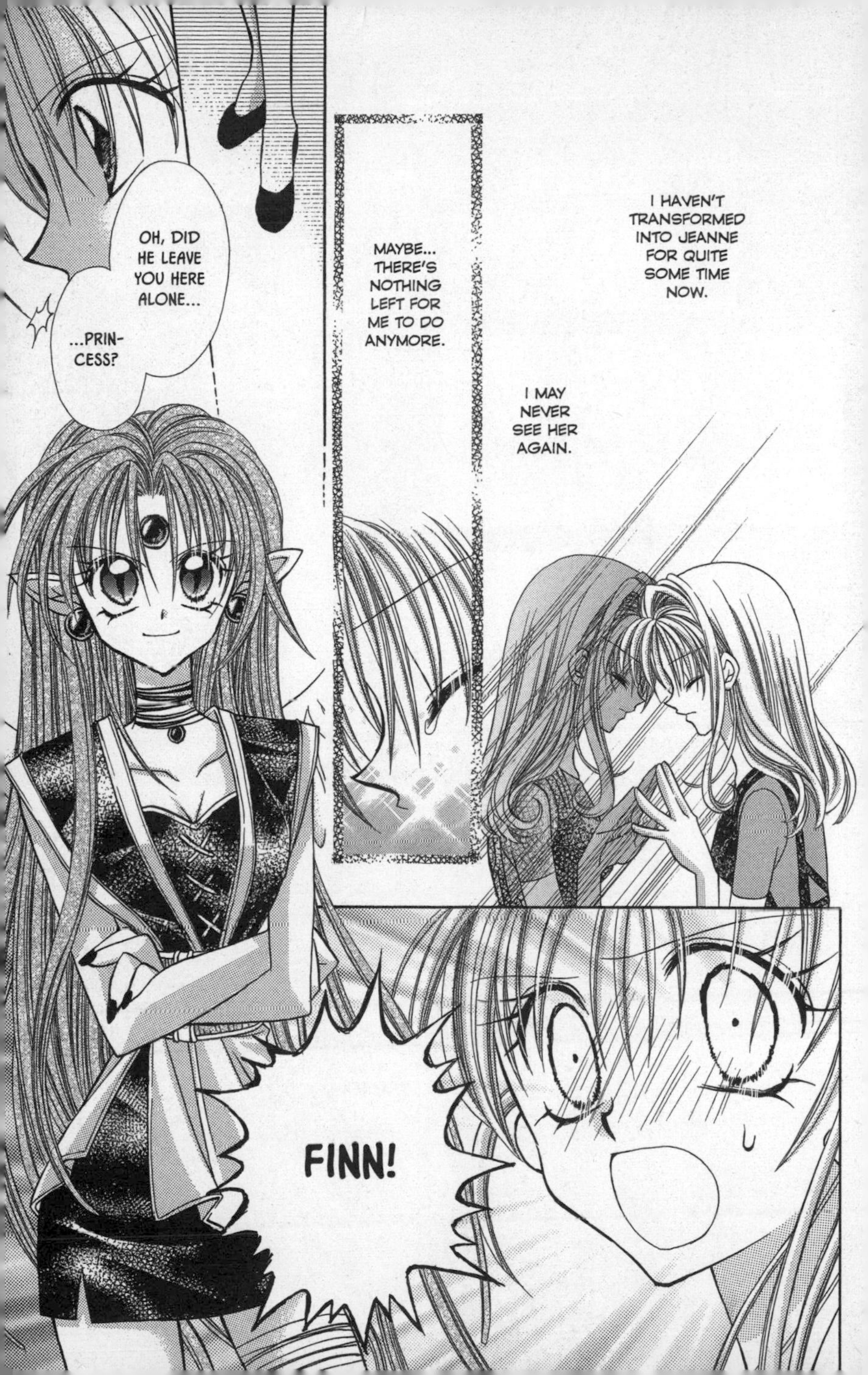
I HAVEN'T TRANSFORMED INTO JEANNE FOR QUITE SOME TIME NOW.
I MAY NEVER SEE HER AGAIN.
MAYBE... THERE'S NOTHING LEFT FOR ME TO DO ANYMORE.
FINN!
OH, DID HE LEAVE YOU HERE ALONE...
...PRIN-CESS?

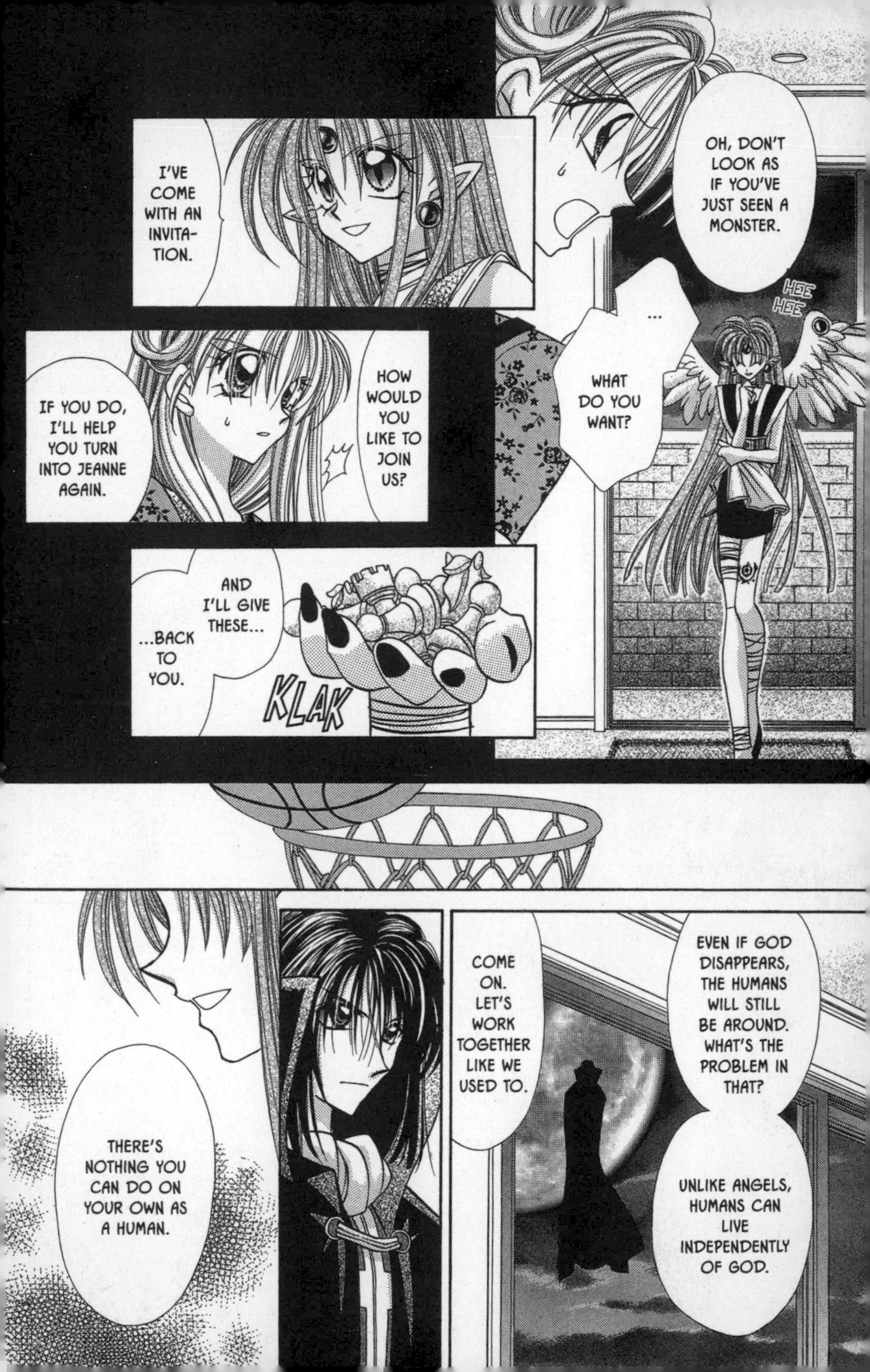
OH, DON'T LOOK AS IF YOU'VE JUST SEEN A MONSTER.
HEE HEE
...
WHAT DO YOU WANT?
I'VE COME WITH AN INVITATION.
HOW WOULD YOU LIKE TO JOIN US?
IF YOU DO, I'LL HELP YOU TURN INTO JEANNE AGAIN.
AND I'LL GIVE THESE...
...BACK TO YOU.
KLAK
EVEN IF GOD DISAPPEARS, THE HUMANS WILL STILL BE AROUND. WHAT'S THE PROBLEM IN THAT?
UNLIKE ANGELS, HUMANS CAN LIVE INDEPENDENTLY OF GOD.
COME ON. LET'S WORK TOGETHER LIKE WE USED TO.
THERE'S NOTHING YOU CAN DO ON YOUR OWN AS A HUMAN.

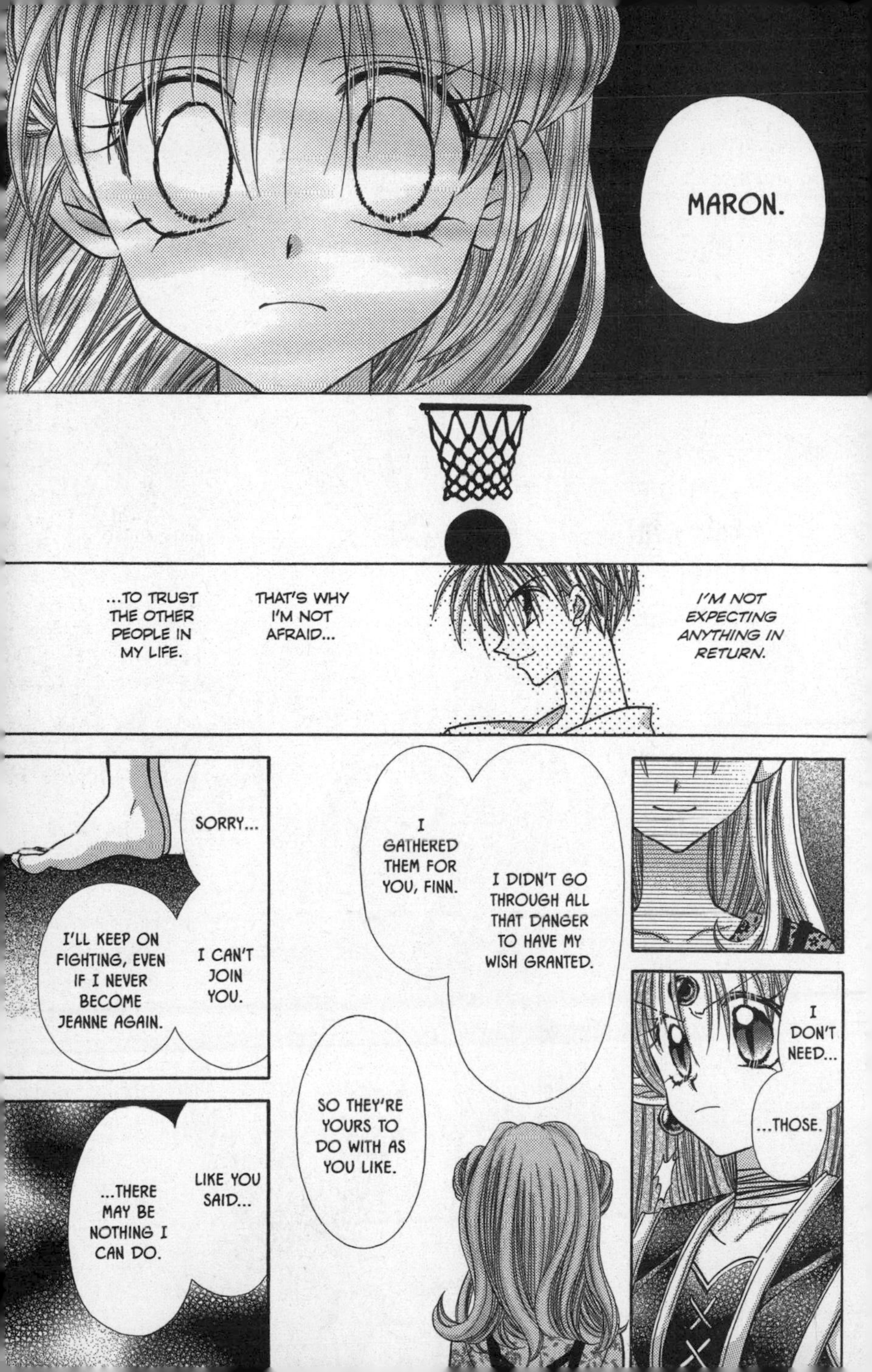
MARON.
I'M NOT EXPECTING ANYTHING IN RETURN.
THAT'S WHY I'M NOT AFRAID...
...TO TRUST THE OTHER PEOPLE IN MY LIFE.
I DON'T NEED...
...THOSE.
I DIDN'T GO THROUGH ALL THAT DANGER TO HAVE MY WISH GRANTED.
I GATHERED THEM FOR YOU, FINN.
SO THEY'RE YOURS TO DO WITH AS YOU LIKE.
SORRY...
I CAN'T JOIN YOU.
I'LL KEEP ON FIGHTING, EVEN IF I NEVER BECOME JEANNE AGAIN.
LIKE YOU SAID...
...THERE MAY BE NOTHING I CAN DO.

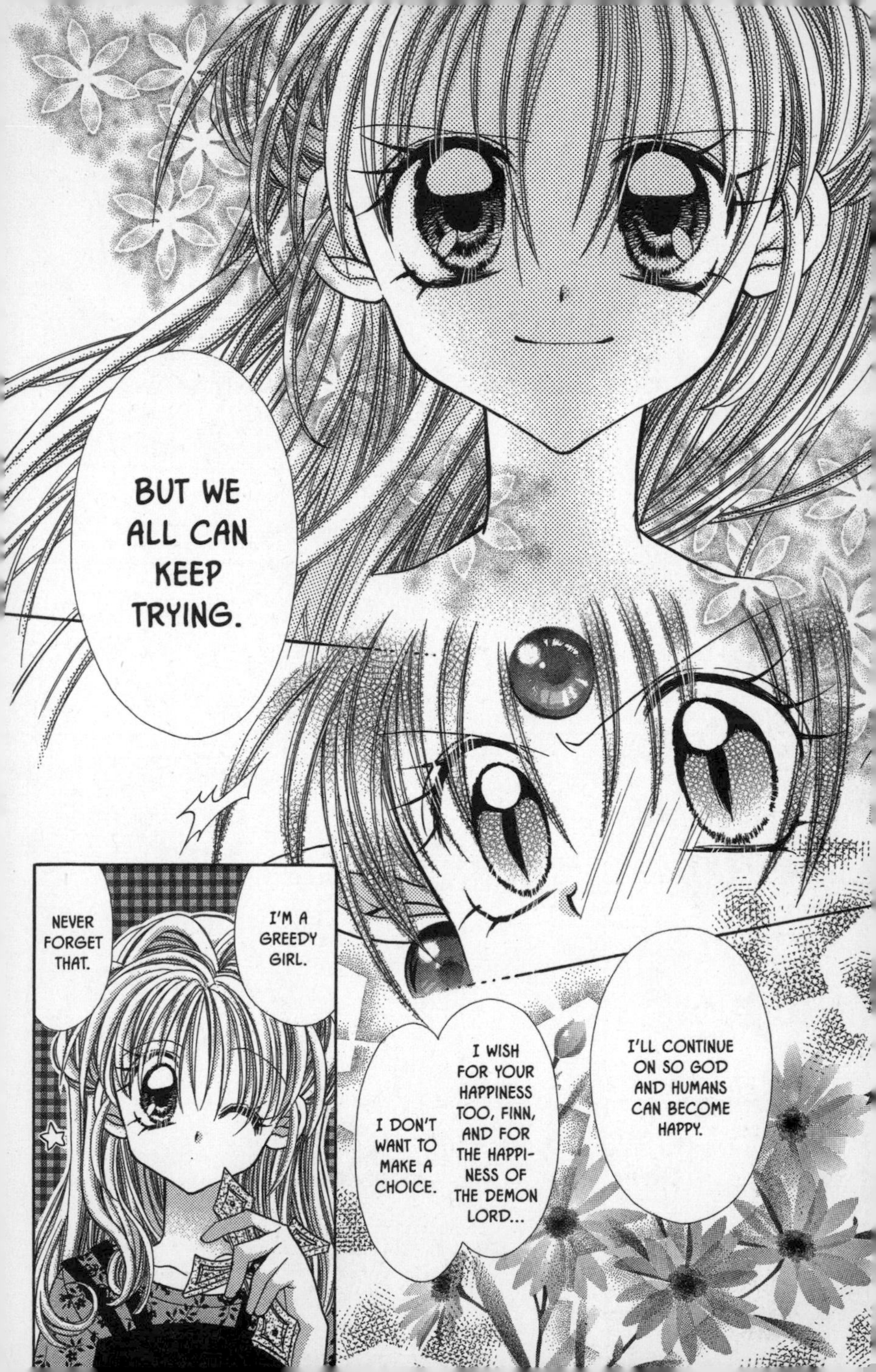
BUT WE ALL CAN KEEP TRYING.
I'LL CONTINUE ON SO GOD AND HUMANS CAN BECOME HAPPY.
I WISH FOR YOUR HAPPINESS TOO, FINN, AND FOR THE HAPPI-NESS OF THE DEMON LORD...
I DON'T WANT TO MAKE A CHOICE.
I'M A GREEDY GIRL.
NEVER FORGET THAT.

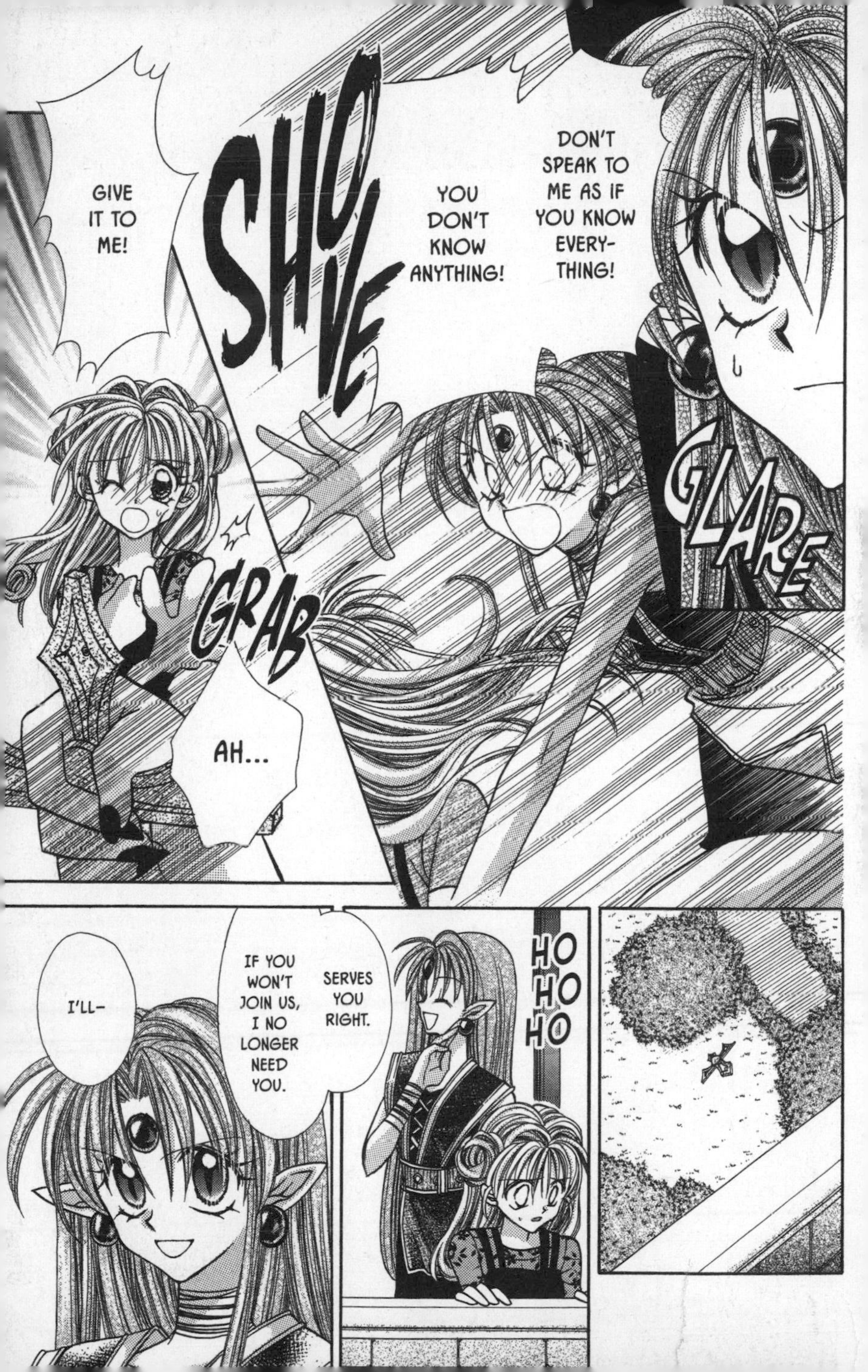
DON'T SPEAK TO ME AS IF YOU KNOW EVERY-THING!
GLARE
YOU DON'T KNOW ANYTHING!
SHOVE
GIVE IT TO ME!
GRAB
AH...
HO HO HO HO HO
SERVES YOU RIGHT.
IF YOU WON'T JOIN US, I NO LONGER NEED YOU.
I'LL-

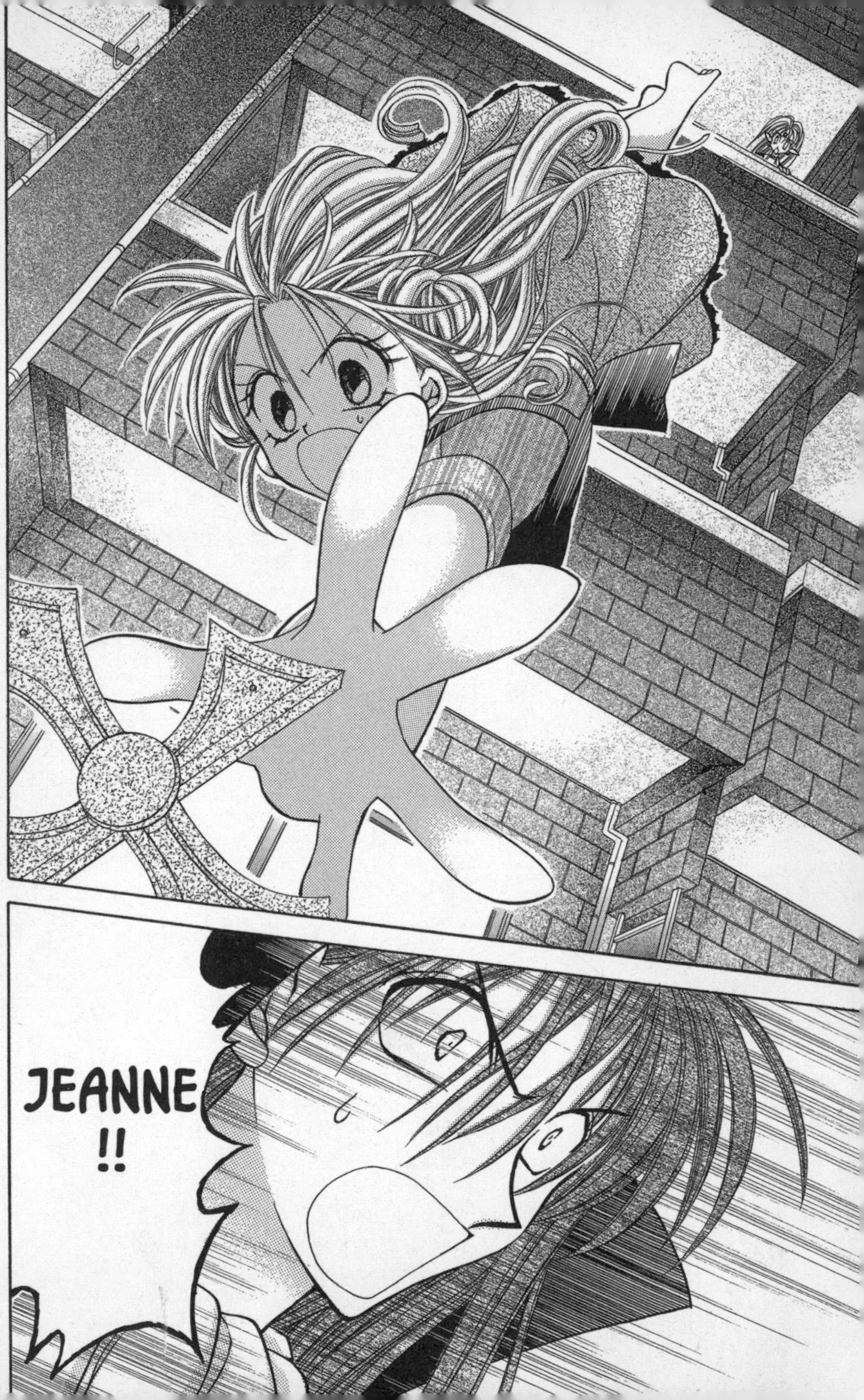
JEANNE
!!

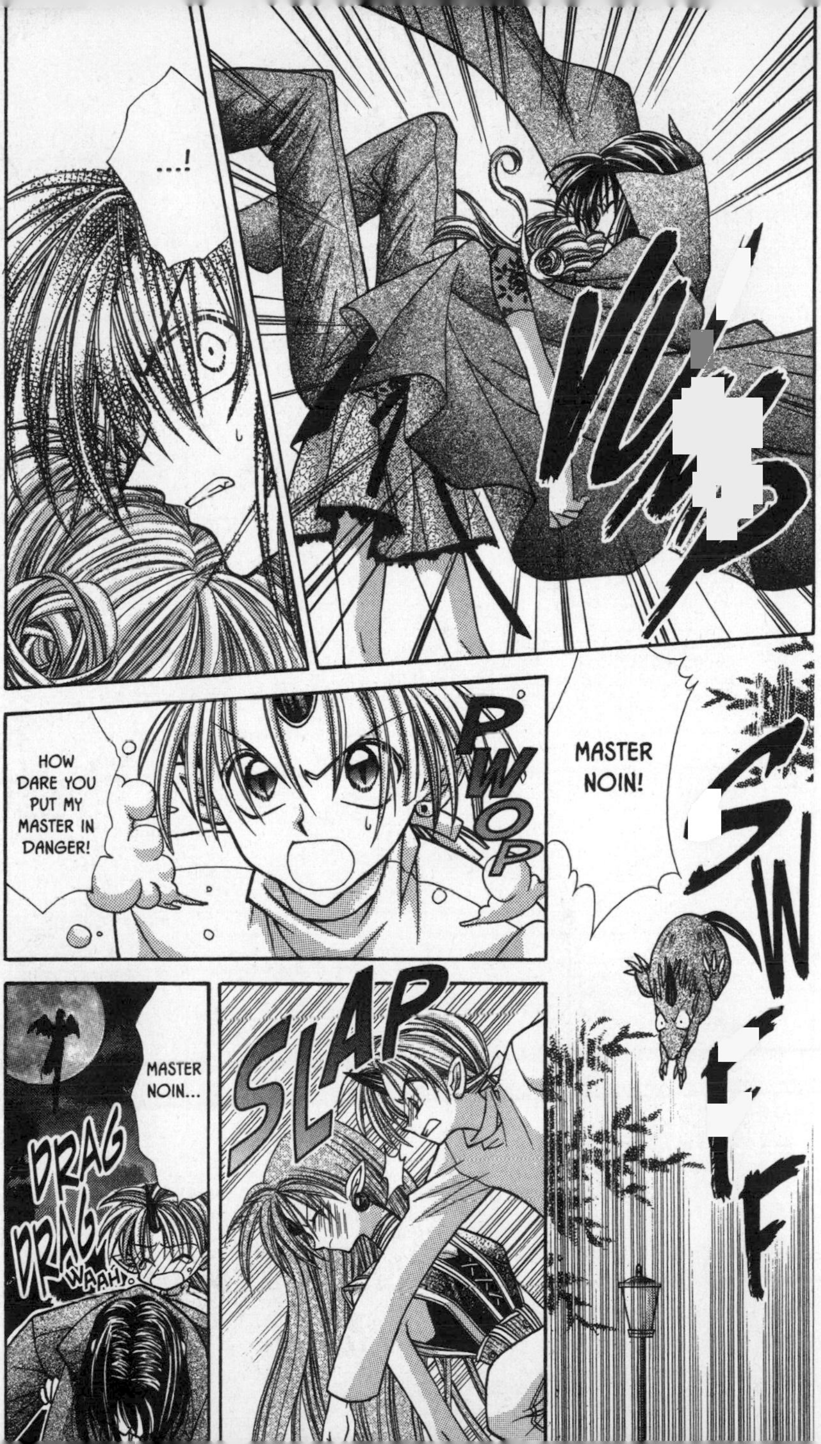

...!
MASTER NOIN!
PWOP
HOW DARE YOU PUT MY MASTER IN DANGER!
SLAP
MASTER NOIN...
DRAG DRAG
WAAH!

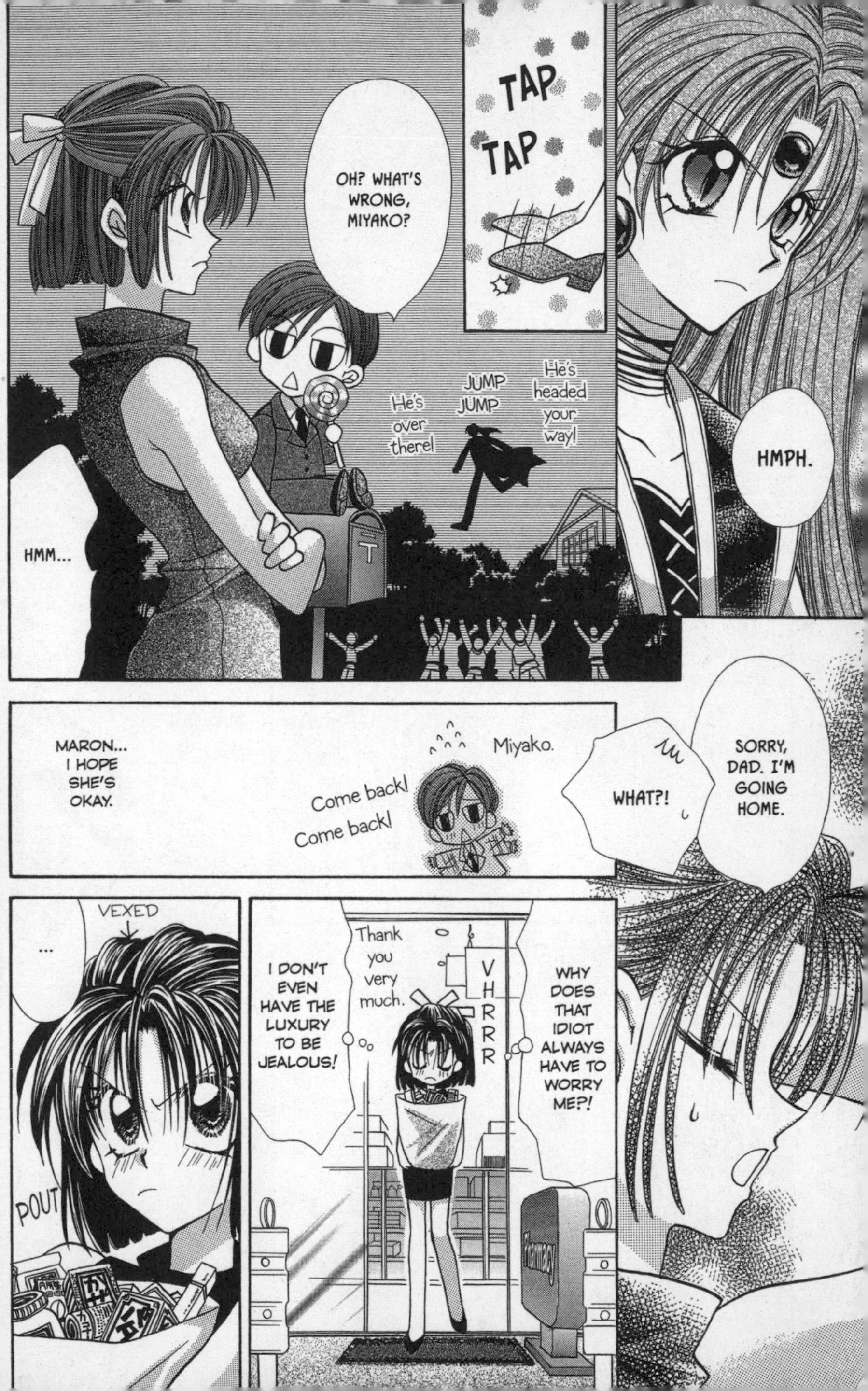
HMPH.
TAP
TAP
OH? WHAT'S WRONG, MIYAKO?
He's headed your way!
JUMP JUMP
He's over there!
HMM...
SORRY, DAD. I'M GOING HOME.
WHAT?!
Miyako.
Come back! Come back!
MARON... I HOPE SHE'S OKAY.
WHY DOES THAT IDIOT ALWAYS HAVE TO WORRY ME?!
VHRR
Thank you very much.
I DON'T EVEN HAVE THE LUXURY TO BE JEALOUS!
VEXED
...
POUT

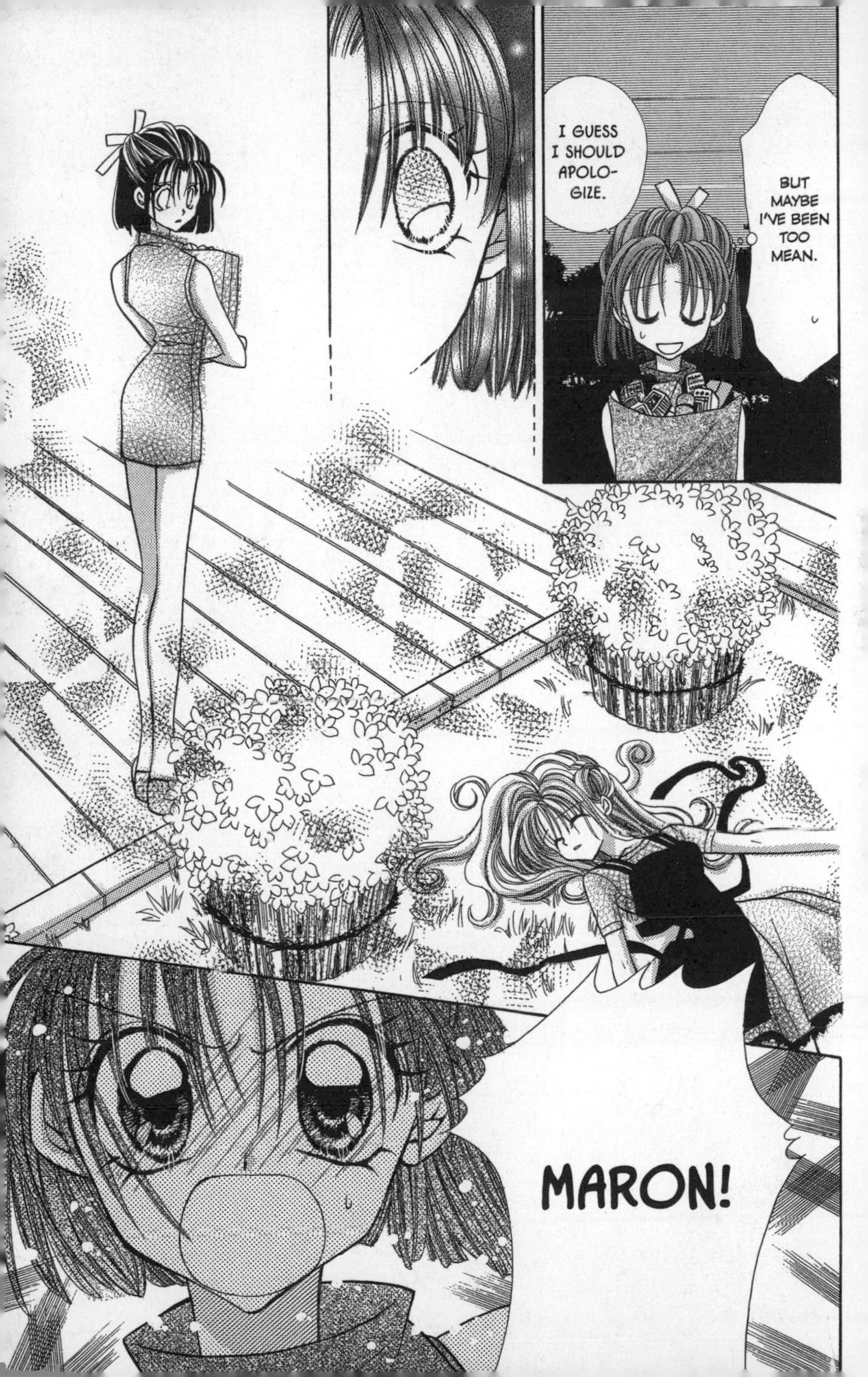
BUT MAYBE I'VE BEEN TOO MEAN.
I GUESS I SHOULD APOLO-GIZE.
MARON!

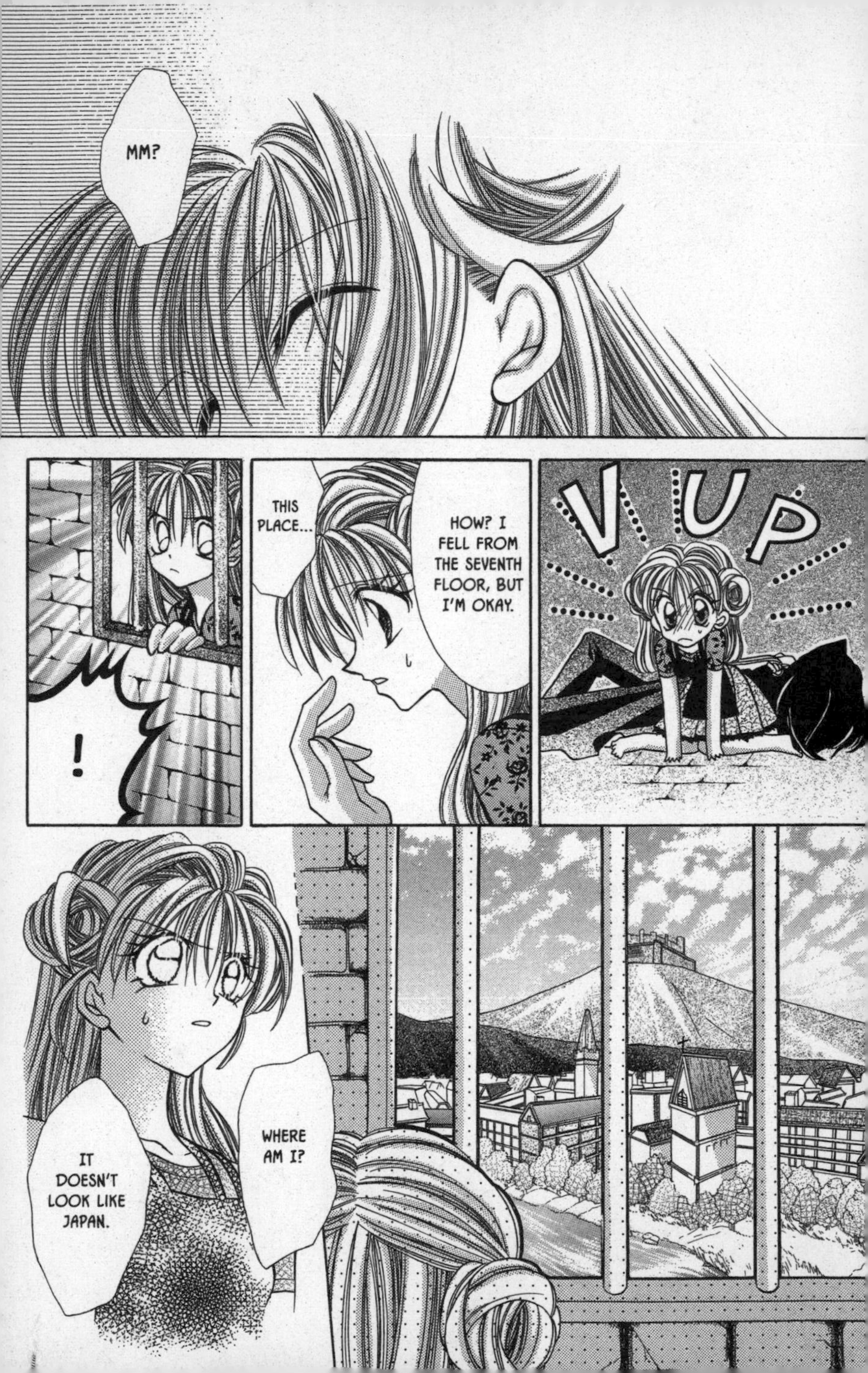
MM?
VUP
HOW? I FELL FROM THE SEVENTH FLOOR, BUT I'M OKAY.
THIS PLACE...
!
WHERE AM I?
IT DOESN'T LOOK LIKE JAPAN.

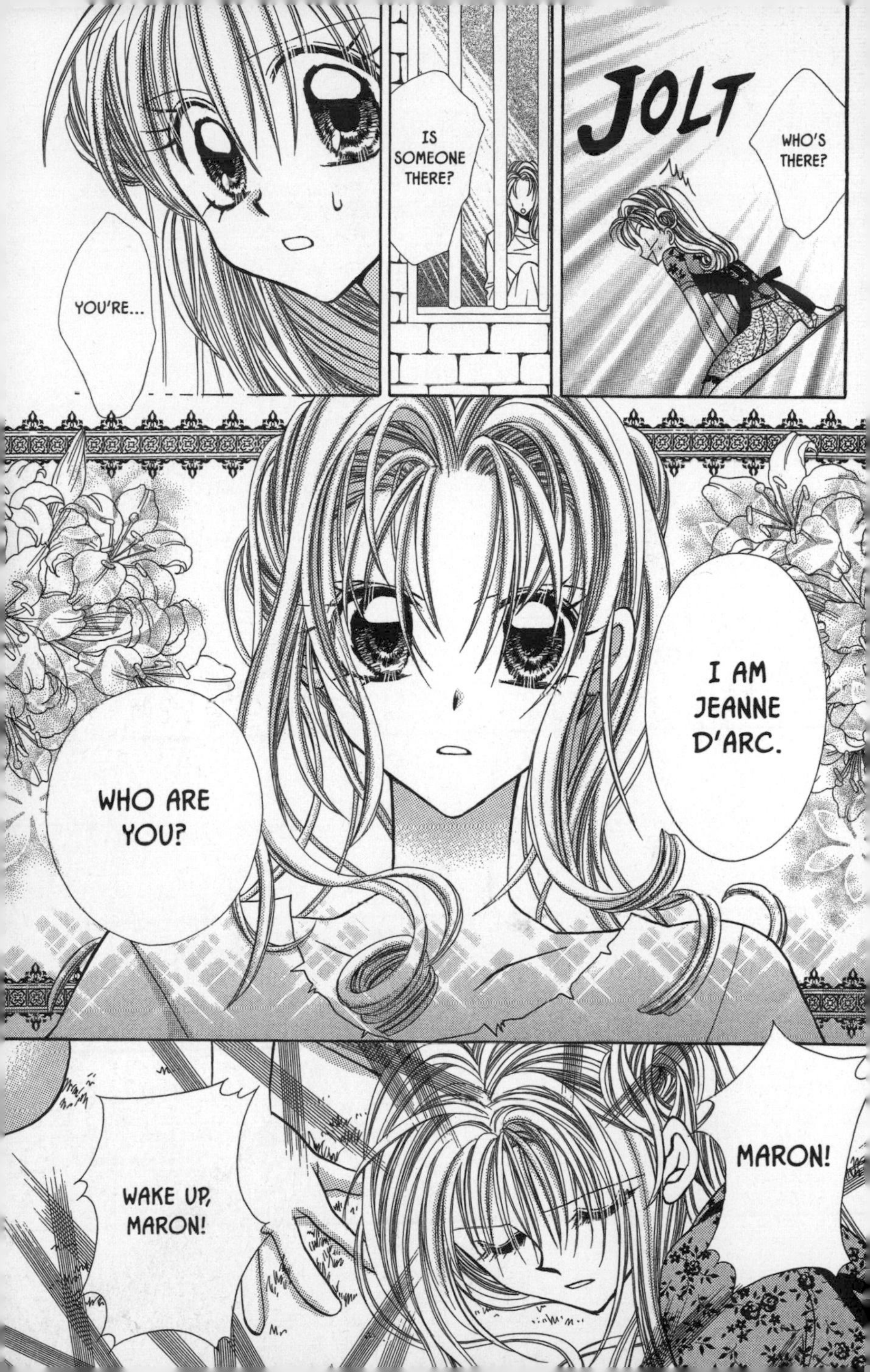
JOLT
WHO'S THERE?
IS SOMEONE THERE?
YOU'RE...
I AM JEANNE D'ARC.
WHO ARE YOU?
MARON!
WAKE UP, MARON!

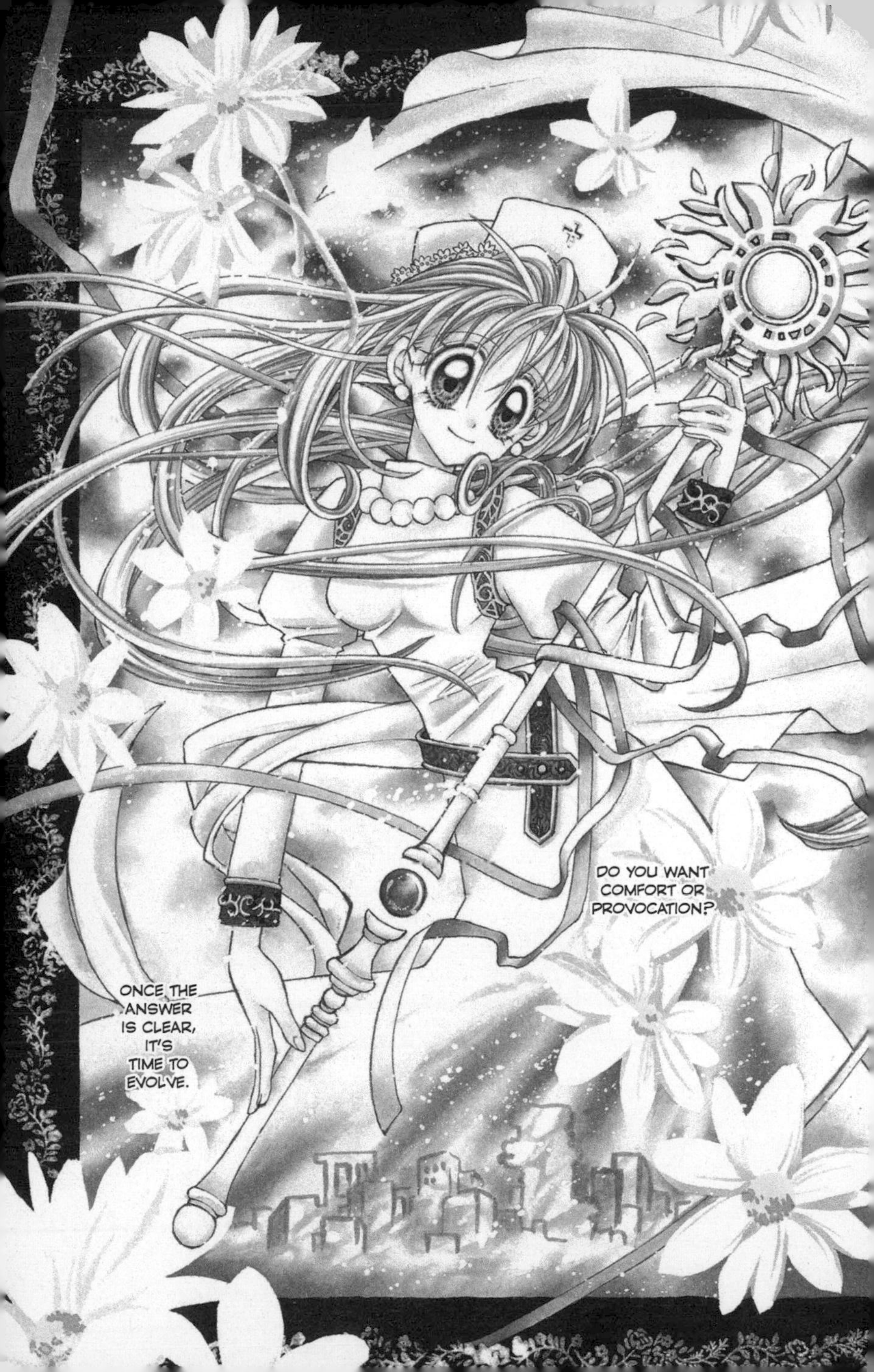
DO YOU WANT COMFORT OR PROVOCATION?
ONCE THE ANSWER IS CLEAR, IT'S TIME TO EVOLVE.

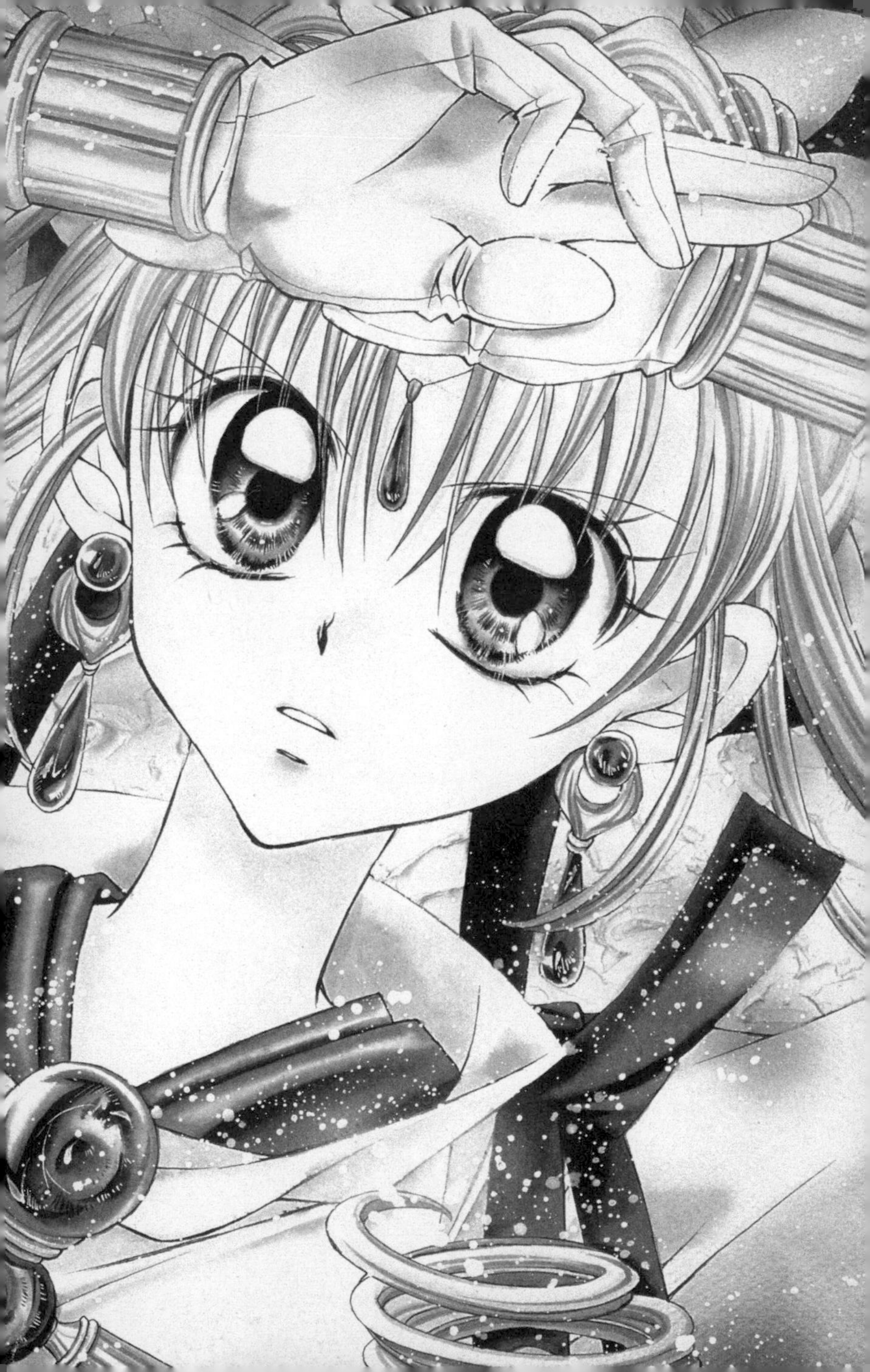

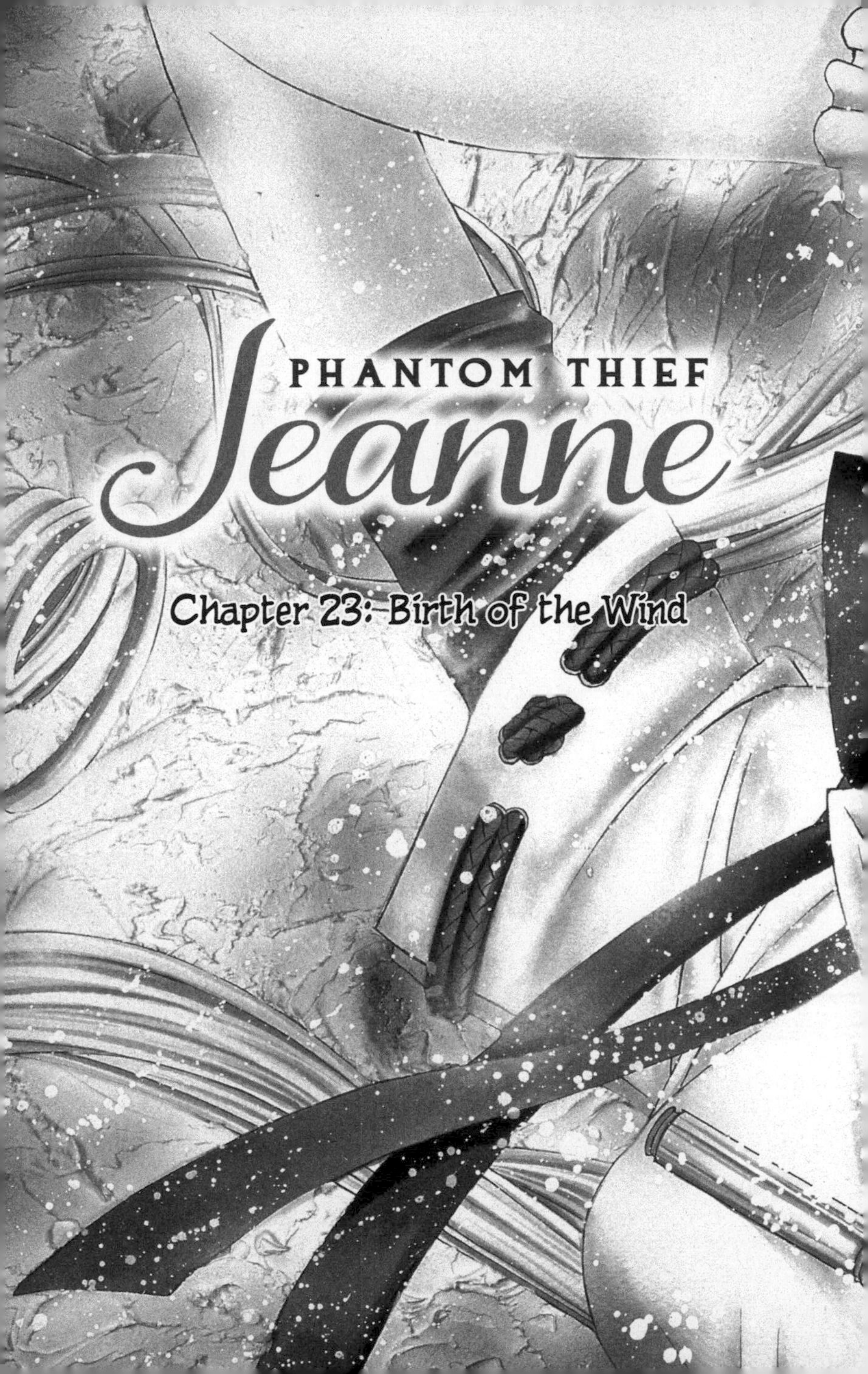
PHANTOM THIEF
Jeanne
Chapter 23: Birth of the Wind

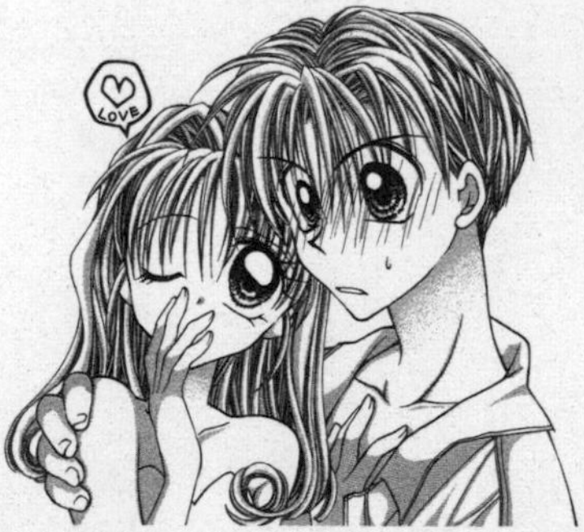
LOVE

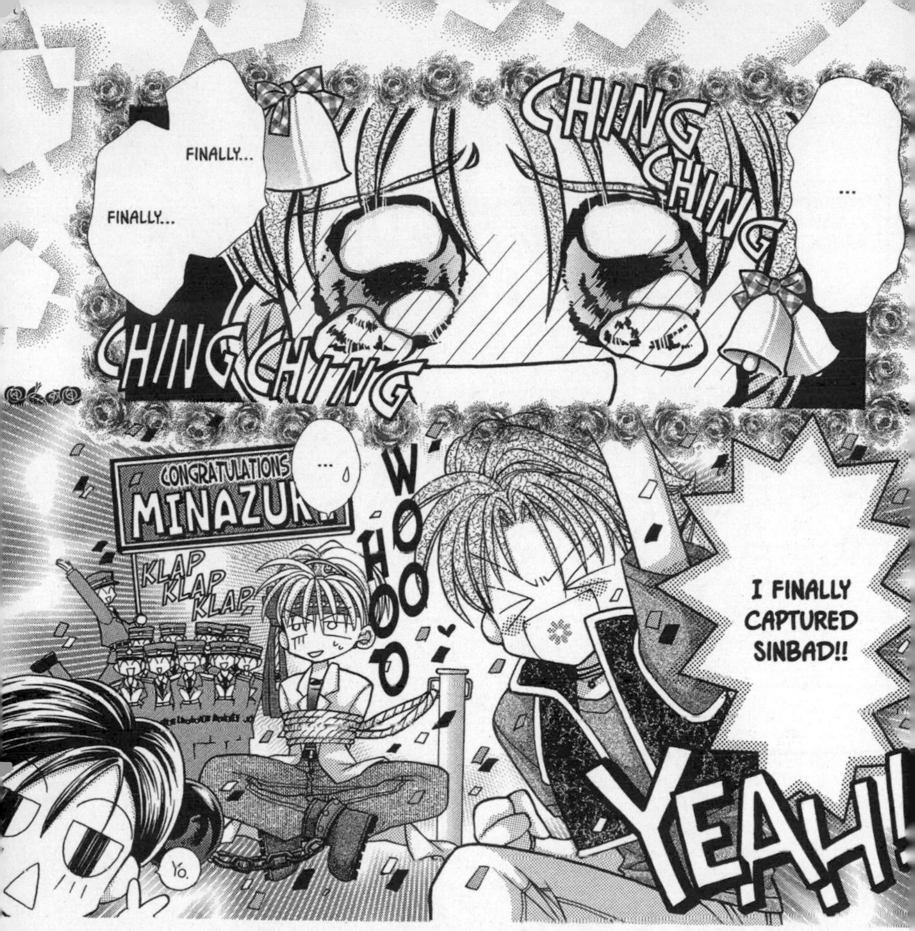
CHING CHING
...
FINALLY...
FINALLY...
CHING CHING
I FINALLY CAPTURED SINBAD!!
YEAH!!
WOO HOO
...
CONGRATULATIONS
MINAZUKI
KLAP KLAP KLAP
Yo.

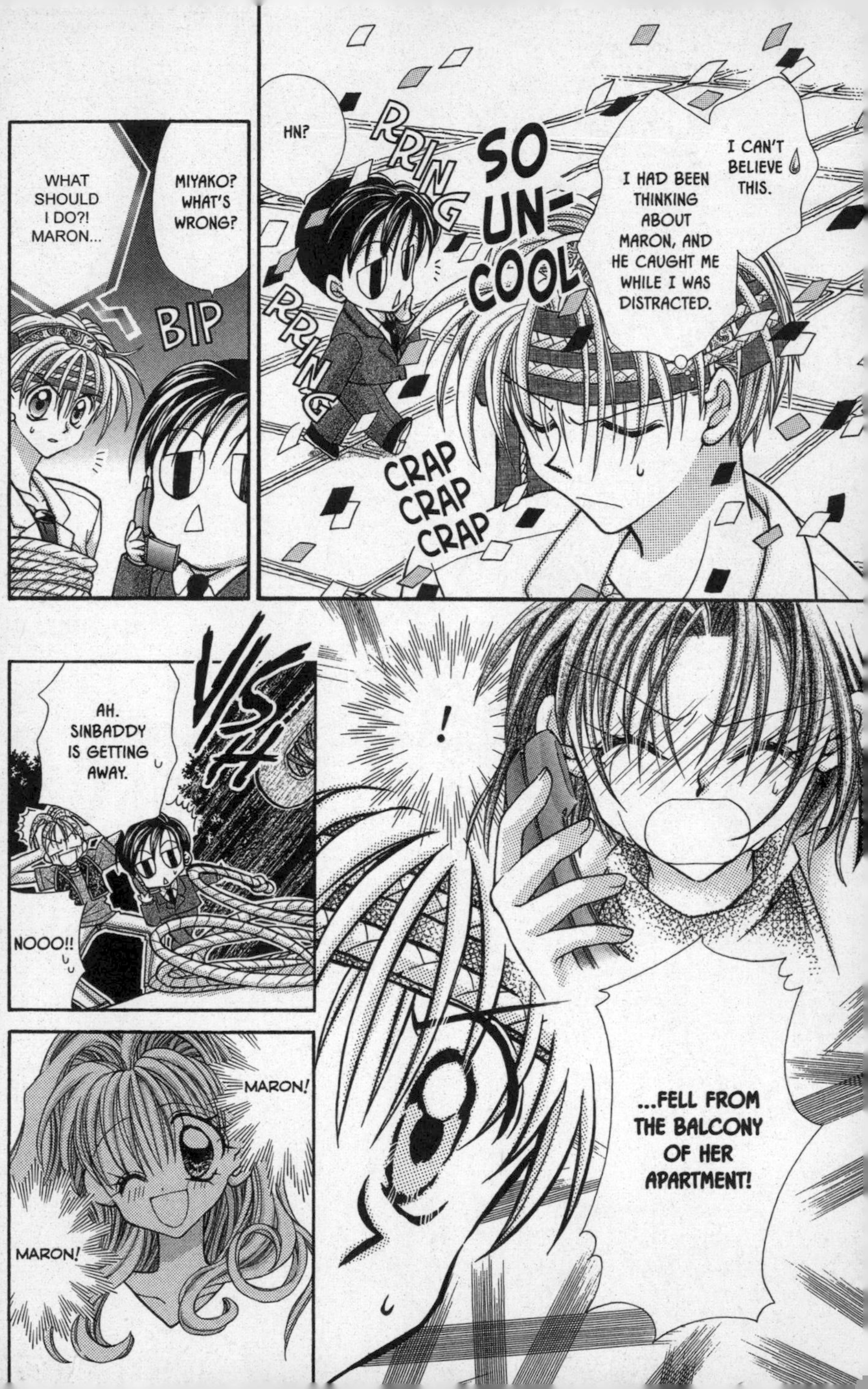
I CAN'T BELIEVE THIS.
I HAD BEEN THINKING ABOUT MARON, AND HE CAUGHT ME WHILE I WAS DISTRACTED.
SO UN-COOL
HN?
RRING
RRING
CRAP CRAP CRAP
MIYAKO? WHAT'S WRONG?
WHAT SHOULD I DO?! MARON...
BIP
!
...FELL FROM THE BALCONY OF HER APARTMENT!
VSSH
AH. SINBADDY IS GETTING AWAY.
NOOO!!
MARON!
MARON!

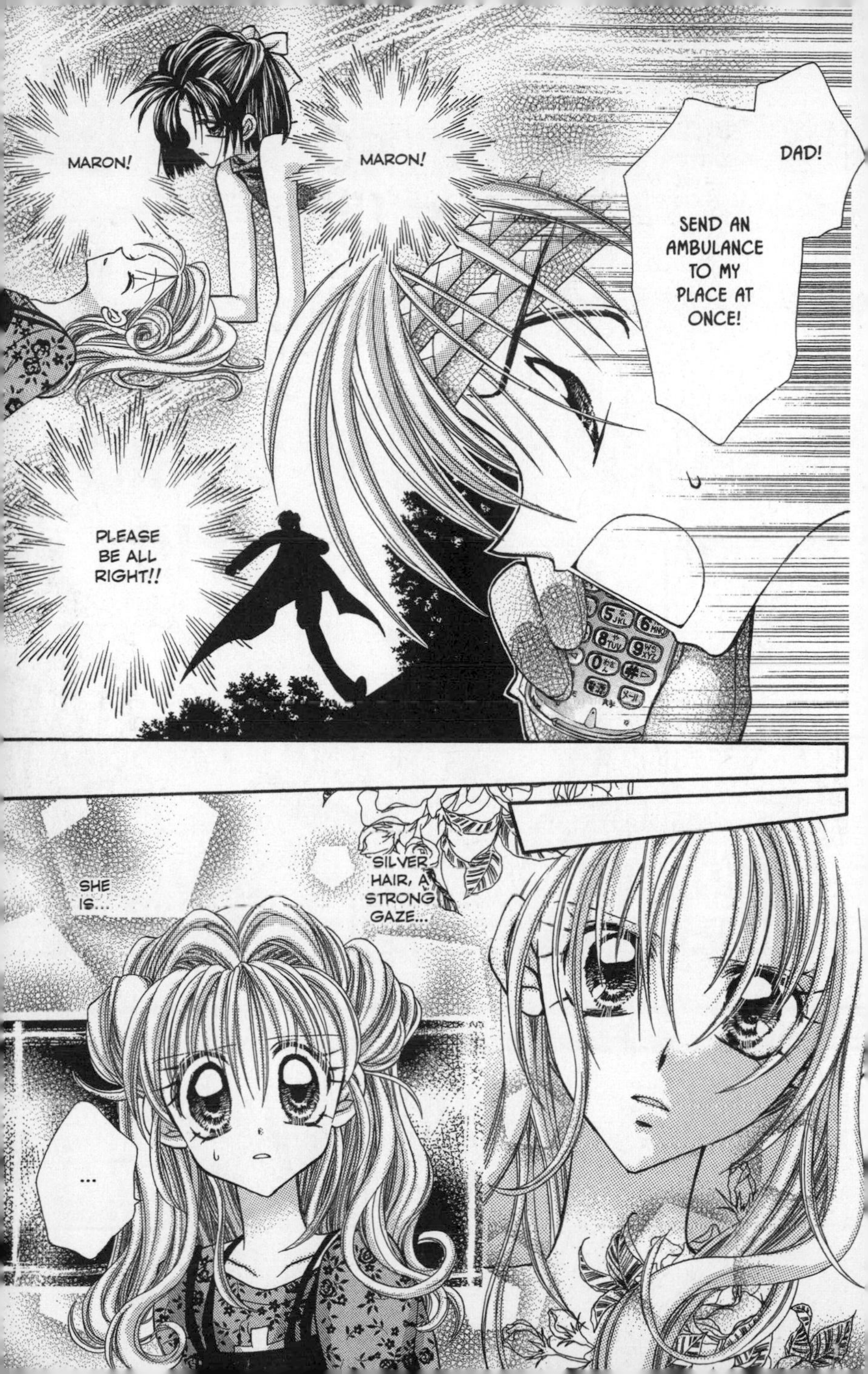
DAD!
SEND AN AMBULANCE TO MY PLACE AT ONCE!
MARON!
MARON!
PLEASE BE ALL RIGHT!!
SILVER HAIR, A STRONG GAZE...
SHE IS...
...

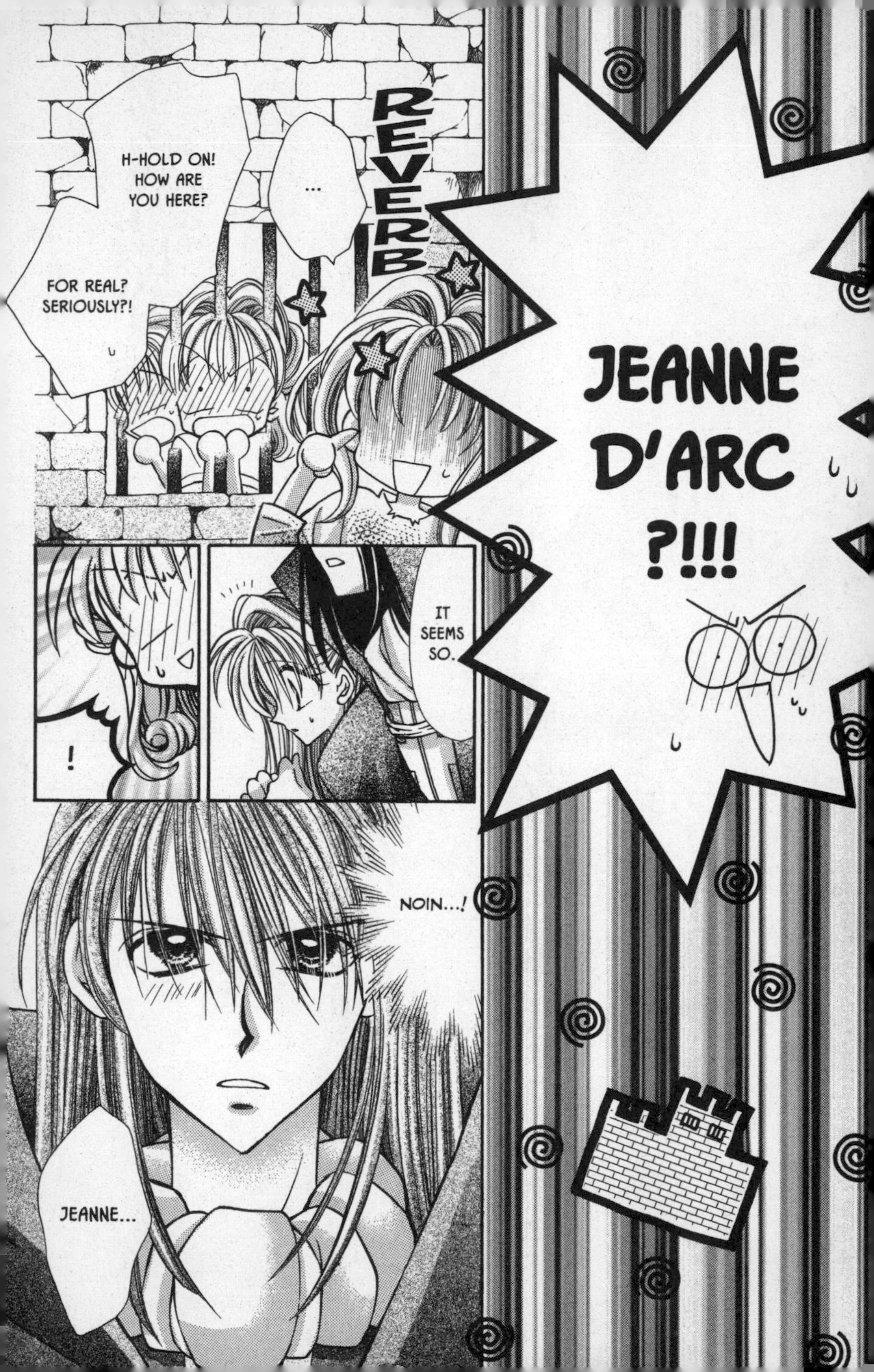
H-HOLD ON! HOW ARE YOU HERE?
...
REVERB
FOR REAL? SERIOUSLY?!
IT SEEMS SO.
!
NOIN...!
JEANNE...
JEANNE D'ARC ?!!!

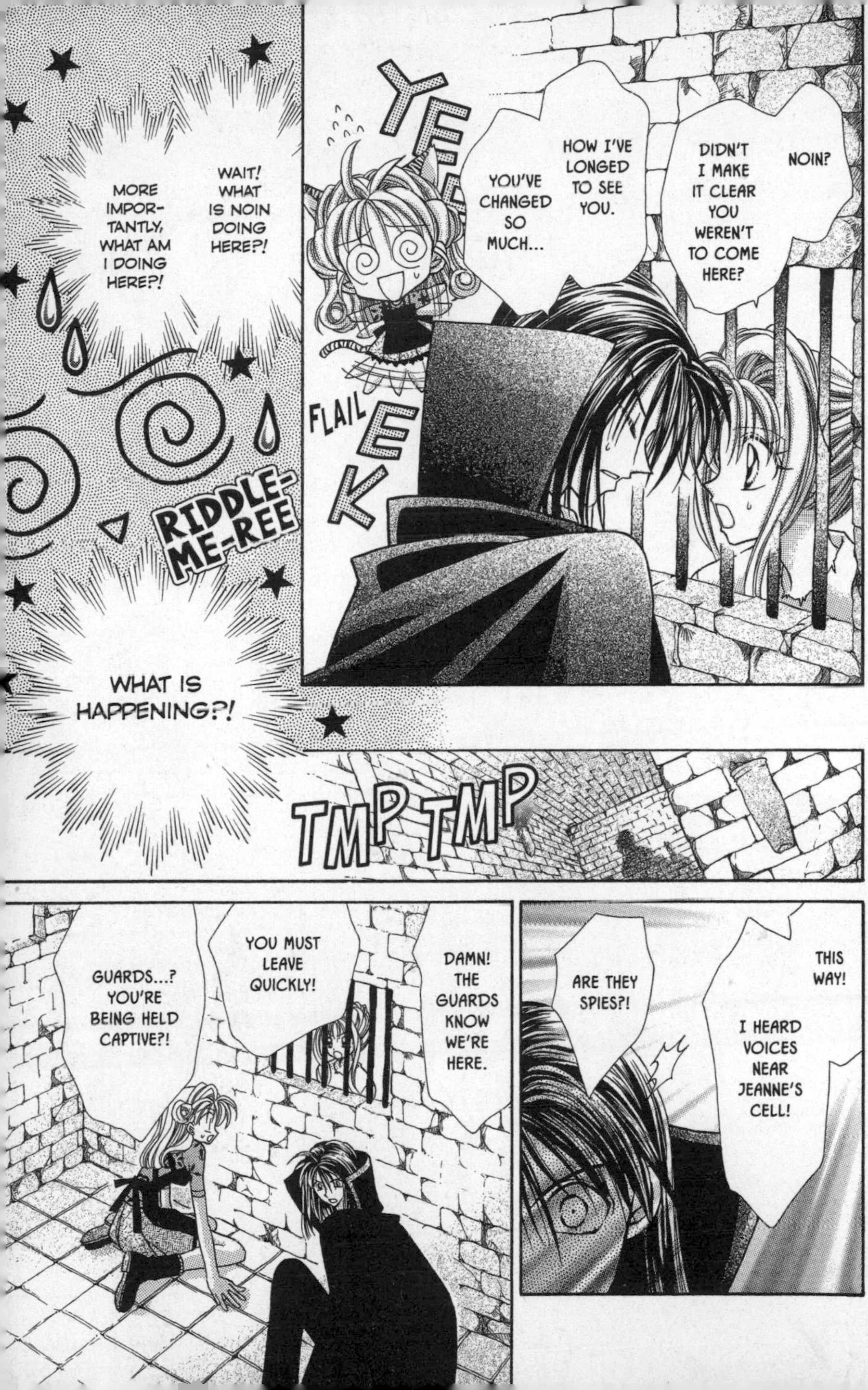

NOIN?
DIDN'T I MAKE IT CLEAR YOU WEREN'T TO COME HERE?
HOW I'VE LONGED TO SEE YOU.
YOU'VE CHANGED SO MUCH...
YEEEK
FLAIL
WAIT! WHAT IS NOIN DOING HERE?!
MORE IMPORTANTLY, WHAT AM I DOING HERE?!
RIDDLE-ME-REE
WHAT IS HAPPENING?!
TMP TMP
THIS WAY!
I HEARD VOICES NEAR JEANNE'S CELL!
ARE THEY SPIES?!
DAMN! THE GUARDS KNOW WE'RE HERE.
YOU MUST LEAVE QUICKLY!
GUARDS...? YOU'RE BEING HELD CAPTIVE?!

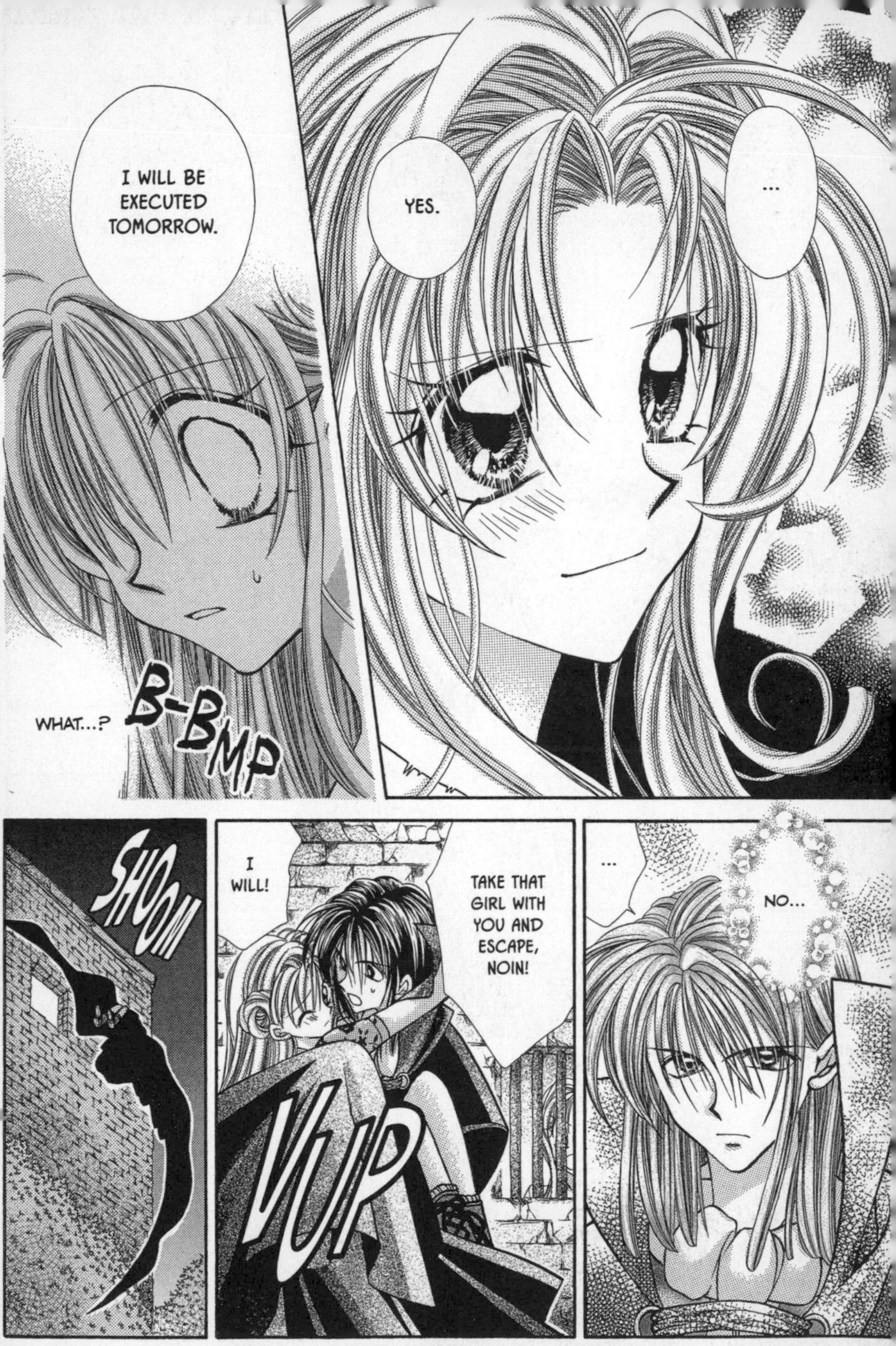
...
YES.
I WILL BE EXECUTED TOMORROW.
B-BMP
WHAT...?
...
NO...
TAKE THAT GIRL WITH YOU AND ESCAPE, NOIN!
I WILL!
VUP
SHOOM

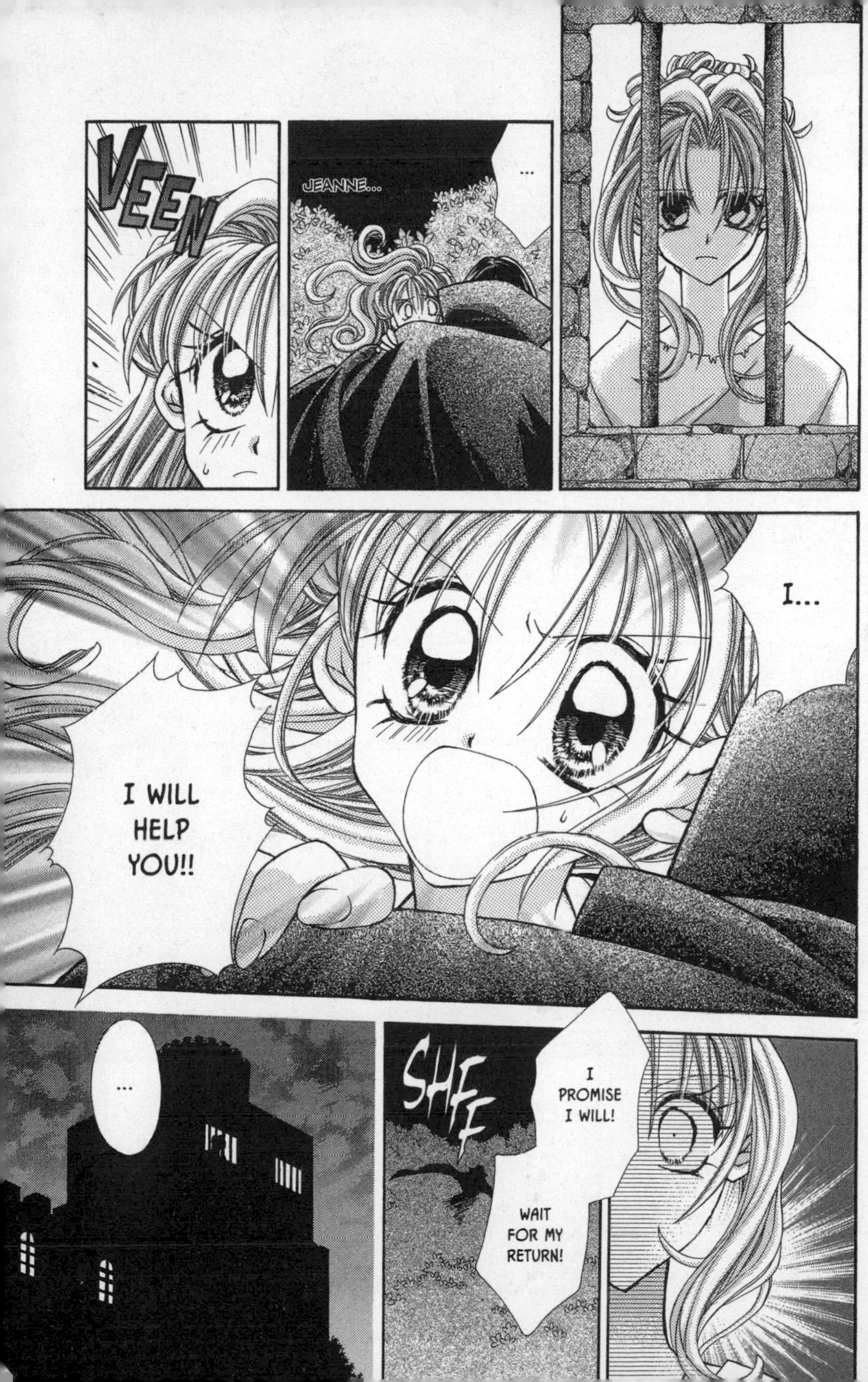
...
JEANNE...
VEEN
I...
I WILL HELP YOU!!
I PROMISE I WILL!
SHFF
WAIT FOR MY RETURN!
...

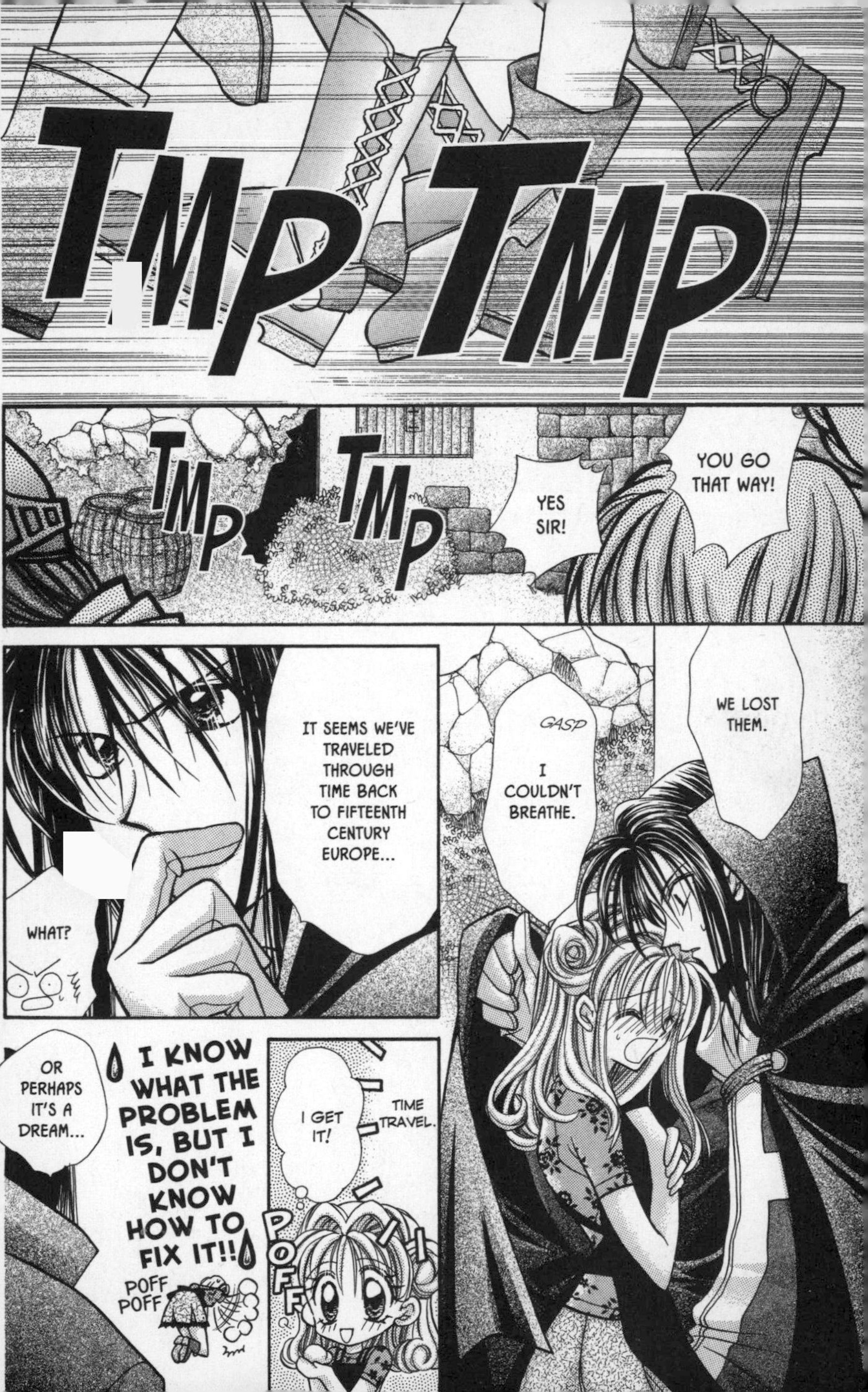
TMP TMP
YOU GO THAT WAY!
YES SIR!
TMP TMP
WE LOST THEM.
GASP
I COULDN'T BREATHE.
IT SEEMS WE'VE TRAVELED THROUGH TIME BACK TO FIFTEENTH CENTURY EUROPE...
WHAT?
TIME TRAVEL.
I GET IT!
POFF
OR PERHAPS IT'S A DREAM...
I KNOW WHAT THE PROBLEM IS, BUT I DON'T KNOW HOW TO FIX IT!!
POFF POFF

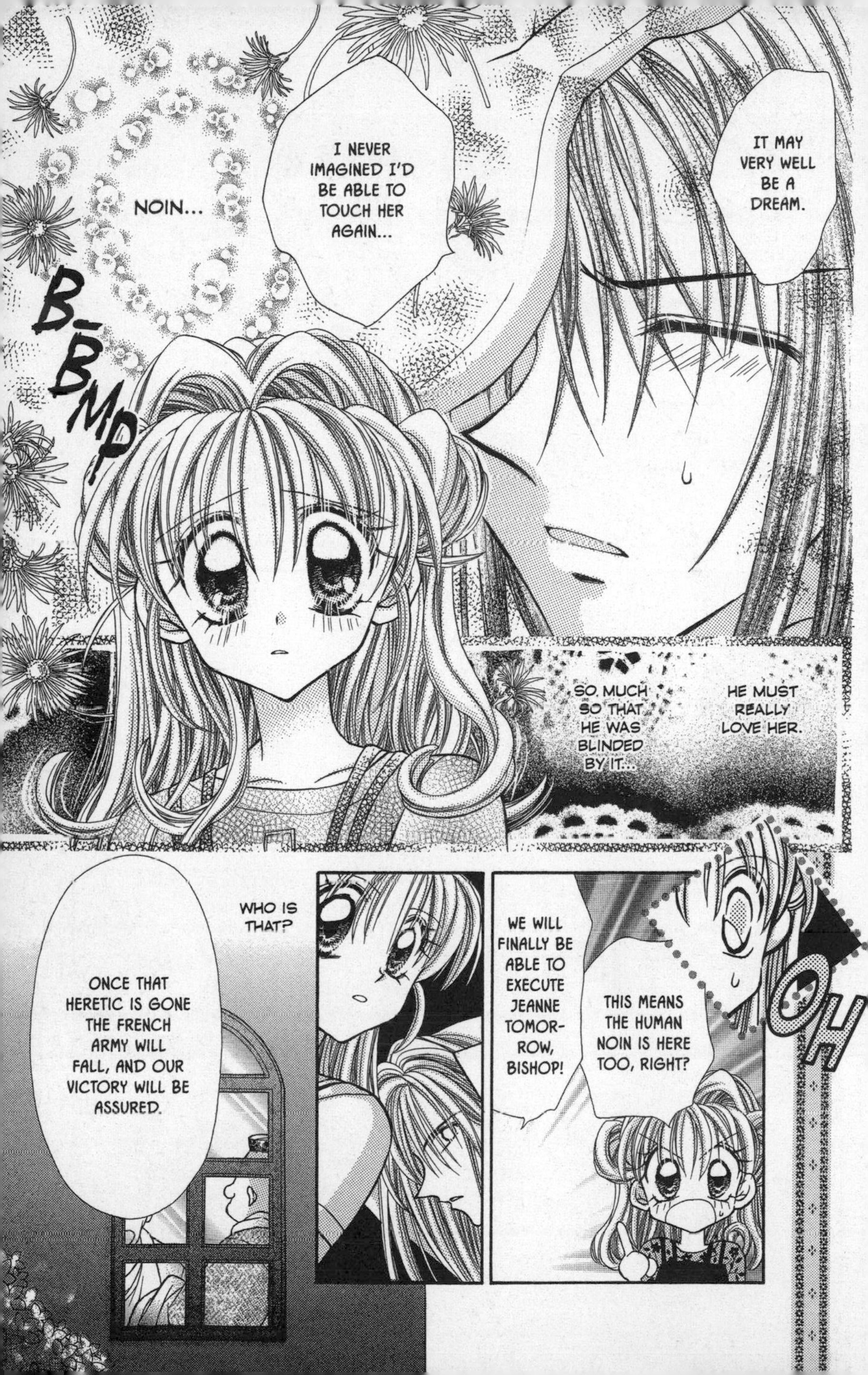
IT MAY VERY WELL BE A DREAM.
I NEVER IMAGINED I'D BE ABLE TO TOUCH HER AGAIN...
NOIN...
B-BMP!
HE MUST REALLY LOVE HER.
SO MUCH SO THAT HE WAS BLINDED BY IT...
OH
THIS MEANS THE HUMAN NOIN IS HERE TOO, RIGHT?
WE WILL FINALLY BE ABLE TO EXECUTE JEANNE TOMOR-ROW, BISHOP!
WHO IS THAT?
ONCE THAT HERETIC IS GONE THE FRENCH ARMY WILL FALL, AND OUR VICTORY WILL BE ASSURED.

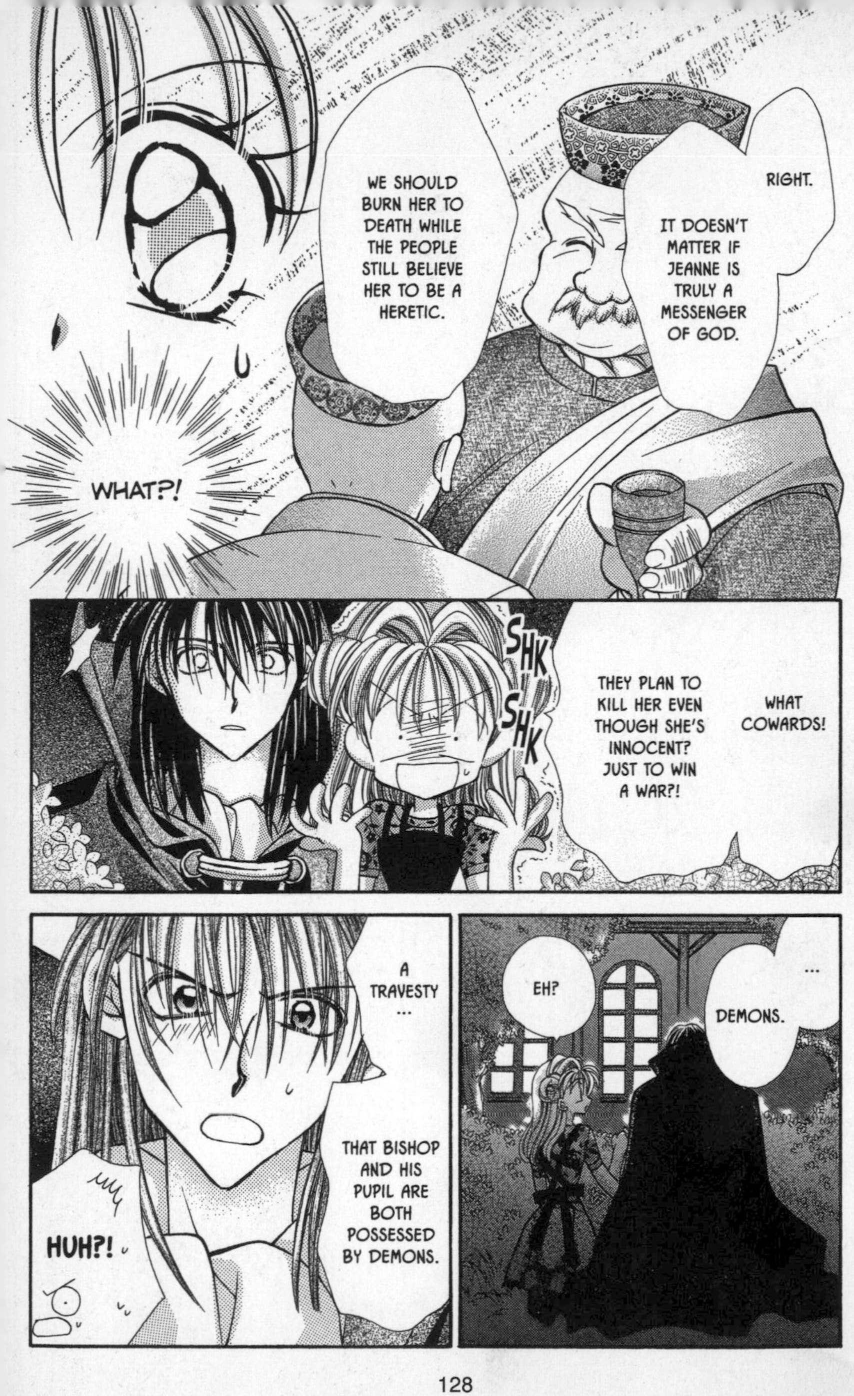
RIGHT.
IT DOESN'T MATTER IF JEANNE IS TRULY A MESSENGER OF GOD.
WE SHOULD BURN HER TO DEATH WHILE THE PEOPLE STILL BELIEVE HER TO BE A HERETIC.
WHAT?!
WHAT COWARDS!
THEY PLAN TO KILL HER EVEN THOUGH SHE'S INNOCENT? JUST TO WIN A WAR?!
SHK SHK
... DEMONS.
EH?
A TRAVESTY ...
THAT BISHOP AND HIS PUPIL ARE BOTH POSSESSED BY DEMONS.
HUH?!

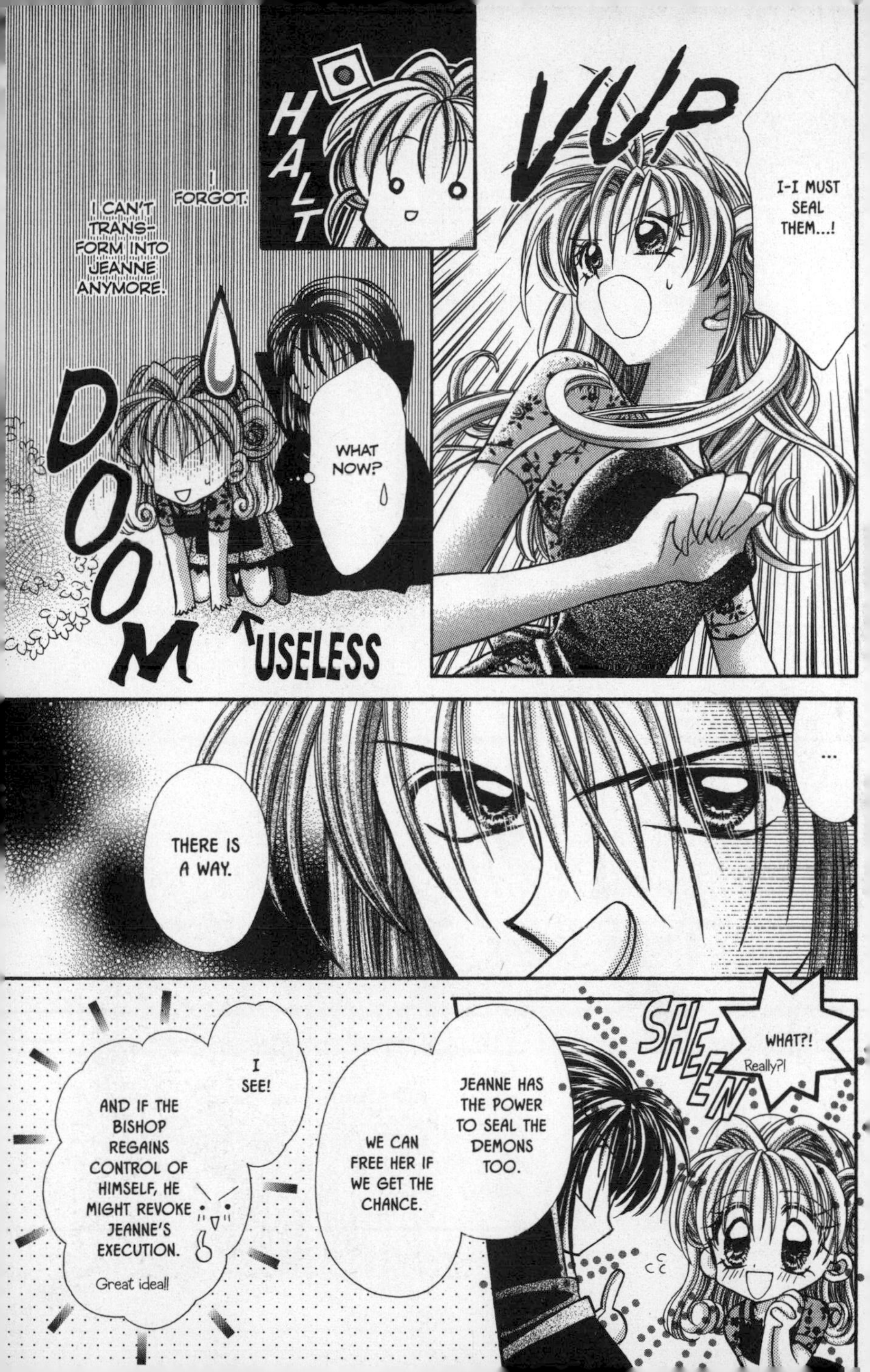
VUP
I-I MUST SEAL THEM...!
HALT
I FORGOT.
I CAN'T TRANSFORM INTO JEANNE ANYMORE.
DOOOM
WHAT NOW?
USELESS
...
THERE IS A WAY.
SHEEN
WHAT?!
Really?!
JEANNE HAS THE POWER TO SEAL THE DEMONS TOO.
WE CAN FREE HER IF WE GET THE CHANCE.
I SEE!
AND IF THE BISHOP REGAINS CONTROL OF HIMSELF, HE MIGHT REVOKE JEANNE'S EXECUTION.
Great idea!

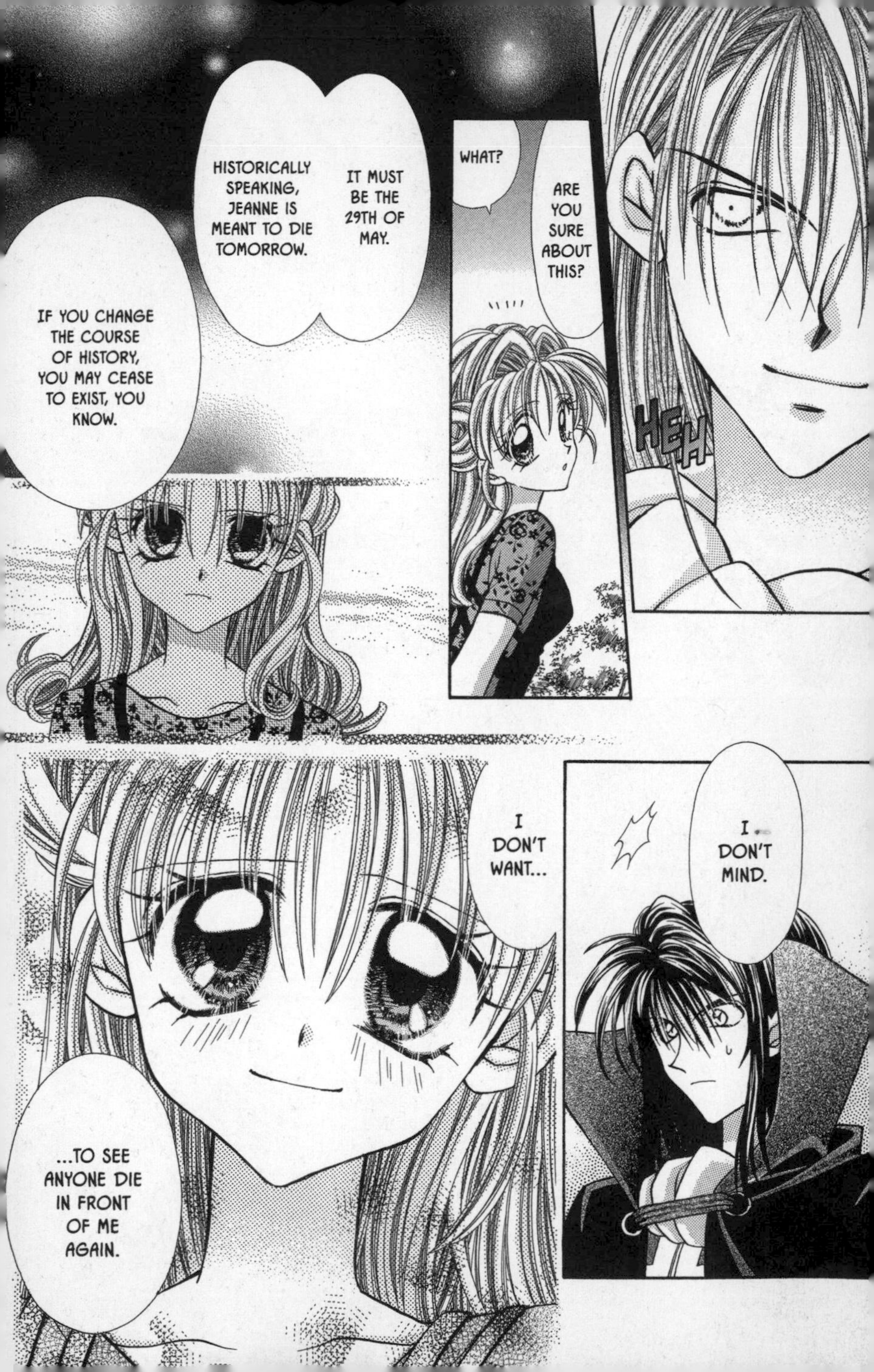
HEH
ARE YOU SURE ABOUT THIS?
WHAT?
IT MUST BE THE 29TH OF MAY.
HISTORICALLY SPEAKING, JEANNE IS MEANT TO DIE TOMORROW.
IF YOU CHANGE THE COURSE OF HISTORY, YOU MAY CEASE TO EXIST, YOU KNOW.
I DON'T MIND.
I DON'T WANT...
...TO SEE ANYONE DIE IN FRONT OF ME AGAIN.

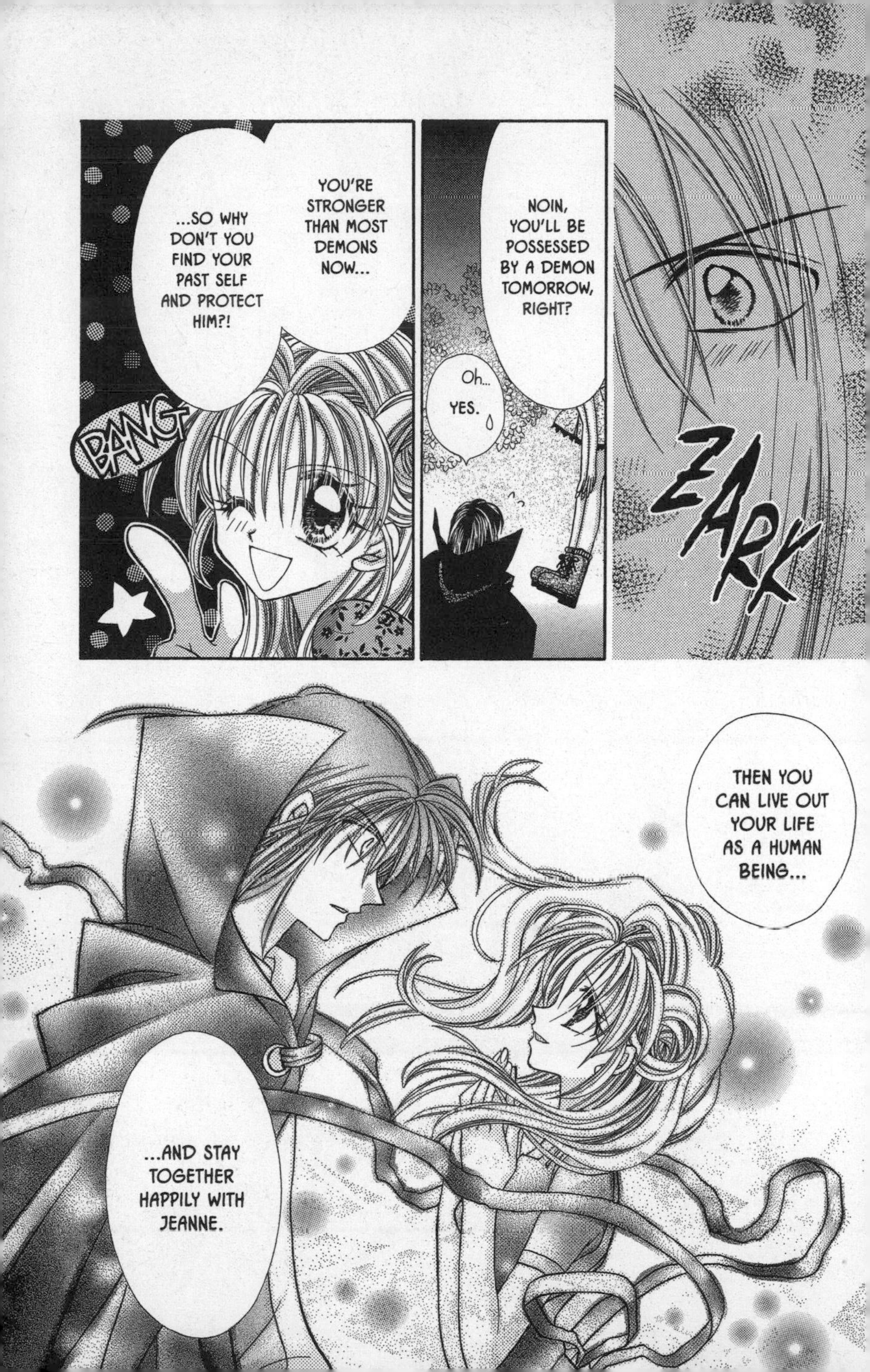
ZARK
NOIN, YOU'LL BE POSSESSED BY A DEMON TOMORROW, RIGHT?
Oh.. YES.
YOU'RE STRONGER THAN MOST DEMONS NOW...
...SO WHY DON'T YOU FIND YOUR PAST SELF AND PROTECT HIM?!
BANG
THEN YOU CAN LIVE OUT YOUR LIFE AS A HUMAN BEING...
...AND STAY TOGETHER HAPPILY WITH JEANNE.

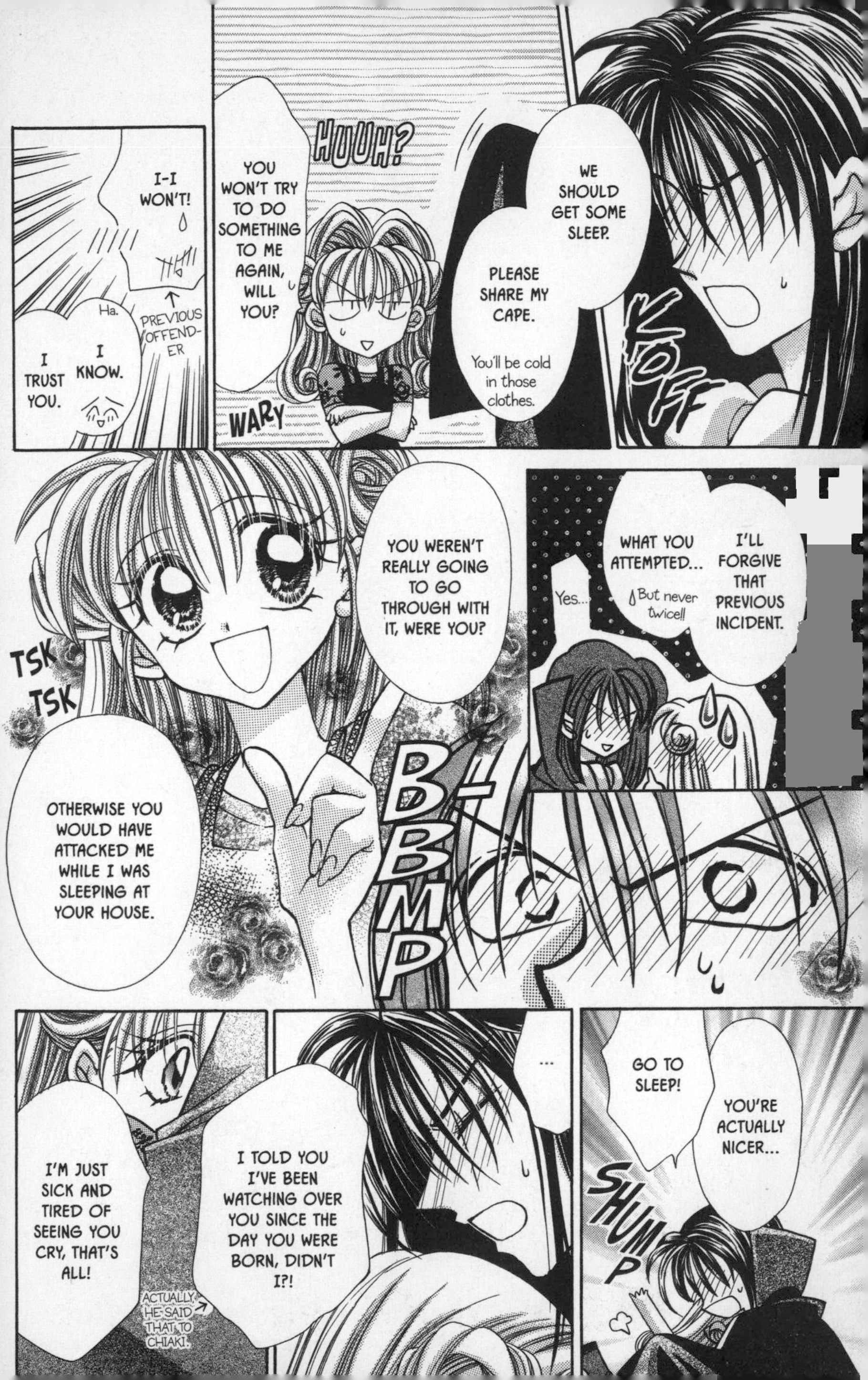
WE SHOULD GET SOME SLEEP.
PLEASE SHARE MY CAPE.
You'll be cold in those clothes.
KOFF
HUUH?
YOU WON'T TRY TO DO SOMETHING TO ME AGAIN, WILL YOU?
WARY
I-I WON'T!
PREVIOUS OFFENDER
Ha.
I KNOW.
I TRUST YOU.
I'LL FORGIVE THAT PREVIOUS INCIDENT.
WHAT YOU ATTEMPTED...
But never twice!!
Yes...
B-BBMP
YOU WEREN'T REALLY GOING TO GO THROUGH WITH IT, WERE YOU?
TSK TSK
OTHERWISE YOU WOULD HAVE ATTACKED ME WHILE I WAS SLEEPING AT YOUR HOUSE.
YOU'RE ACTUALLY NICER...
GO TO SLEEP!
SHUMP
...
I TOLD YOU I'VE BEEN WATCHING OVER YOU SINCE THE DAY YOU WERE BORN, DIDN'T I?!
ACTUALLY, HE SAID THAT TO CHIAKI.
I'M JUST SICK AND TIRED OF SEEING YOU CRY, THAT'S ALL!

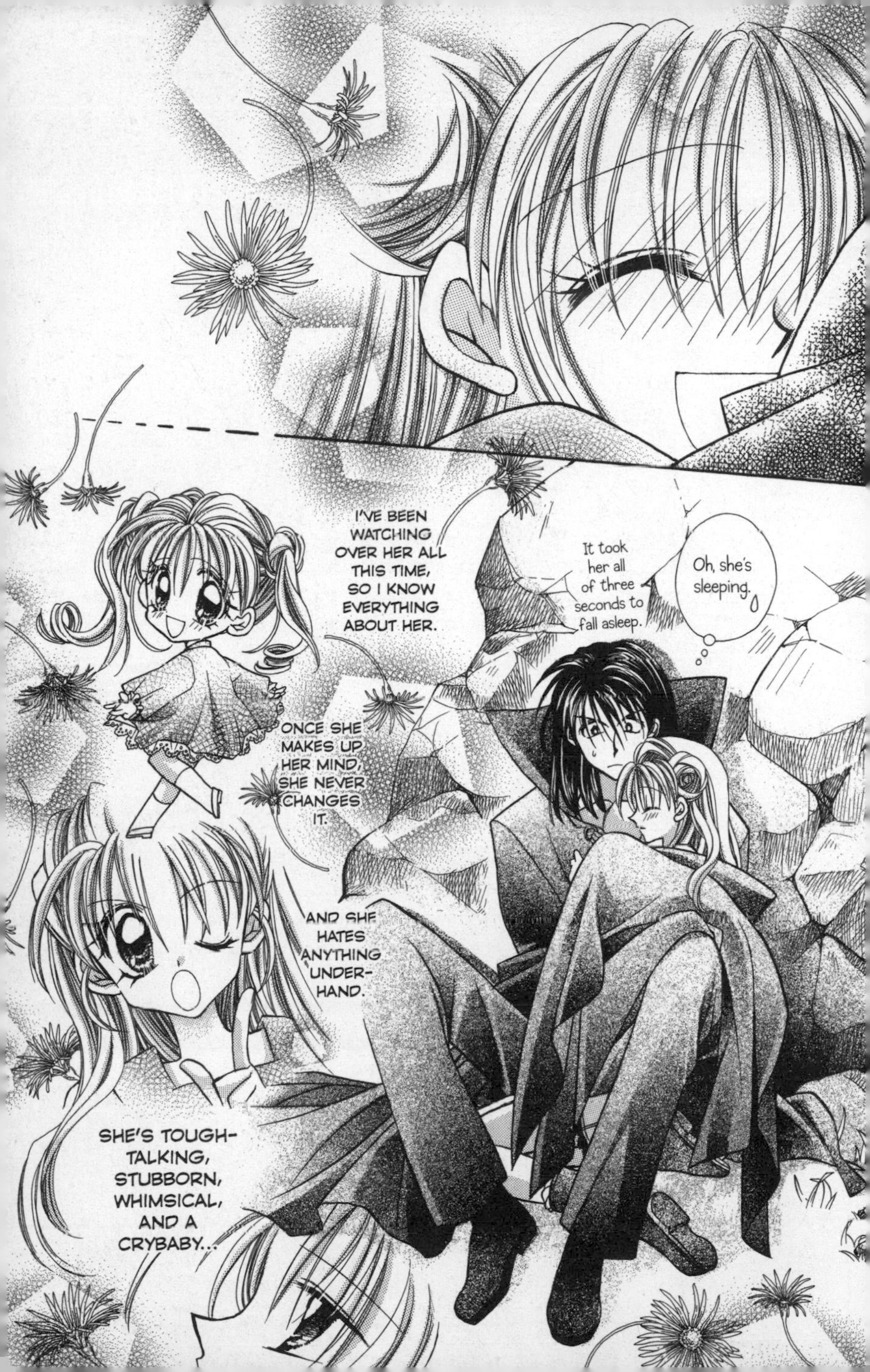
Oh, she's sleeping.
It took her all of three seconds to fall asleep.
I'VE BEEN WATCHING OVER HER ALL THIS TIME, SO I KNOW EVERYTHING ABOUT HER.
ONCE SHE MAKES UP HER MIND, SHE NEVER CHANGES IT.
AND SHE HATES ANYTHING UNDER-HAND.
SHE'S TOUGH-TALKING, STUBBORN, WHIMSICAL, AND A CRYBABY...

AND...

HE WAS RIGHT. SHE'S ENTIRELY DIFFERENT FROM JEANNE...

HEH

ZZZ

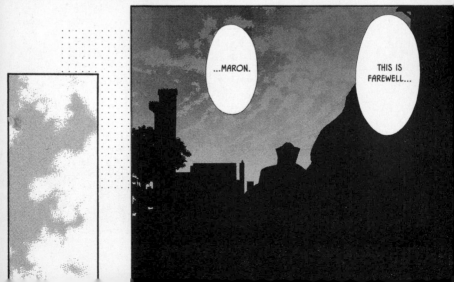

...MARON.

THIS IS FAREWELL...

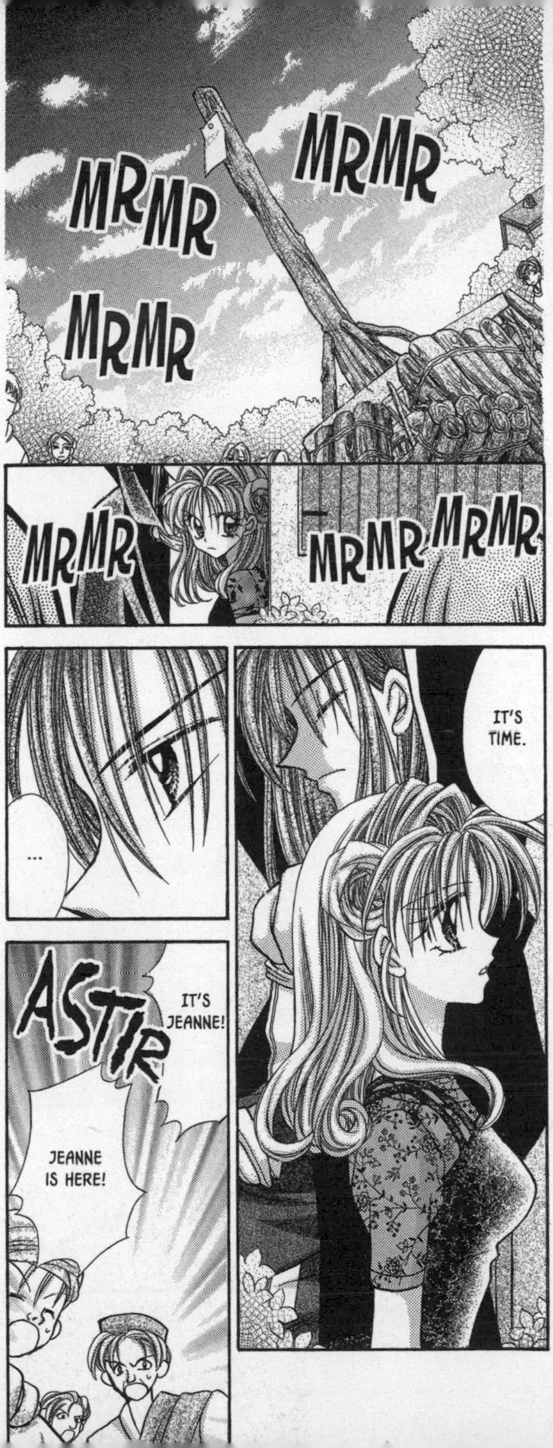
MRMR
MRMR
MRMR
MRMR
MRMR
MRMR
IT'S TIME.
...
ASTIR
IT'S JEANNE!
JEANNE IS HERE!

PHANTOM
THIEF
JEANNE

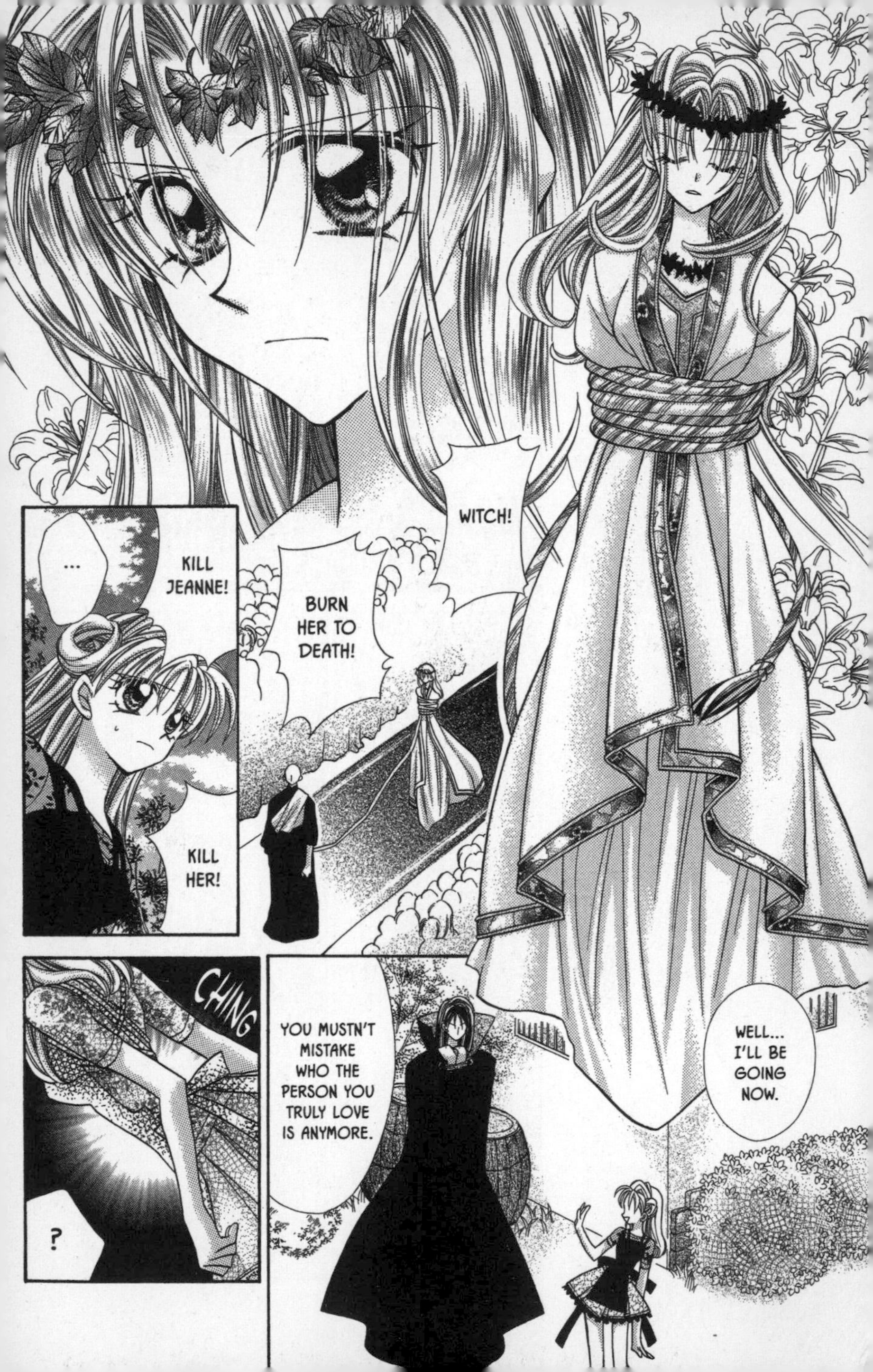
WITCH!
BURN HER TO DEATH!
KILL JEANNE!
...
KILL HER!
WELL... I'LL BE GOING NOW.
YOU MUSTN'T MISTAKE WHO THE PERSON YOU TRULY LOVE IS ANYMORE.
CHING
?

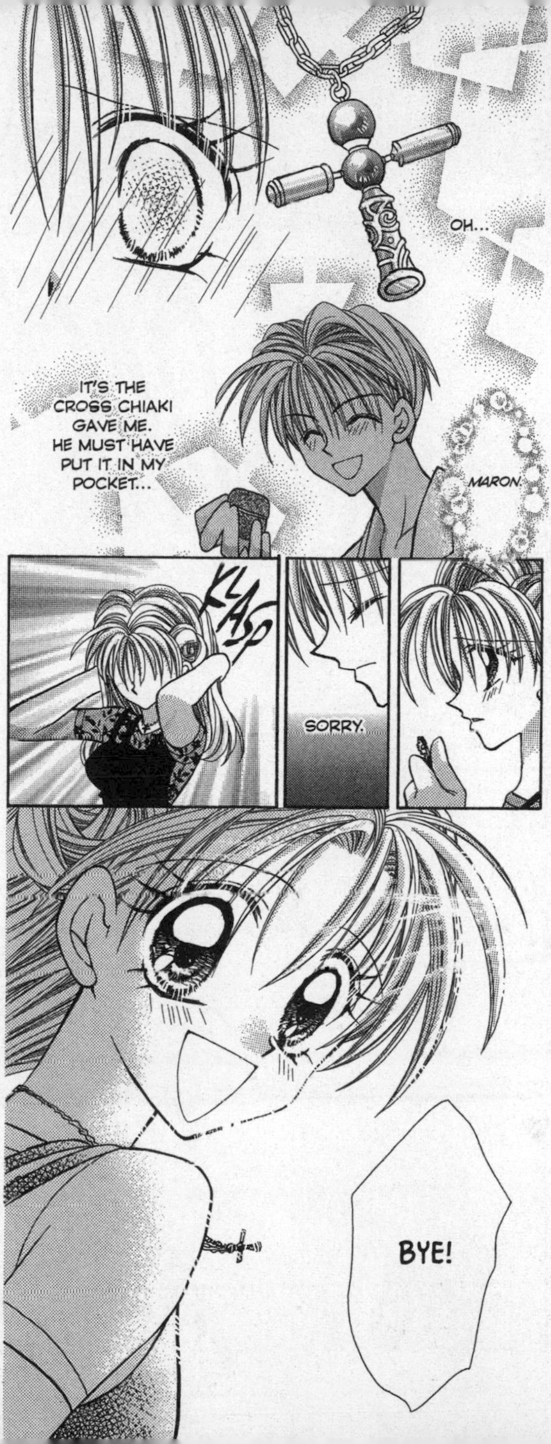
OH...
IT'S THE CROSS CHIAKI GAVE ME. HE MUST HAVE PUT IT IN MY POCKET...
MARON.
SORRY.
KLASP
BYE!

PHANTOM
THIEF
JEANNE

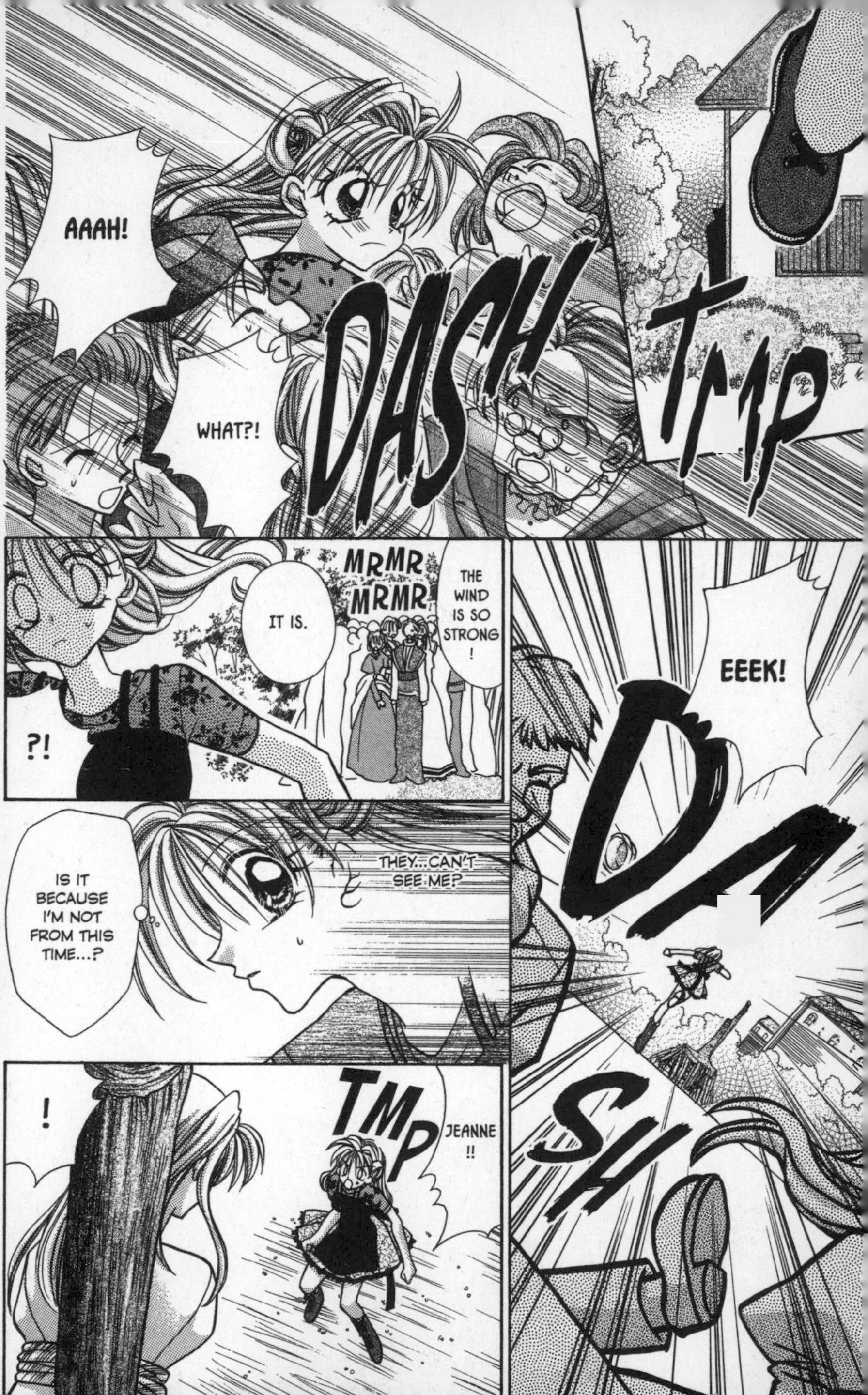
TRIP
DASH
AAAH!
WHAT?!
EEEK!
DASH
THE WIND IS SO STRONG!
MRMR MRMR
IT IS.
?!
THEY...CAN'T SEE ME?
IS IT BECAUSE I'M NOT FROM THIS TIME...?
JEANNE!!
TMP
!

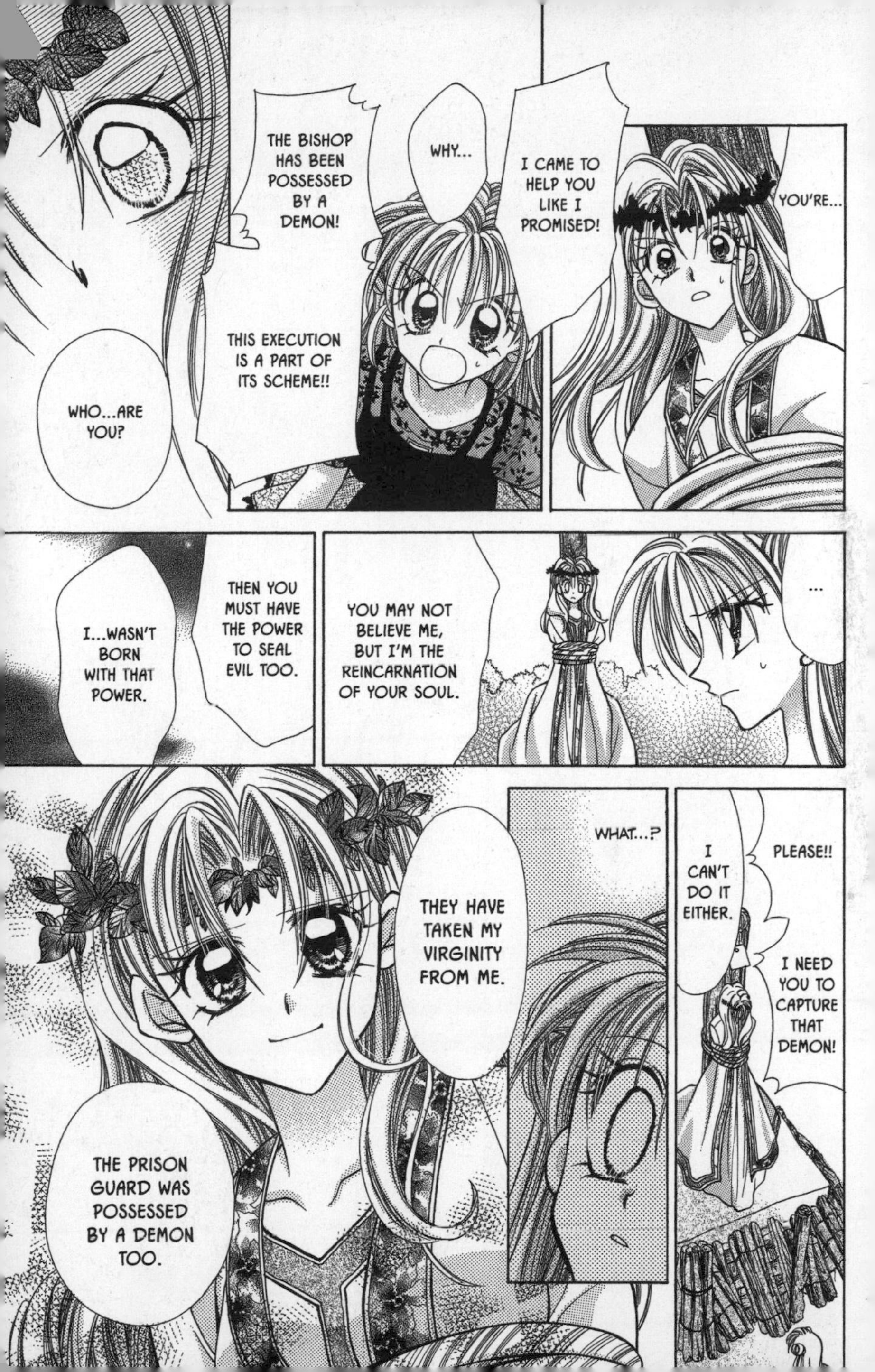
YOU'RE...
I CAME TO HELP YOU LIKE I PROMISED!
WHY...
THE BISHOP HAS BEEN POSSESSED BY A DEMON!
THIS EXECUTION IS A PART OF ITS SCHEME!!
WHO...ARE YOU?
...
YOU MAY NOT BELIEVE ME, BUT I'M THE REINCARNATION OF YOUR SOUL.
THEN YOU MUST HAVE THE POWER TO SEAL EVIL TOO.
I...WASN'T BORN WITH THAT POWER.
PLEASE!!
I NEED YOU TO CAPTURE THAT DEMON!
I CAN'T DO IT EITHER.
WHAT...?
THEY HAVE TAKEN MY VIRGINITY FROM ME.
THE PRISON GUARD WAS POSSESSED BY A DEMON TOO.

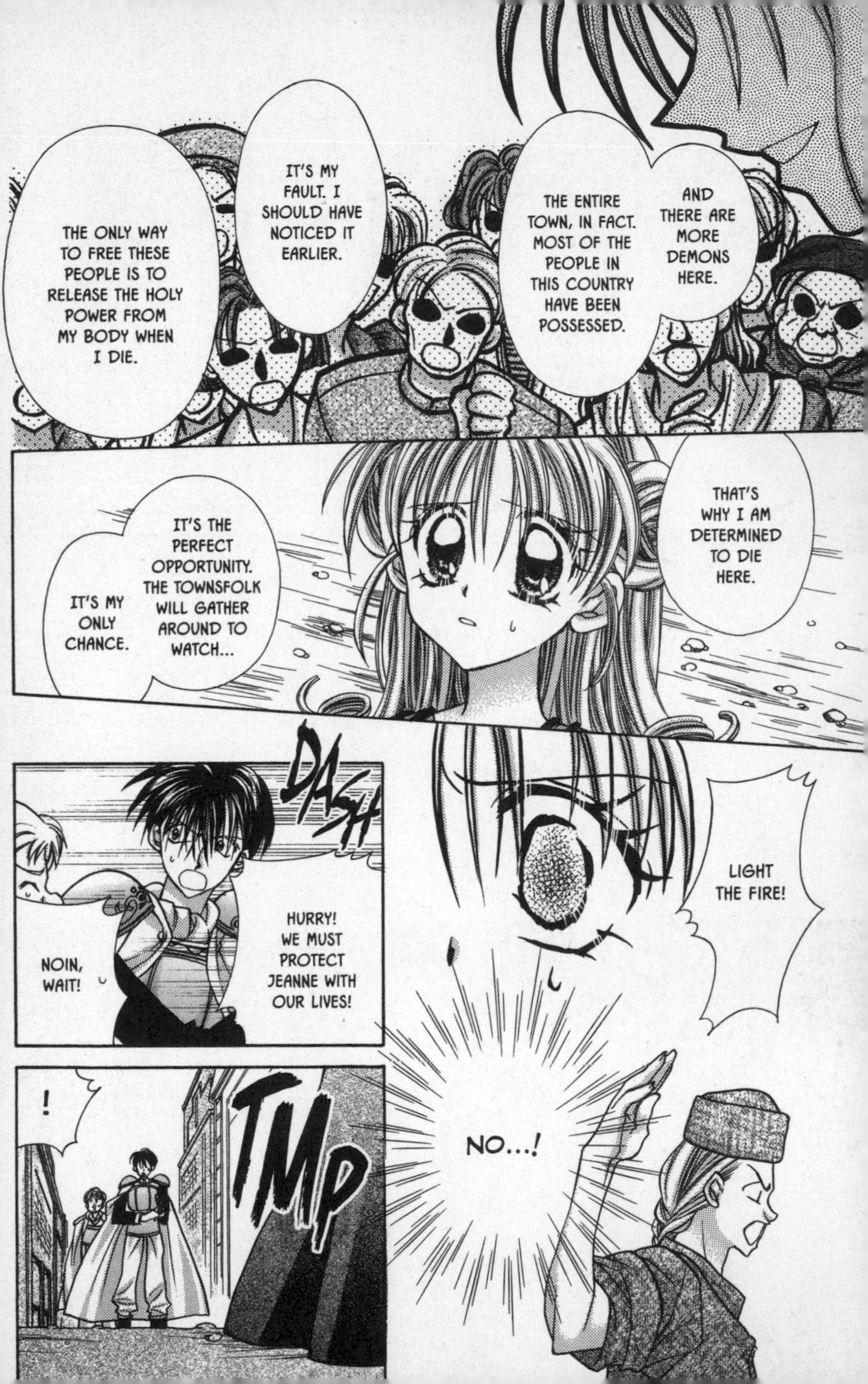
AND THERE ARE MORE DEMONS HERE.
THE ENTIRE TOWN, IN FACT. MOST OF THE PEOPLE IN THIS COUNTRY HAVE BEEN POSSESSED.
IT'S MY FAULT. I SHOULD HAVE NOTICED IT EARLIER.
THE ONLY WAY TO FREE THESE PEOPLE IS TO RELEASE THE HOLY POWER FROM MY BODY WHEN I DIE.
THAT'S WHY I AM DETERMINED TO DIE HERE.
IT'S THE PERFECT OPPORTUNITY. THE TOWNSFOLK WILL GATHER AROUND TO WATCH...
IT'S MY ONLY CHANCE.
LIGHT THE FIRE!
NO...!
DASH
HURRY! WE MUST PROTECT JEANNE WITH OUR LIVES!
NOIN, WAIT!
!
TMP

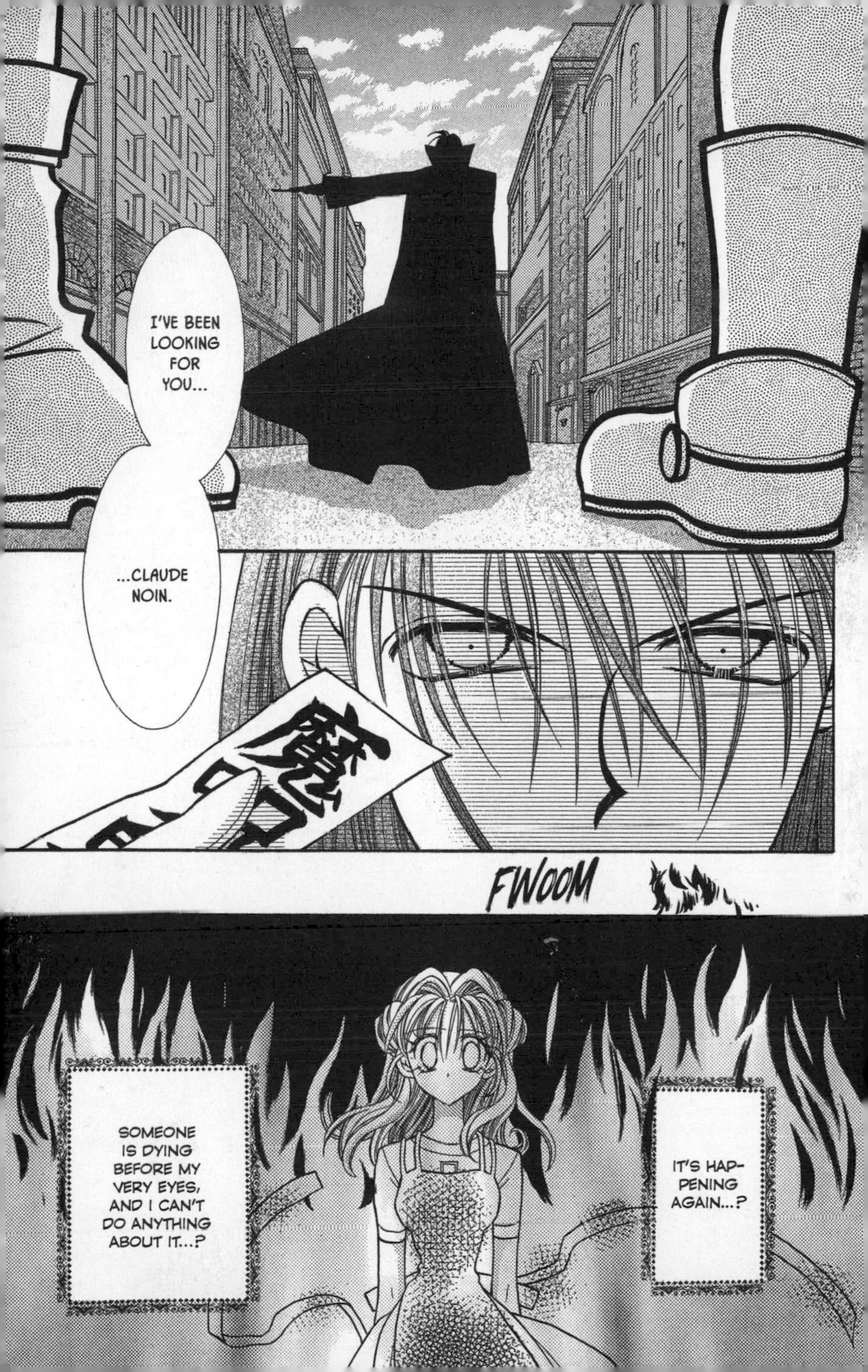
I'VE BEEN LOOKING FOR YOU...
...CLAUDE NOIN.
FWOOM
IT'S HAP-PENING AGAIN...?
SOMEONE IS DYING BEFORE MY VERY EYES, AND I CAN'T DO ANYTHING ABOUT IT...?

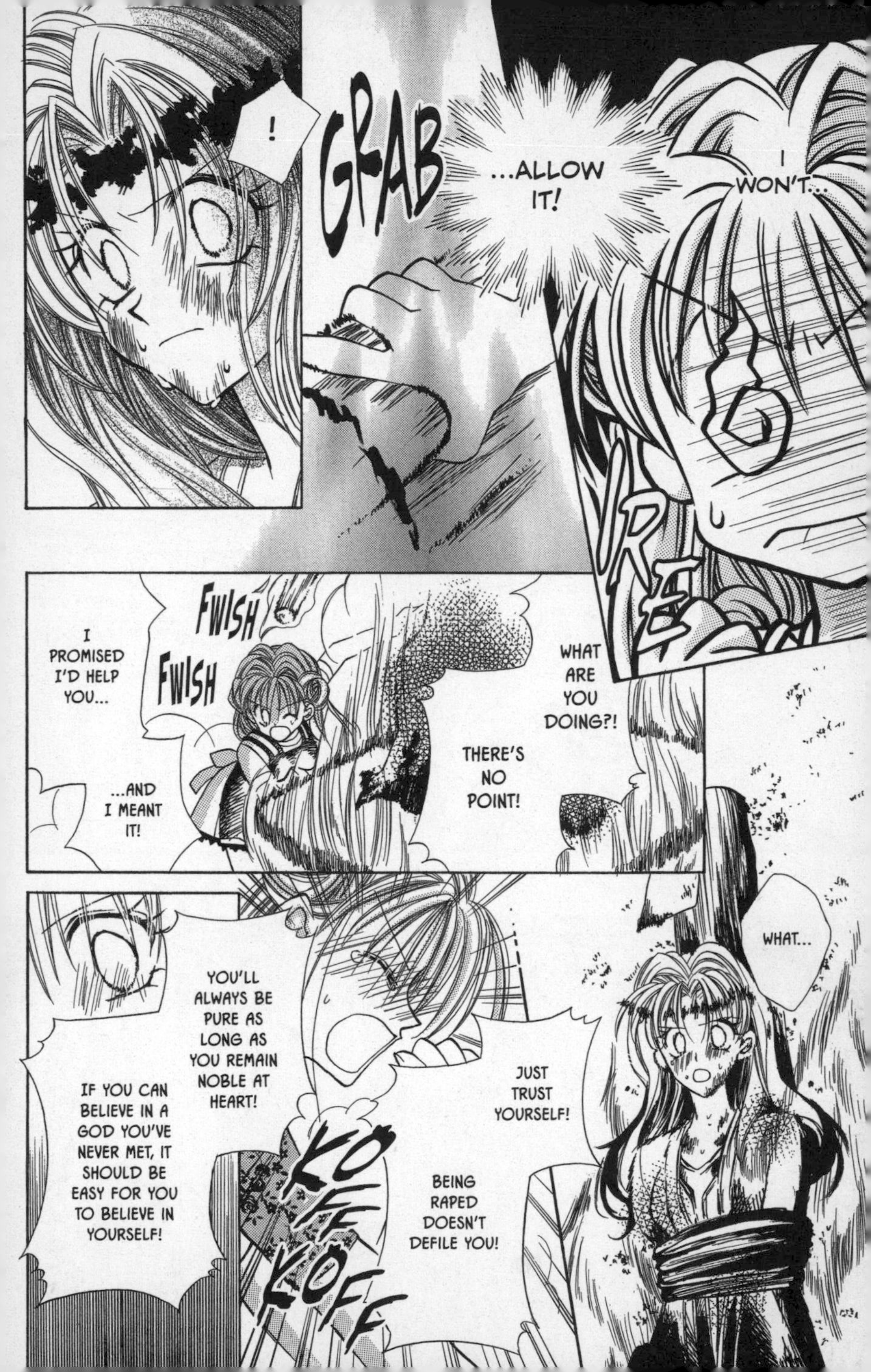
I WON'T...
...ALLOW IT!
GRAB
!
WHAT ARE YOU DOING?!
THERE'S NO POINT!
FWISH
FWISH
I PROMISED I'D HELP YOU...
...AND I MEANT IT!
WHAT...
JUST TRUST YOURSELF!
YOU'LL ALWAYS BE PURE AS LONG AS YOU REMAIN NOBLE AT HEART!
BEING RAPED DOESN'T DEFILE YOU!
KOFF
KOFF
IF YOU CAN BELIEVE IN A GOD YOU'VE NEVER MET, IT SHOULD BE EASY FOR YOU TO BELIEVE IN YOURSELF!

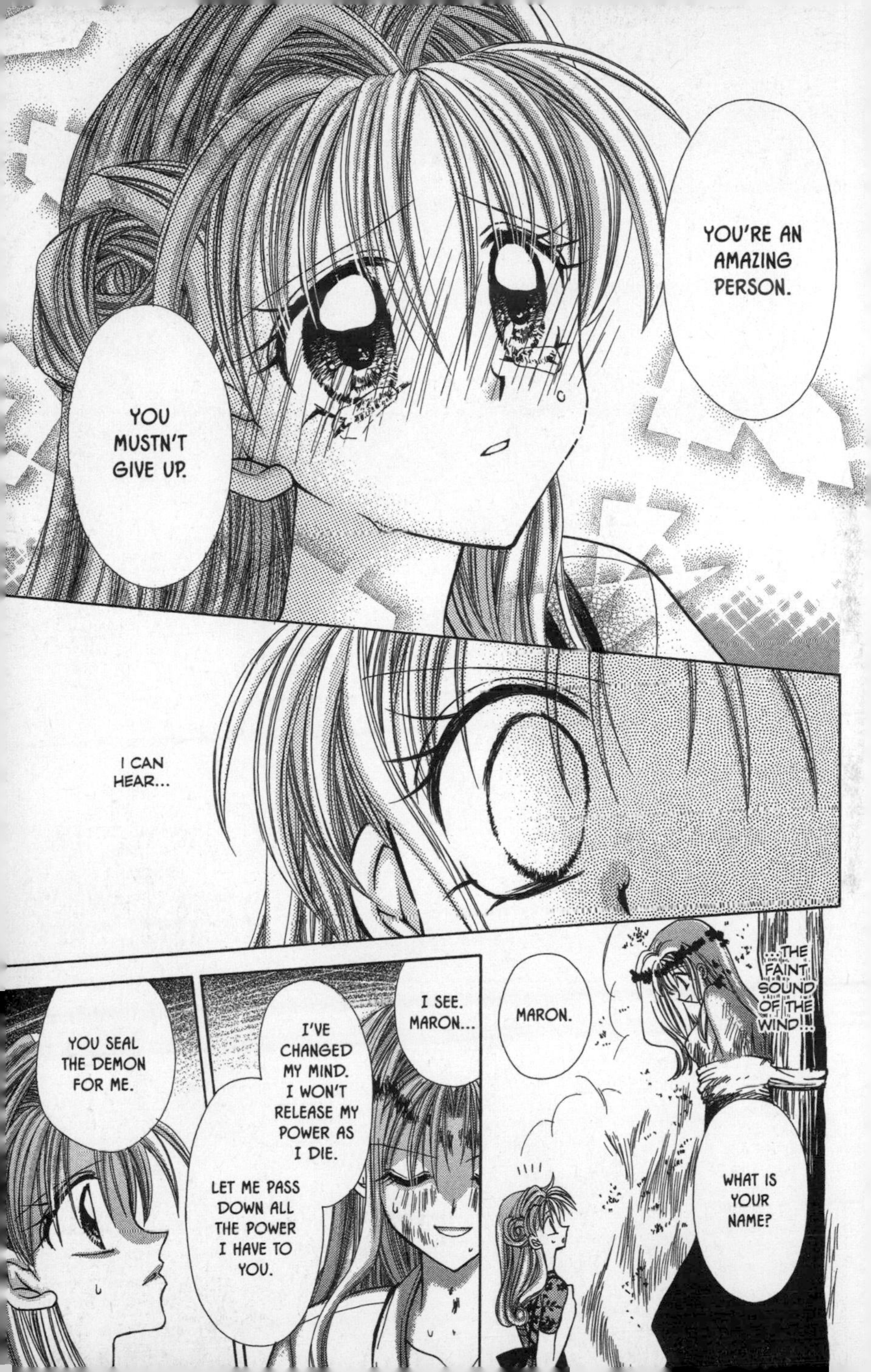
YOU'RE AN AMAZING PERSON.
YOU MUSTN'T GIVE UP.
I CAN HEAR...
...THE FAINT SOUND OF THE WIND...
WHAT IS YOUR NAME?
MARON.
I SEE. MARON...
I'VE CHANGED MY MIND. I WON'T RELEASE MY POWER AS I DIE.
LET ME PASS DOWN ALL THE POWER I HAVE TO YOU.
YOU SEAL THE DEMON FOR ME.

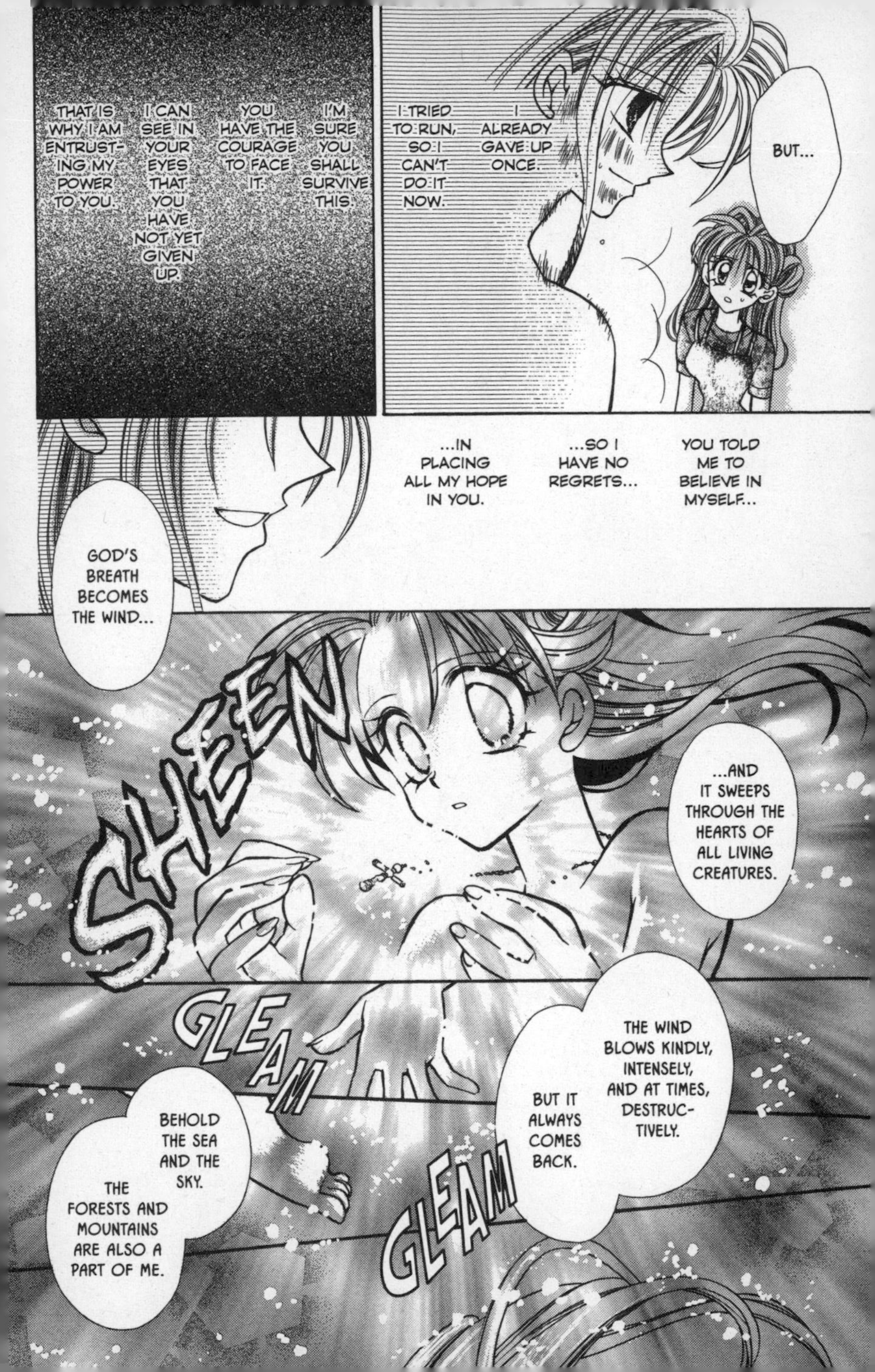
BUT...
I ALREADY GAVE UP ONCE.
I TRIED TO RUN, SO I CAN'T DO IT NOW.
I'M SURE YOU SHALL SURVIVE THIS.
YOU HAVE THE COURAGE TO FACE IT.
I CAN SEE IN YOUR EYES THAT YOU HAVE NOT YET GIVEN UP.
THAT IS WHY I AM ENTRUSTING MY POWER TO YOU.
YOU TOLD ME TO BELIEVE IN MYSELF...
...SO I HAVE NO REGRETS...
...IN PLACING ALL MY HOPE IN YOU.
GOD'S BREATH BECOMES THE WIND...
...AND IT SWEEPS THROUGH THE HEARTS OF ALL LIVING CREATURES.
SHEEN
THE WIND BLOWS KINDLY, INTENSELY, AND AT TIMES, DESTRUCTIVELY.
BUT IT ALWAYS COMES BACK.
GLEAM
GLEAM
BEHOLD THE SEA AND THE SKY.
THE FORESTS AND MOUNTAINS ARE ALSO A PART OF ME.

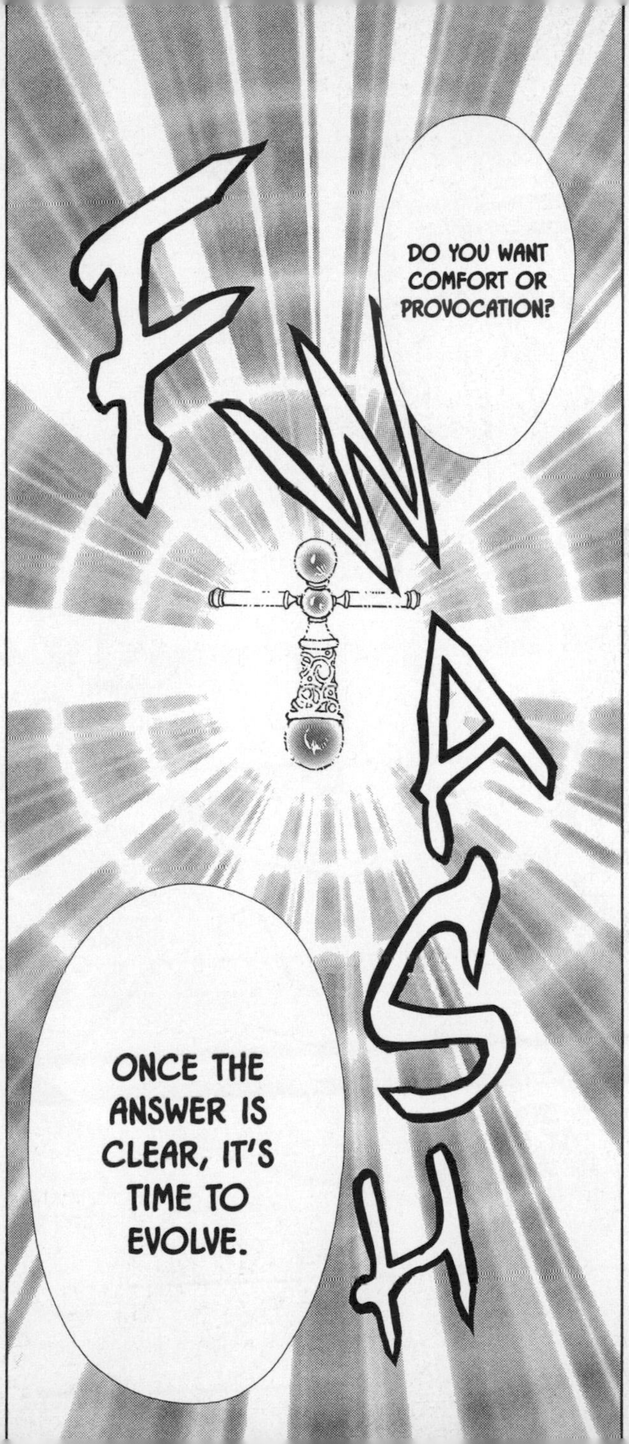
DO YOU WANT COMFORT OR PROVOCATION?
FWASH
ONCE THE ANSWER IS CLEAR, IT'S TIME TO EVOLVE.

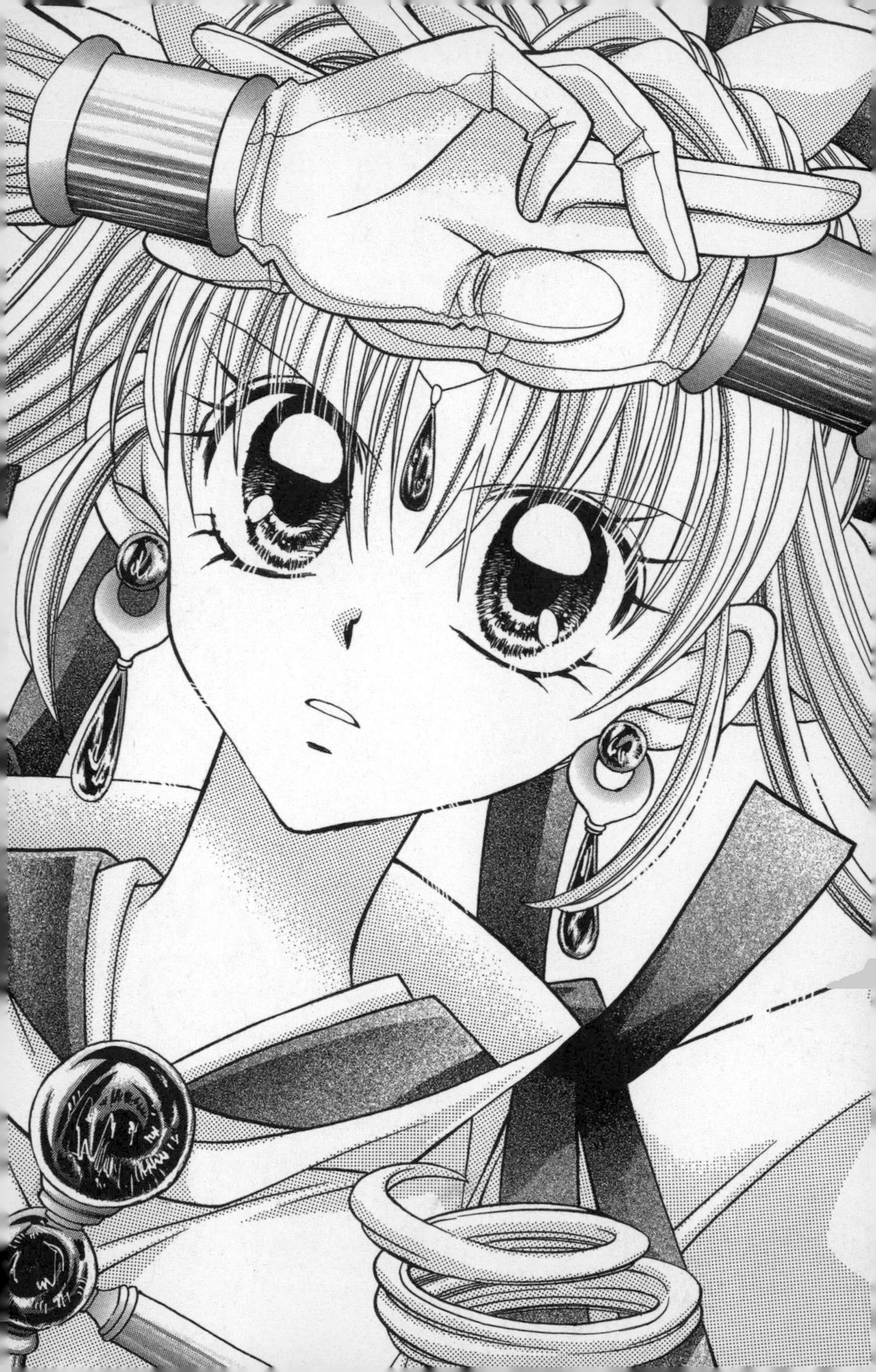

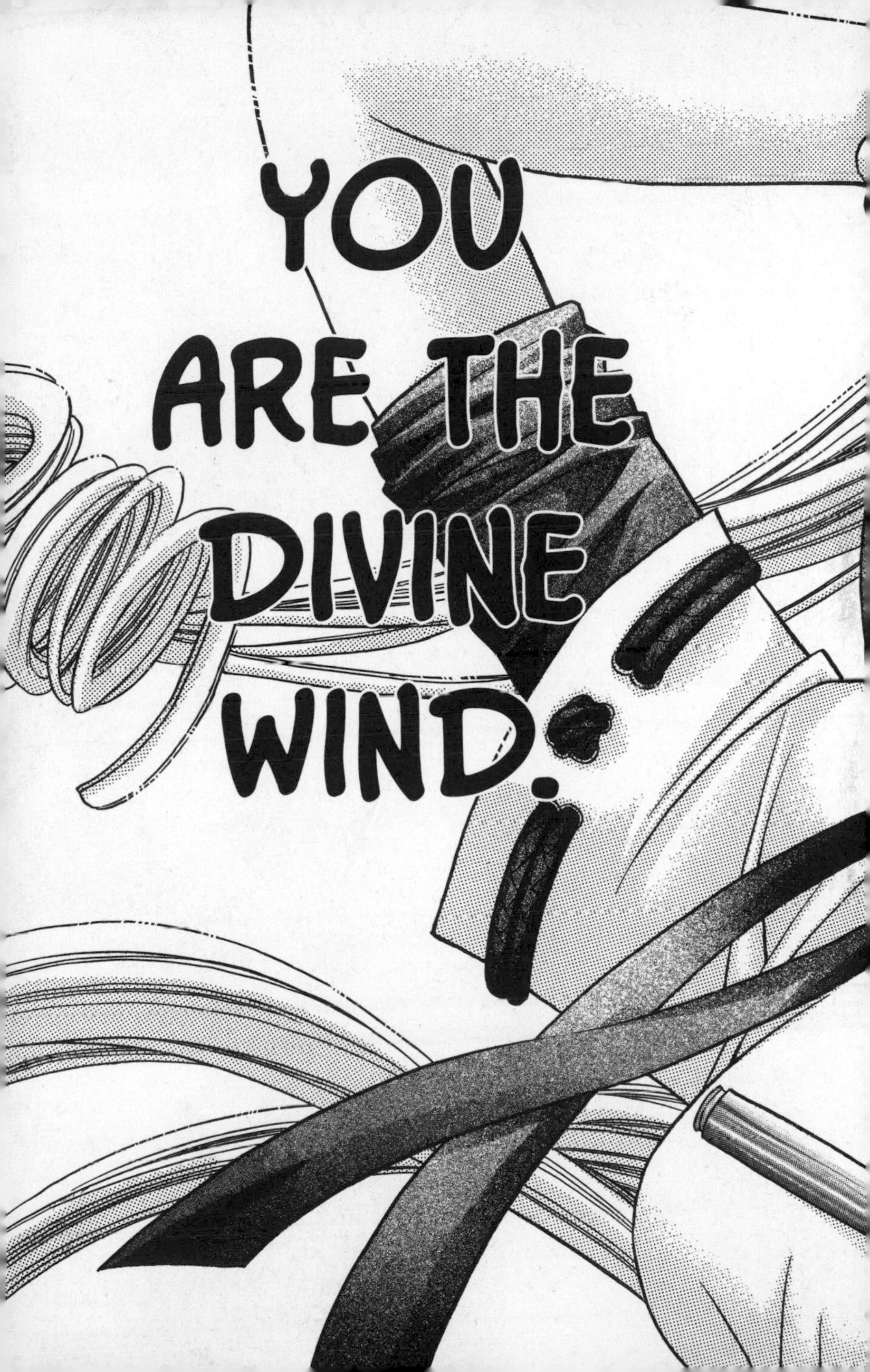
YOU ARE THE DIVINE WIND!

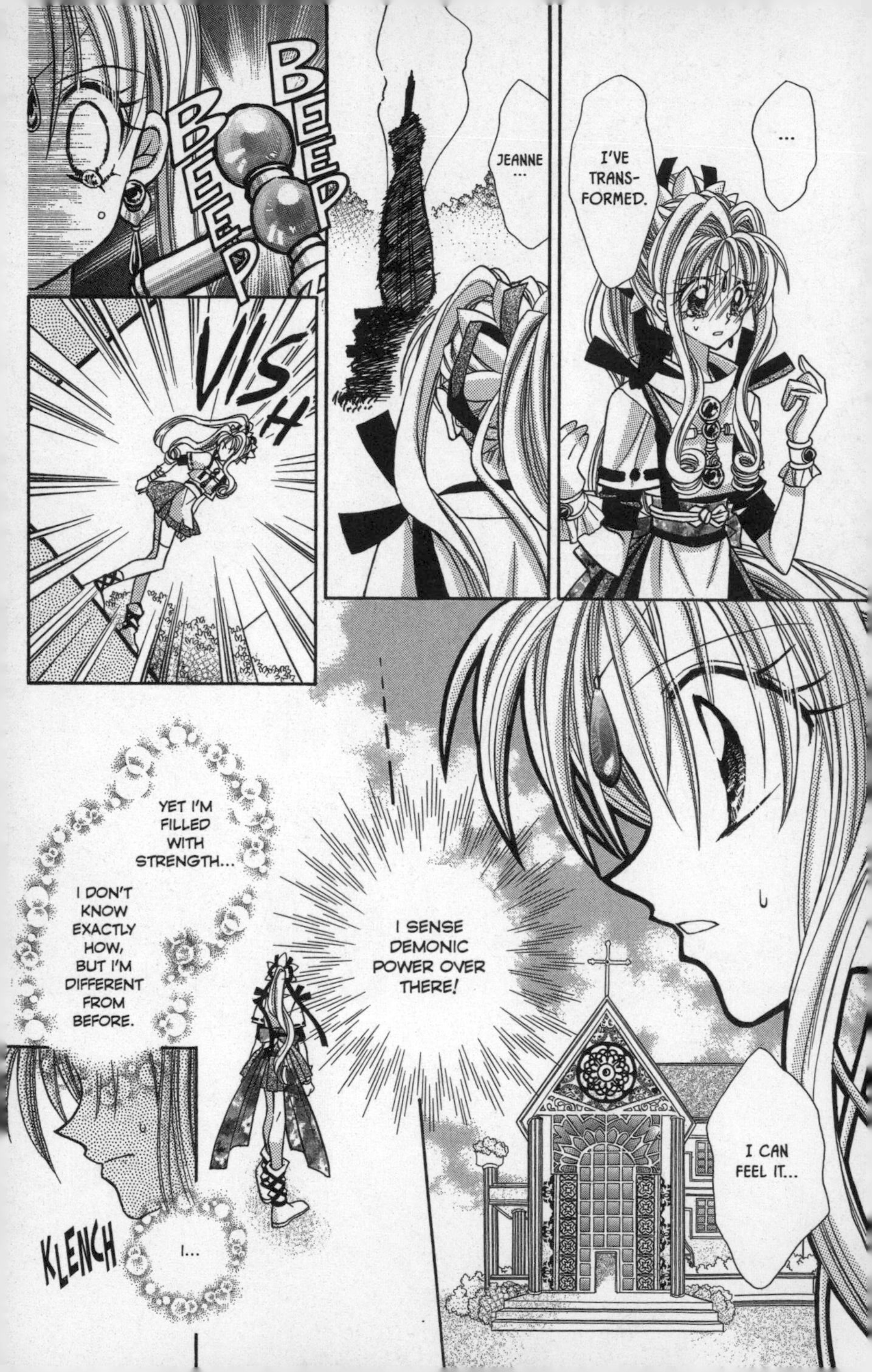
...
I'VE TRANS-FORMED.
JEANNE ...
BEEP
BEEP
VISH
I CAN FEEL IT...
I SENSE DEMONIC POWER OVER THERE!
YET I'M FILLED WITH STRENGTH...
I DON'T KNOW EXACTLY HOW, BUT I'M DIFFERENT FROM BEFORE.
I...
KLENCH

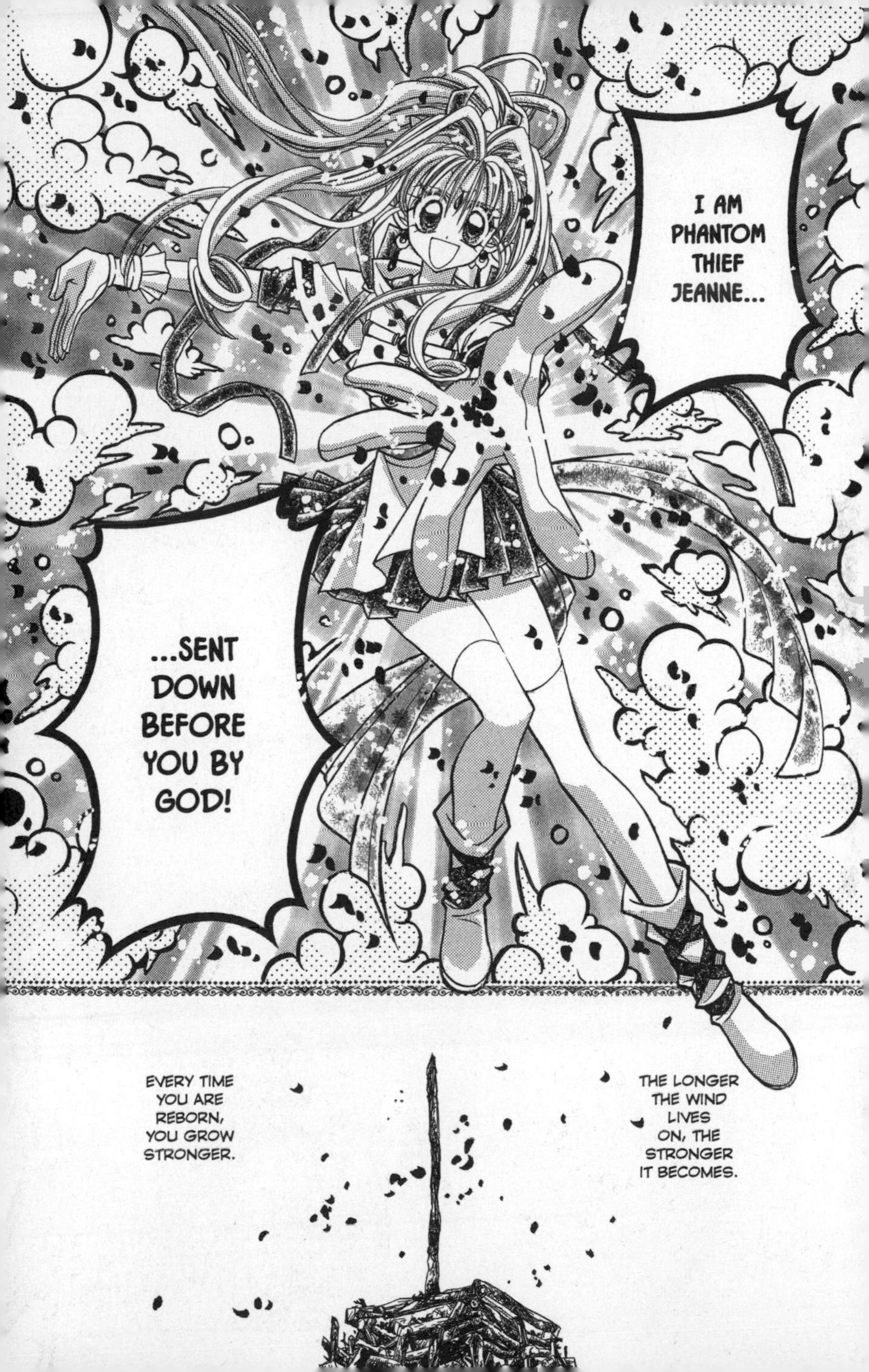
I AM PHANTOM THIEF JEANNE...
...SENT DOWN BEFORE YOU BY GOD!
THE LONGER THE WIND LIVES ON, THE STRONGER IT BECOMES.
EVERY TIME YOU ARE REBORN, YOU GROW STRONGER.

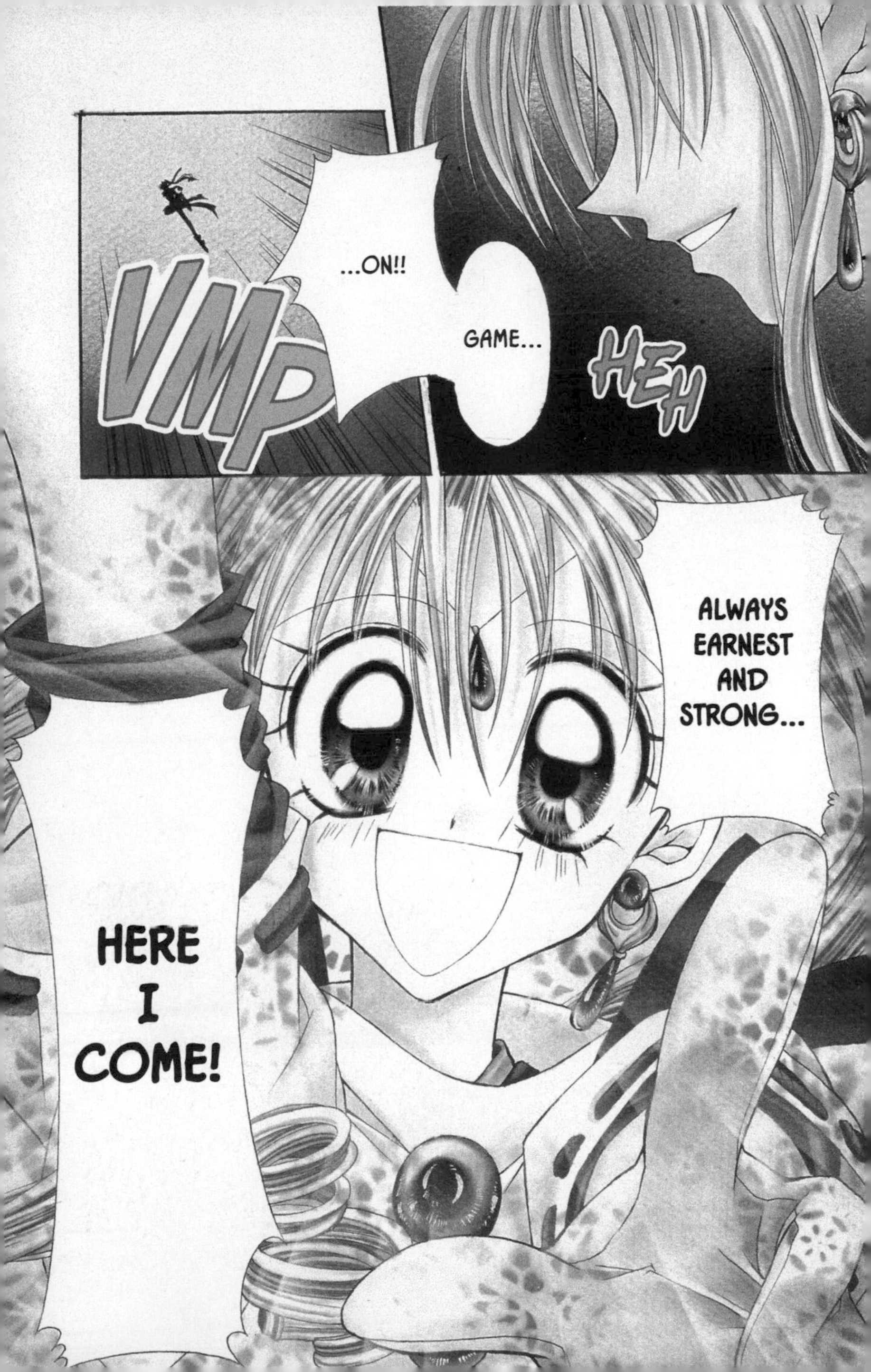
HEH
GAME...
...ON!!
VMP
ALWAYS EARNEST AND STRONG...
HERE I COME!

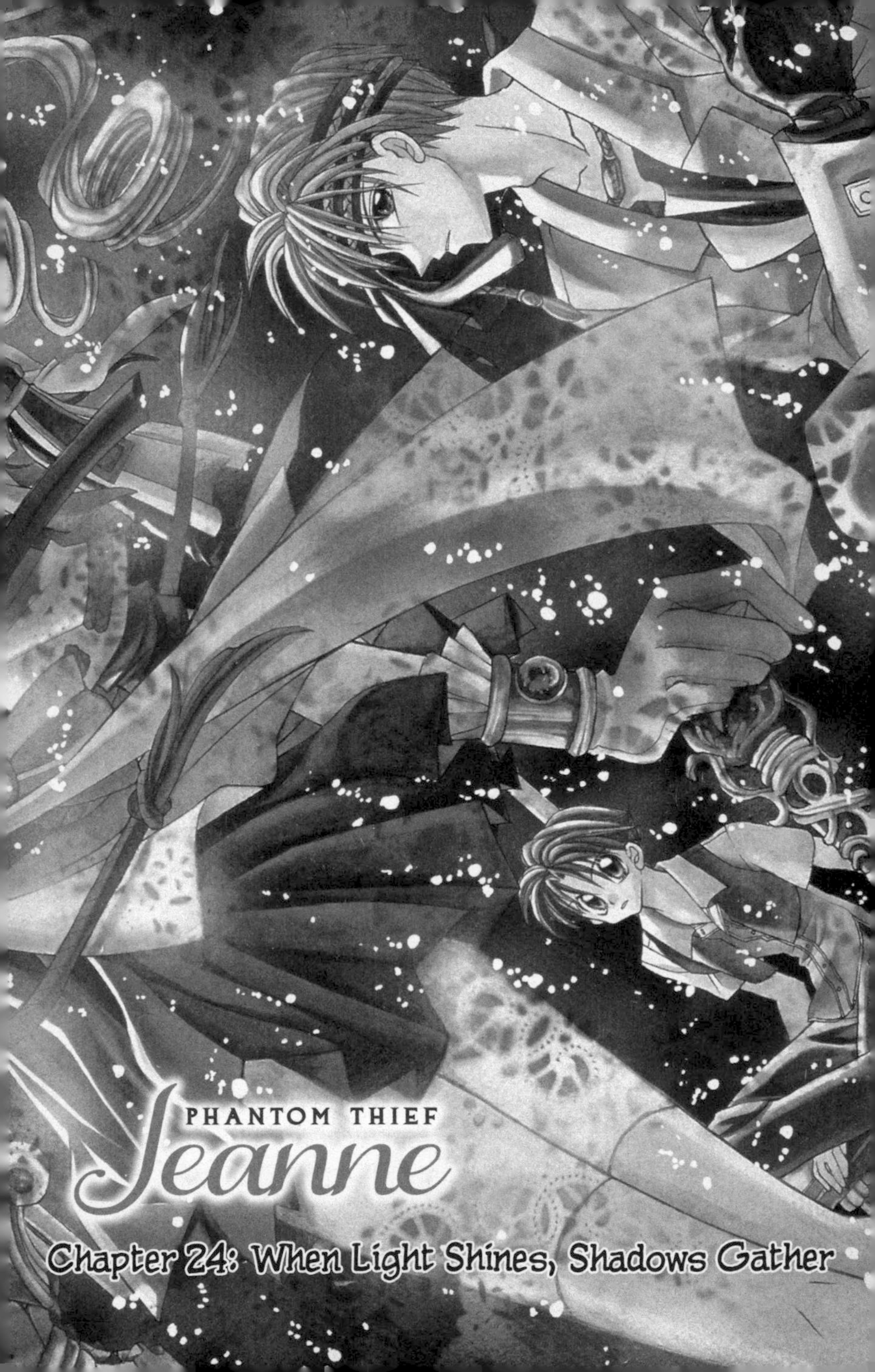
PHANTOM THIEF
Jeanne
Chapter 24: When Light Shines, Shadows Gather

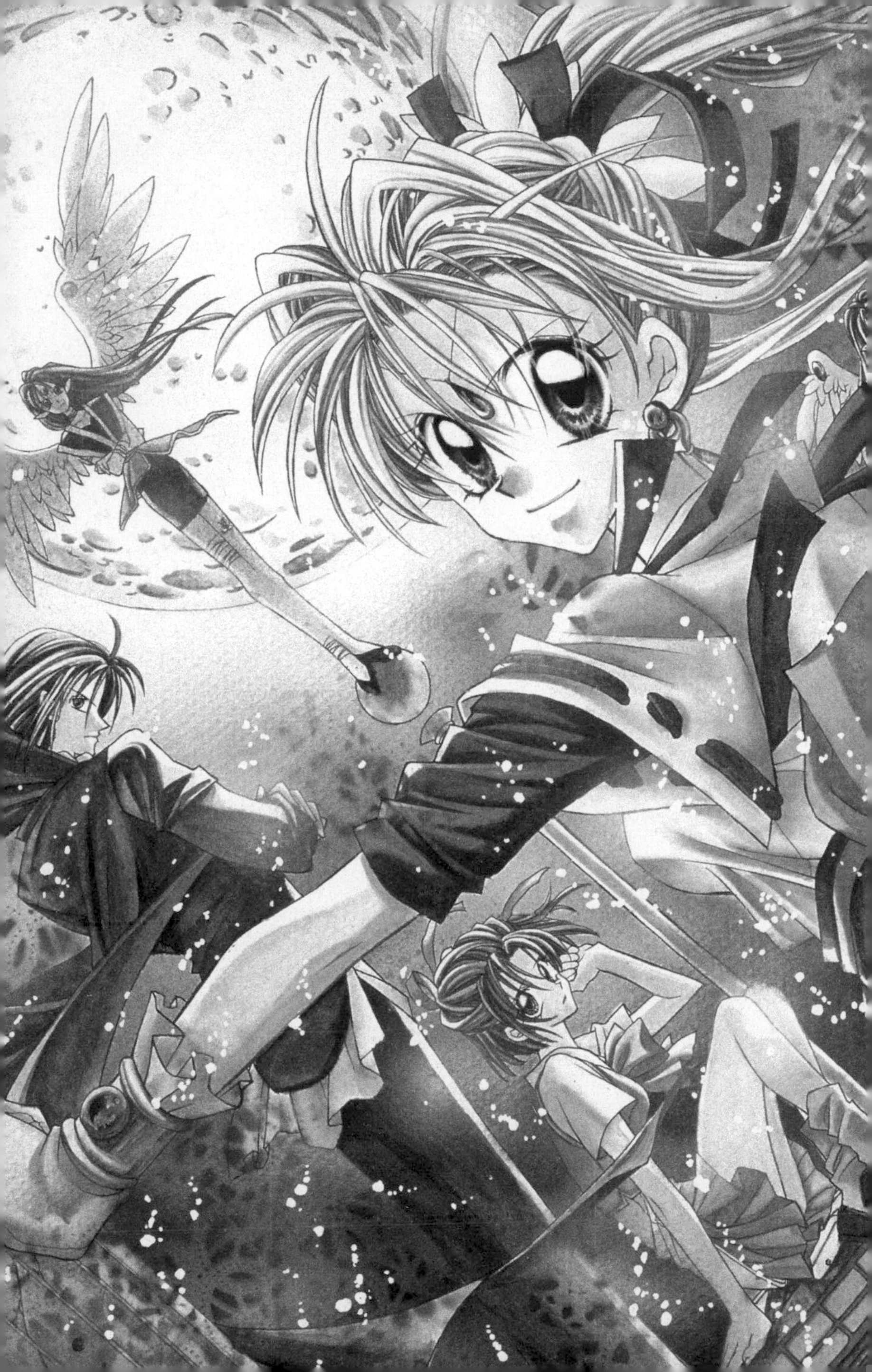

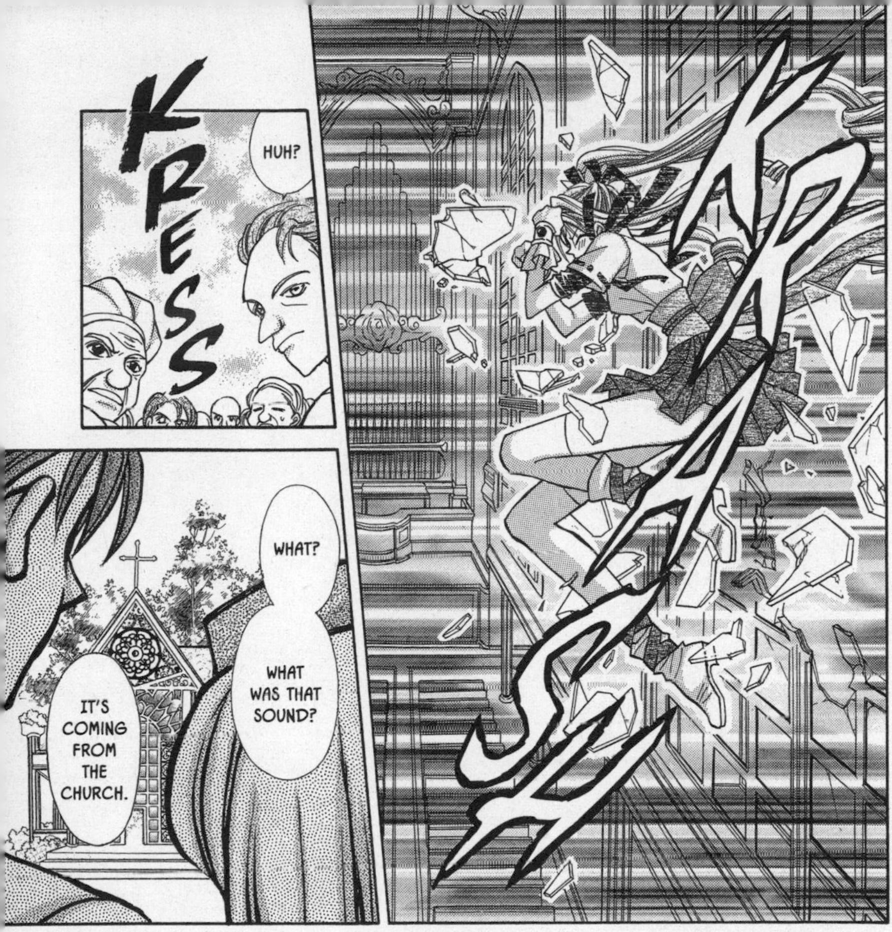
KRASSH
KRESS
HUH?
WHAT?
WHAT WAS THAT SOUND?
IT'S COMING FROM THE CHURCH.

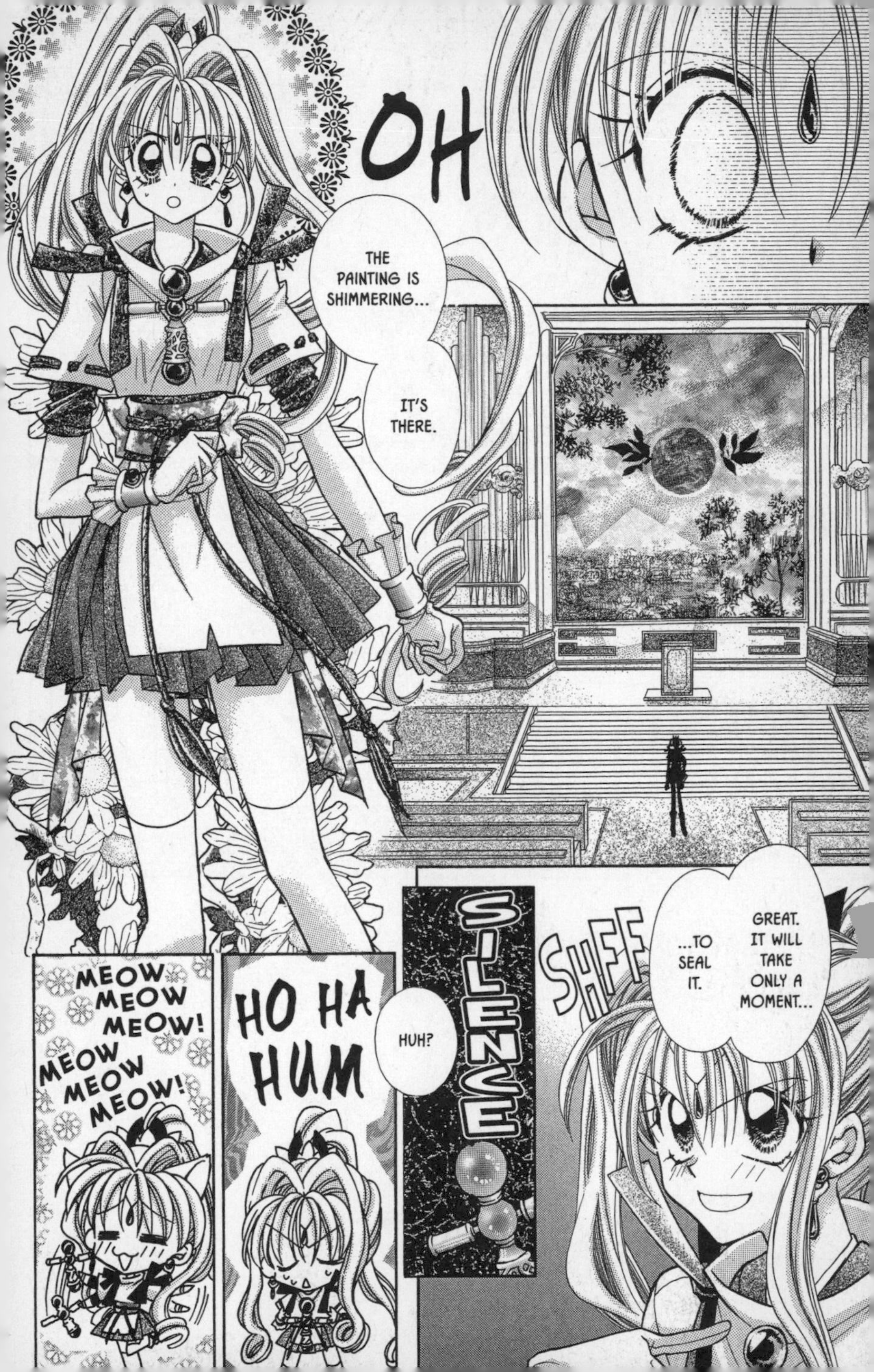
OH
THE PAINTING IS SHIMMERING...
IT'S THERE.
SHFF
GREAT. IT WILL TAKE ONLY A MOMENT...
...TO SEAL IT.
SILENCE
HUH?
HO HA HUM
MEOW MEOW MEOW! MEOW MEOW MEOW!

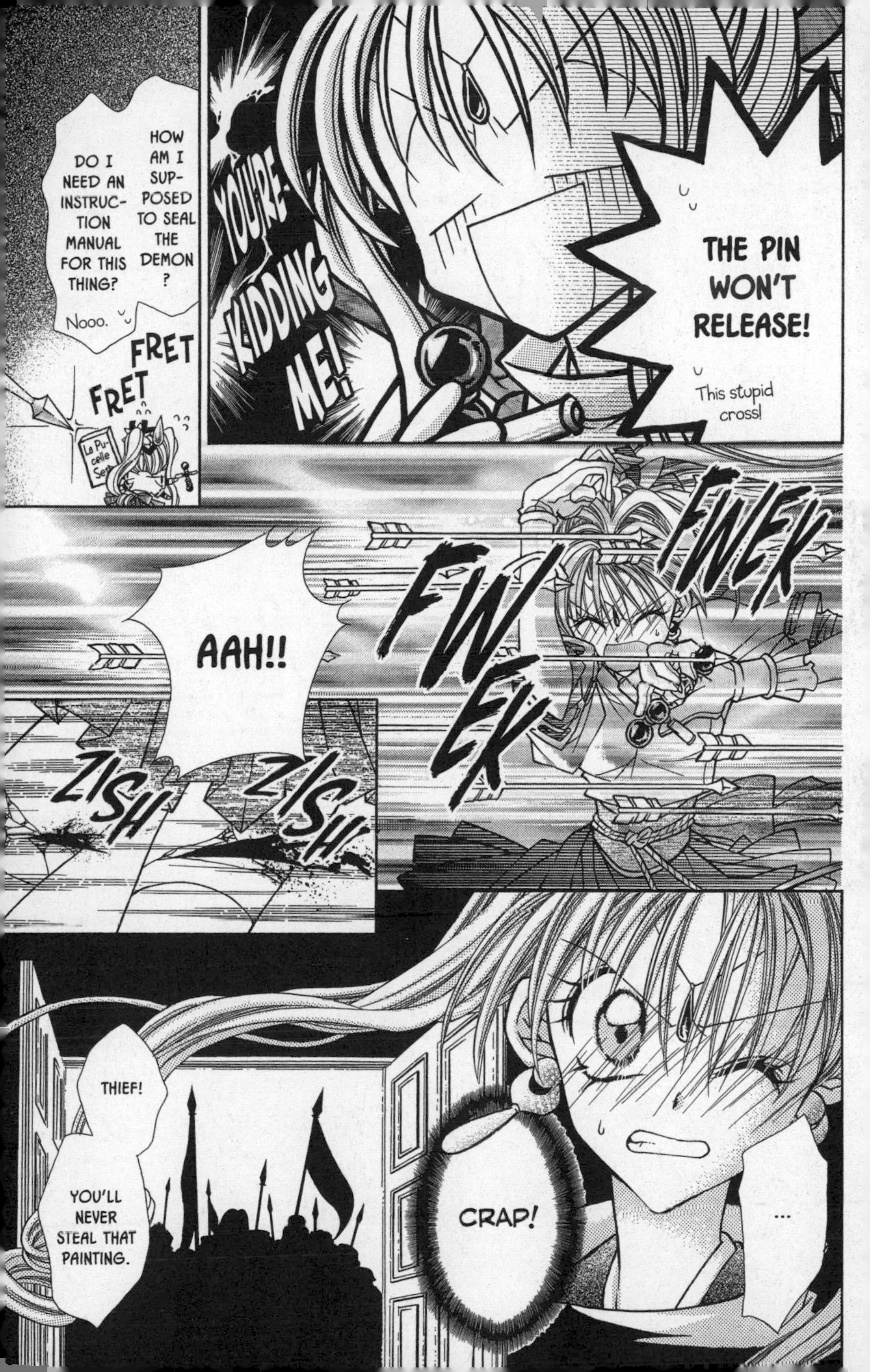
THE PIN WON'T RELEASE!
This stupid cross!
YOU'RE KIDDING ME!
HOW AM I SUP-POSED TO SEAL THE DEMON?
DO I NEED AN INSTRUC-TION MANUAL FOR THIS THING?
Nooo.
FRET FRET
La Pucelle Set
FWEK FWEK
AAH!!
ZISH ZISH
...
CRAP!
THIEF!
YOU'LL NEVER STEAL THAT PAINTING.

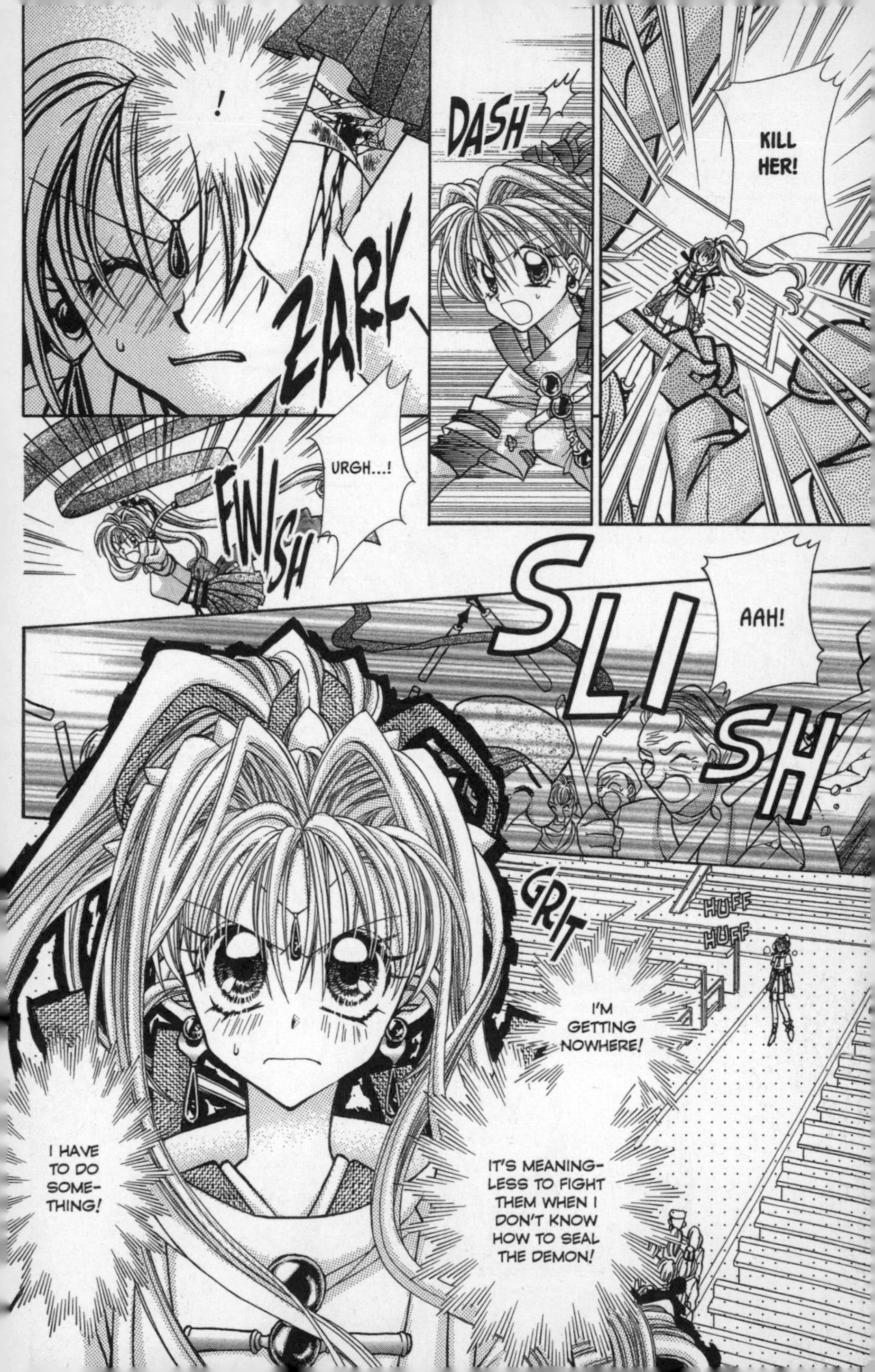
KILL HER!
DASH
!
ZARK
URGH...!
FWISH
AAH!
SLISH
GRIT
HUFF HUFF
I'M GETTING NOWHERE!
IT'S MEANING-LESS TO FIGHT THEM WHEN I DON'T KNOW HOW TO SEAL THE DEMON!
I HAVE TO DO SOME-THING!

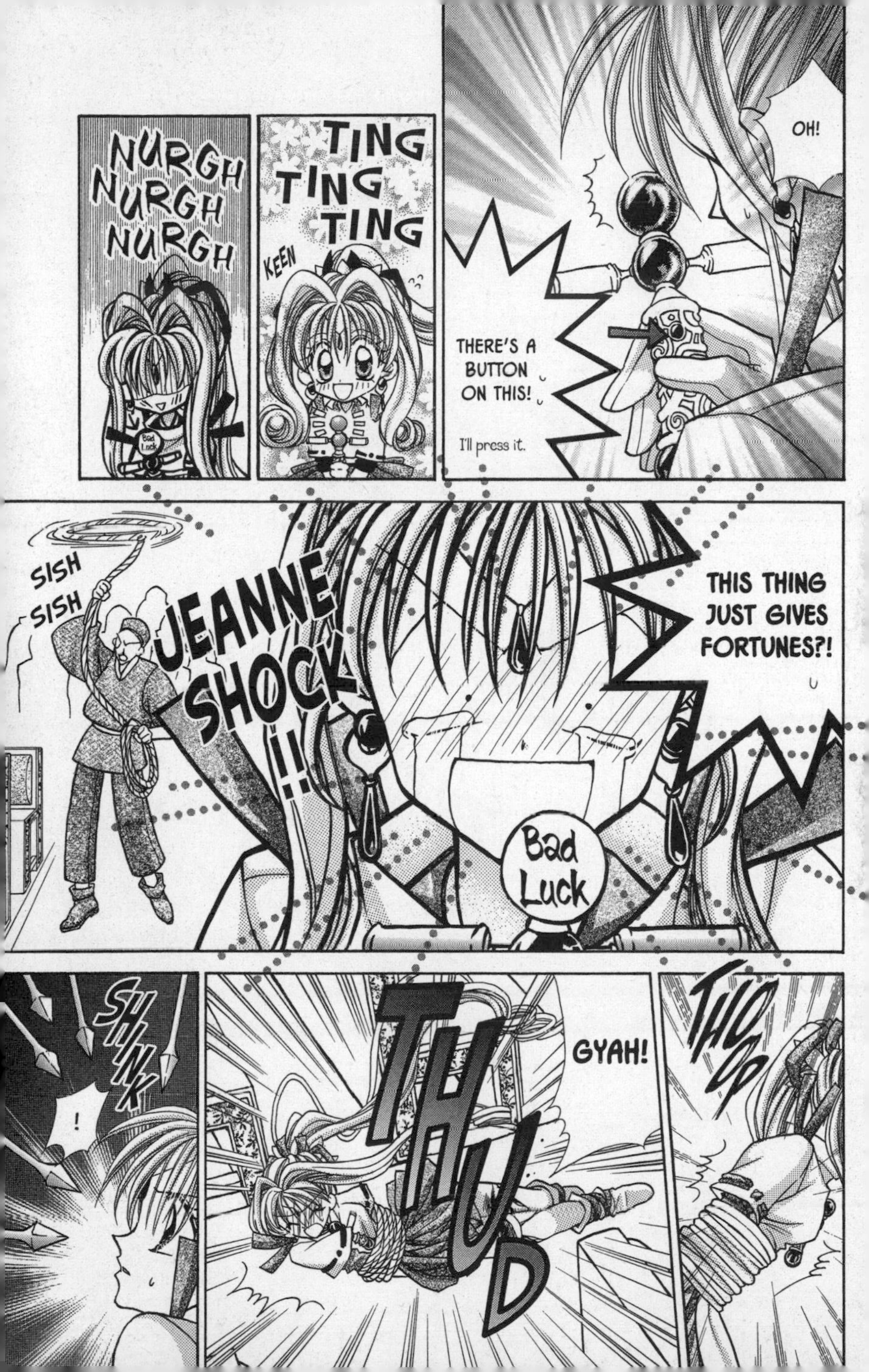
OH!
THERE'S A BUTTON ON THIS!
I'll press it.
TING TING TING
KEEN
NURGH NURGH NURGH
Bad Luck
THIS THING JUST GIVES FORTUNES?!
Bad Luck
JEANNE SHOCK!!
SISH SISH
THUD
GYAH!
THUD
SHINK
!

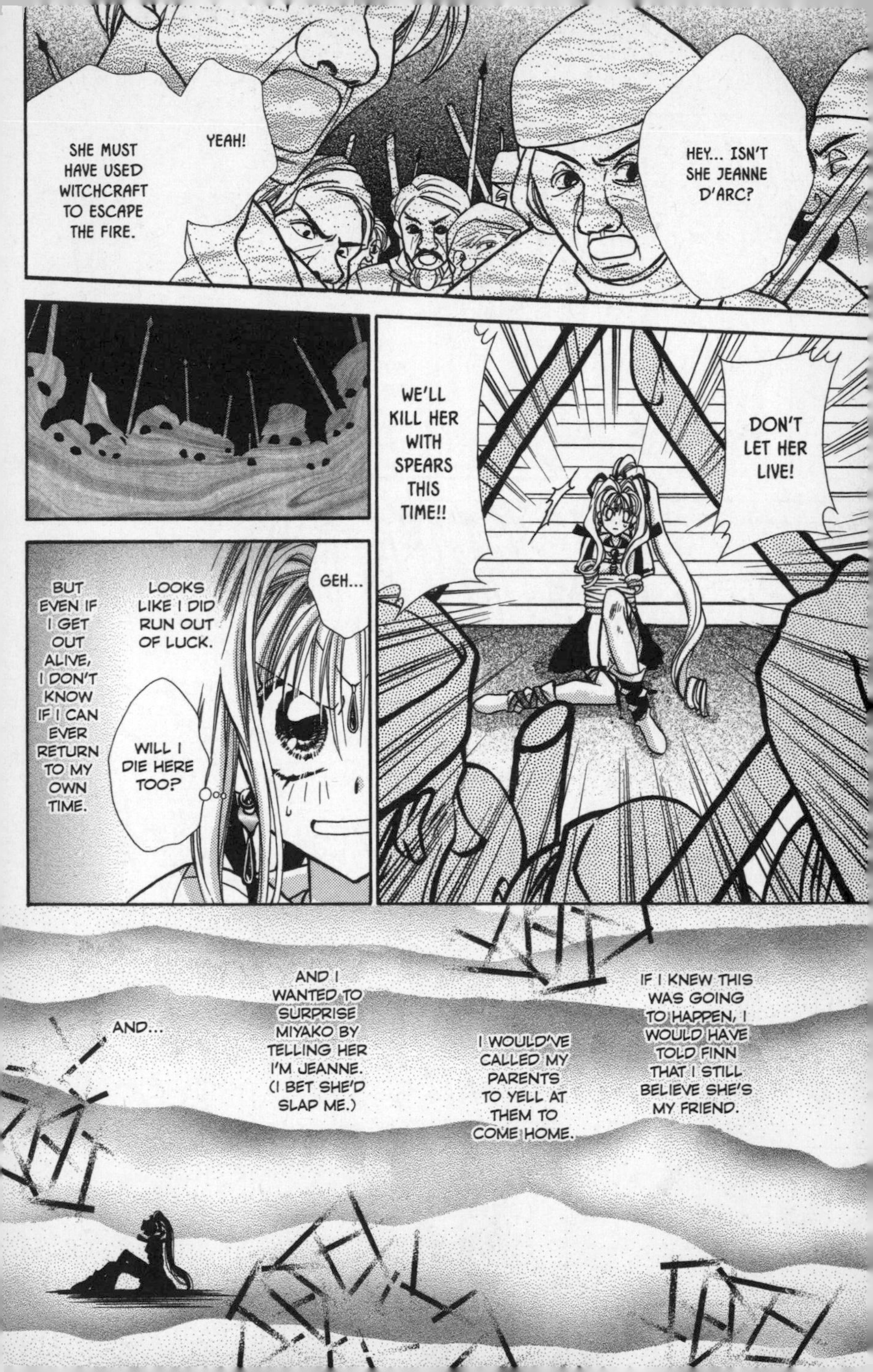
HEY... ISN'T SHE JEANNE D'ARC?
YEAH!
SHE MUST HAVE USED WITCHCRAFT TO ESCAPE THE FIRE.
DON'T LET HER LIVE!
WE'LL KILL HER WITH SPEARS THIS TIME!!
GEH...
LOOKS LIKE I DID RUN OUT OF LUCK.
BUT EVEN IF I GET OUT ALIVE, I DON'T KNOW IF I CAN EVER RETURN TO MY OWN TIME.
WILL I DIE HERE TOO?
IF I KNEW THIS WAS GOING TO HAPPEN, I WOULD HAVE TOLD FINN THAT I STILL BELIEVE SHE'S MY FRIEND.
I WOULD'VE CALLED MY PARENTS TO YELL AT THEM TO COME HOME.
AND I WANTED TO SURPRISE MIYAKO BY TELLING HER I'M JEANNE. (I BET SHE'D SLAP ME.)
AND...

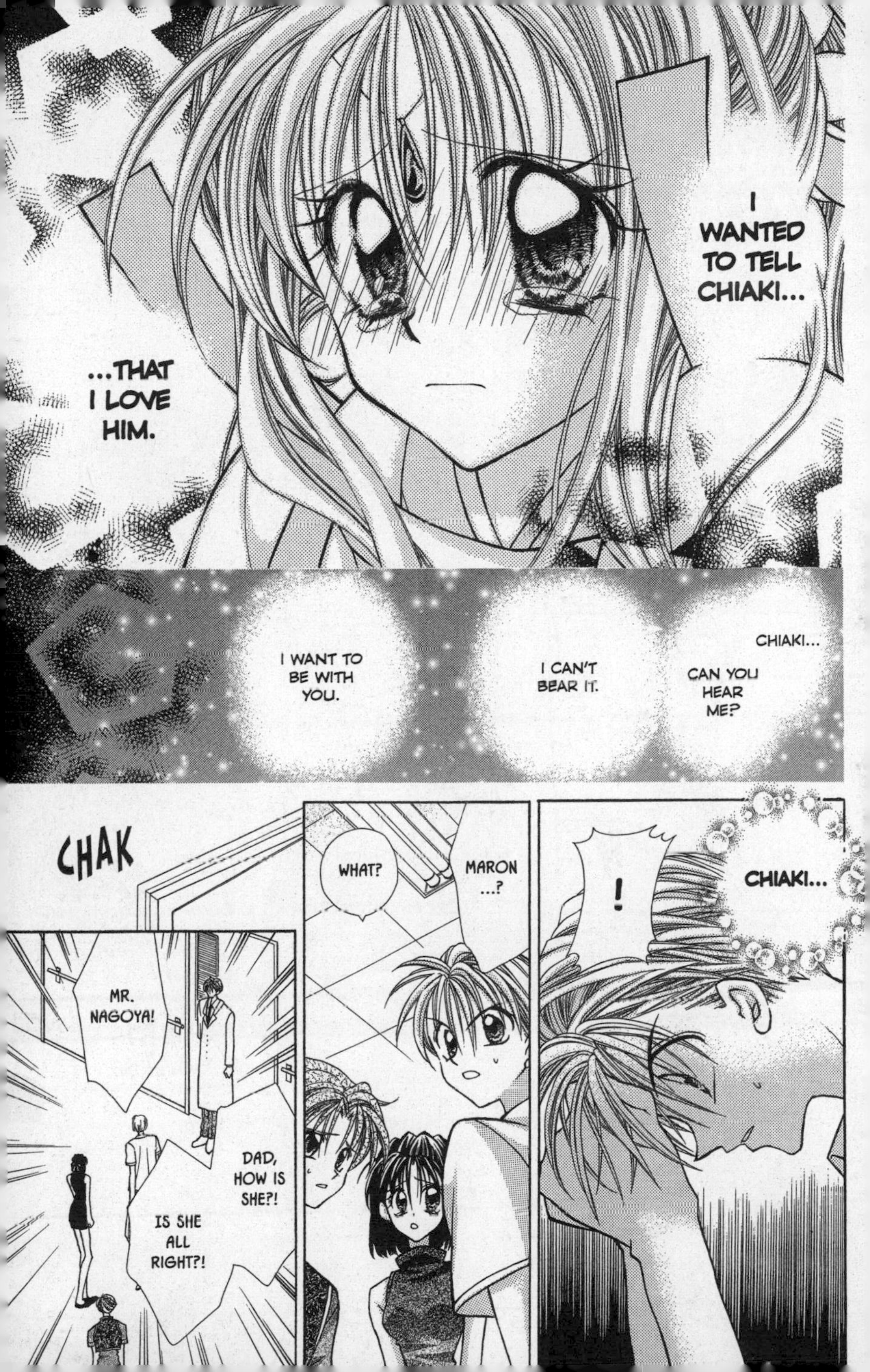
I WANTED TO TELL CHIAKI...
...THAT I LOVE HIM.
CHIAKI...
CAN YOU HEAR ME?
I CAN'T BEAR IT.
I WANT TO BE WITH YOU.
!
CHIAKI...
MARON ...?
WHAT?
CHAK
MR. NAGOYA!
DAD, HOW IS SHE?!
IS SHE ALL RIGHT?!

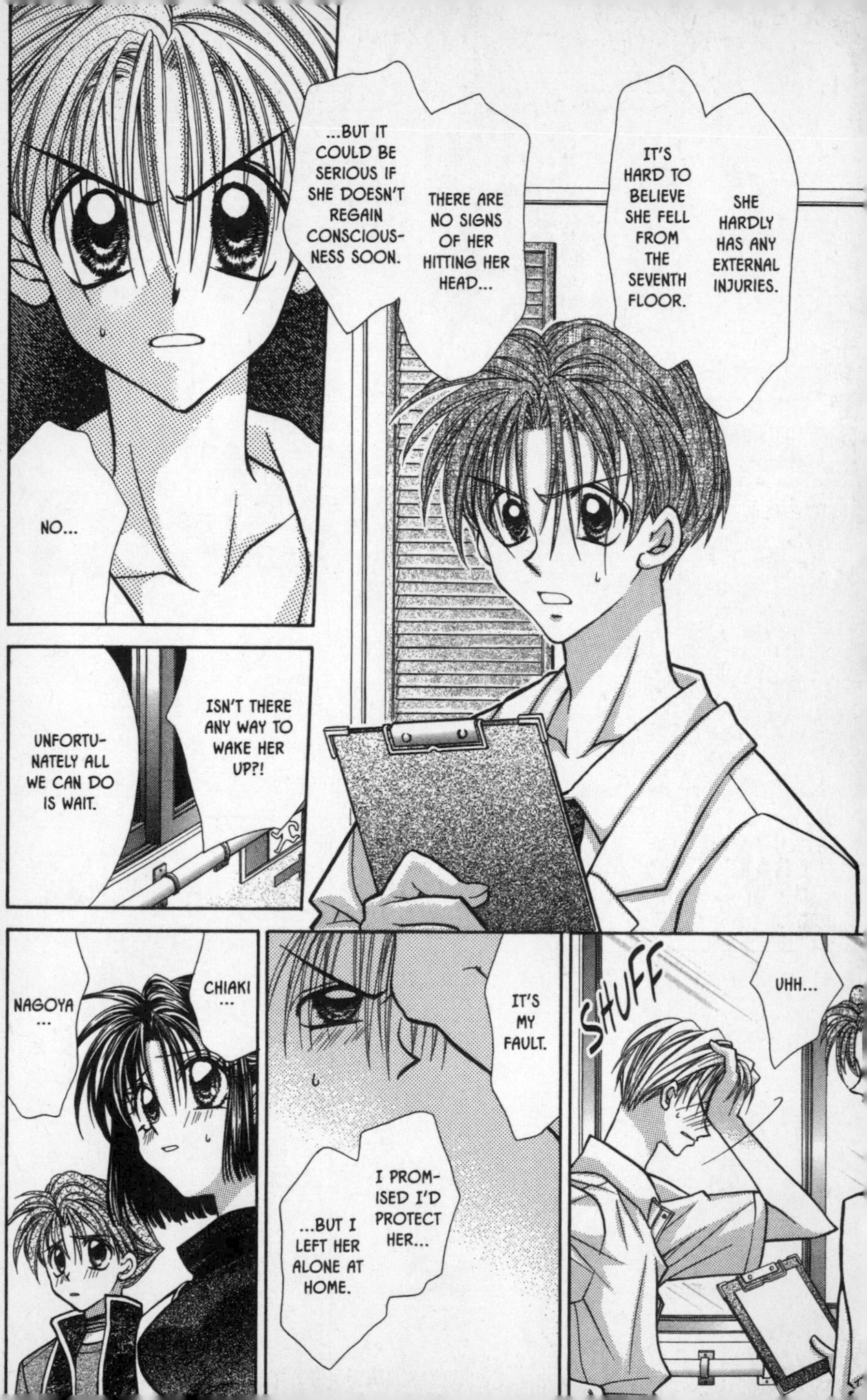
SHE HARDLY HAS ANY EXTERNAL INJURIES.
IT'S HARD TO BELIEVE SHE FELL FROM THE SEVENTH FLOOR.
THERE ARE NO SIGNS OF HER HITTING HER HEAD...
...BUT IT COULD BE SERIOUS IF SHE DOESN'T REGAIN CONSCIOUS-NESS SOON.
NO...
ISN'T THERE ANY WAY TO WAKE HER UP?!
UNFORTU-NATELY ALL WE CAN DO IS WAIT.
UHH...
SHUFF
IT'S MY FAULT.
I PROM-ISED I'D PROTECT HER...
...BUT I LEFT HER ALONE AT HOME.
CHIAKI ...
NAGOYA ...

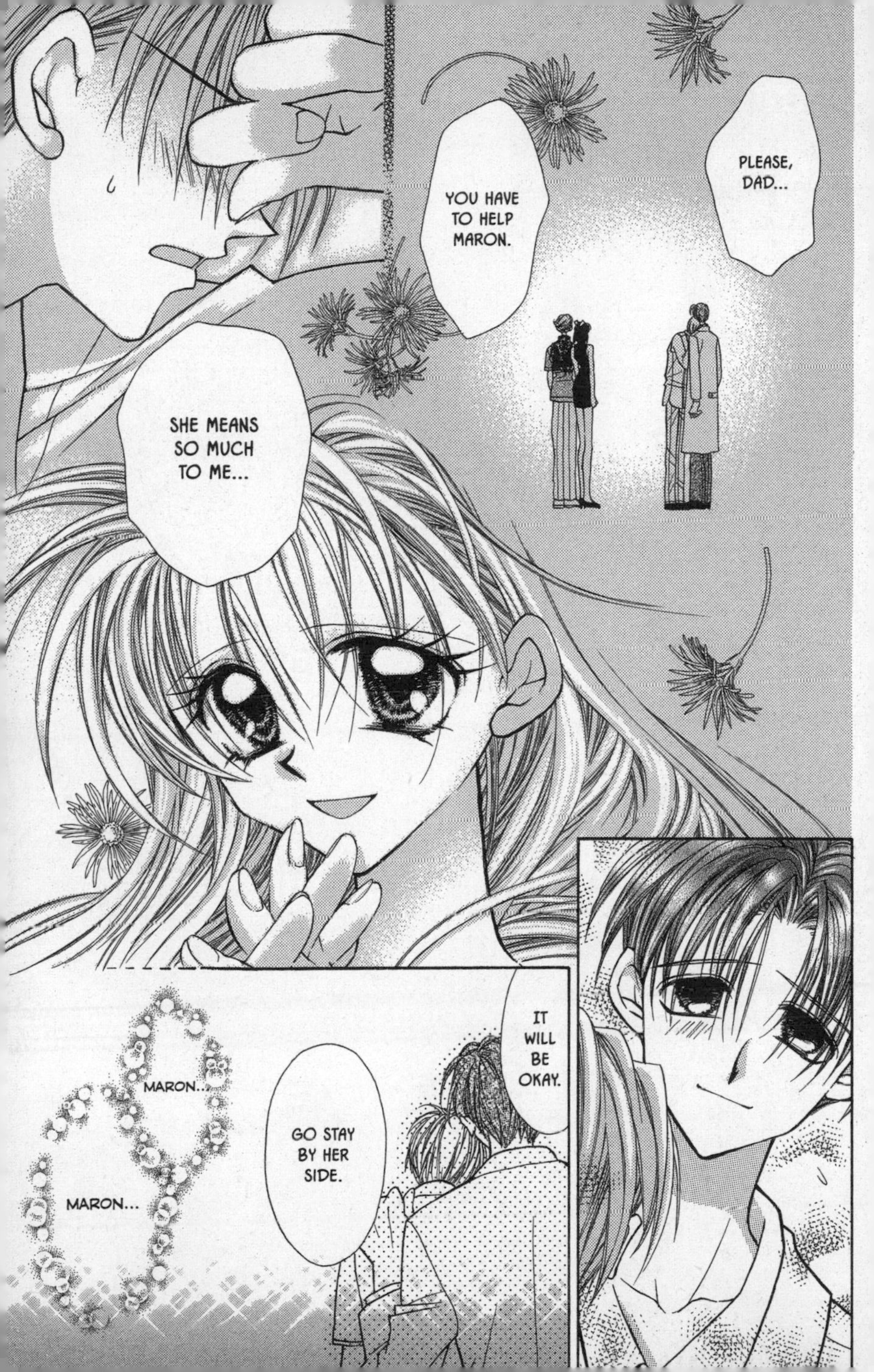
PLEASE, DAD...
YOU HAVE TO HELP MARON.
SHE MEANS SO MUCH TO ME...
IT WILL BE OKAY.
GO STAY BY HER SIDE.
MARON...
MARON...

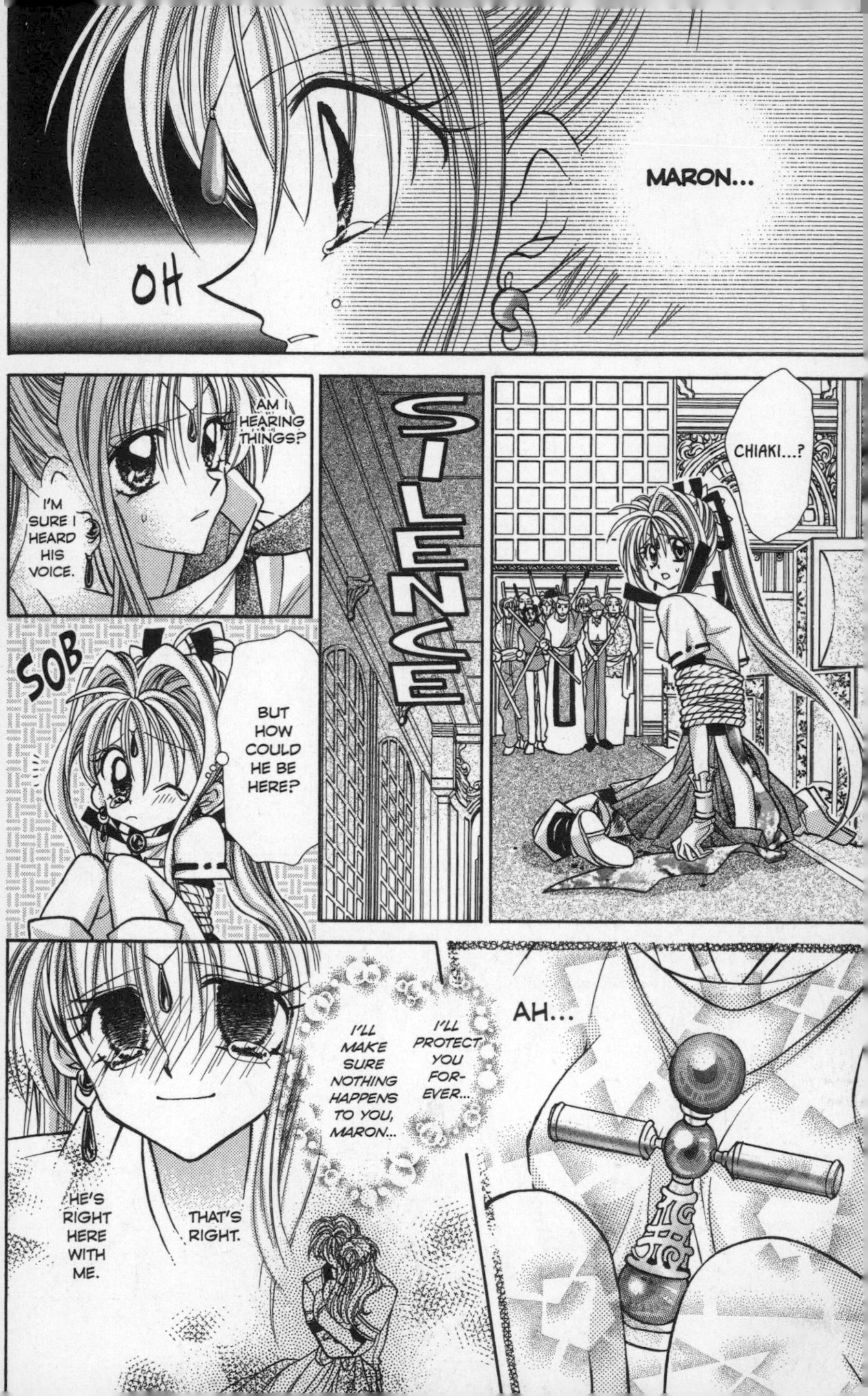
MARON...
OH
CHIAKI...?
SILENCE
AM I HEARING THINGS?
I'M SURE I HEARD HIS VOICE.
SOB
BUT HOW COULD HE BE HERE?
AH...
I'LL PROTECT YOU FOR-EVER...
I'LL MAKE SURE NOTHING HAPPENS TO YOU, MARON...
THAT'S RIGHT.
HE'S RIGHT HERE WITH ME.

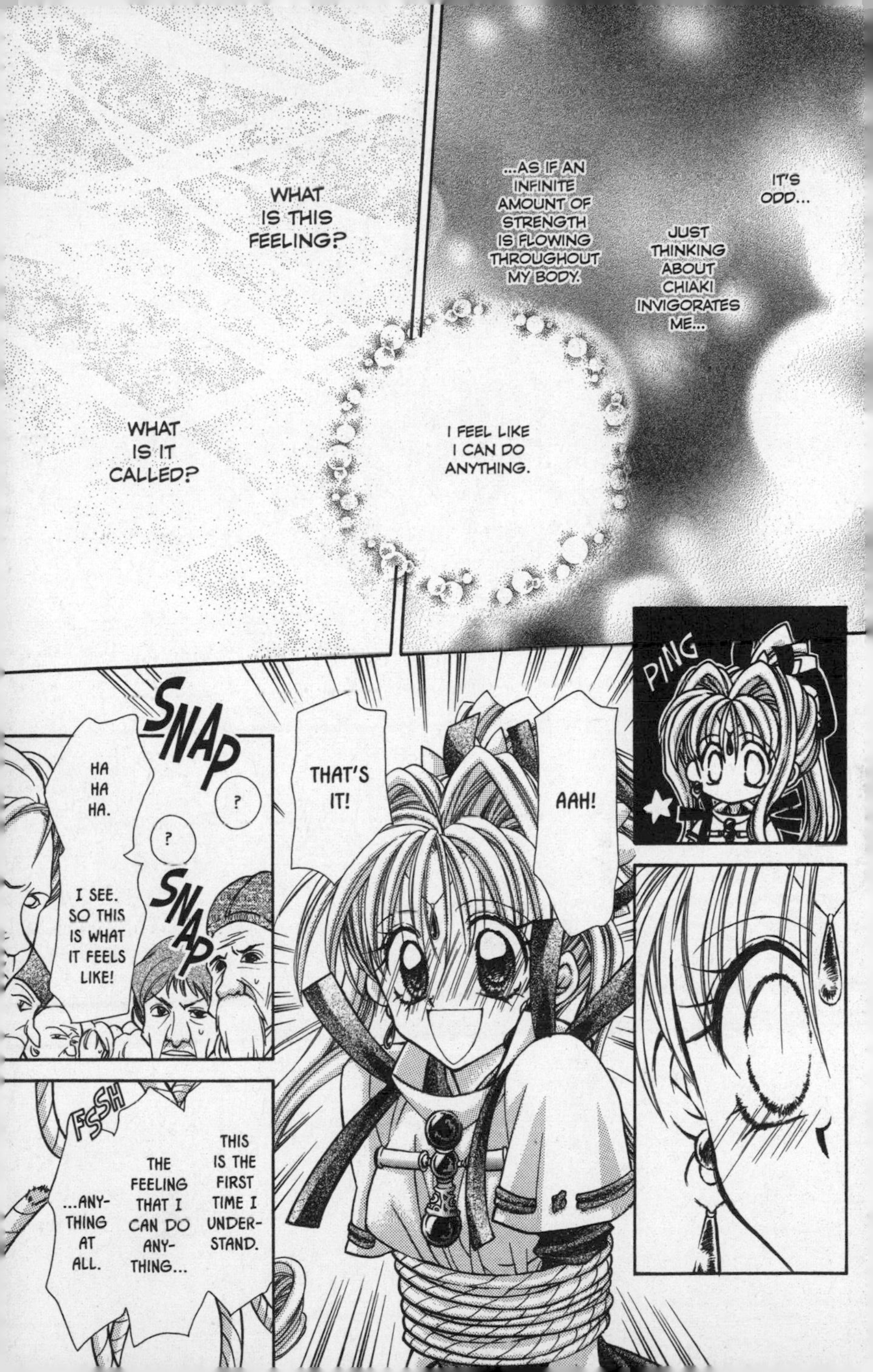
IT'S ODD...
JUST THINKING ABOUT CHIAKI INVIGORATES ME...
...AS IF AN INFINITE AMOUNT OF STRENGTH IS FLOWING THROUGHOUT MY BODY.
I FEEL LIKE I CAN DO ANYTHING.
WHAT IS THIS FEELING?
WHAT IS IT CALLED?
PING
AAH!
THAT'S IT!
SNAP
?
?
HA HA HA.
SNAP
I SEE. SO THIS IS WHAT IT FEELS LIKE!
FSSH
THIS IS THE FIRST TIME I UNDERSTAND.
THE FEELING THAT I CAN DO ANYTHING...
...ANYTHING AT ALL.

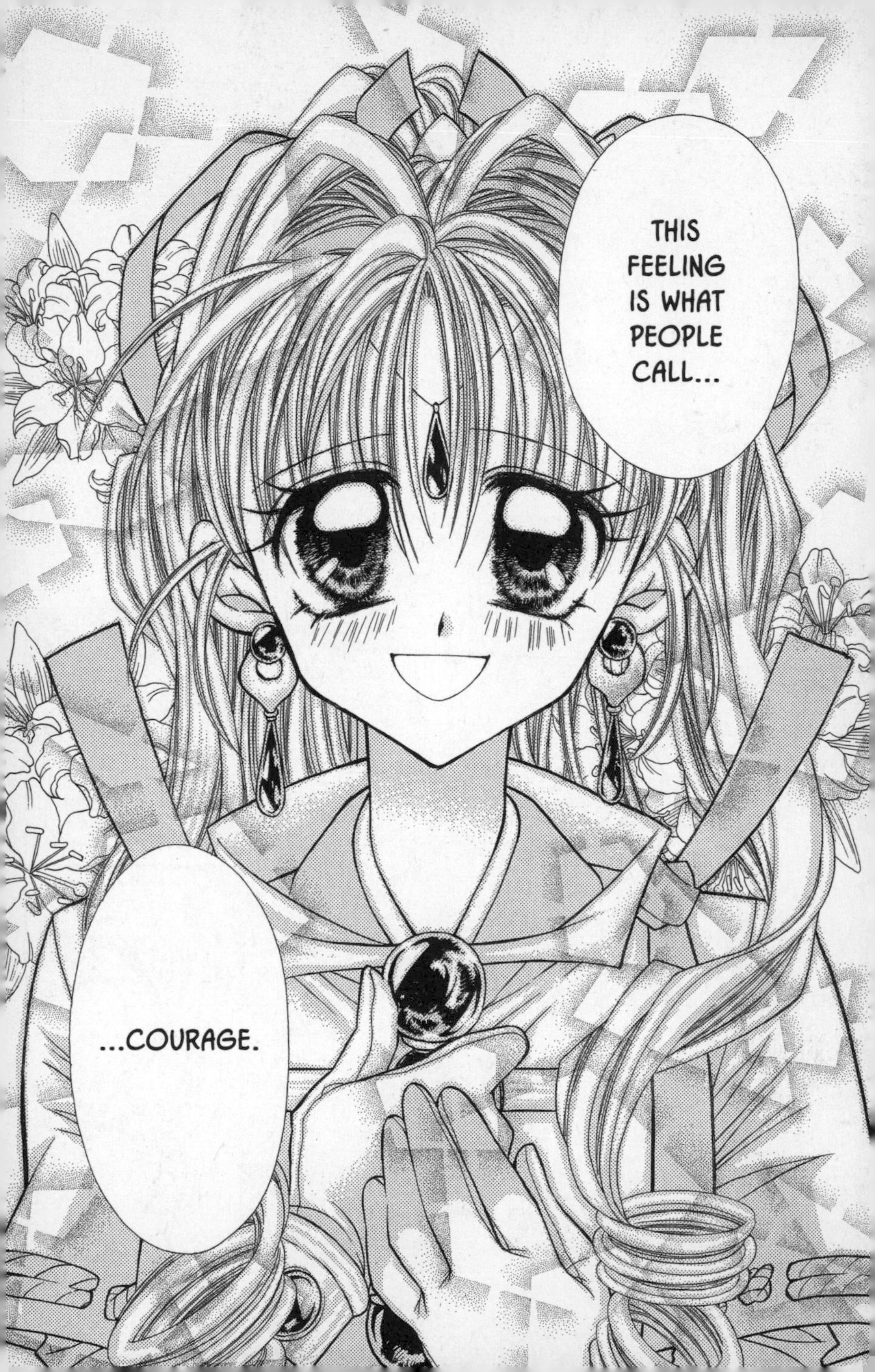
THIS FEELING IS WHAT PEOPLE CALL...
...COURAGE.

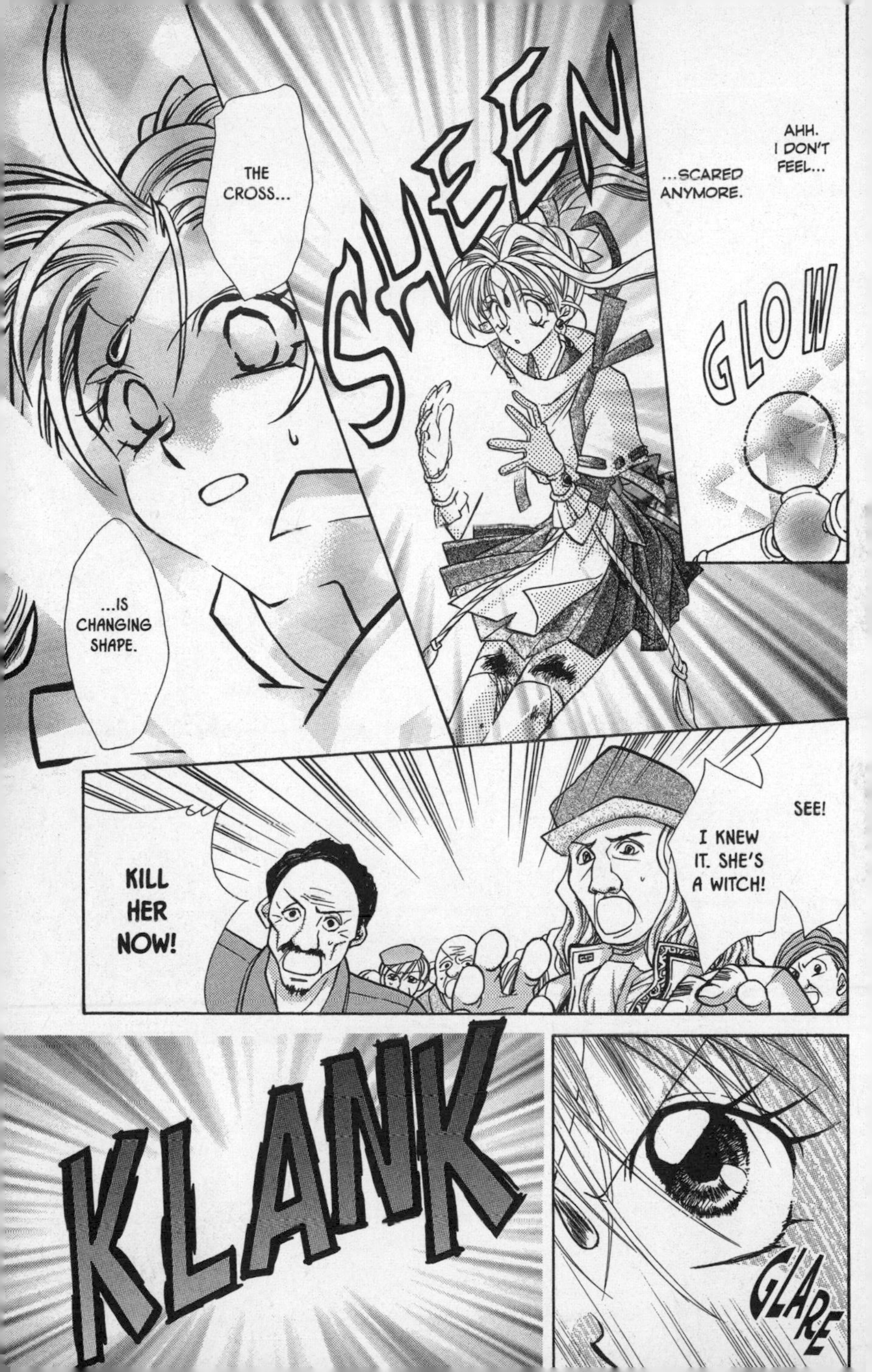
AHH. I DON'T FEEL...
...SCARED ANYMORE.
GLOW
SHEEN
THE CROSS...
...IS CHANGING SHAPE.
SEE!
I KNEW IT. SHE'S A WITCH!
KILL HER NOW!
GLARE
KLANK

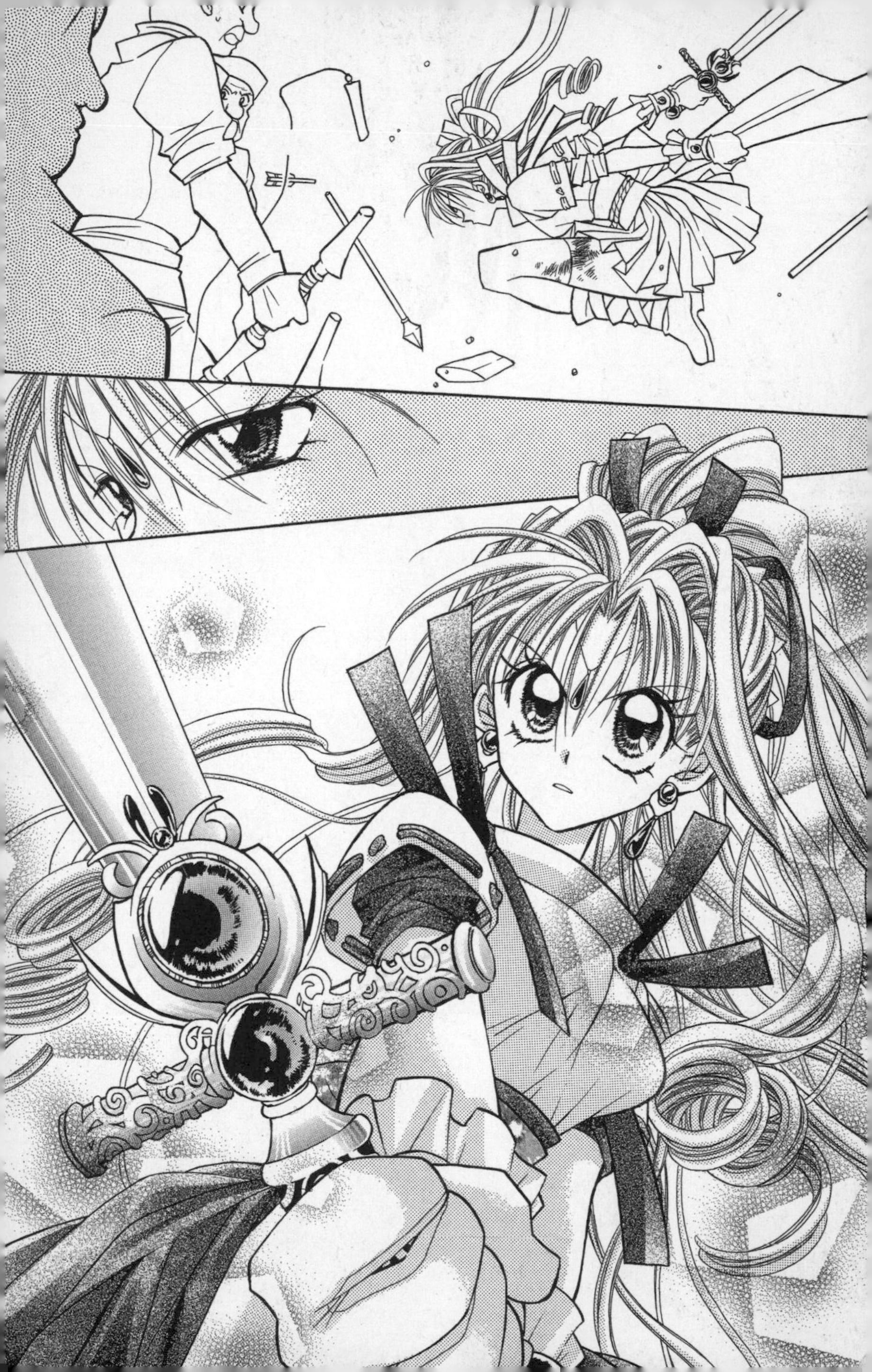

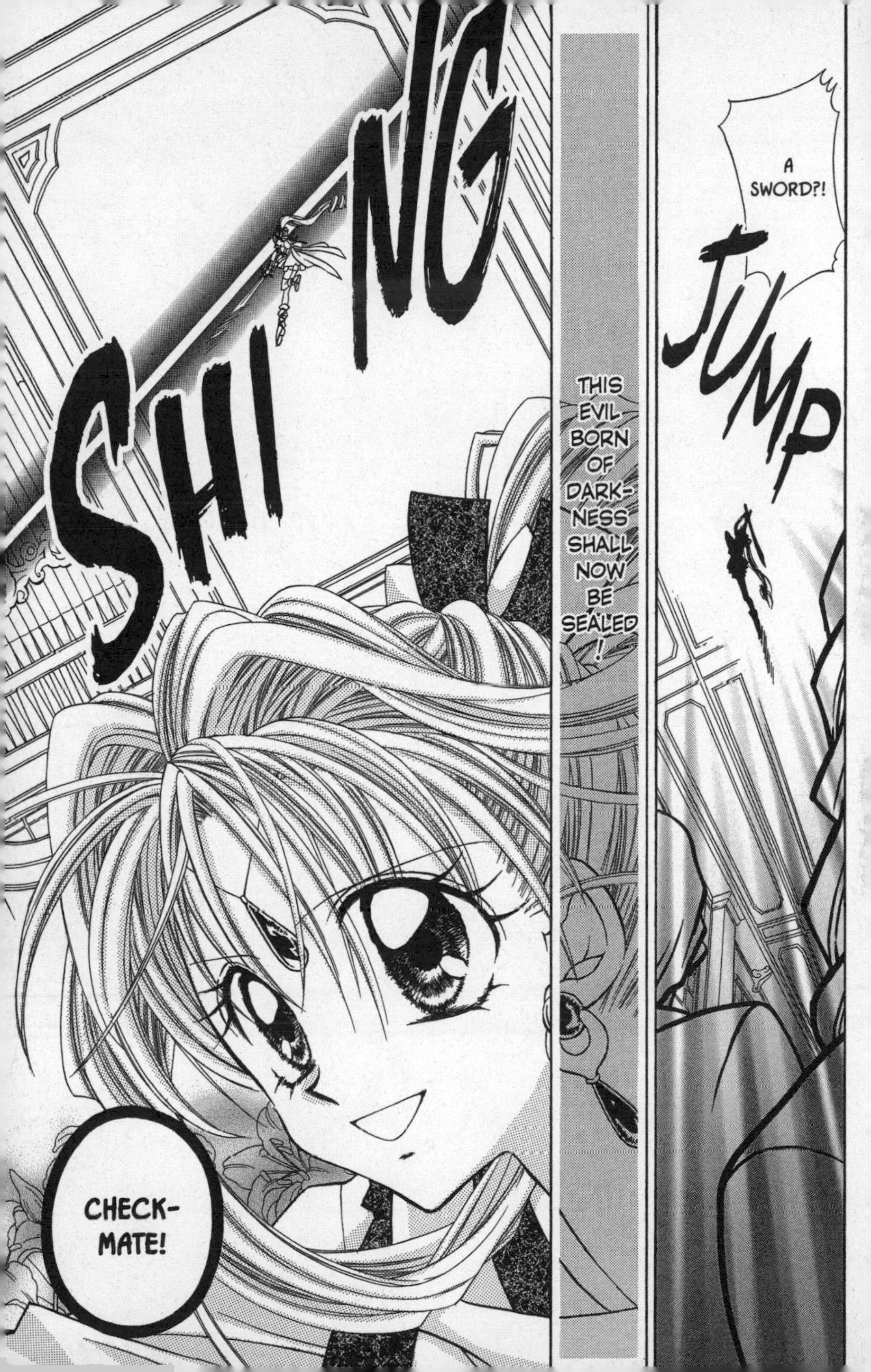
A SWORD?!
JUMP
THIS EVIL BORN OF DARK-NESS SHALL NOW BE SEALED!
SHING
CHECK-MATE!

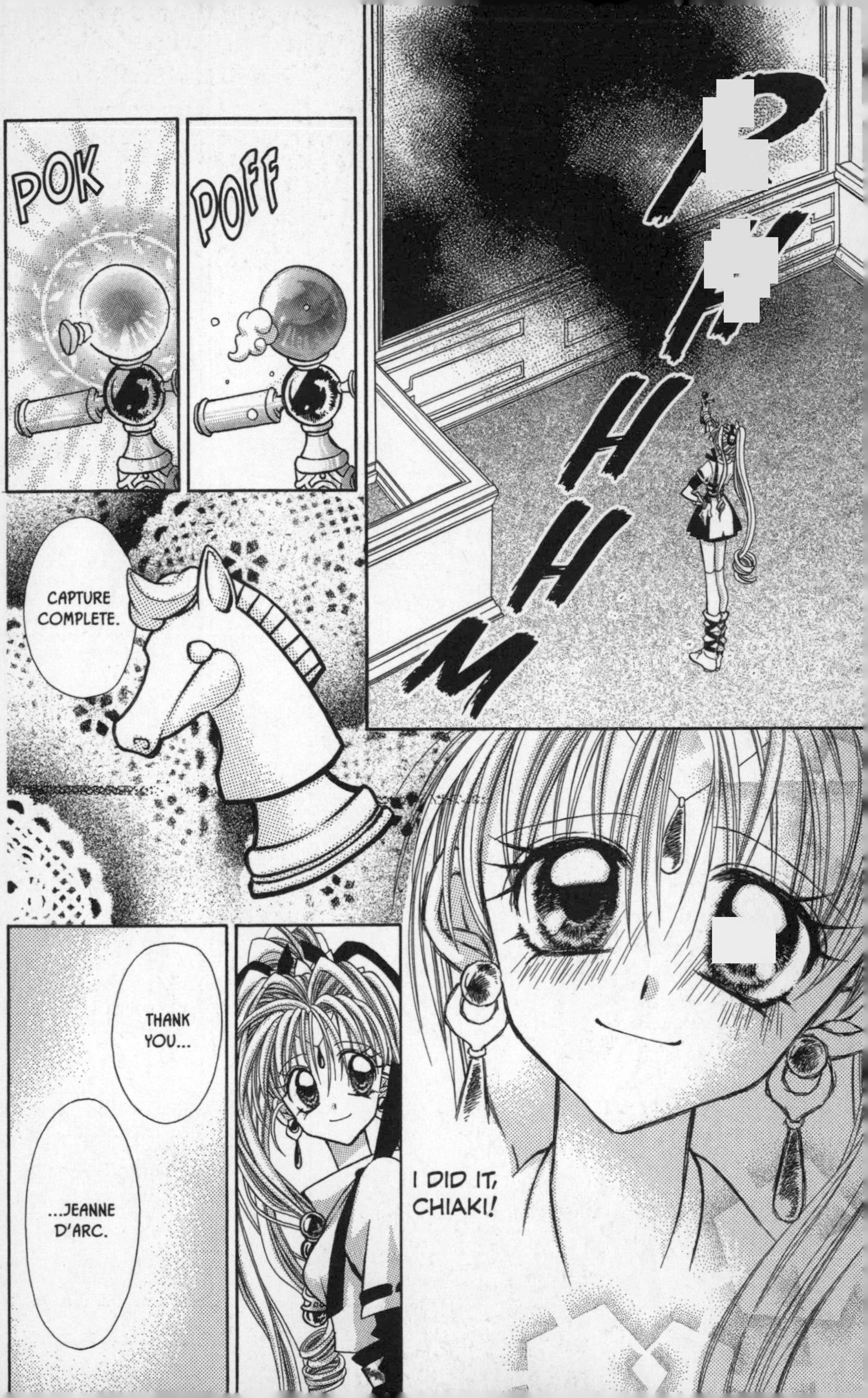
POFF
POK
CAPTURE COMPLETE.
I DID IT, CHIAKI!
THANK YOU...
...JEANNE D'ARC.

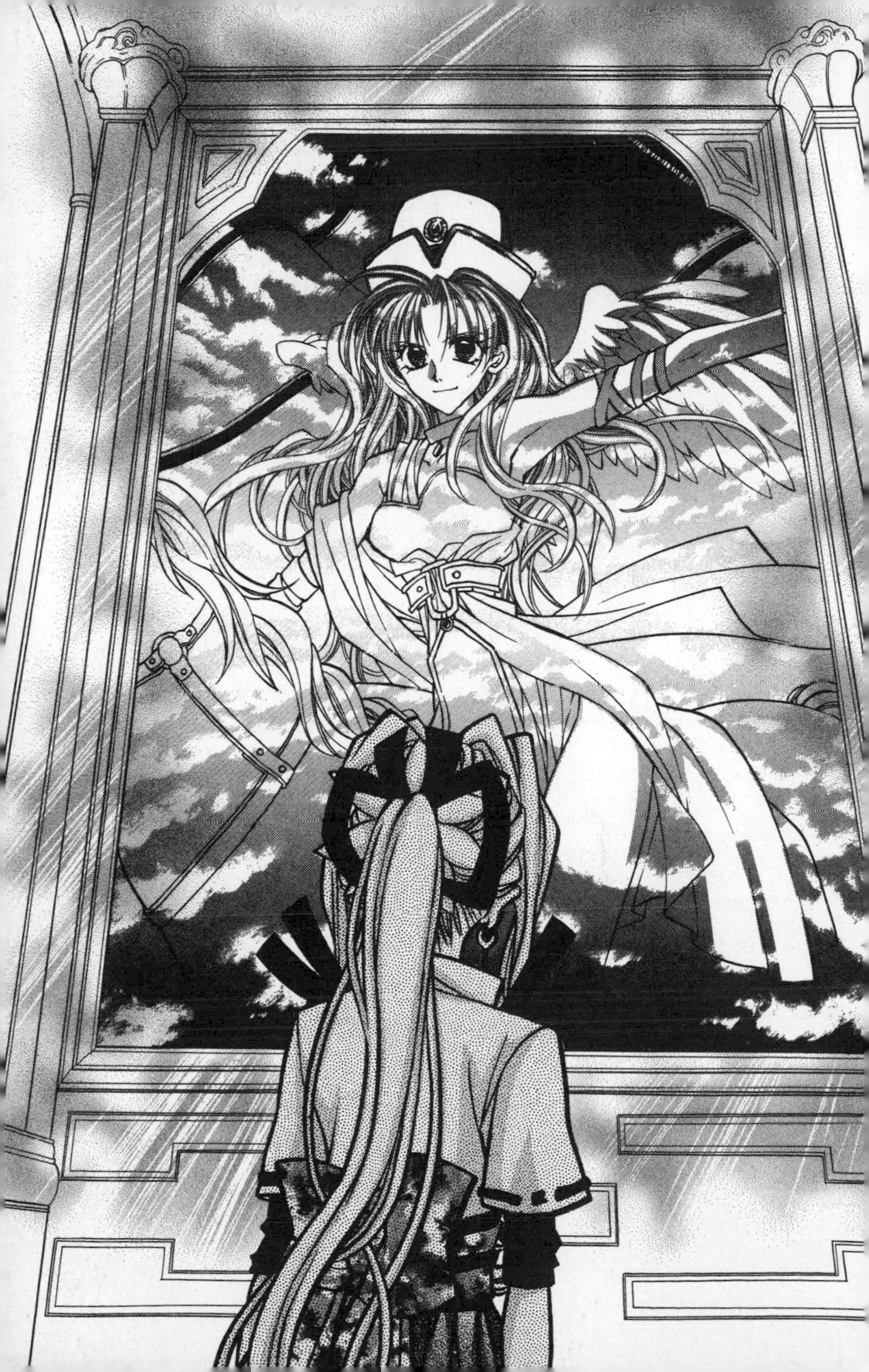

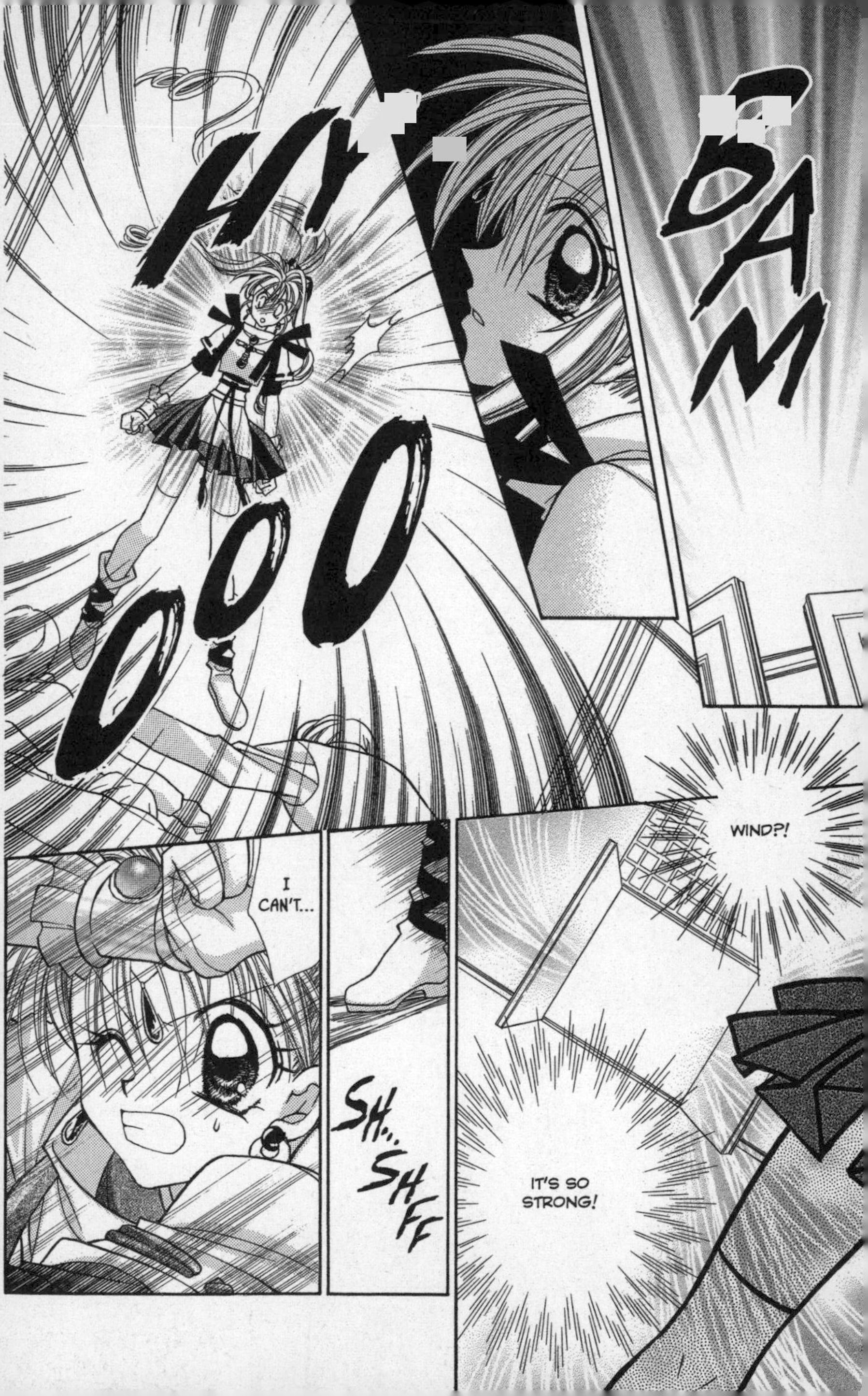
BAM
HYOOOO
WIND?!
IT'S SO STRONG!
SH... SHFF
I CAN'T...

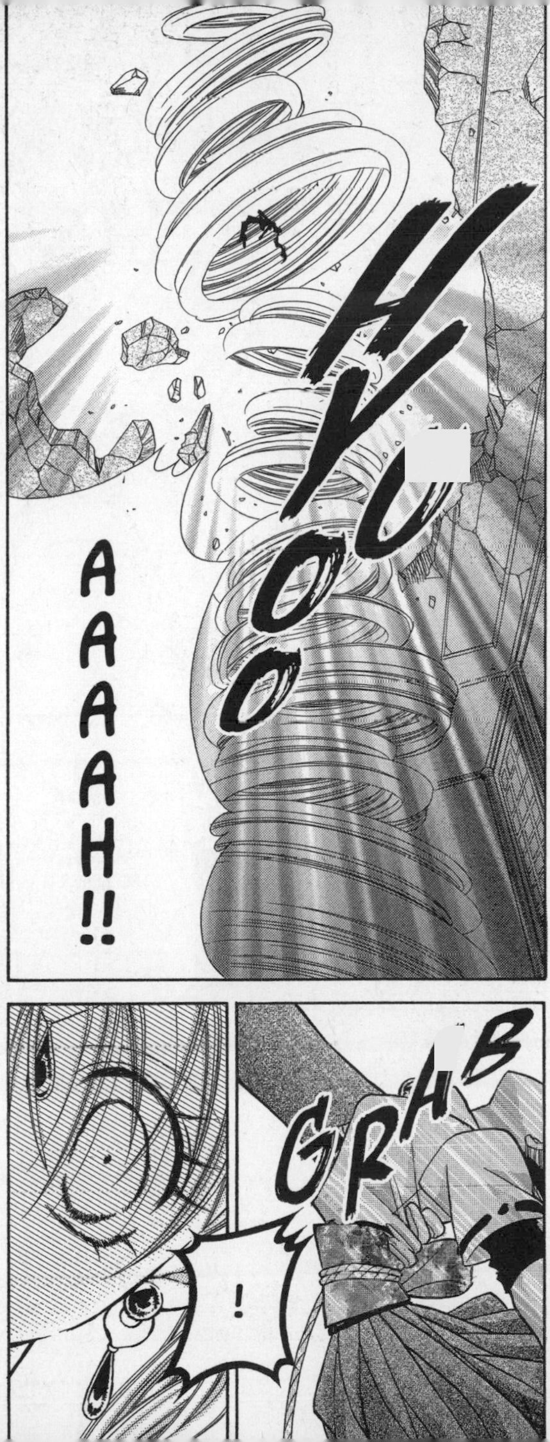
HYUOO
AAAAAH!!
GRAB
!

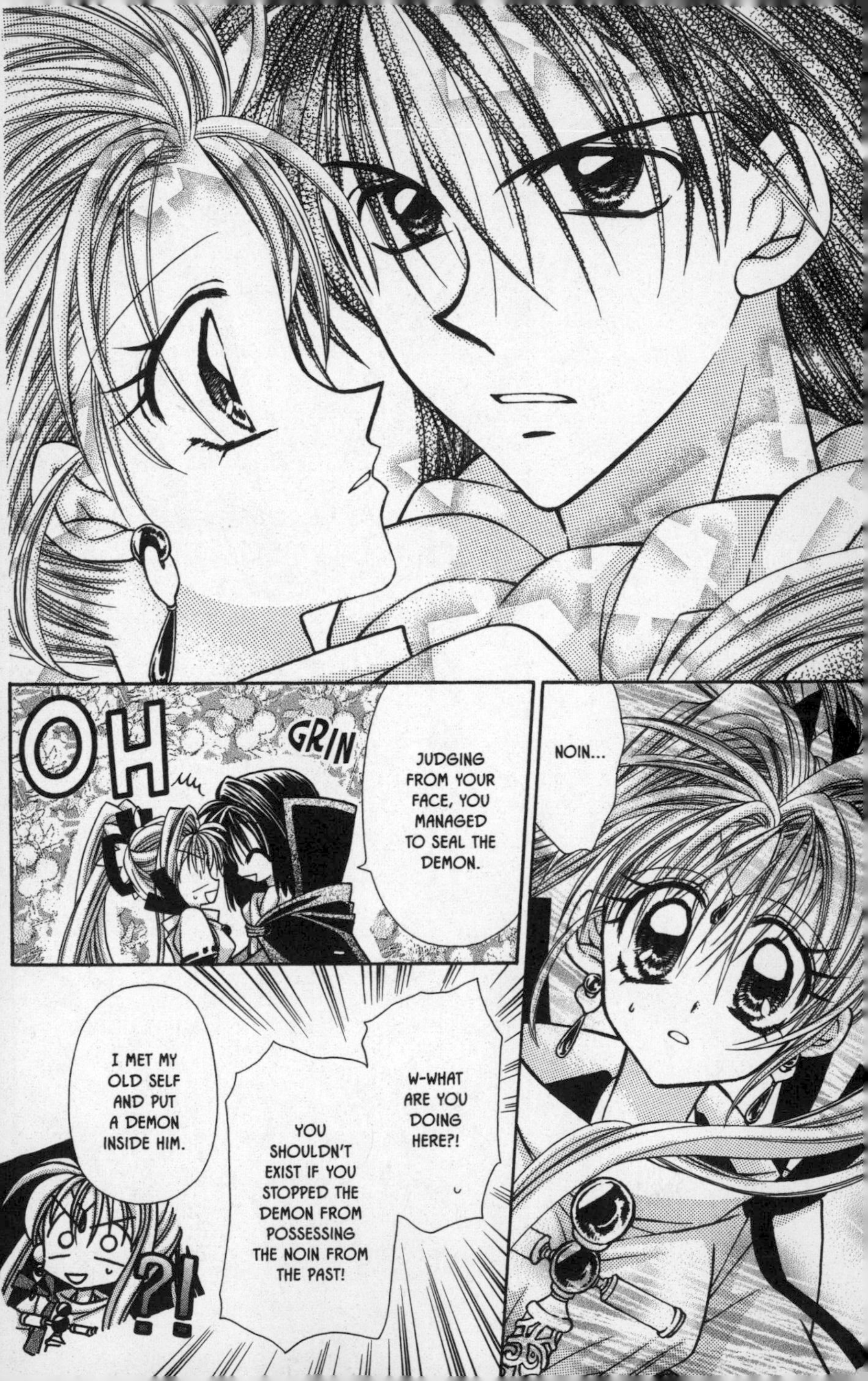
NOIN...
JUDGING FROM YOUR FACE, YOU MANAGED TO SEAL THE DEMON.
GRIN
OH
W-WHAT ARE YOU DOING HERE?!
YOU SHOULDN'T EXIST IF YOU STOPPED THE DEMON FROM POSSESSING THE NOIN FROM THE PAST!
I MET MY OLD SELF AND PUT A DEMON INSIDE HIM.
?!

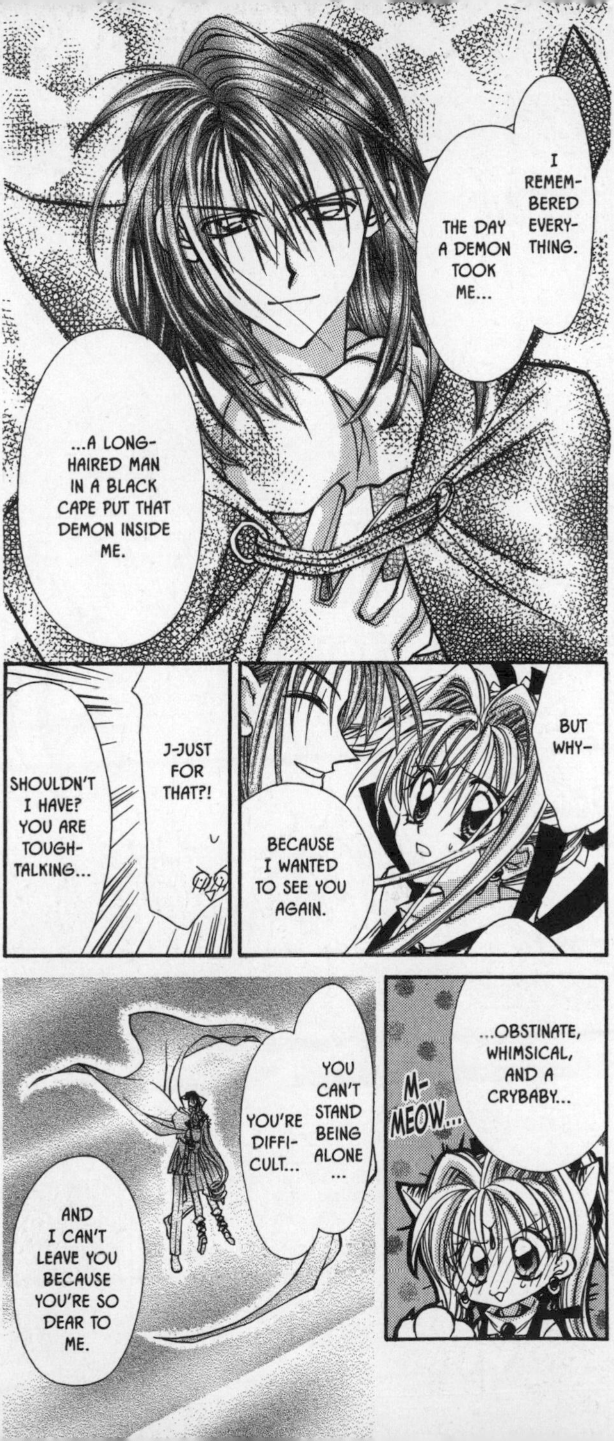
I REMEMBERED EVERYTHING.
THE DAY A DEMON TOOK ME...
...A LONG-HAIRED MAN IN A BLACK CAPE PUT THAT DEMON INSIDE ME.
BUT WHY-
BECAUSE I WANTED TO SEE YOU AGAIN.
J-JUST FOR THAT?!
SHOULDN'T I HAVE? YOU ARE TOUGH-TALKING...
...OBSTINATE, WHIMSICAL, AND A CRYBABY...
M-MEOW...
YOU CAN'T STAND BEING ALONE...
YOU'RE DIFFICULT...
AND I CAN'T LEAVE YOU BECAUSE YOU'RE SO DEAR TO ME.

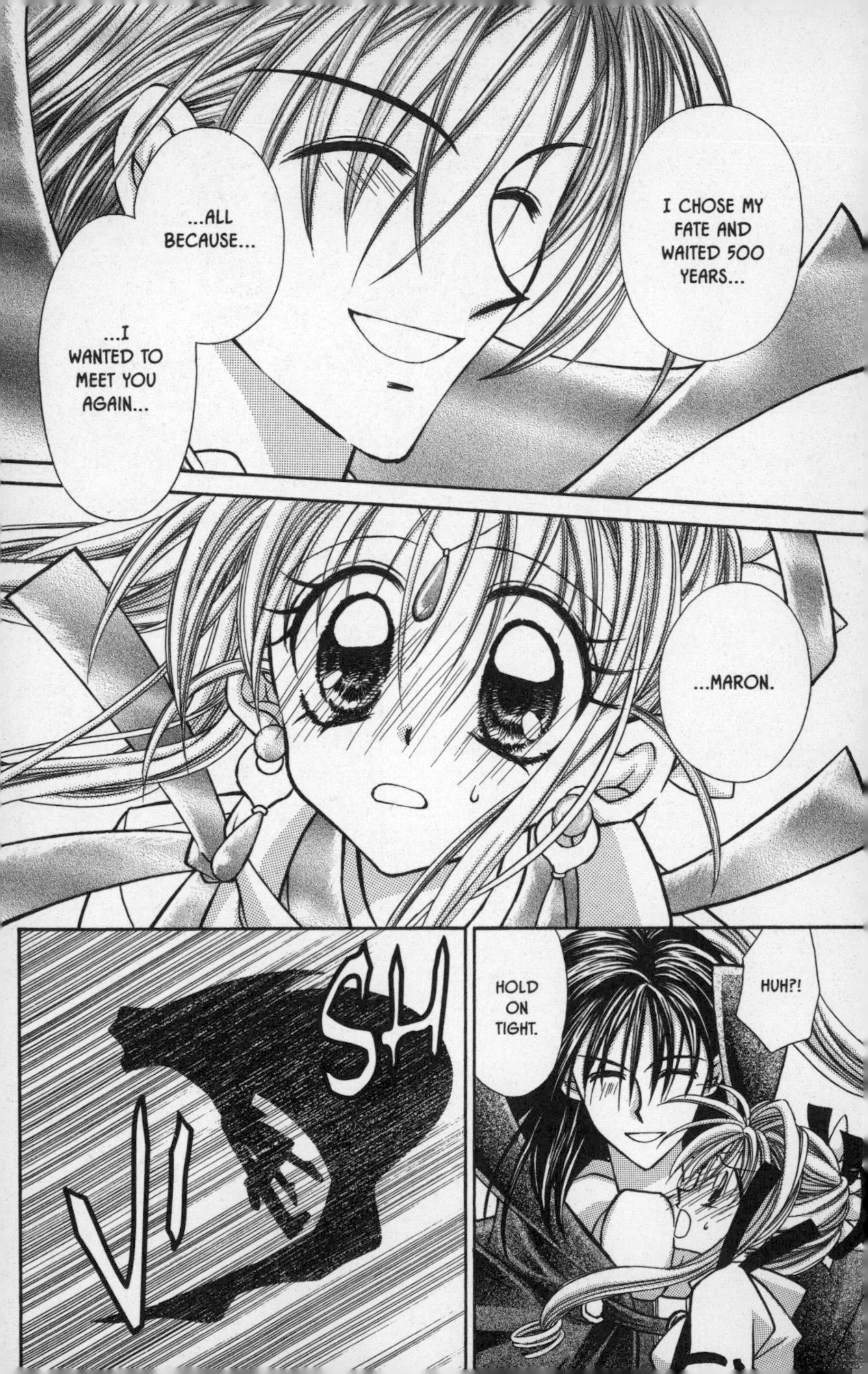
I CHOSE MY FATE AND WAITED 500 YEARS...
...ALL BECAUSE...
...I WANTED TO MEET YOU AGAIN...
...MARON.
HUH?!
HOLD ON TIGHT.
VISH

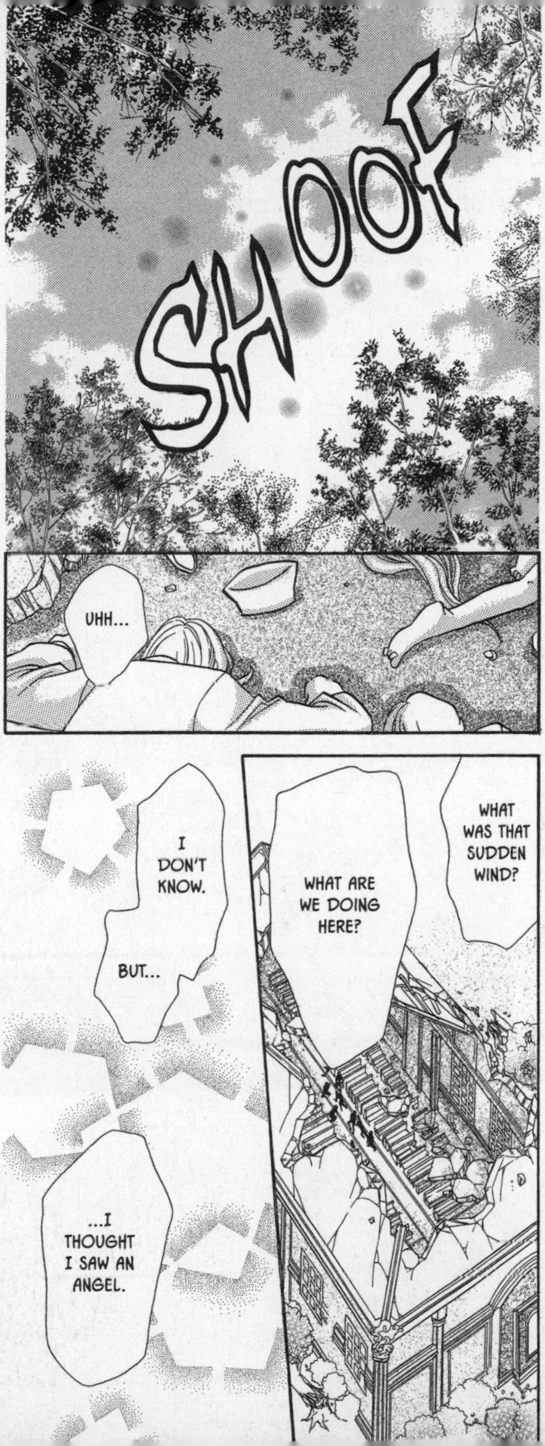
SHOOF
UHH...
WHAT WAS THAT SUDDEN WIND?
WHAT ARE WE DOING HERE?
I DON'T KNOW.
BUT...
...I THOUGHT I SAW AN ANGEL.

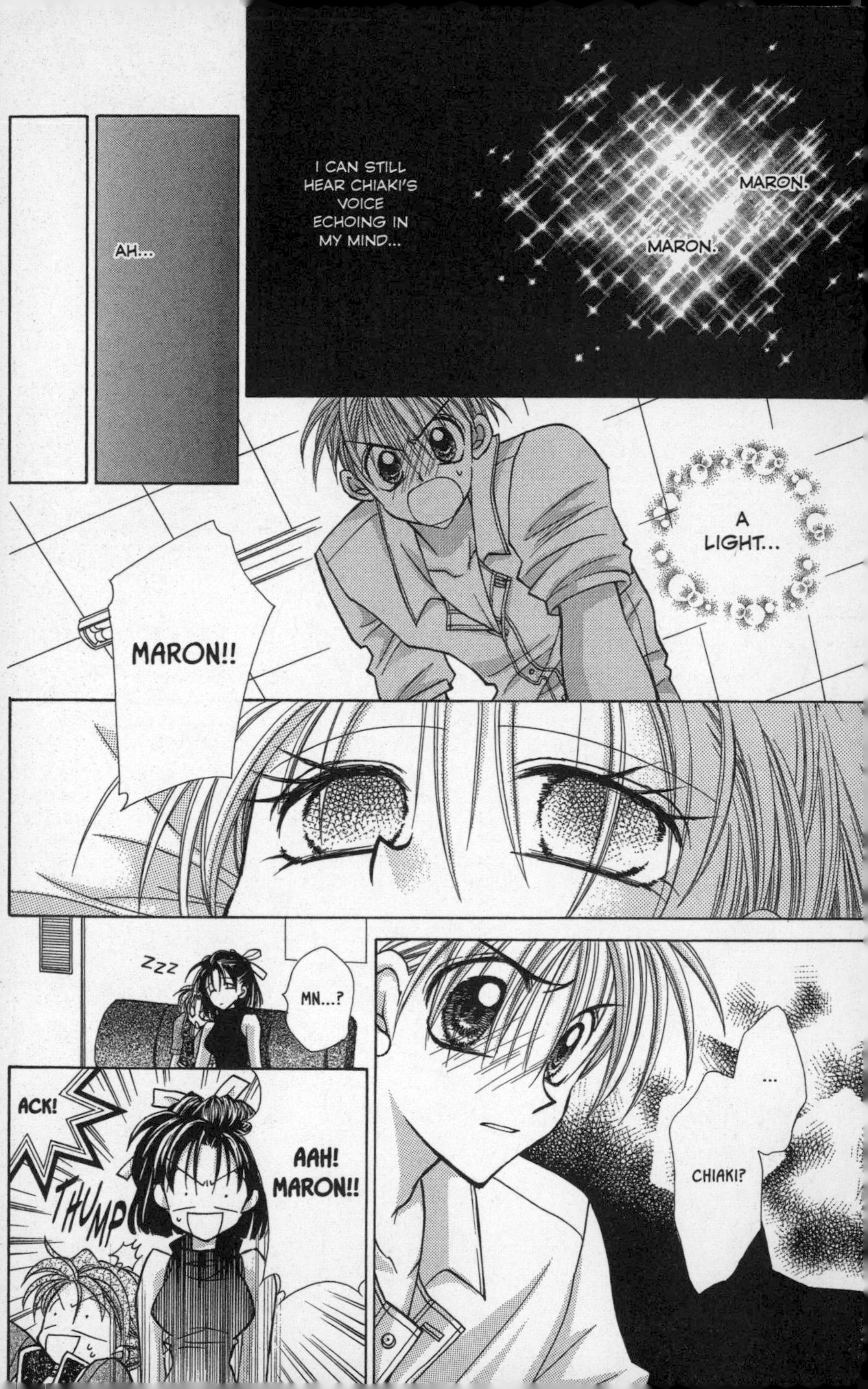
MARON.
MARON.
I CAN STILL HEAR CHIAKI'S VOICE ECHOING IN MY MIND...
AH...
A LIGHT...
MARON!!
...
CHIAKI?
MN...?
ZZZ
AAH! MARON!!
ACK!
THUMP

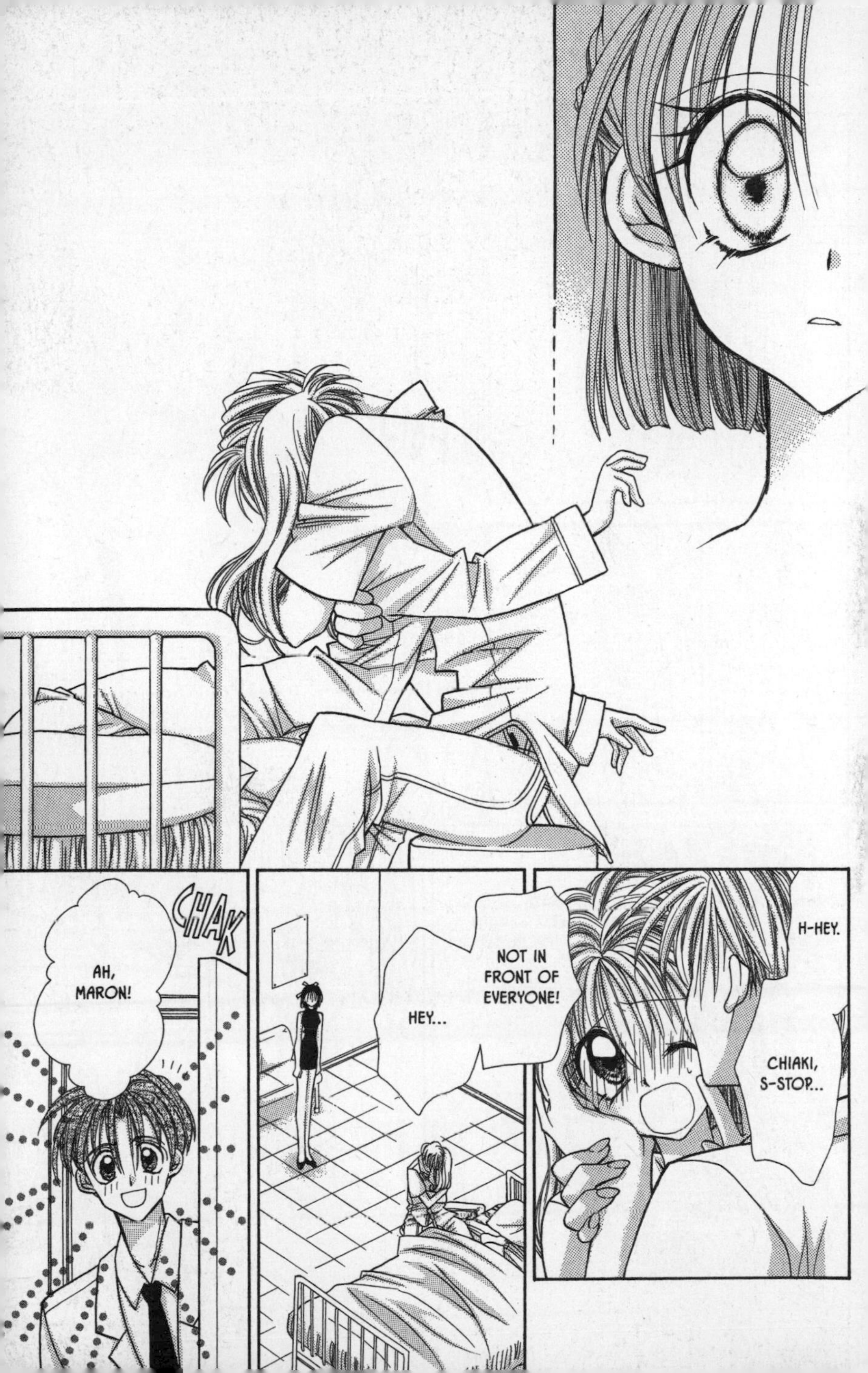
H-HEY.
CHIAKI, S-STOP...
NOT IN FRONT OF EVERYONE!
HEY...
CHAK
AH, MARON!

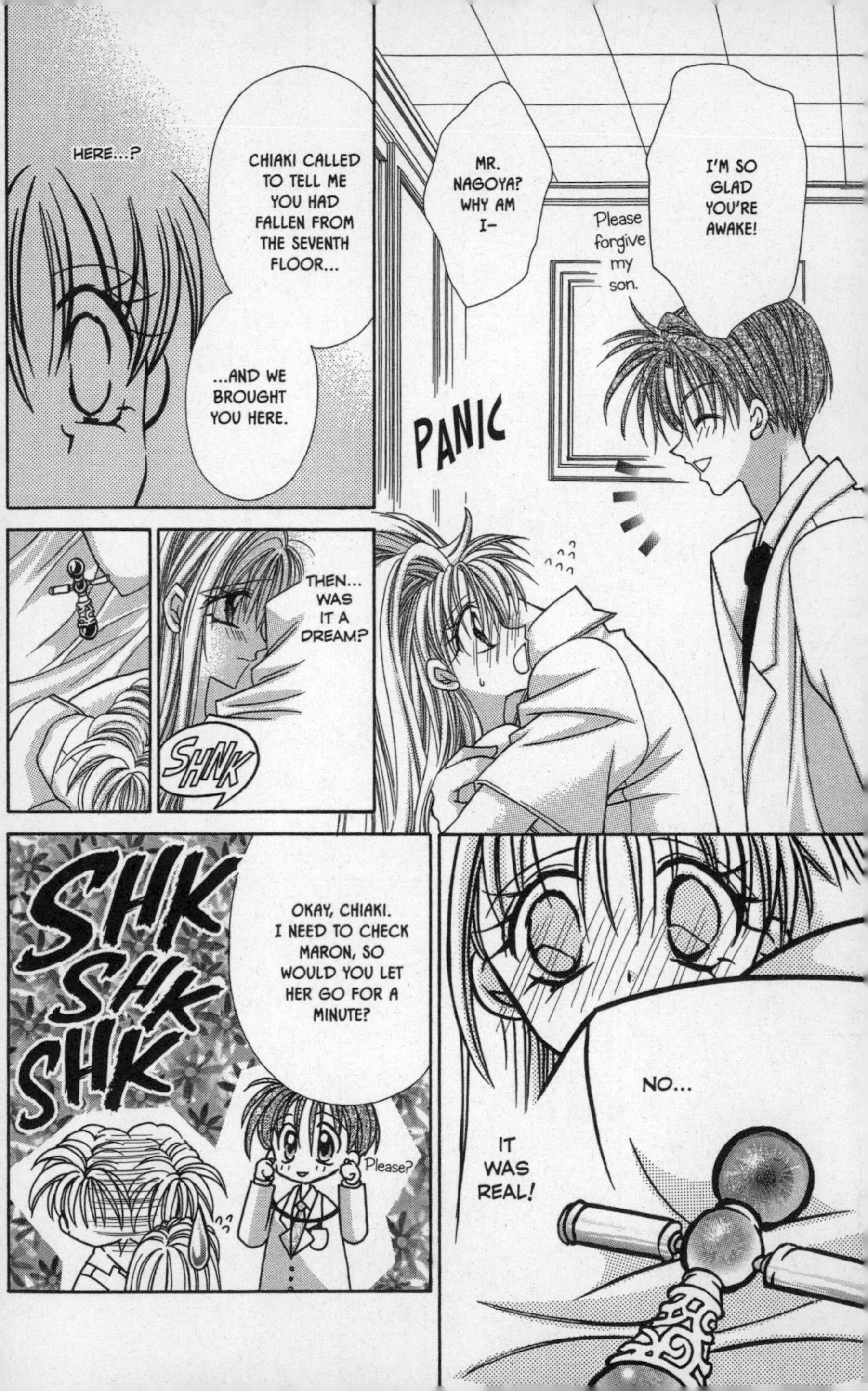
I'M SO GLAD YOU'RE AWAKE!
Please forgive my son.
MR. NAGOYA? WHY AM I–
PANIC
CHIAKI CALLED TO TELL ME YOU HAD FALLEN FROM THE SEVENTH FLOOR...
...AND WE BROUGHT YOU HERE.
HERE...?
THEN... WAS IT A DREAM?
SHNK
NO...
IT WAS REAL!
OKAY, CHIAKI. I NEED TO CHECK MARON, SO WOULD YOU LET HER GO FOR A MINUTE?
Please?
SHK SHK SHK

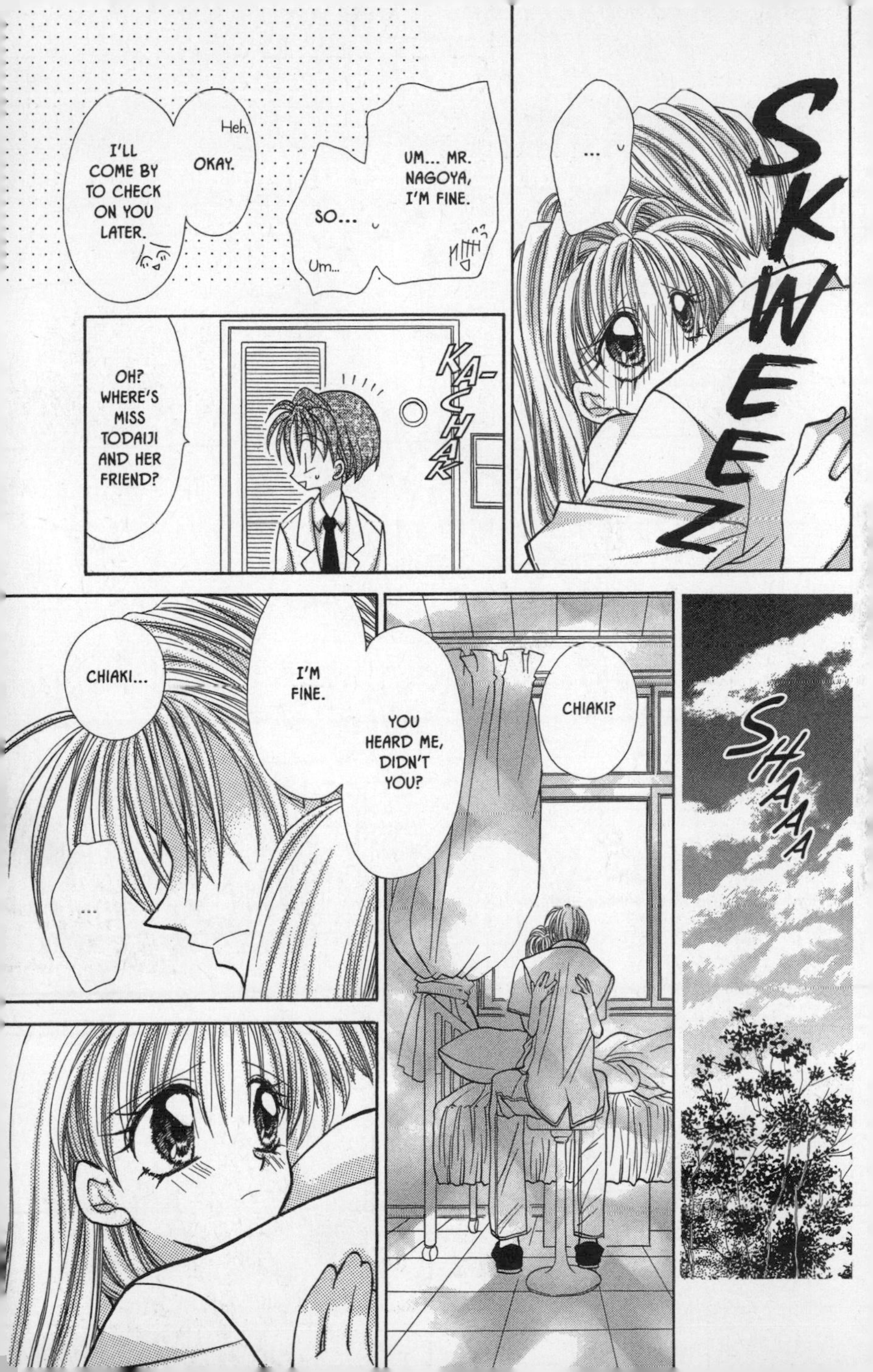
...
SKWEEZ
UM... MR. NAGOYA, I'M FINE.
SO...
Um...
Heh.
OKAY.
I'LL COME BY TO CHECK ON YOU LATER.
KA-CHAK
OH? WHERE'S MISS TODAIJI AND HER FRIEND?
SHAAA
CHIAKI?
I'M FINE.
YOU HEARD ME, DIDN'T YOU?
CHIAKI...
...

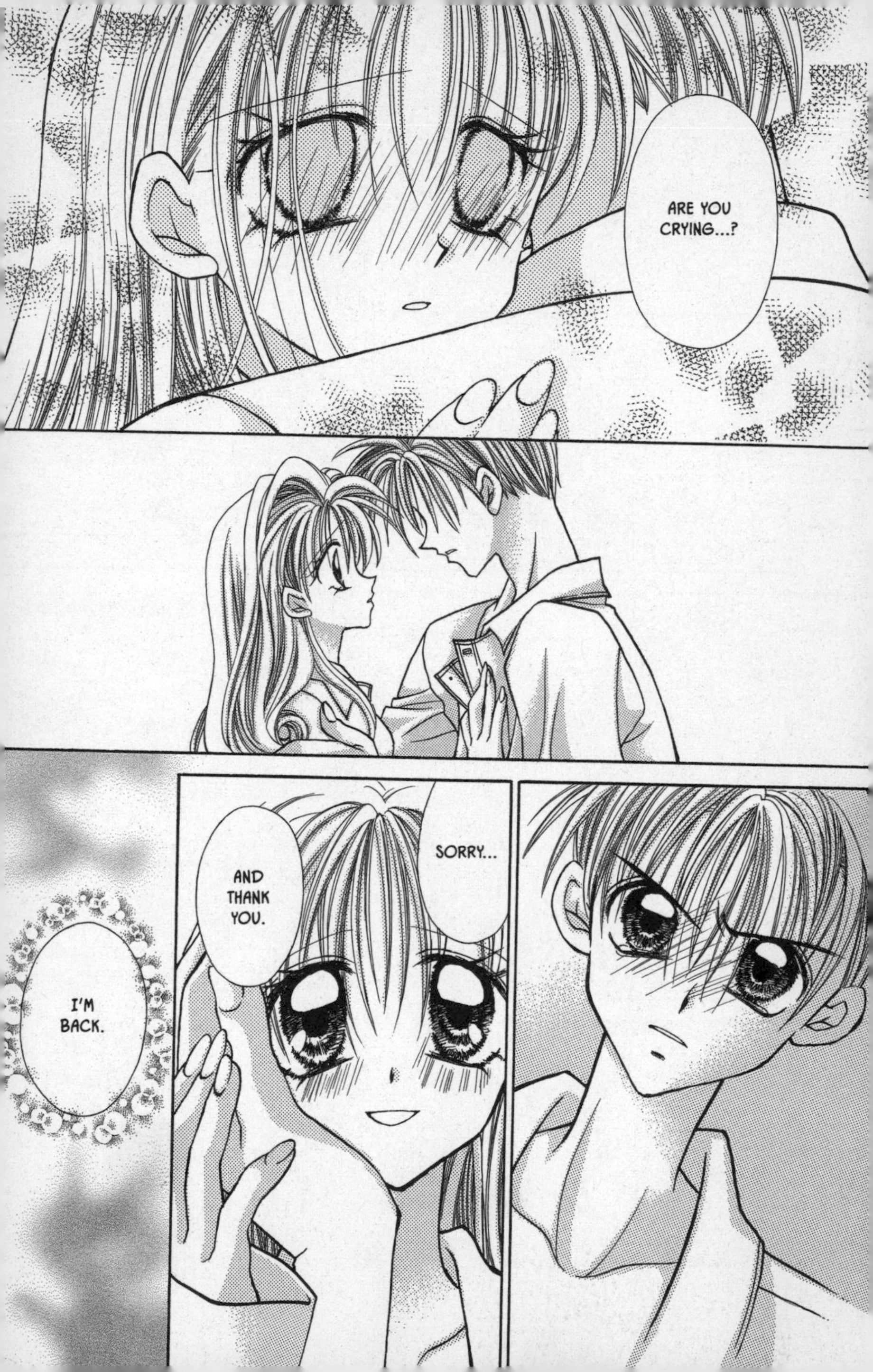
ARE YOU CRYING...?
SORRY...
AND THANK YOU.
I'M BACK.

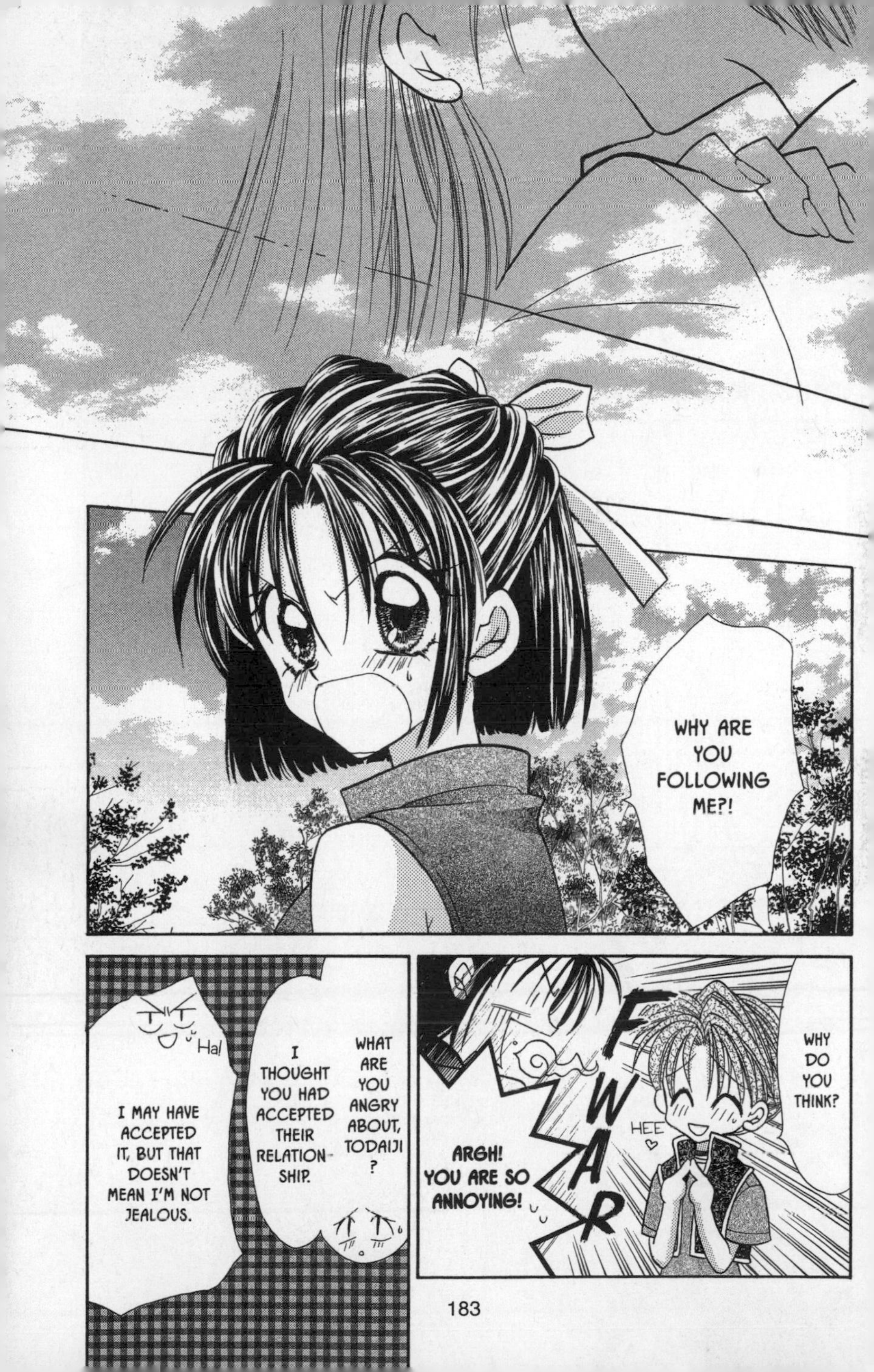
WHY ARE YOU FOLLOWING ME?!
WHY DO YOU THINK?
HEE
FWAR
ARGH! YOU ARE SO ANNOYING!
WHAT ARE YOU ANGRY ABOUT, TODAIJI?
I THOUGHT YOU HAD ACCEPTED THEIR RELATIONSHIP.
Ha!
I MAY HAVE ACCEPTED IT, BUT THAT DOESN'T MEAN I'M NOT JEALOUS.

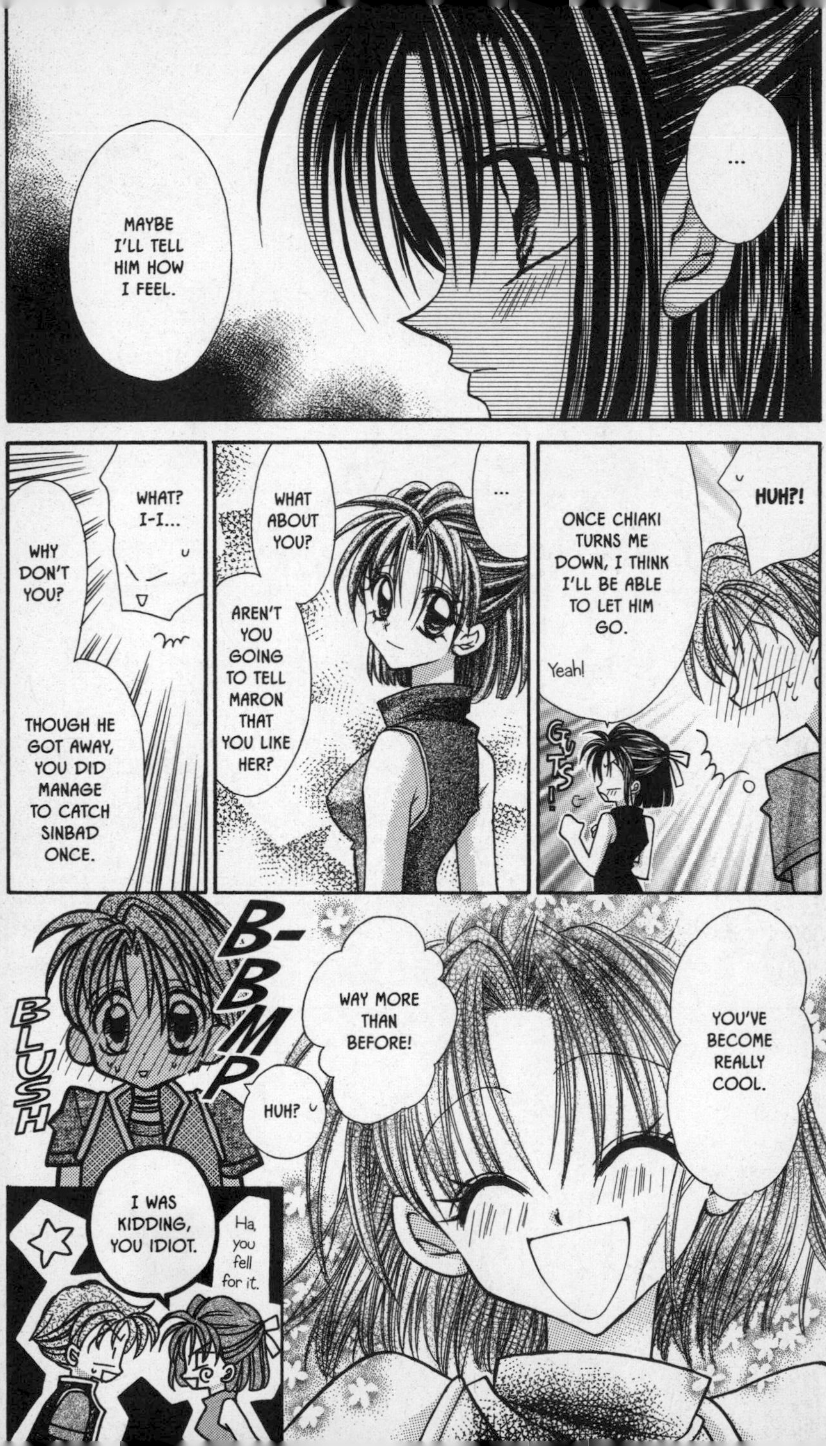
...
MAYBE I'LL TELL HIM HOW I FEEL.
HUH?!
ONCE CHIAKI TURNS ME DOWN, I THINK I'LL BE ABLE TO LET HIM GO.
Yeah!
GUTS!
...
WHAT ABOUT YOU?
AREN'T YOU GOING TO TELL MARON THAT YOU LIKE HER?
WHAT? I-I...
WHY DON'T YOU?
THOUGH HE GOT AWAY, YOU DID MANAGE TO CATCH SINBAD ONCE.
YOU'VE BECOME REALLY COOL.
WAY MORE THAN BEFORE!
HUH?
B-BMP
BLUSH
I WAS KIDDING, YOU IDIOT.
Ha, you fell for it.

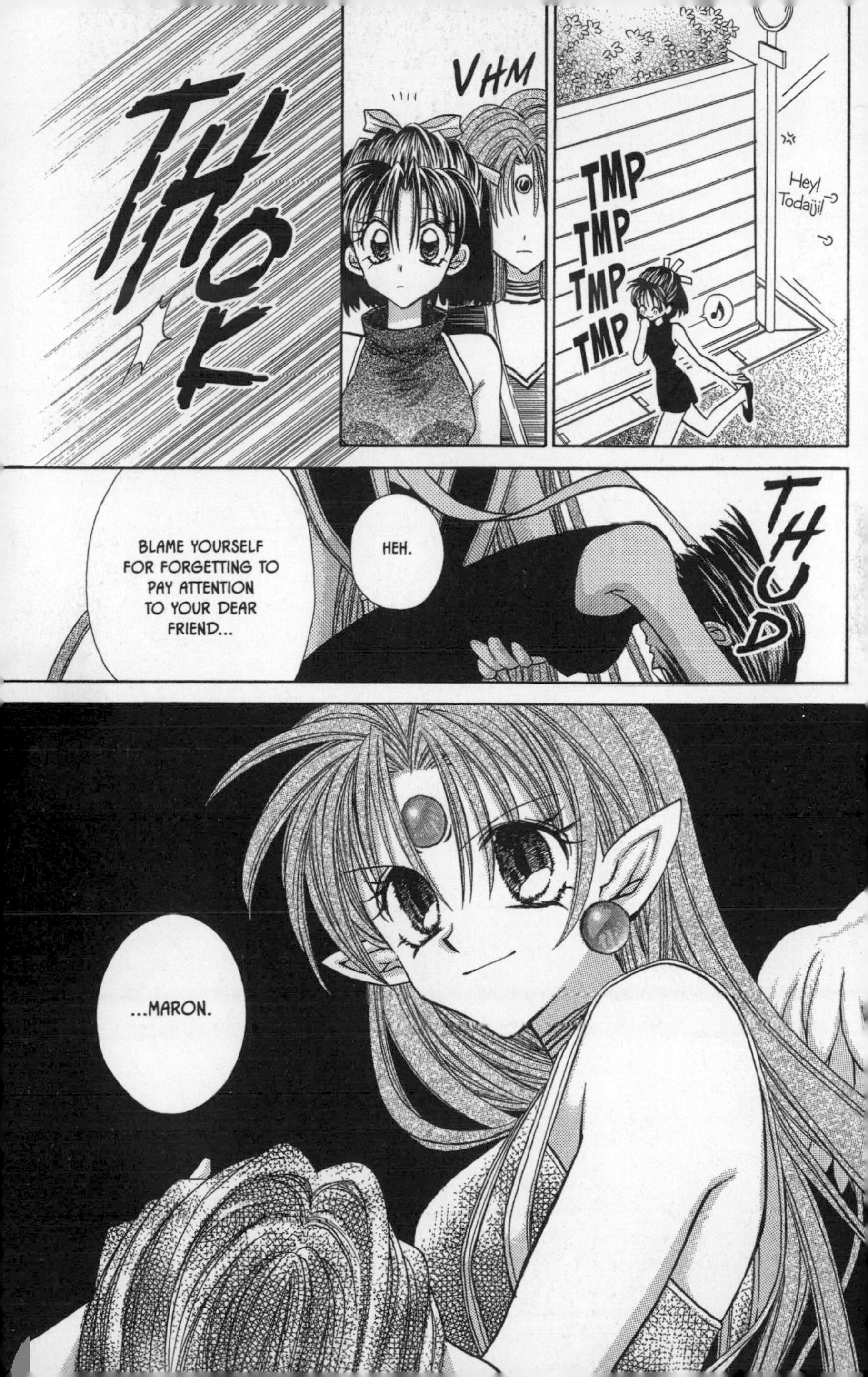
Hey! Todaiji!
TMP TMP TMP TMP
VHM
THOK
THUD
HEH.
BLAME YOURSELF FOR FORGETTING TO PAY ATTENTION TO YOUR DEAR FRIEND...
...MARON.

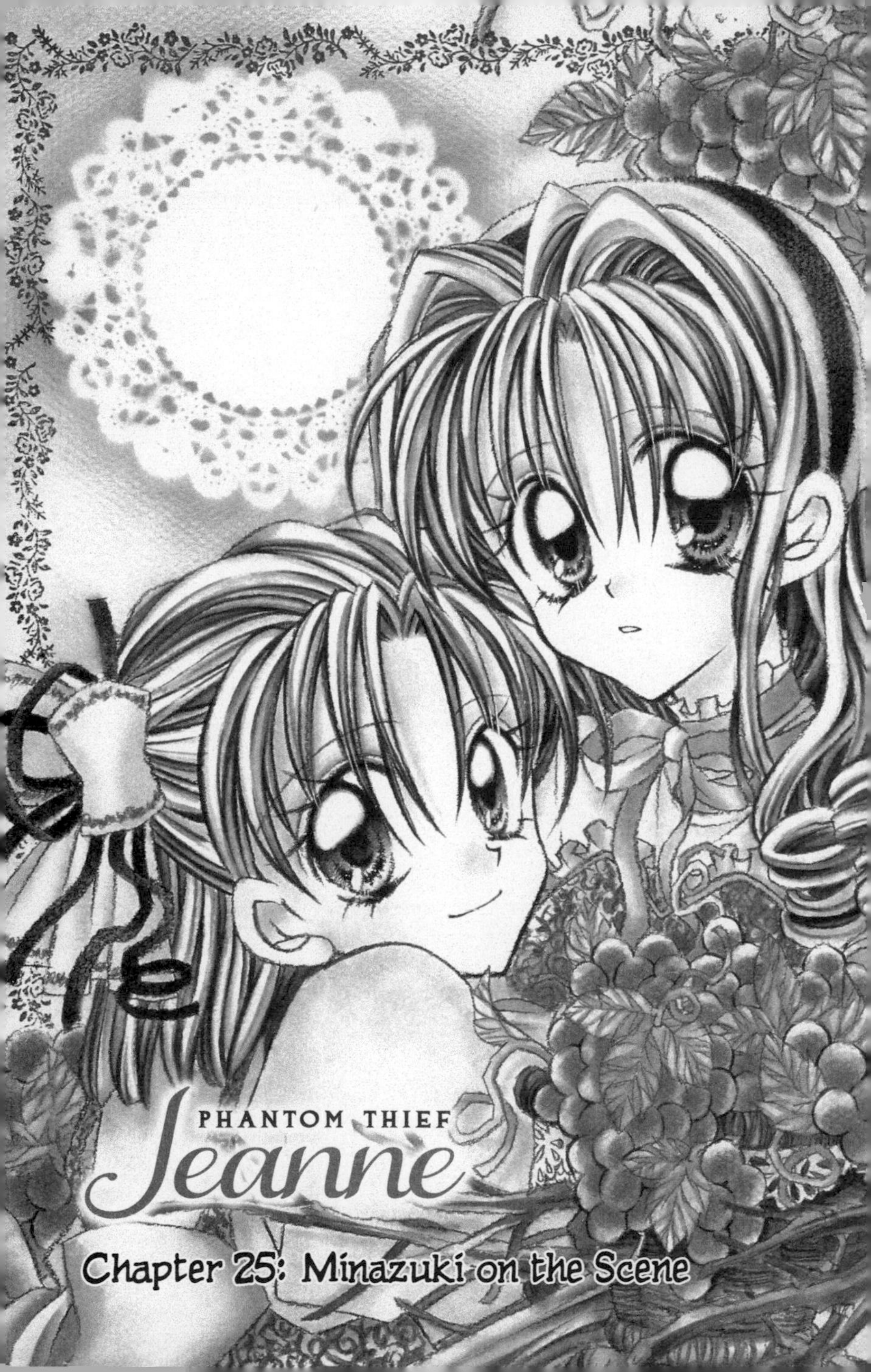
PHANTOM THIEF
Jeanne
Chapter 25: Minazuki on the Scene

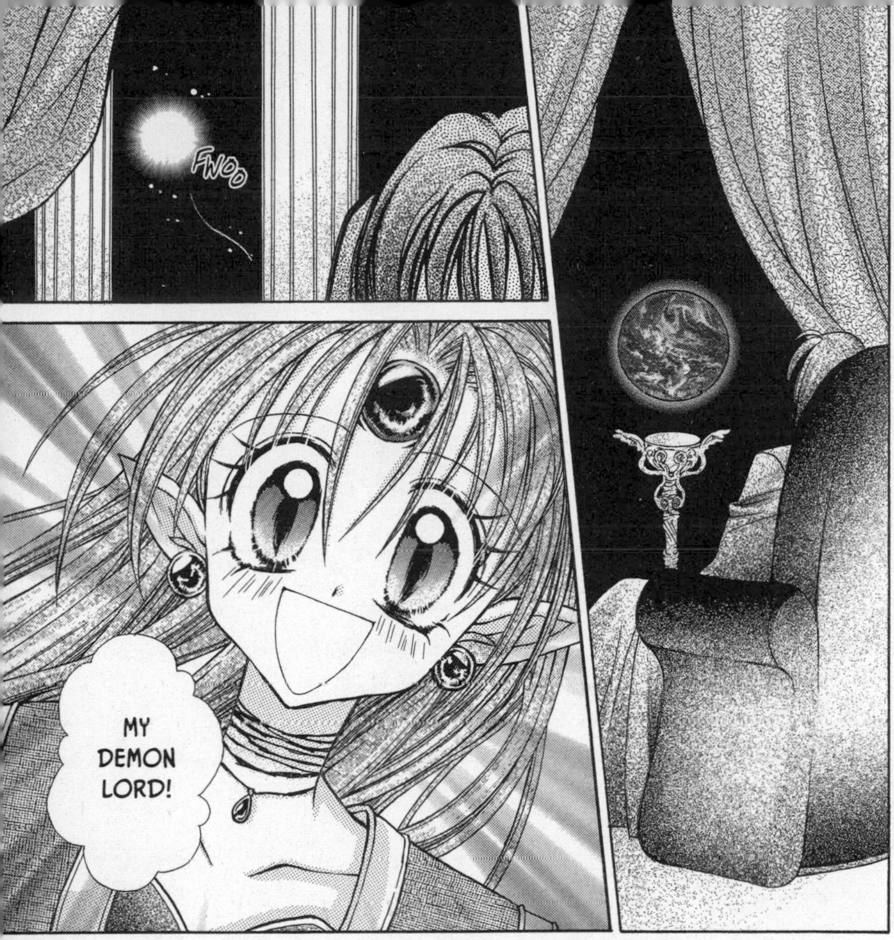
FWOO
MY DEMON LORD!

PHANTOM
THIEF
JEANNE

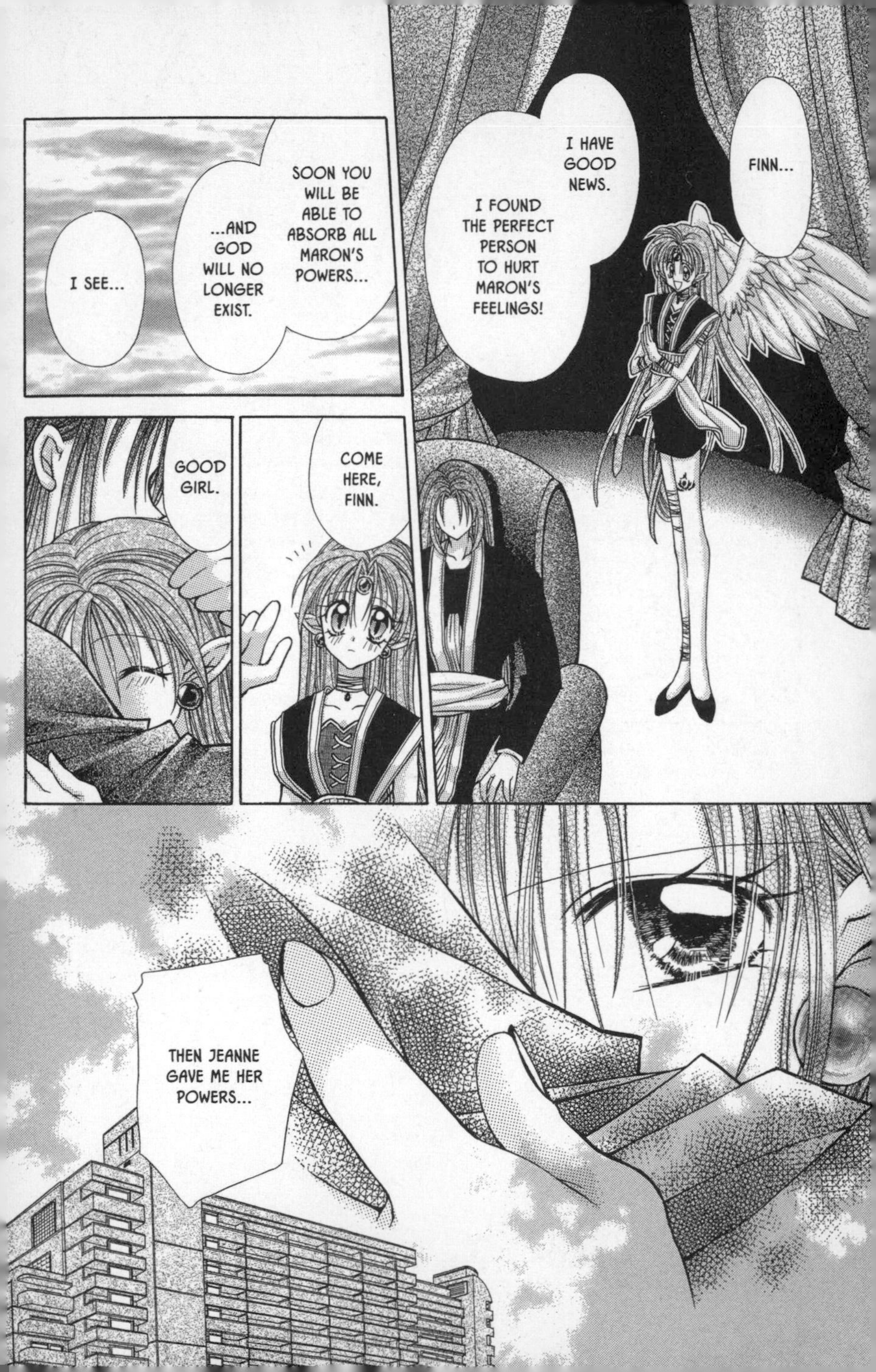
FINN...
I HAVE GOOD NEWS.
I FOUND THE PERFECT PERSON TO HURT MARON'S FEELINGS!
SOON YOU WILL BE ABLE TO ABSORB ALL MARON'S POWERS...
...AND GOD WILL NO LONGER EXIST.
I SEE...
COME HERE, FINN.
GOOD GIRL.
THEN JEANNE GAVE ME HER POWERS...

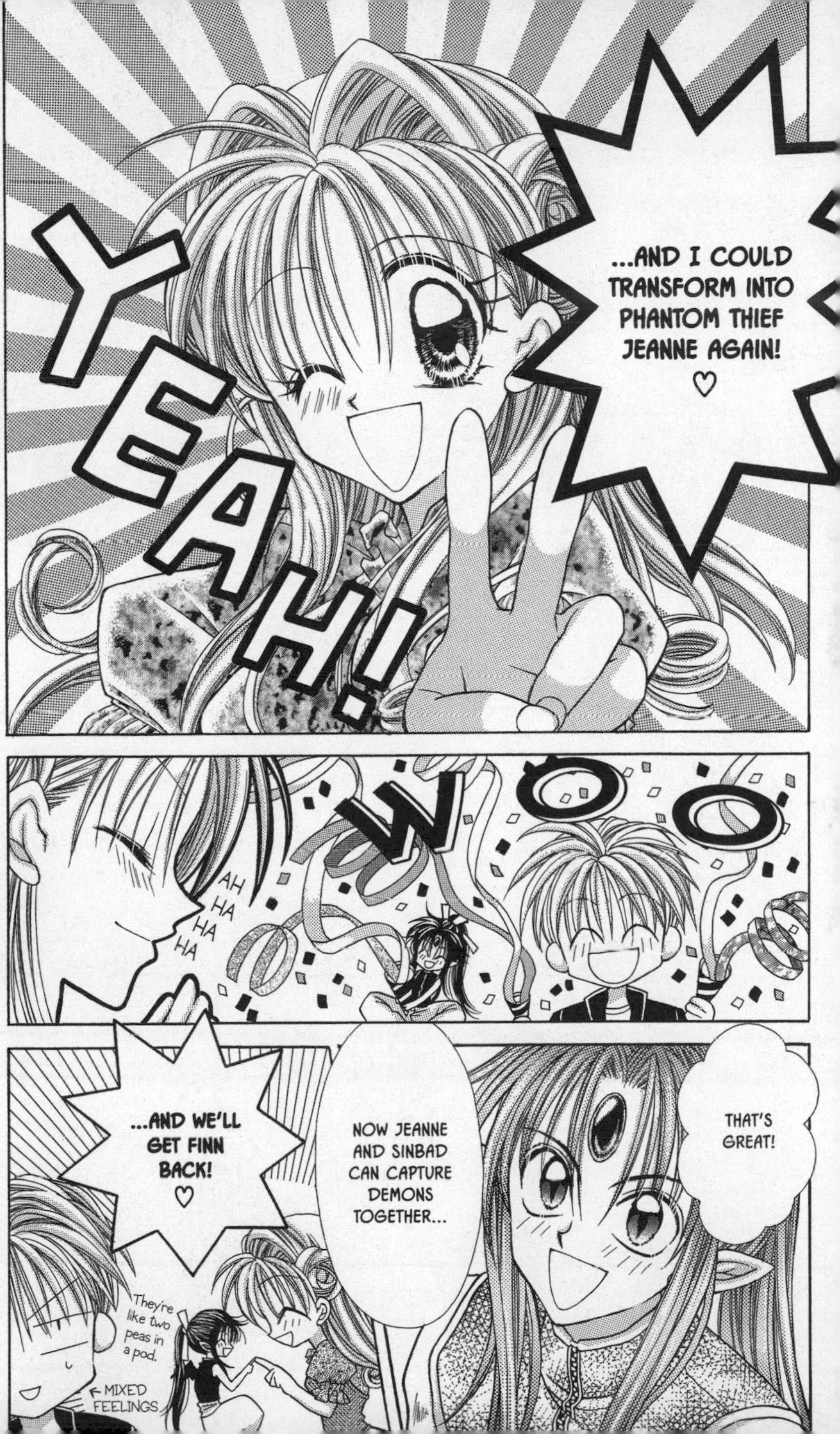
...AND I COULD TRANSFORM INTO PHANTOM THIEF JEANNE AGAIN! ♡
YEAH!
WOOO
AH HA HA HA
THAT'S GREAT!
NOW JEANNE AND SINBAD CAN CAPTURE DEMONS TOGETHER...
...AND WE'LL GET FINN BACK! ♡
They're like two peas in a pod.
MIXED FEELINGS

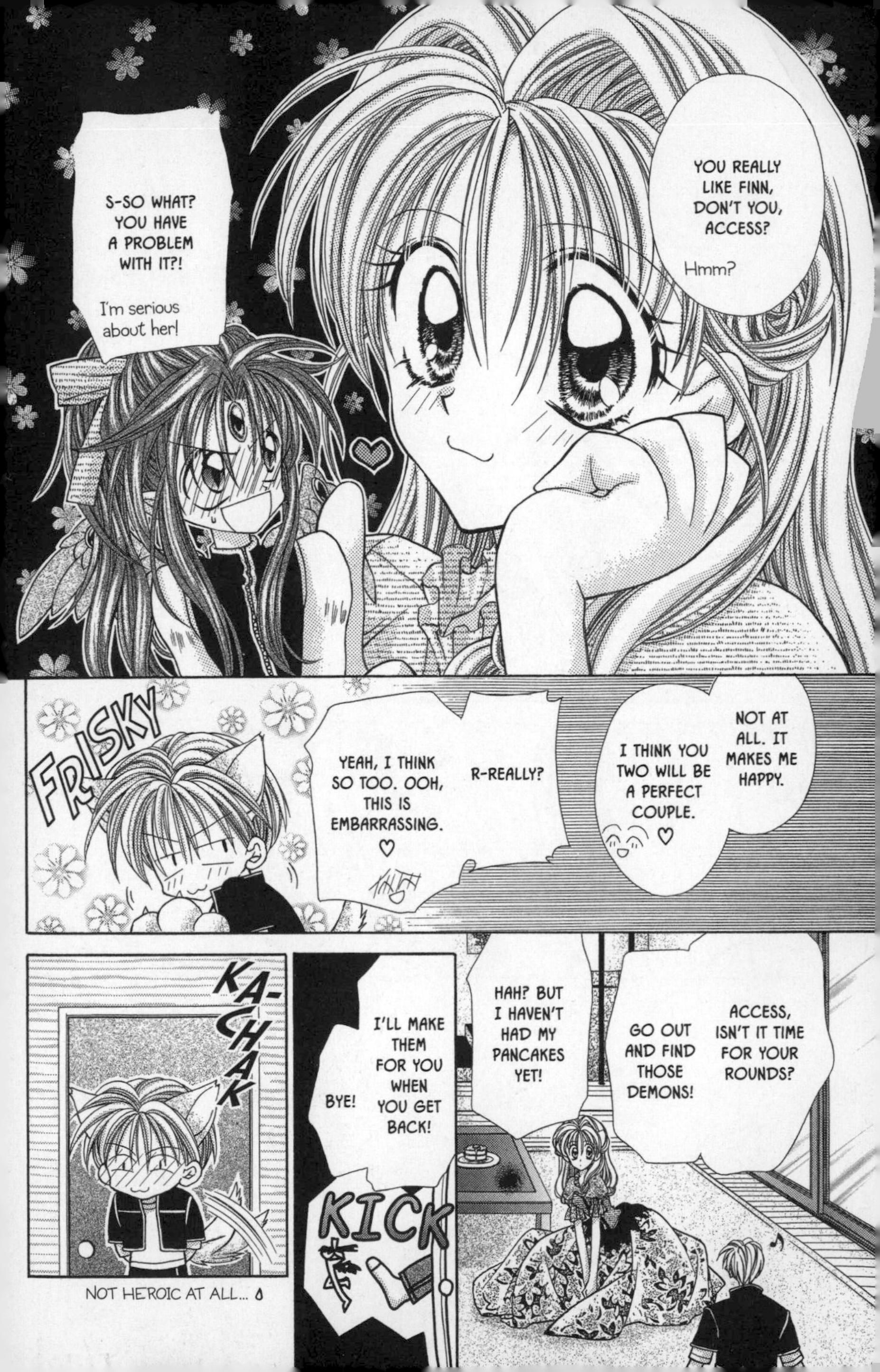
YOU REALLY LIKE FINN, DON'T YOU, ACCESS?
Hmm?
S-SO WHAT? YOU HAVE A PROBLEM WITH IT?!
I'm serious about her!
NOT AT ALL. IT MAKES ME HAPPY.
I THINK YOU TWO WILL BE A PERFECT COUPLE. ♡
R-REALLY?
YEAH, I THINK SO TOO. OOH, THIS IS EMBARRASSING. ♡
FRISKY
ACCESS, ISN'T IT TIME FOR YOUR ROUNDS?
GO OUT AND FIND THOSE DEMONS!
HAH? BUT I HAVEN'T HAD MY PANCAKES YET!
I'LL MAKE THEM FOR YOU WHEN YOU GET BACK!
BYE!
KICK
KA-CHAK
NOT HEROIC AT ALL...

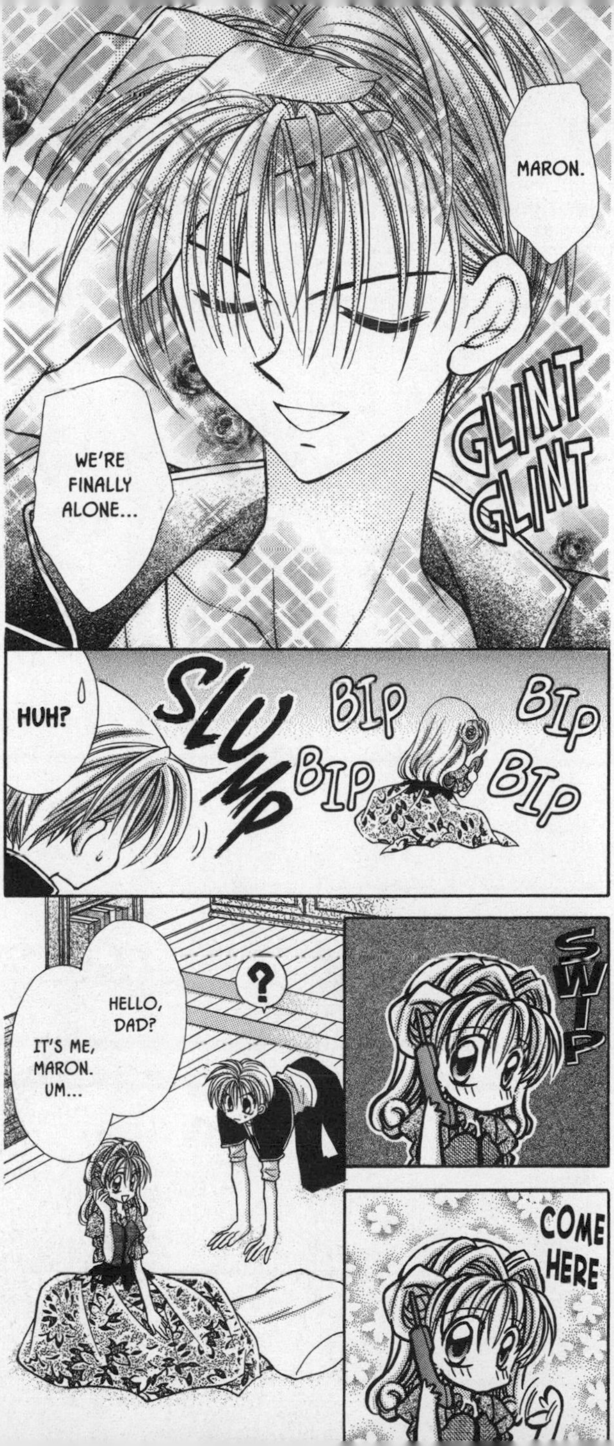
MARON.
WE'RE FINALLY ALONE...
GLINT GLINT
BIP BIP BIP BIP
SLUMP
HUH?
SWIP
COME HERE
HELLO, DAD?
IT'S ME, MARON. UM...
?

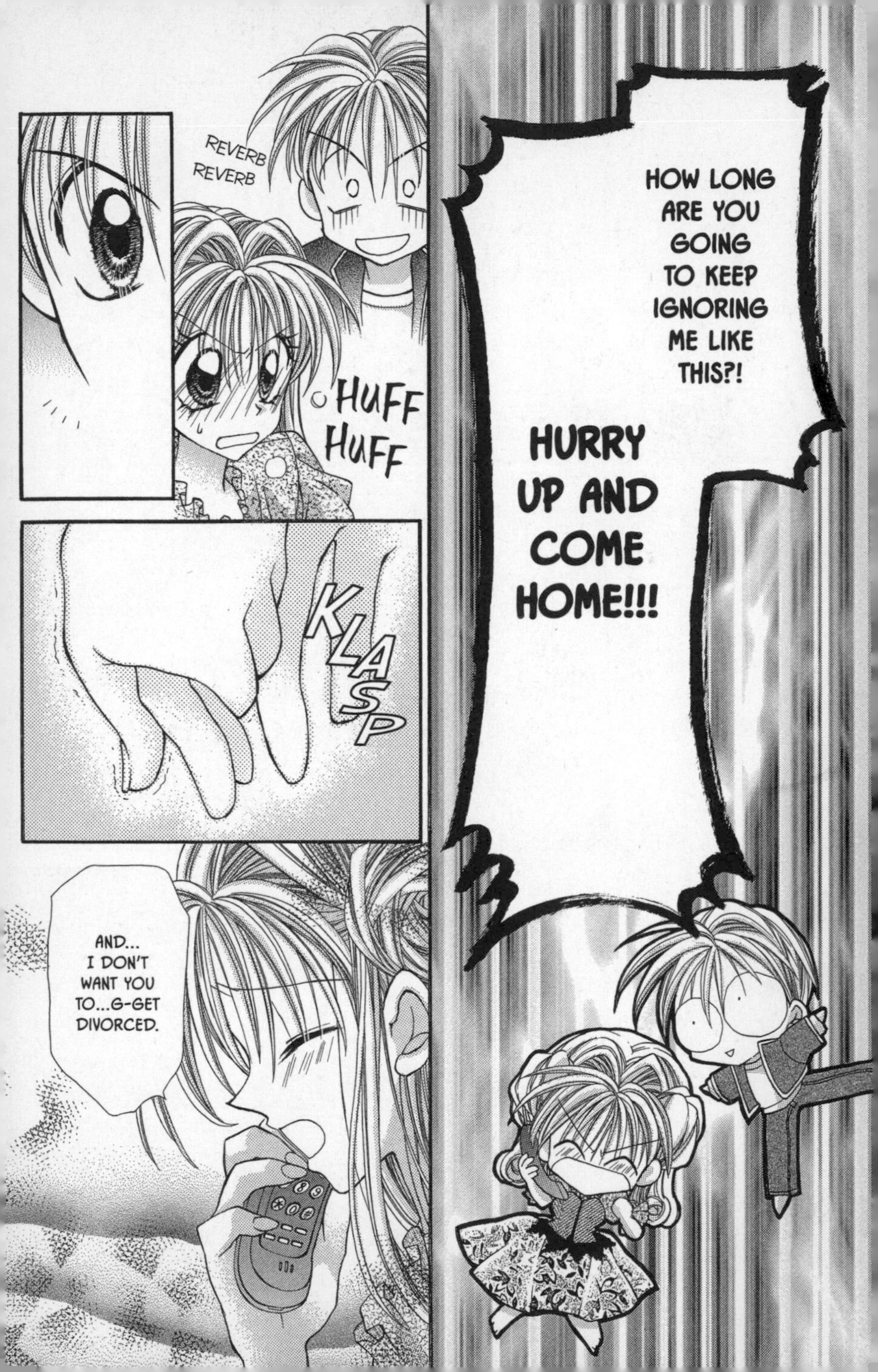
HOW LONG ARE YOU GOING TO KEEP IGNORING ME LIKE THIS?!
HURRY UP AND COME HOME!!!
REVERB REVERB
HUFF HUFF
KLASP
AND... I DON'T WANT YOU TO...G-GET DIVORCED.

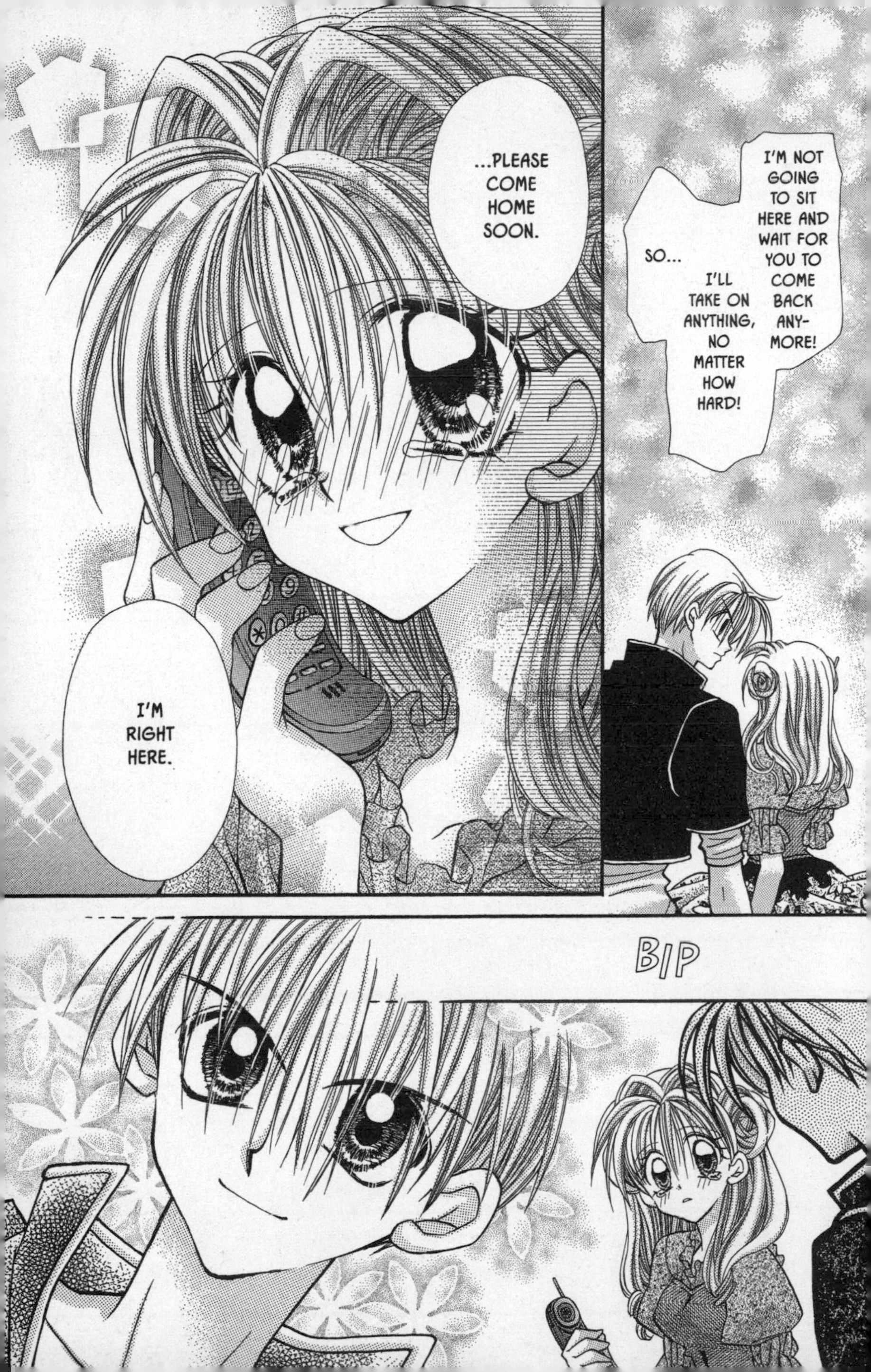
I'M NOT GOING TO SIT HERE AND WAIT FOR YOU TO COME BACK ANY-MORE!
SO...
I'LL TAKE ON ANYTHING, NO MATTER HOW HARD!
...PLEASE COME HOME SOON.
I'M RIGHT HERE.
BIP

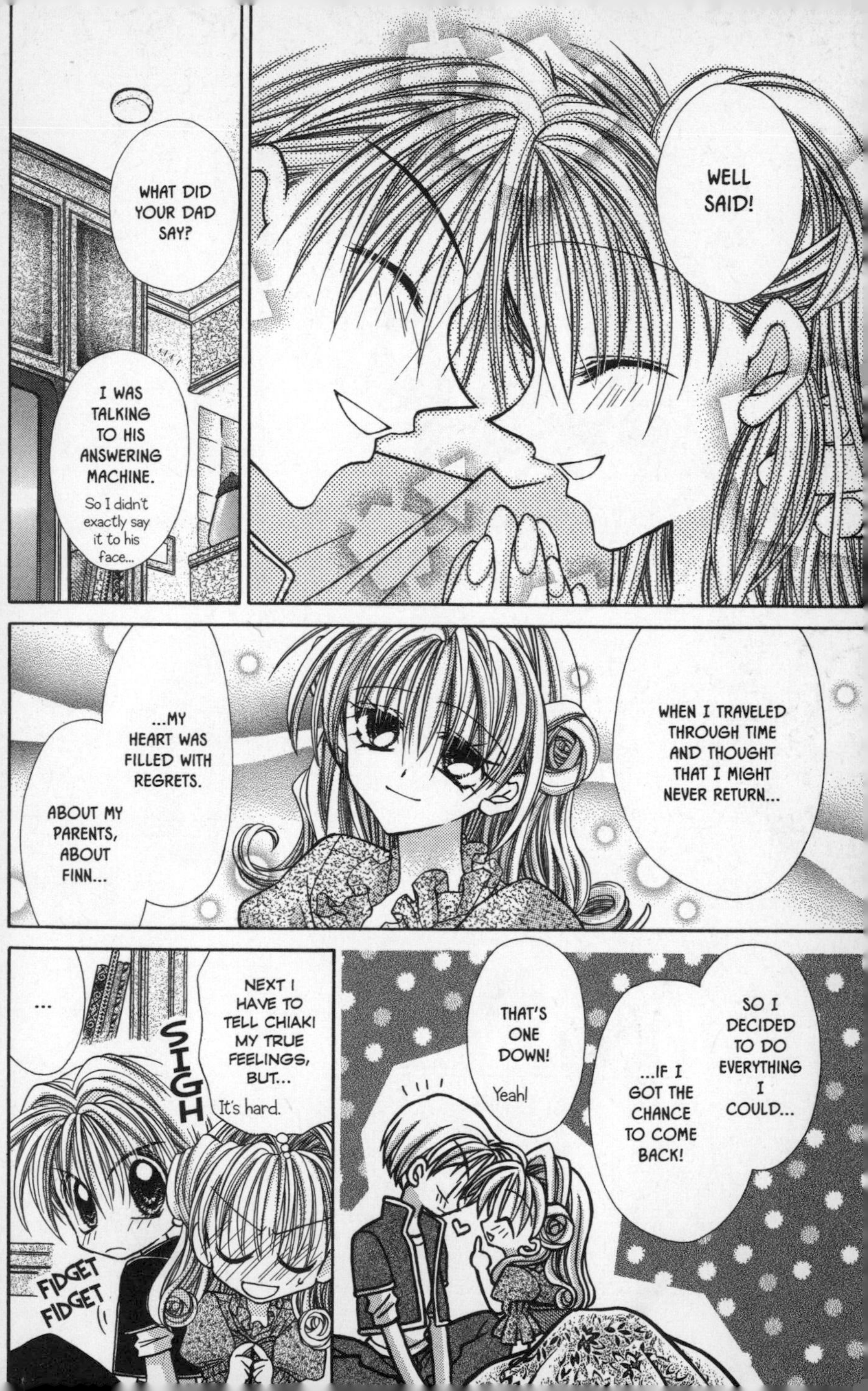
WELL SAID!
WHAT DID YOUR DAD SAY?
I WAS TALKING TO HIS ANSWERING MACHINE.
So I didn't exactly say it to his face...
WHEN I TRAVELED THROUGH TIME AND THOUGHT THAT I MIGHT NEVER RETURN...
...MY HEART WAS FILLED WITH REGRETS.
ABOUT MY PARENTS, ABOUT FINN...
SO I DECIDED TO DO EVERYTHING I COULD...
...IF I GOT THE CHANCE TO COME BACK!
THAT'S ONE DOWN!
Yeah!
NEXT I HAVE TO TELL CHIAKI MY TRUE FEELINGS, BUT...
It's hard.
SIGH
...
FIDGET FIDGET

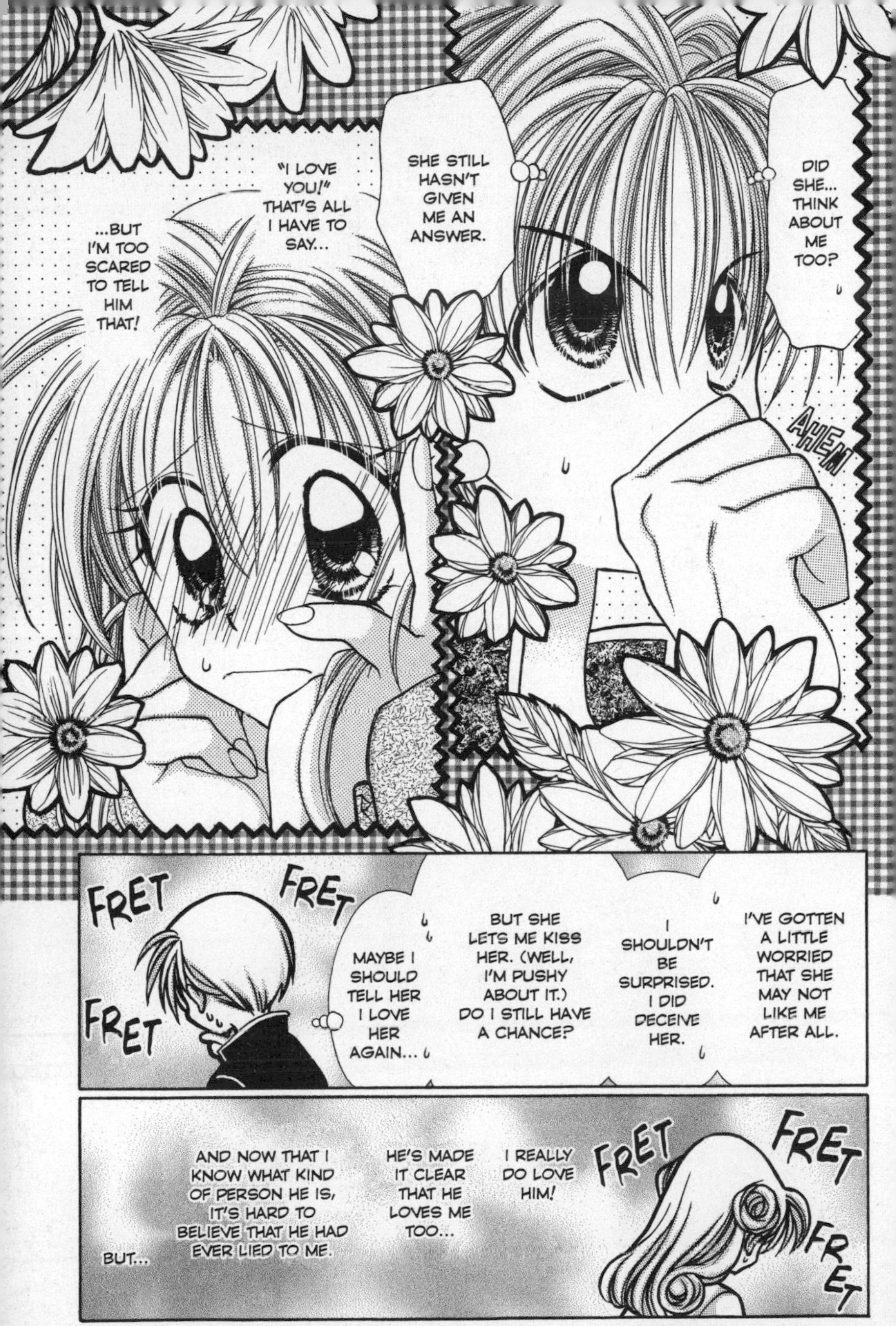
DID SHE... THINK ABOUT ME TOO?
SHE STILL HASN'T GIVEN ME AN ANSWER.
AHEM
"I LOVE YOU!" THAT'S ALL I HAVE TO SAY...
...BUT I'M TOO SCARED TO TELL HIM THAT!
I'VE GOTTEN A LITTLE WORRIED THAT SHE MAY NOT LIKE ME AFTER ALL.
I SHOULDN'T BE SURPRISED. I DID DECEIVE HER.
BUT SHE LETS ME KISS HER. (WELL, I'M PUSHY ABOUT IT.) DO I STILL HAVE A CHANCE?
MAYBE I SHOULD TELL HER I LOVE HER AGAIN...
FRET
FRET
FRET
FRET
FRET
FRET
I REALLY DO LOVE HIM!
HE'S MADE IT CLEAR THAT HE LOVES ME TOO...
AND NOW THAT I KNOW WHAT KIND OF PERSON HE IS, IT'S HARD TO BELIEVE THAT HE HAD EVER LIED TO ME.
BUT...

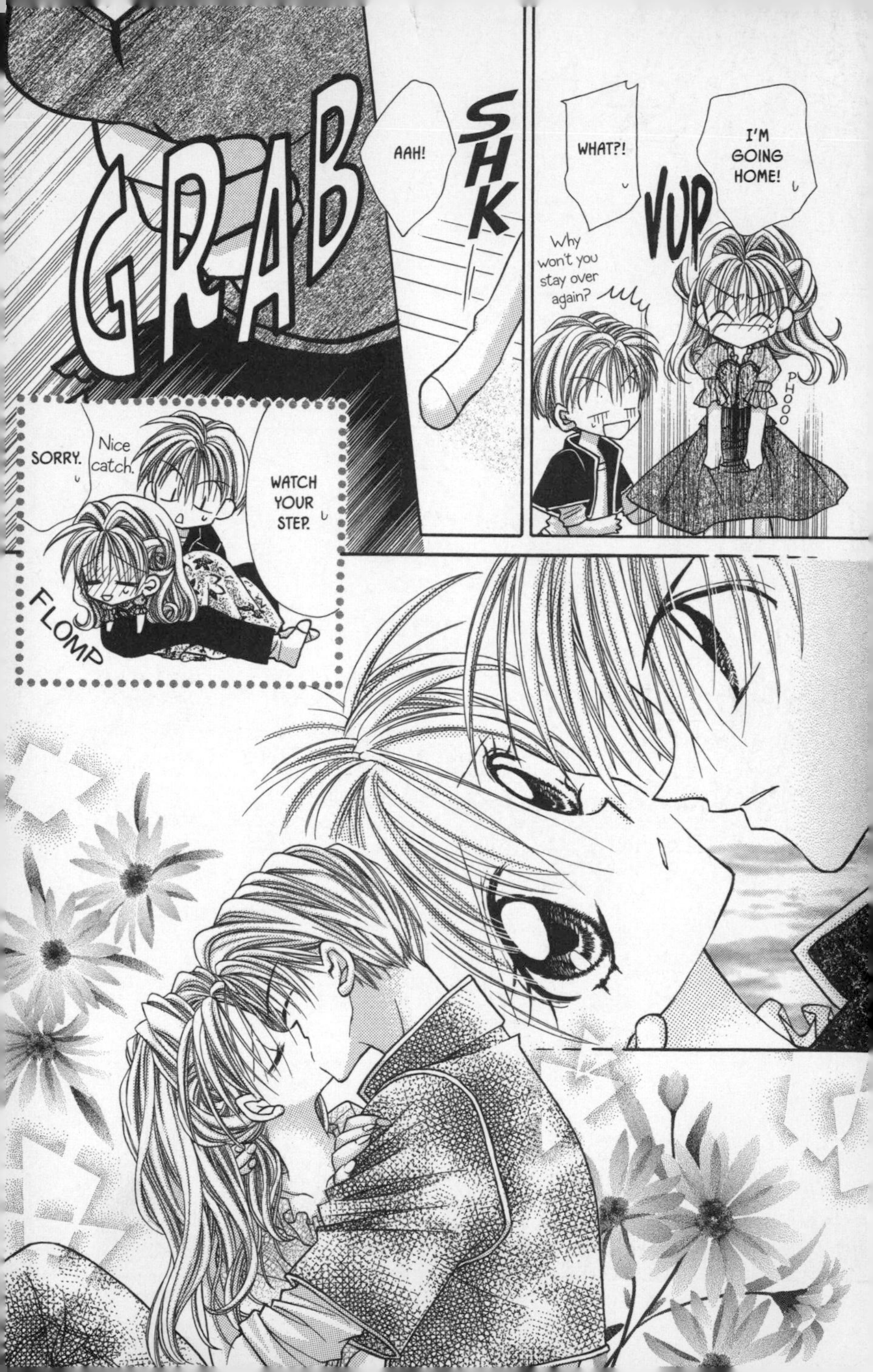
I'M GOING HOME!
WHAT?!
VUP
Why won't you stay over again?
PHOOO
AAH!
SHK
GRAB
WATCH YOUR STEP.
Nice catch.
SORRY.
FLOMP

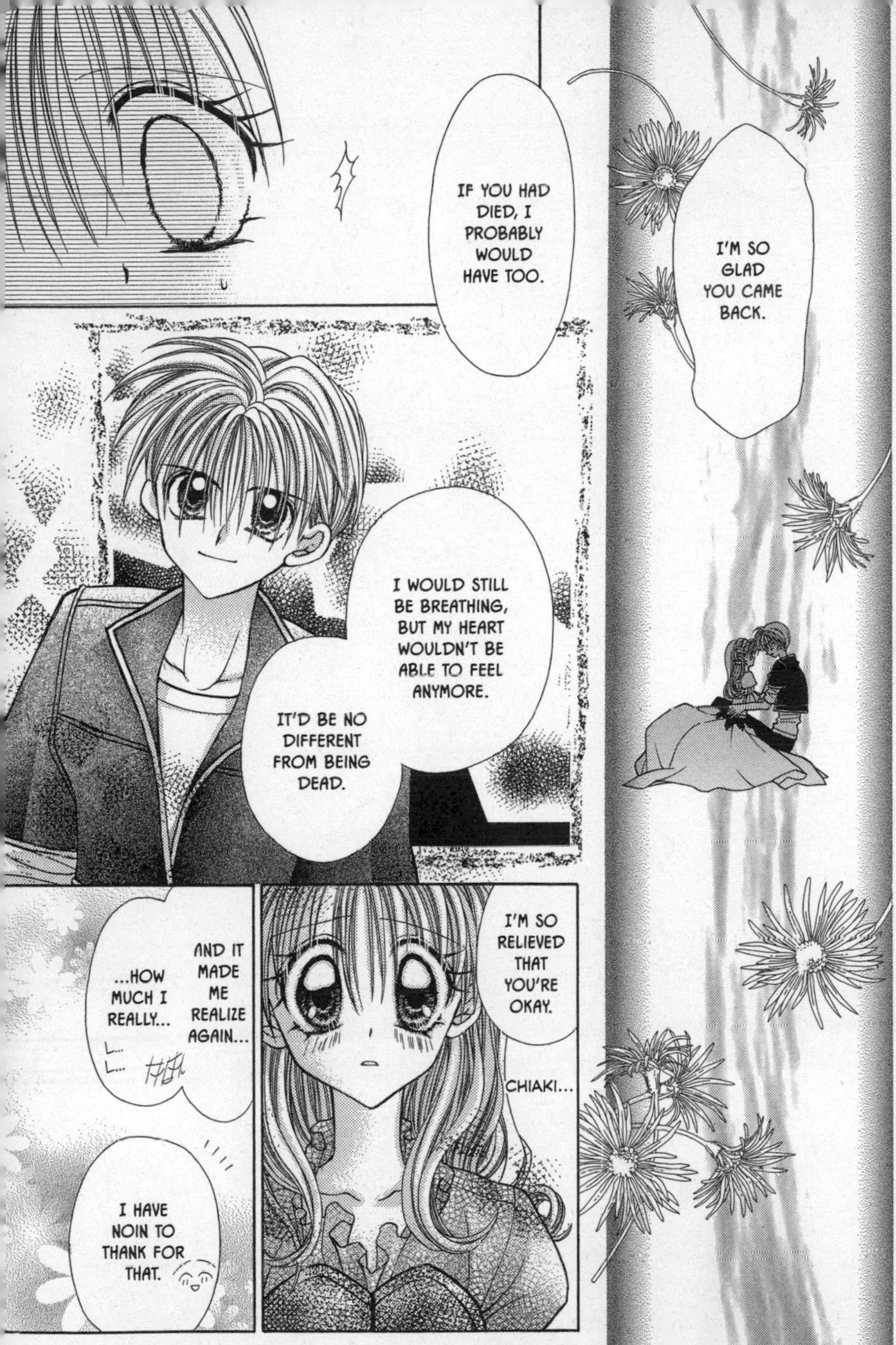
I'M SO GLAD YOU CAME BACK.
IF YOU HAD DIED, I PROBABLY WOULD HAVE TOO.
I WOULD STILL BE BREATHING, BUT MY HEART WOULDN'T BE ABLE TO FEEL ANYMORE.
IT'D BE NO DIFFERENT FROM BEING DEAD.
I'M SO RELIEVED THAT YOU'RE OKAY.
CHIAKI...
AND IT MADE ME REALIZE AGAIN...
...HOW MUCH I REALLY...
L... L...
I HAVE NOIN TO THANK FOR THAT.

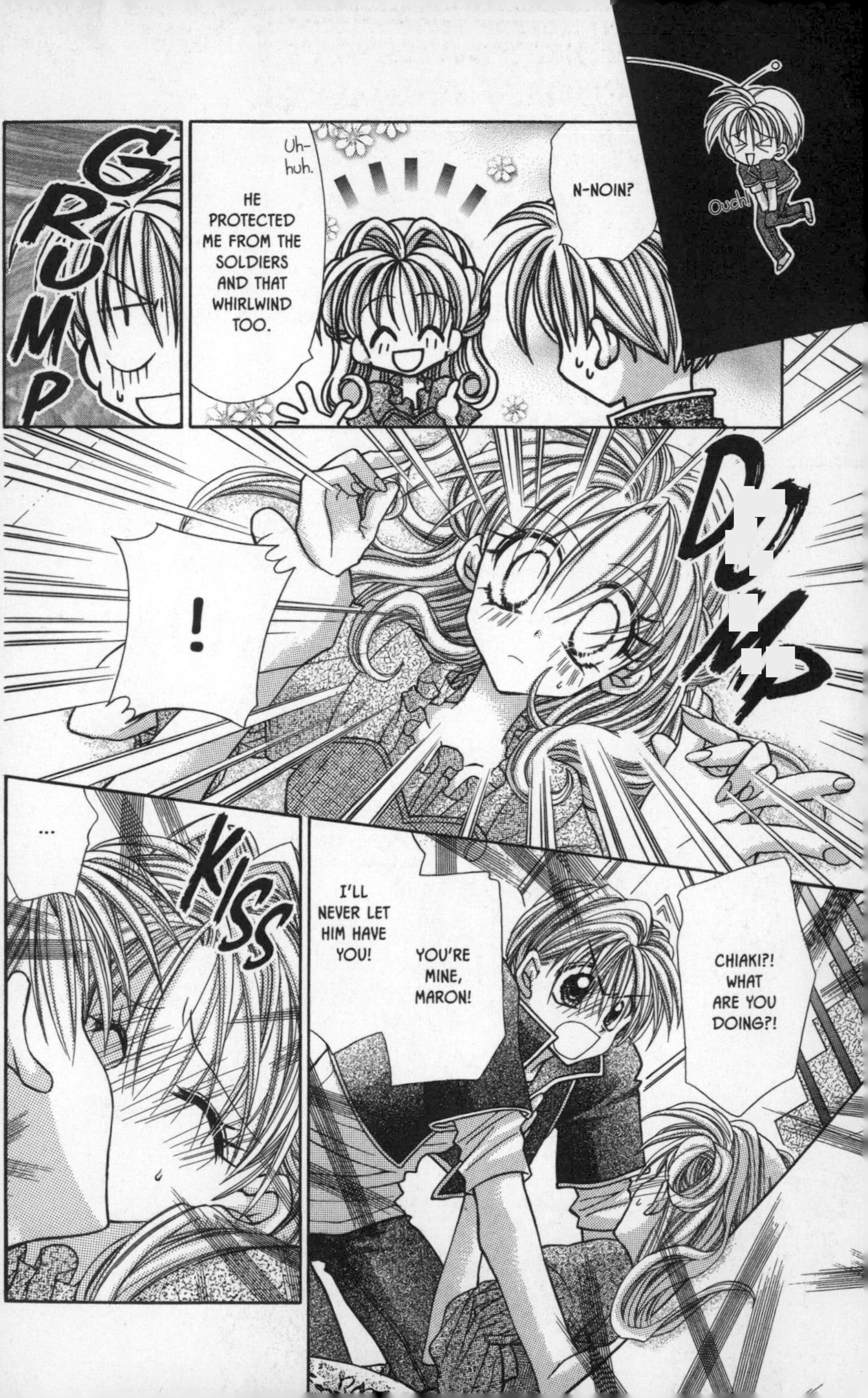
Ouch!
N-NOIN?
Uh-huh.
HE PROTECTED ME FROM THE SOLDIERS AND THAT WHIRLWIND TOO.
GRUMP
DOMP
!
CHIAKI?! WHAT ARE YOU DOING?!
YOU'RE MINE, MARON!
I'LL NEVER LET HIM HAVE YOU!
KISS
...

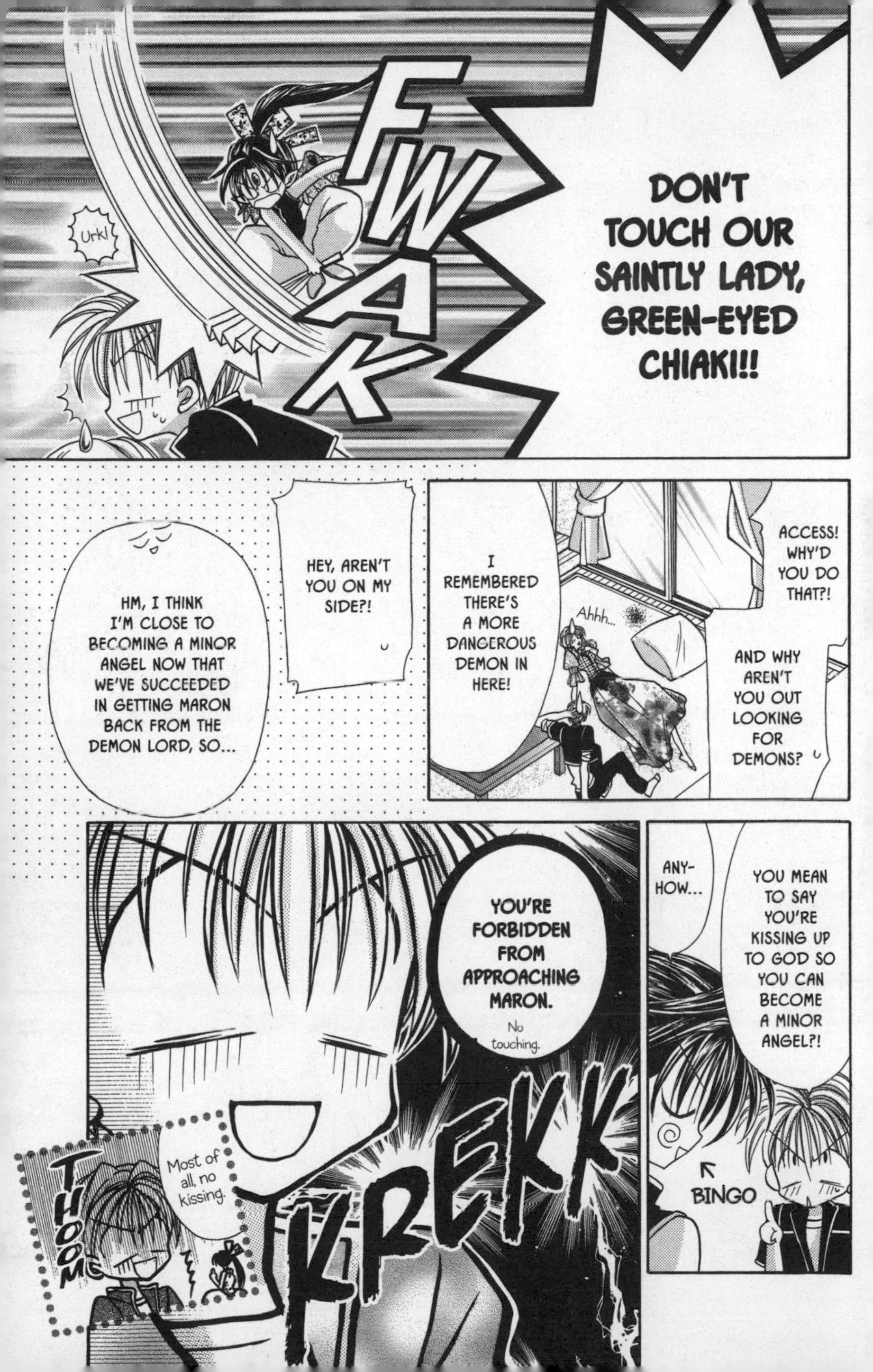
DON'T TOUCH OUR SAINTLY LADY, GREEN-EYED CHIAKI!!
FWAK
Urk!
ACCESS! WHY'D YOU DO THAT?!
AND WHY AREN'T YOU OUT LOOKING FOR DEMONS?
Ahhh...
I REMEMBERED THERE'S A MORE DANGEROUS DEMON IN HERE!
HEY, AREN'T YOU ON MY SIDE?!
HM, I THINK I'M CLOSE TO BECOMING A MINOR ANGEL NOW THAT WE'VE SUCCEEDED IN GETTING MARON BACK FROM THE DEMON LORD, SO...
YOU MEAN TO SAY YOU'RE KISSING UP TO GOD SO YOU CAN BECOME A MINOR ANGEL?!
ANY-HOW...
BINGO
YOU'RE FORBIDDEN FROM APPROACHING MARON.
No touching.
KREKK
Most of all, no kissing.
THOOM

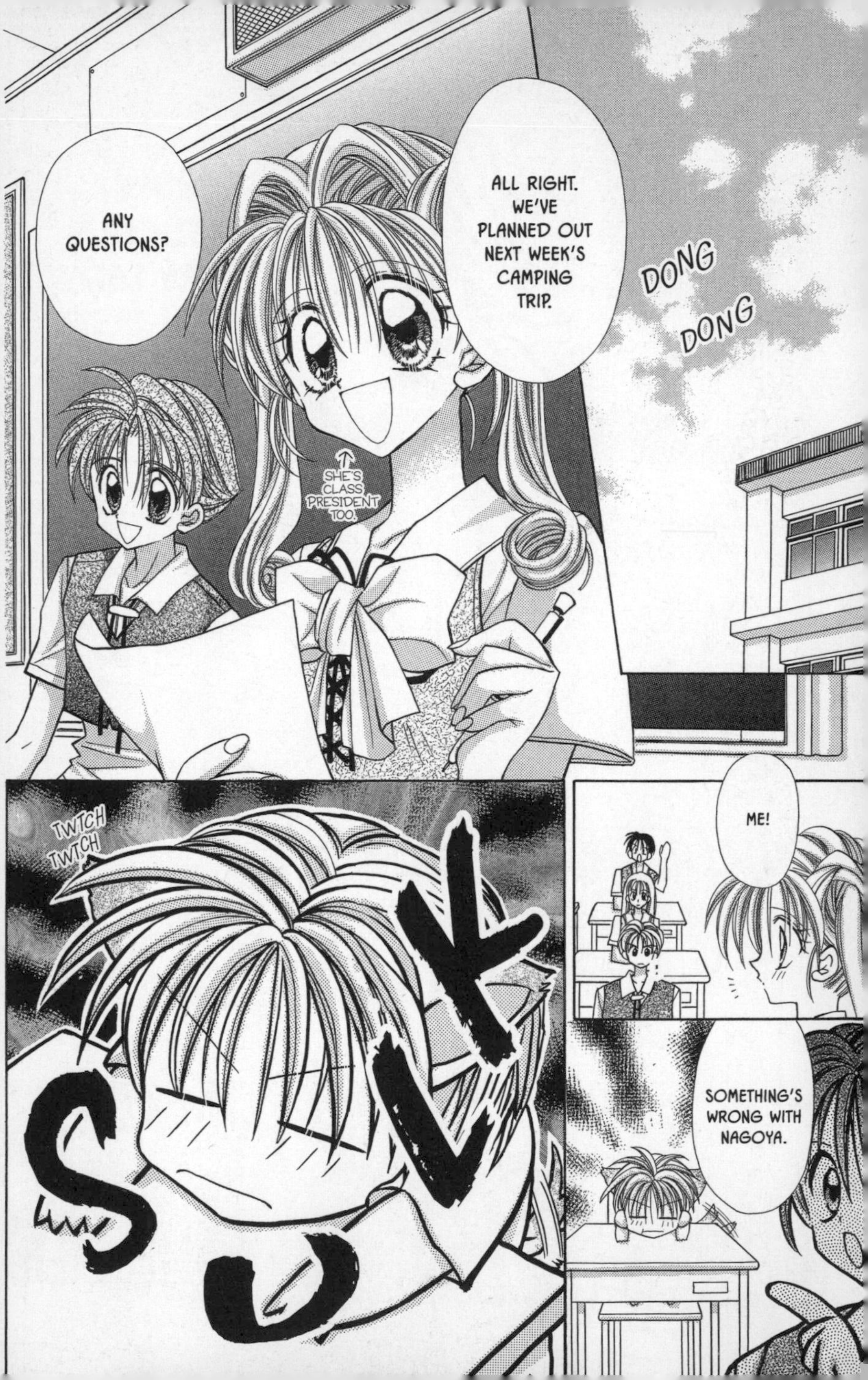
DONG
DONG
ALL RIGHT. WE'VE PLANNED OUT NEXT WEEK'S CAMPING TRIP.
ANY QUESTIONS?
SHE'S CLASS PRESIDENT TOO.
ME!
SOMETHING'S WRONG WITH NAGOYA.
TWITCH TWITCH
SULK

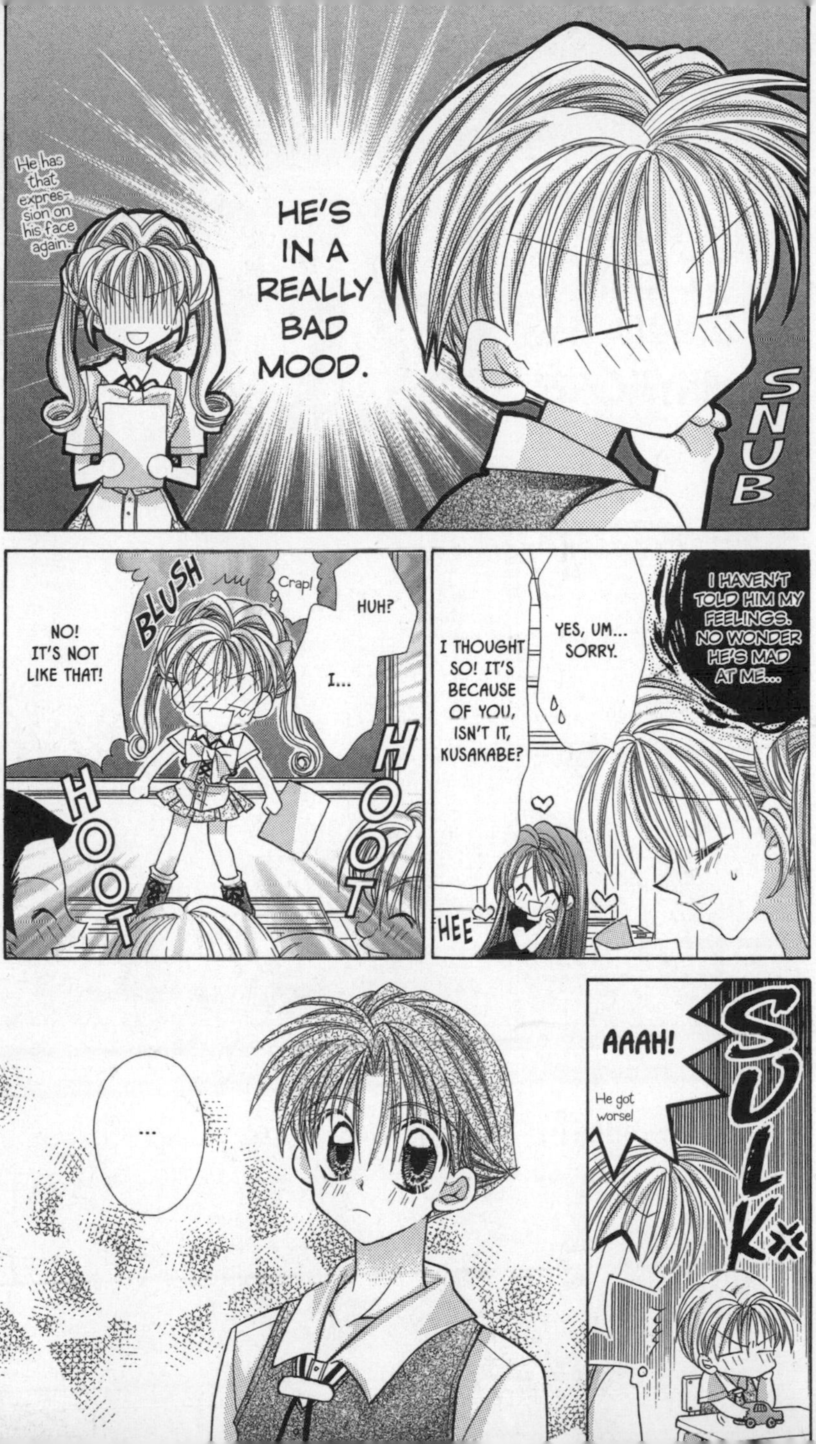
SNUB
HE'S IN A REALLY BAD MOOD.
He has that expression on his face again.
I HAVEN'T TOLD HIM MY FEELINGS. NO WONDER HE'S MAD AT ME...
YES, UM... SORRY.
I THOUGHT SO! IT'S BECAUSE OF YOU, ISN'T IT, KUSAKABE?
HEE
HOOT
HUH?
I...
Crap!
BLUSH
NO! IT'S NOT LIKE THAT!
HOOT
SULK
AAAH!
He got worse!
...

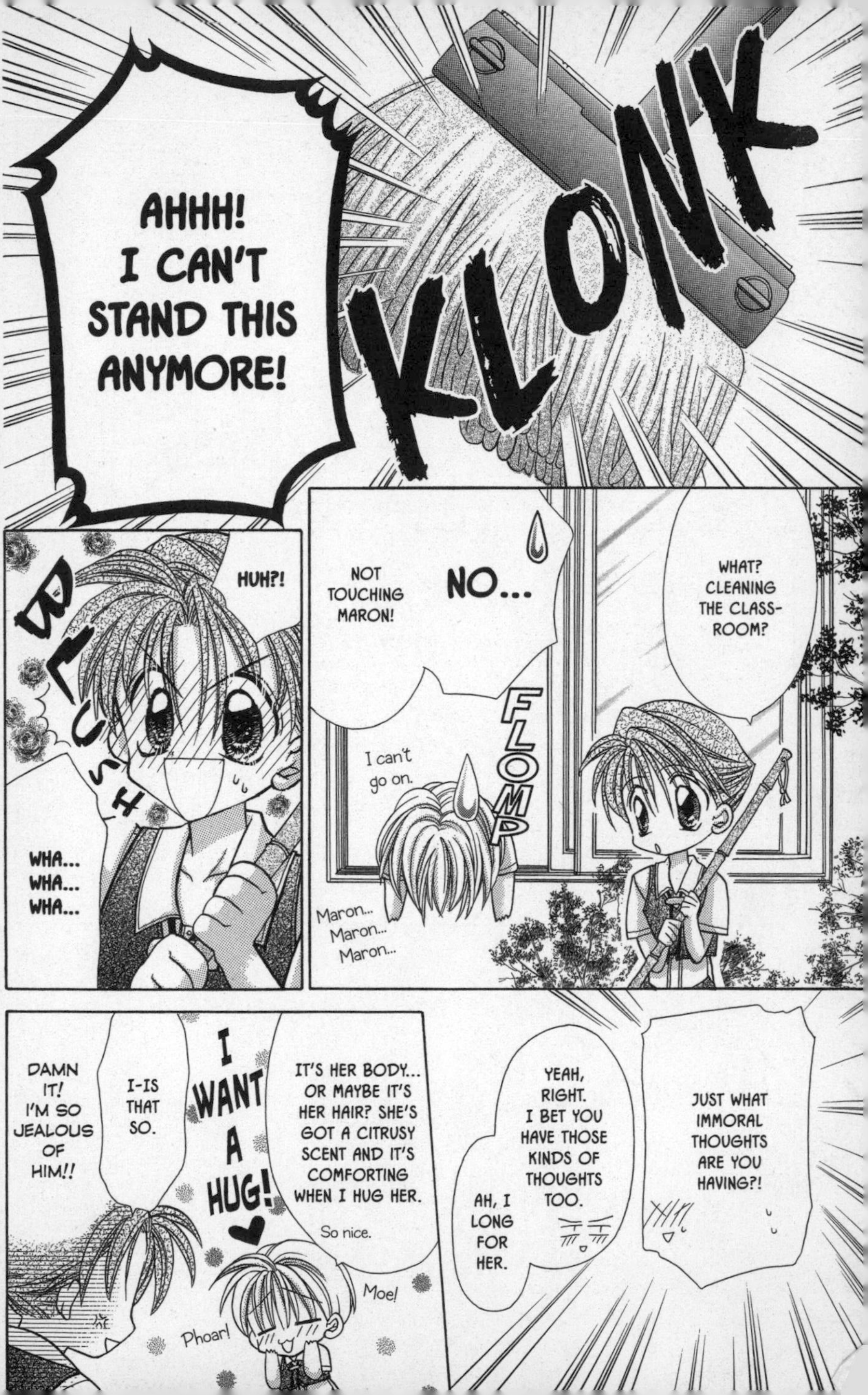
AHHH! I CAN'T STAND THIS ANYMORE!
KLONK
WHAT? CLEANING THE CLASS-ROOM?
NO...
NOT TOUCHING MARON!
FLOMP
I can't go on.
Maron... Maron... Maron...
HUH?!
BLUSH
WHA... WHA... WHA...
JUST WHAT IMMORAL THOUGHTS ARE YOU HAVING?!
YEAH, RIGHT. I BET YOU HAVE THOSE KINDS OF THOUGHTS TOO.
AH, I LONG FOR HER.
IT'S HER BODY... OR MAYBE IT'S HER HAIR? SHE'S GOT A CITRUSY SCENT AND IT'S COMFORTING WHEN I HUG HER.
So nice.
Moe!
I WANT A HUG!
I-IS THAT SO.
DAMN IT! I'M SO JEALOUS OF HIM!!
Phoar!

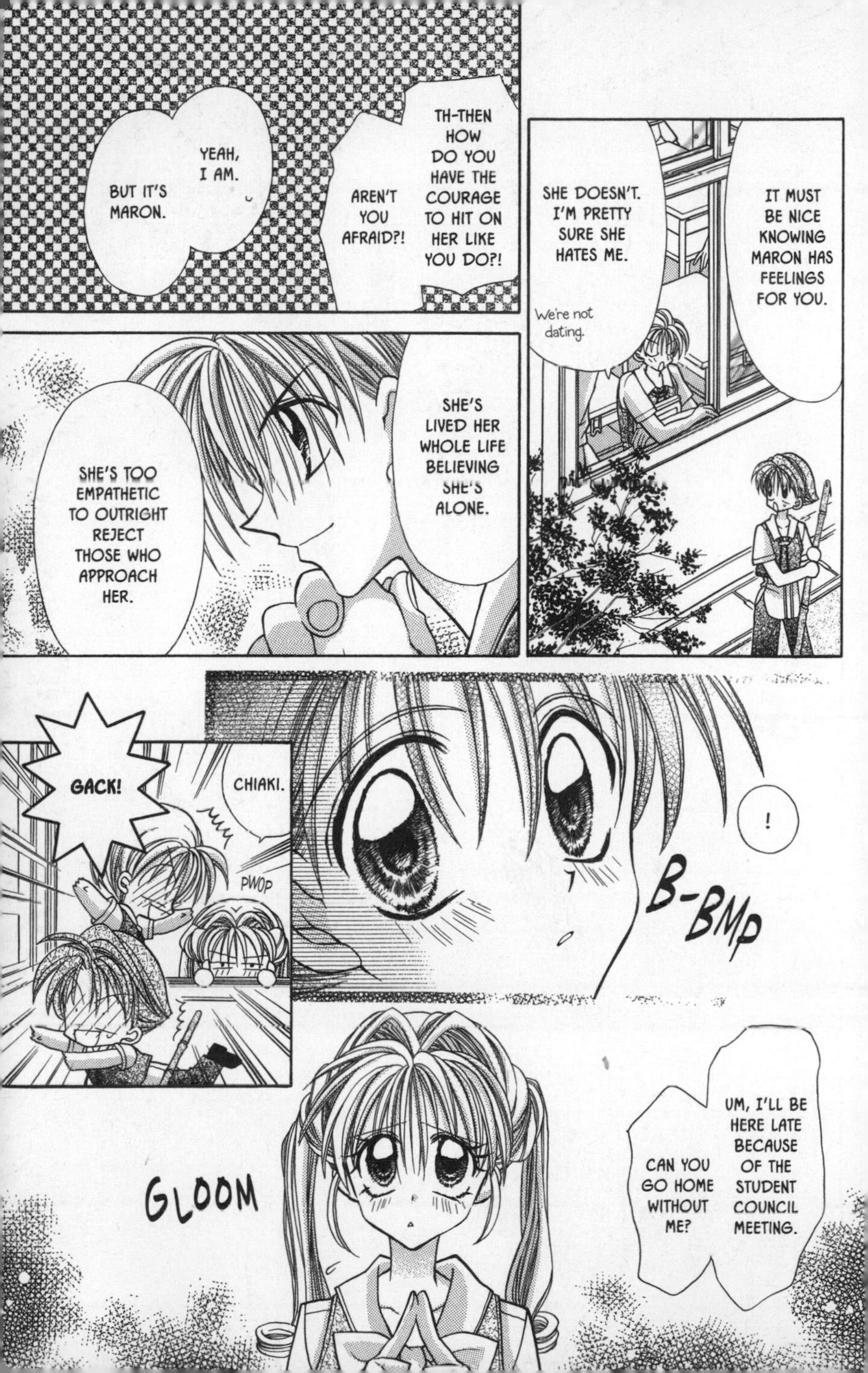
IT MUST BE NICE KNOWING MARON HAS FEELINGS FOR YOU.
SHE DOESN'T. I'M PRETTY SURE SHE HATES ME.
We're not dating.
TH-THEN HOW DO YOU HAVE THE COURAGE TO HIT ON HER LIKE YOU DO?!
AREN'T YOU AFRAID?!
YEAH, I AM.
BUT IT'S MARON.
SHE'S LIVED HER WHOLE LIFE BELIEVING SHE'S ALONE.
SHE'S TOO EMPATHETIC TO OUTRIGHT REJECT THOSE WHO APPROACH HER.
!
B-BMP
CHIAKI.
GACK!
PWOP
UM, I'LL BE HERE LATE BECAUSE OF THE STUDENT COUNCIL MEETING.
CAN YOU GO HOME WITHOUT ME?
GLOOM

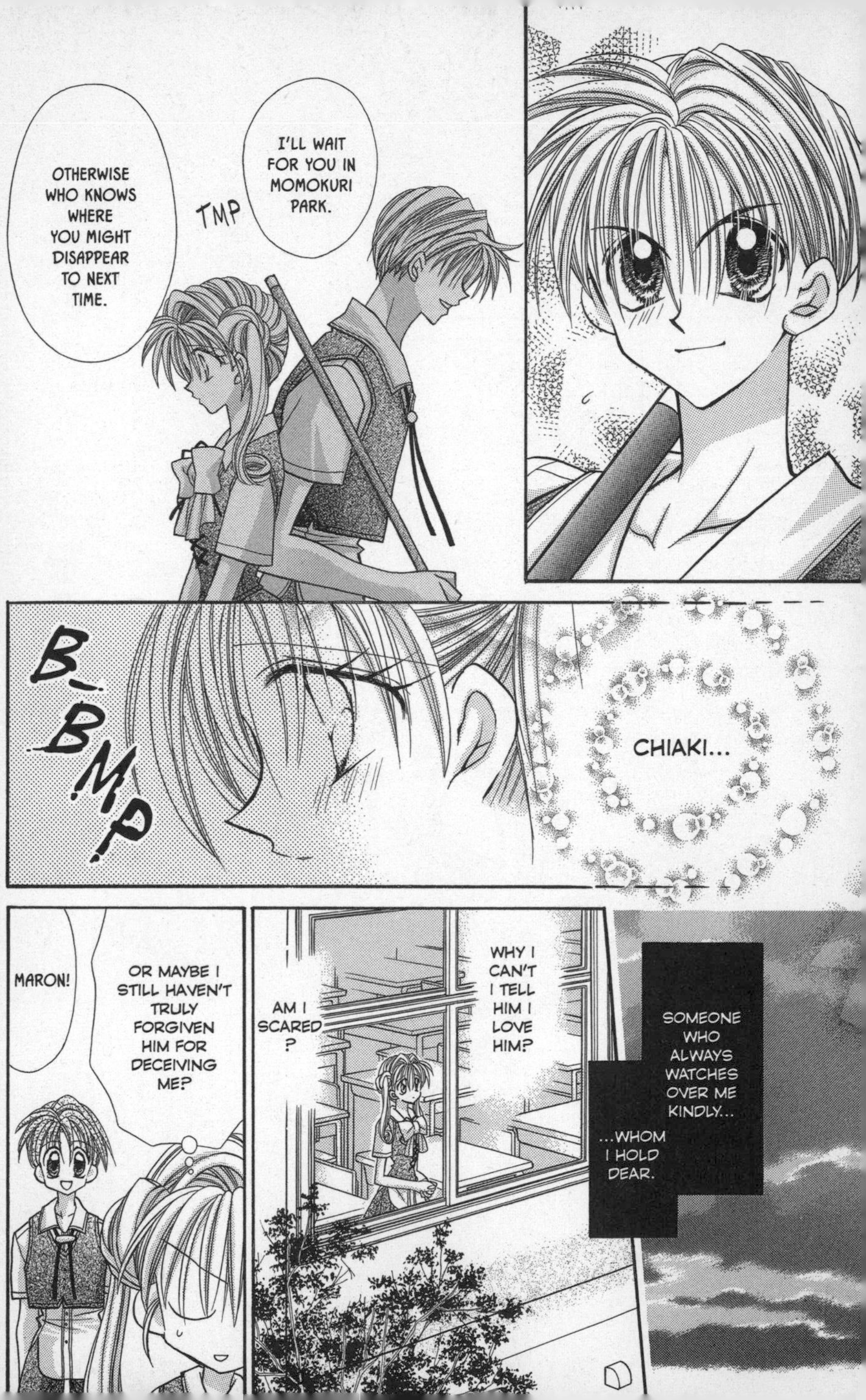
I'LL WAIT FOR YOU IN MOMOKURI PARK.
TMP
OTHERWISE WHO KNOWS WHERE YOU MIGHT DISAPPEAR TO NEXT TIME.
CHIAKI...
B-BMP
SOMEONE WHO ALWAYS WATCHES OVER ME KINDLY...
...WHOM I HOLD DEAR.
WHY I CAN'T I TELL HIM I LOVE HIM?
AM I SCARED?
OR MAYBE I STILL HAVEN'T TRULY FORGIVEN HIM FOR DECEIVING ME?
MARON!

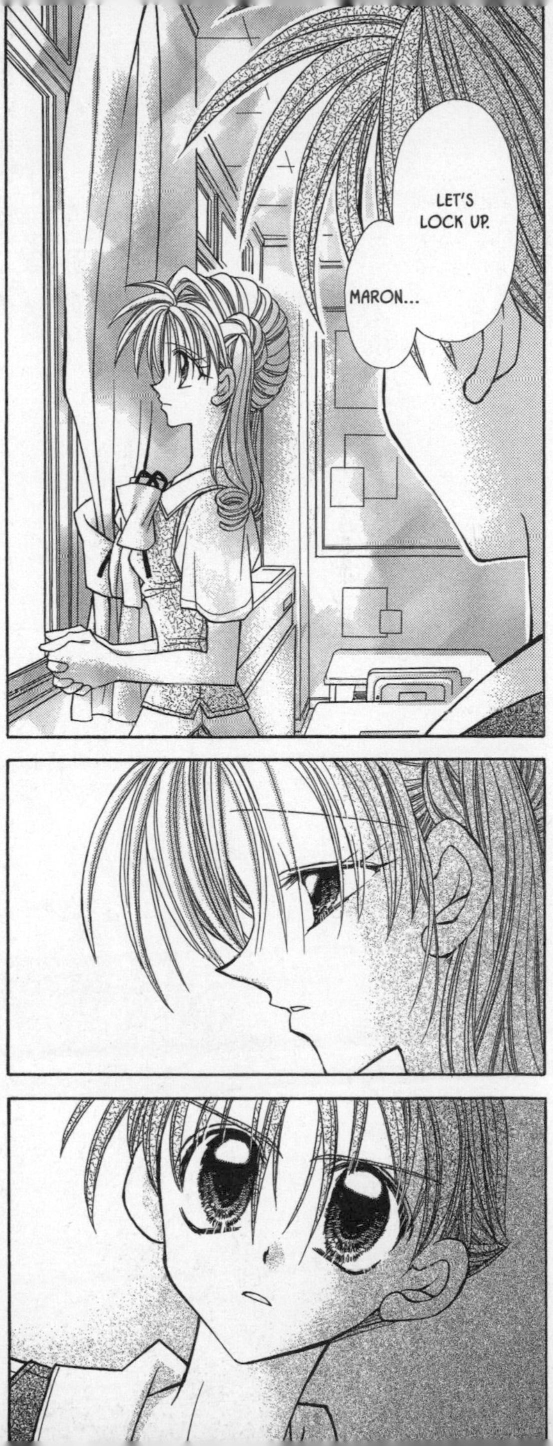
LET'S LOCK UP.
MARON...

PHANTOM THIEF JEANNE

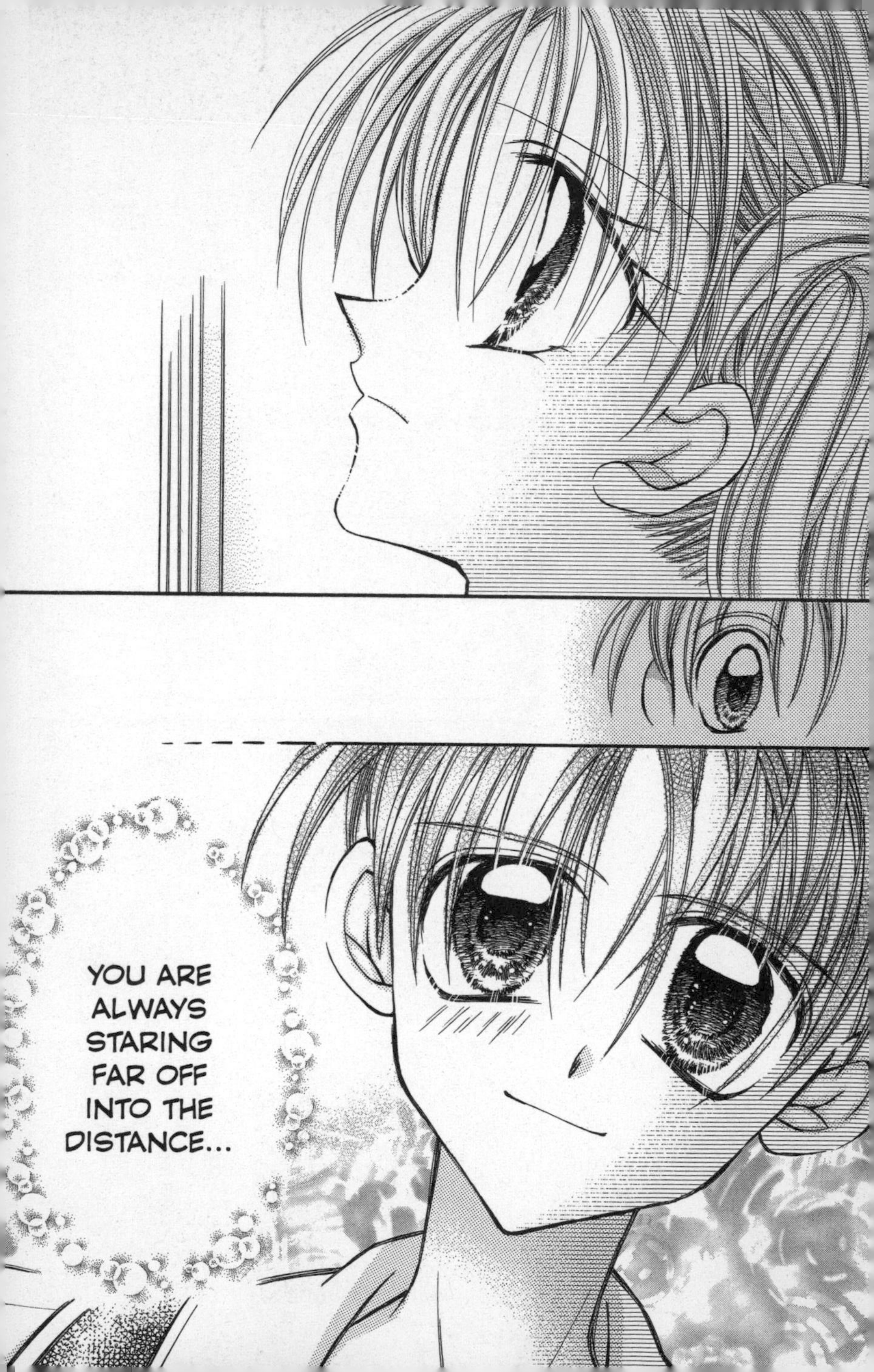
YOU ARE ALWAYS STARING FAR OFF INTO THE DISTANCE...

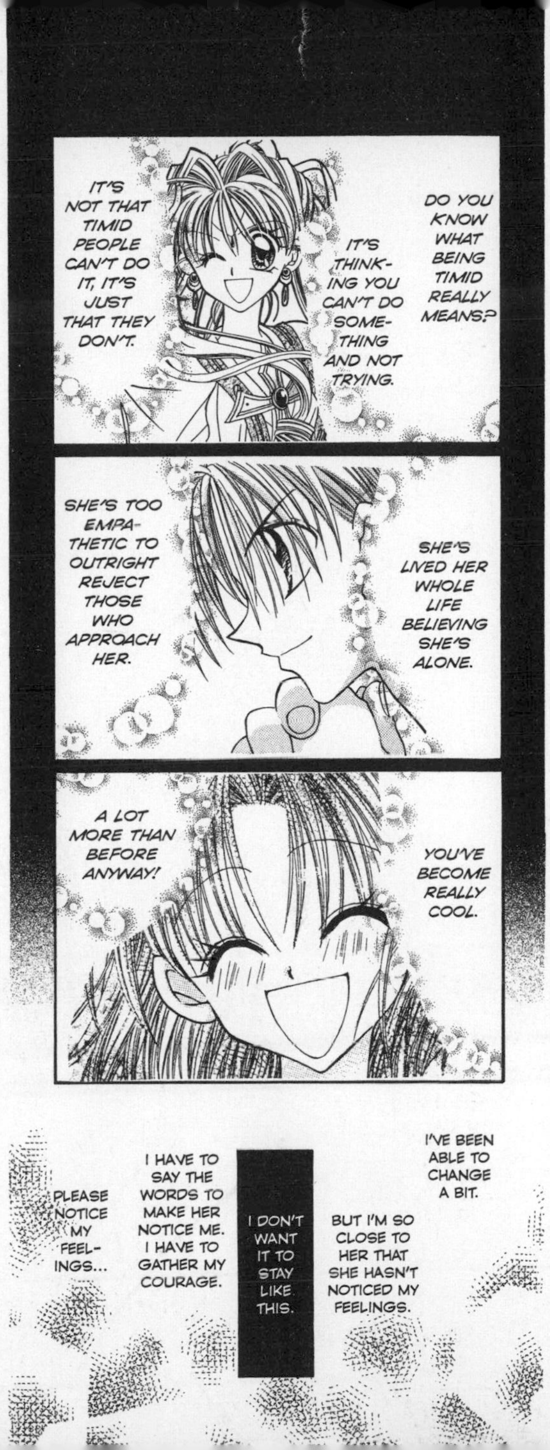
DO YOU KNOW WHAT BEING TIMID REALLY MEANS?
IT'S THINK-ING YOU CAN'T DO SOME-THING AND NOT TRYING.
IT'S NOT THAT TIMID PEOPLE CAN'T DO IT, IT'S JUST THAT THEY DON'T.
SHE'S LIVED HER WHOLE LIFE BELIEVING SHE'S ALONE.
SHE'S TOO EMPA-THETIC TO OUTRIGHT REJECT THOSE WHO APPROACH HER.
YOU'VE BECOME REALLY COOL.
A LOT MORE THAN BEFORE ANYWAY!
I'VE BEEN ABLE TO CHANGE A BIT.
BUT I'M SO CLOSE TO HER THAT SHE HASN'T NOTICED MY FEELINGS.
I DON'T WANT IT TO STAY LIKE THIS.
I HAVE TO SAY THE WORDS TO MAKE HER NOTICE ME. I HAVE TO GATHER MY COURAGE.
PLEASE NOTICE MY FEEL-INGS...

PHANTOM
THIEF
JEANNE

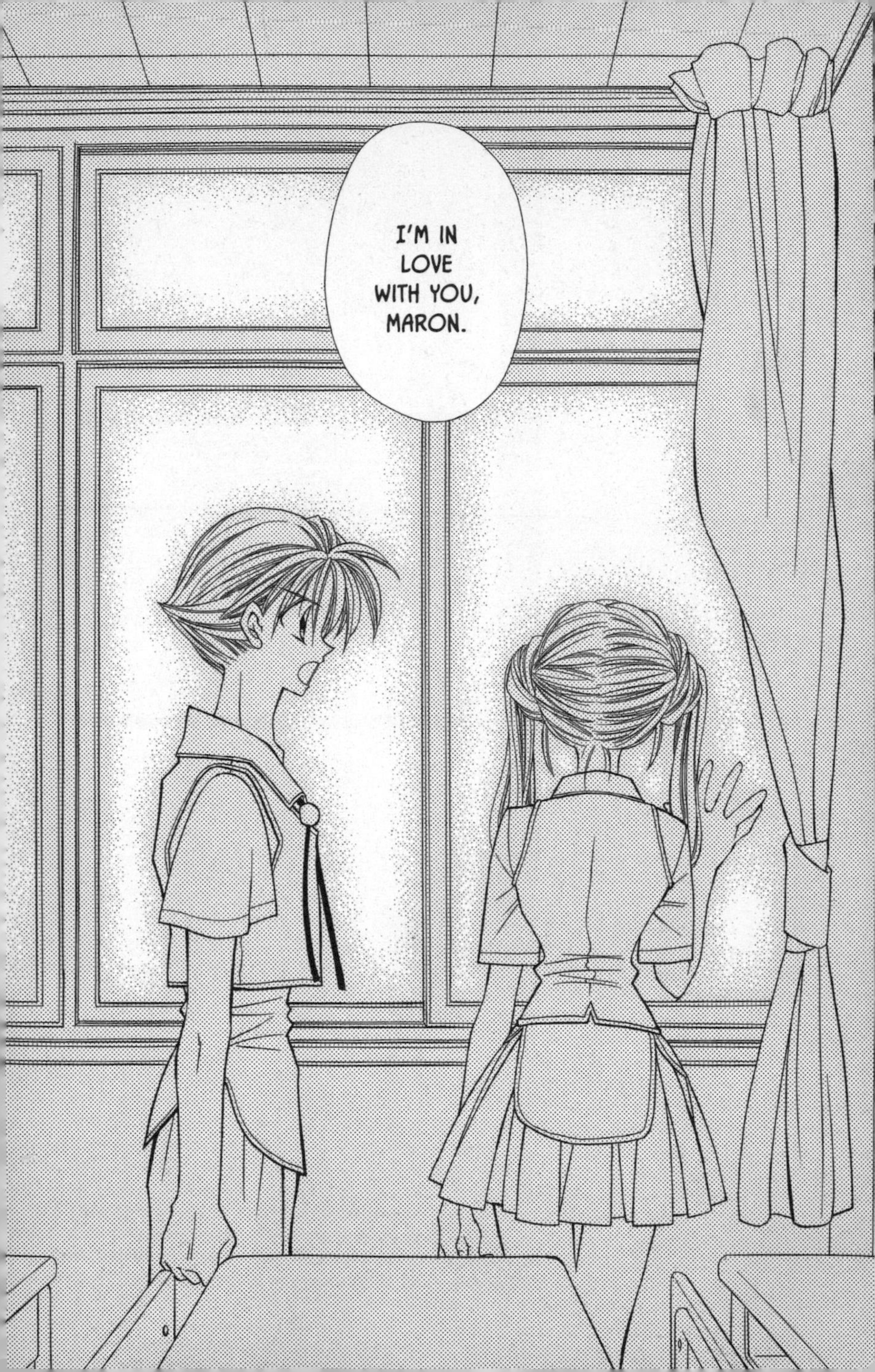
I'M IN LOVE WITH YOU, MARON.

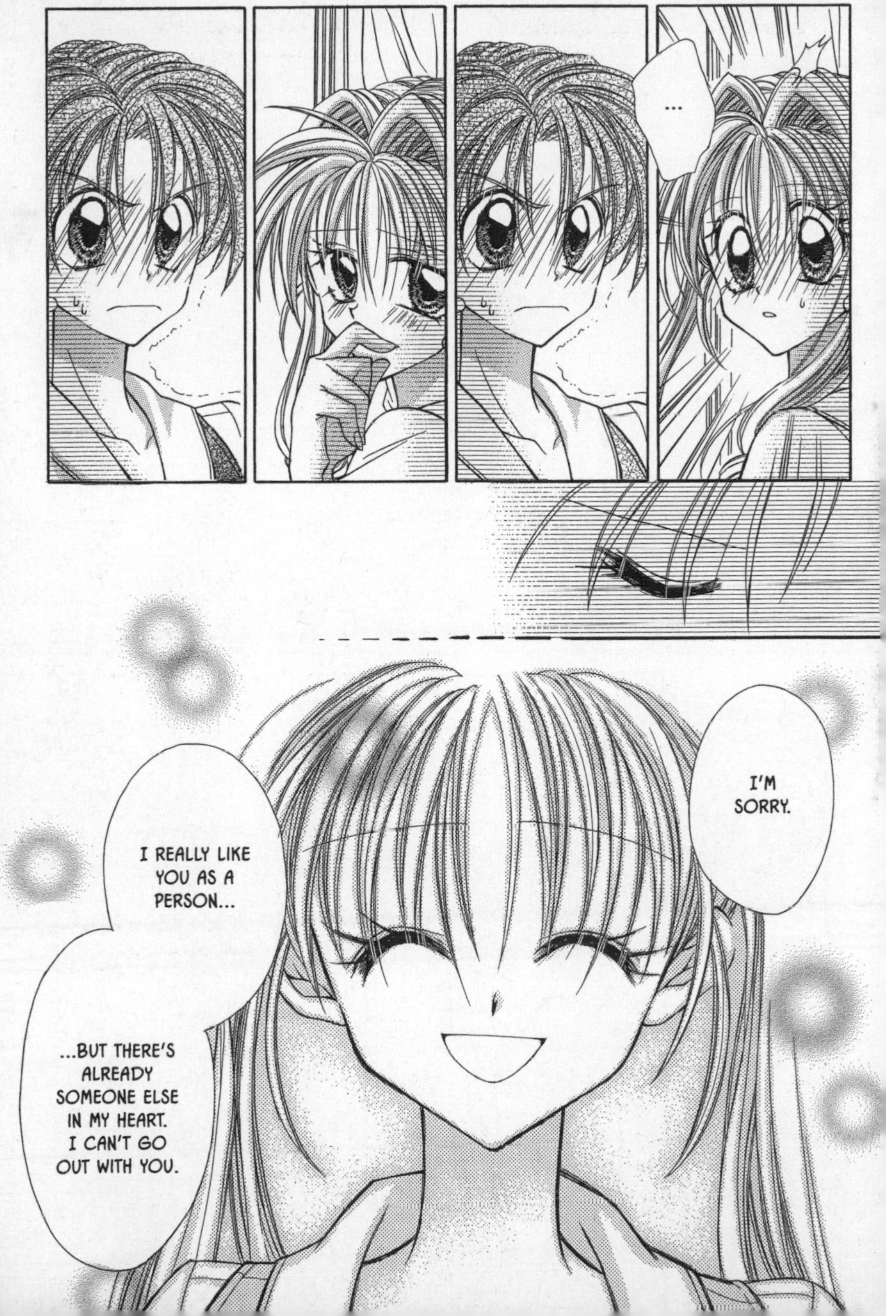
...
I'M SORRY.
I REALLY LIKE YOU AS A PERSON...
...BUT THERE'S ALREADY SOMEONE ELSE IN MY HEART. I CAN'T GO OUT WITH YOU.

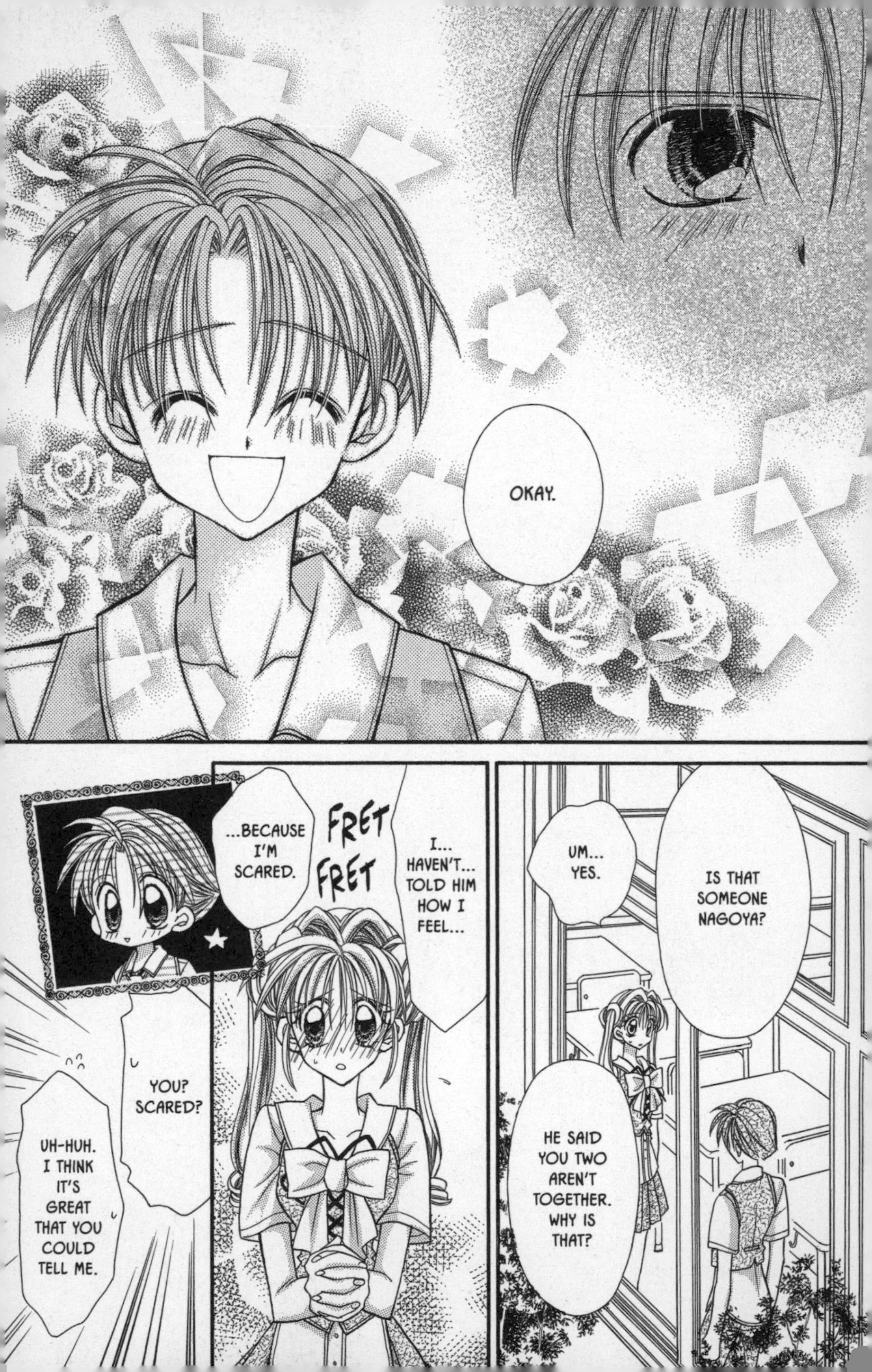
OKAY.
IS THAT SOMEONE NAGOYA?
UM... YES.
HE SAID YOU TWO AREN'T TOGETHER. WHY IS THAT?
I... HAVEN'T... TOLD HIM HOW I FEEL...
FRET FRET
...BECAUSE I'M SCARED.
YOU? SCARED?
UH-HUH. I THINK IT'S GREAT THAT YOU COULD TELL ME.

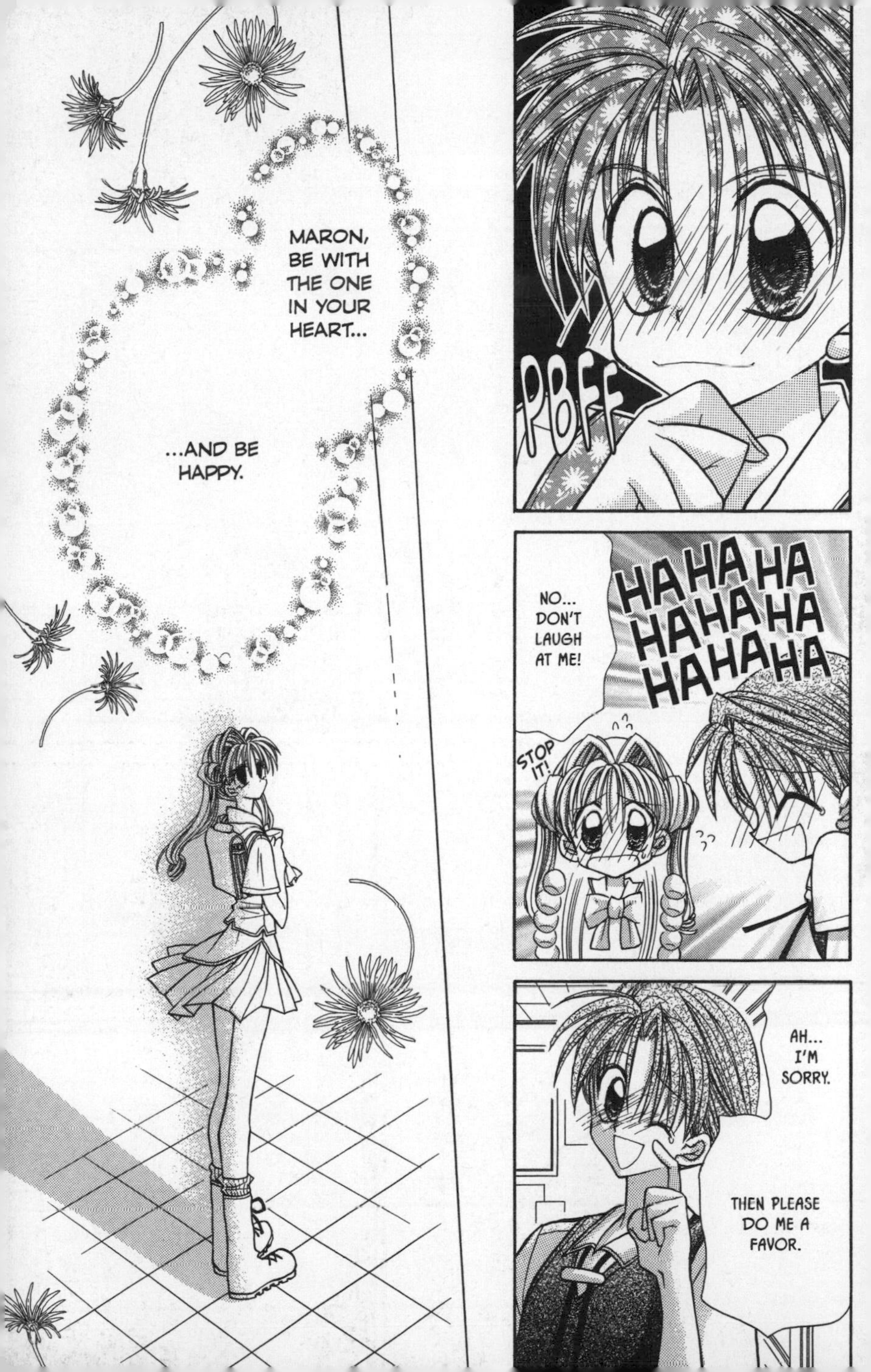
PBFF
HAHA HA HAHA HA HAHAHA
NO... DON'T LAUGH AT ME!
STOP IT!
AH... I'M SORRY.
THEN PLEASE DO ME A FAVOR.
MARON, BE WITH THE ONE IN YOUR HEART...
...AND BE HAPPY.

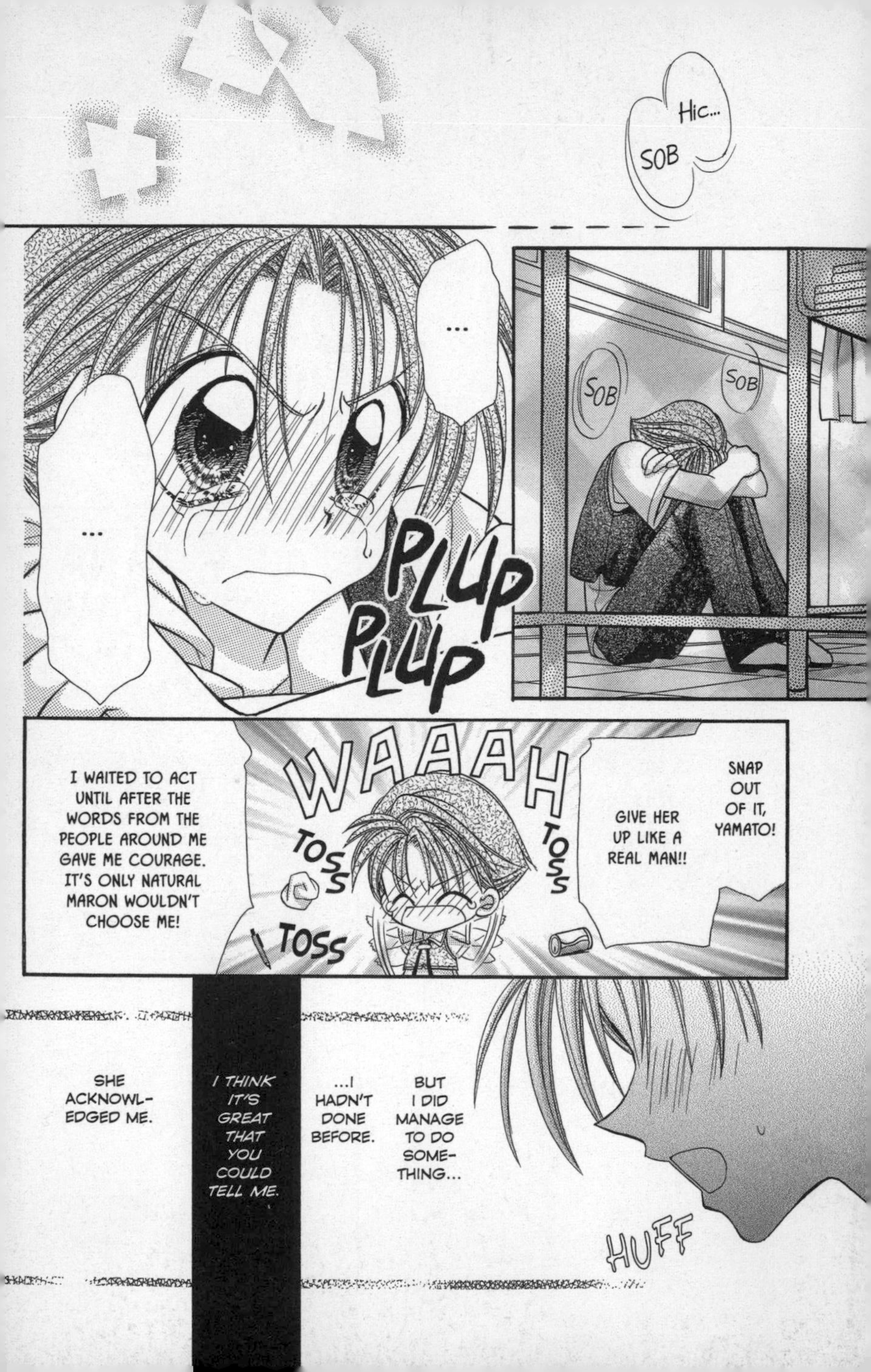
Hic... SOB
SOB
SOB
...
...
PLUP PLUP
SNAP OUT OF IT, YAMATO!
GIVE HER UP LIKE A REAL MAN!!
WAAAH
TOSS
TOSS
TOSS
I WAITED TO ACT UNTIL AFTER THE WORDS FROM THE PEOPLE AROUND ME GAVE ME COURAGE. IT'S ONLY NATURAL MARON WOULDN'T CHOOSE ME!
HUFF
BUT I DID MANAGE TO DO SOME-THING...
...I HADN'T DONE BEFORE.
I THINK IT'S GREAT THAT YOU COULD TELL ME.
SHE ACKNOWL-EDGED ME.

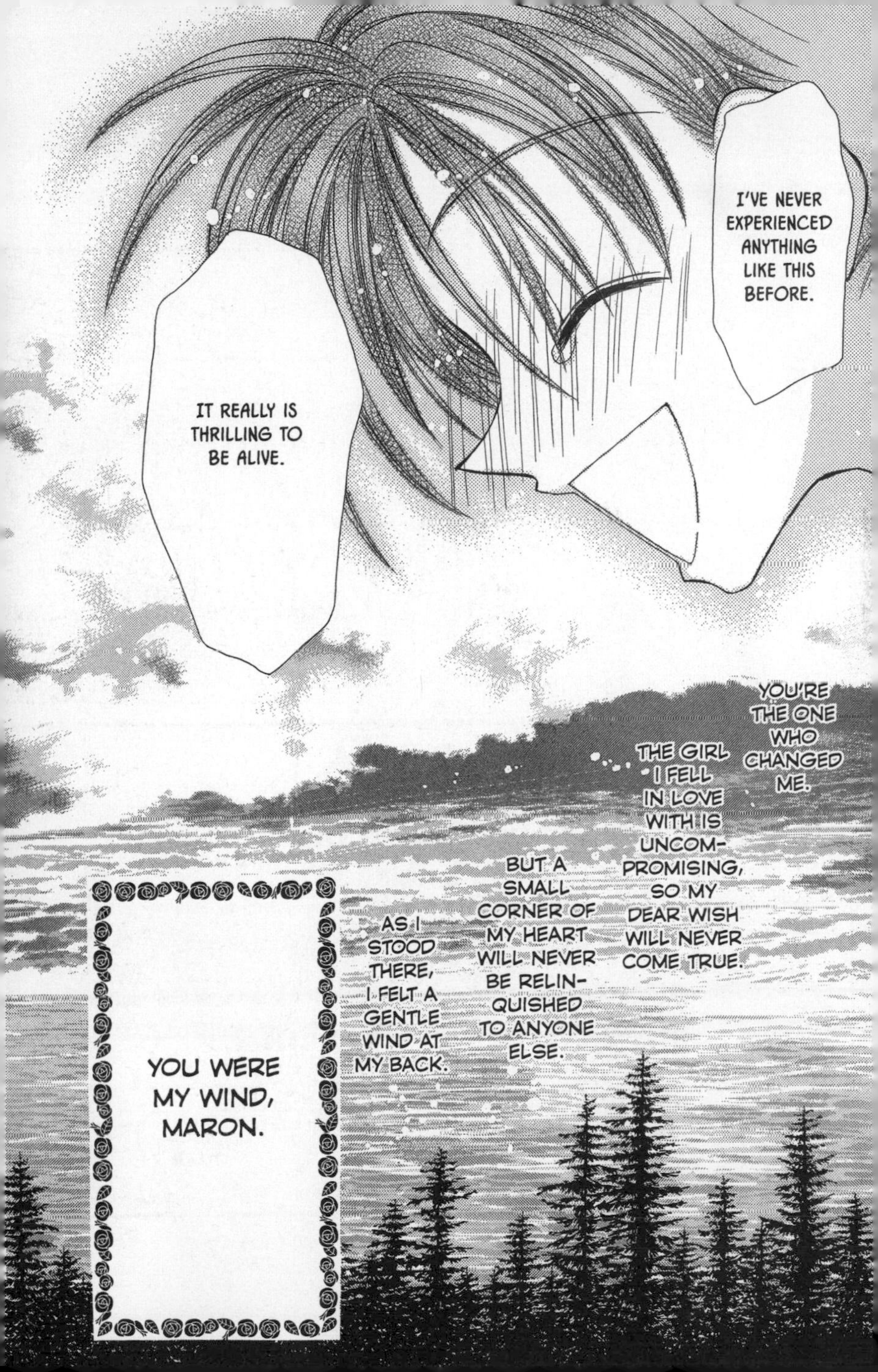
I'VE NEVER EXPERIENCED ANYTHING LIKE THIS BEFORE.
IT REALLY IS THRILLING TO BE ALIVE.
YOU'RE THE ONE WHO CHANGED ME.
THE GIRL I FELL IN LOVE WITH IS UNCOM-PROMISING, SO MY DEAR WISH WILL NEVER COME TRUE.
BUT A SMALL CORNER OF MY HEART WILL NEVER BE RELIN-QUISHED TO ANYONE ELSE.
AS I STOOD THERE, I FELT A GENTLE WIND AT MY BACK.
YOU WERE MY WIND, MARON.

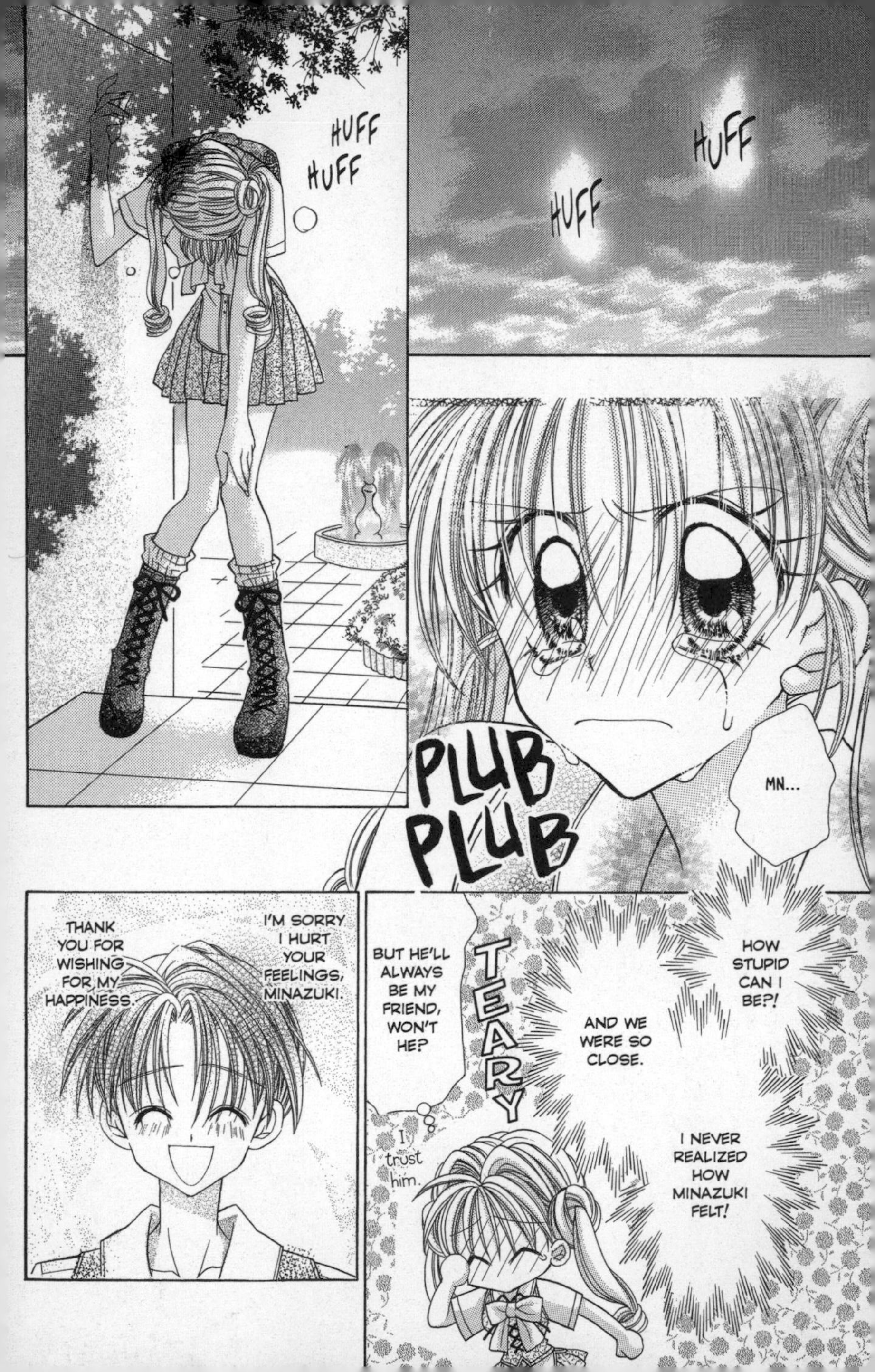
HUFF
HUFF
MN...
PLUB PLUB
HUFF
HUFF
HOW STUPID CAN I BE?!
AND WE WERE SO CLOSE.
BUT HE'LL ALWAYS BE MY FRIEND, WON'T HE?
TEARY
I NEVER REALIZED HOW MINAZUKI FELT!
I trust him.
I'M SORRY I HURT YOUR FEELINGS, MINAZUKI.
THANK YOU FOR WISHING FOR MY HAPPINESS.

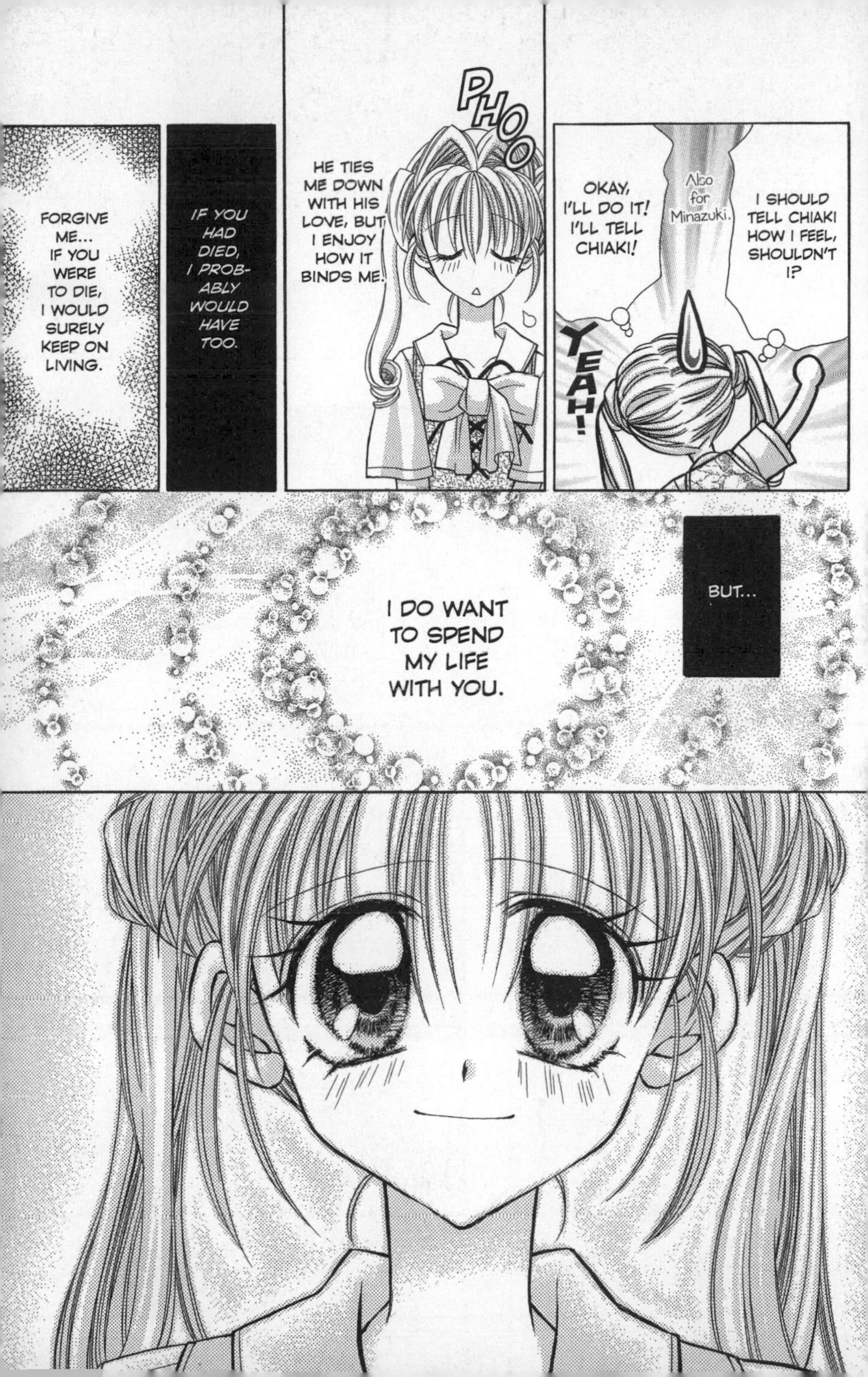
I SHOULD TELL CHIAKI HOW I FEEL, SHOULDN'T I?
Also for Minazuki.
OKAY, I'LL DO IT! I'LL TELL CHIAKI!
YEAH!
PHOO
HE TIES ME DOWN WITH HIS LOVE, BUT I ENJOY HOW IT BINDS ME.
IF YOU HAD DIED, I PROBABLY WOULD HAVE TOO.
FORGIVE ME... IF YOU WERE TO DIE, I WOULD SURELY KEEP ON LIVING.
BUT...
I DO WANT TO SPEND MY LIFE WITH YOU.

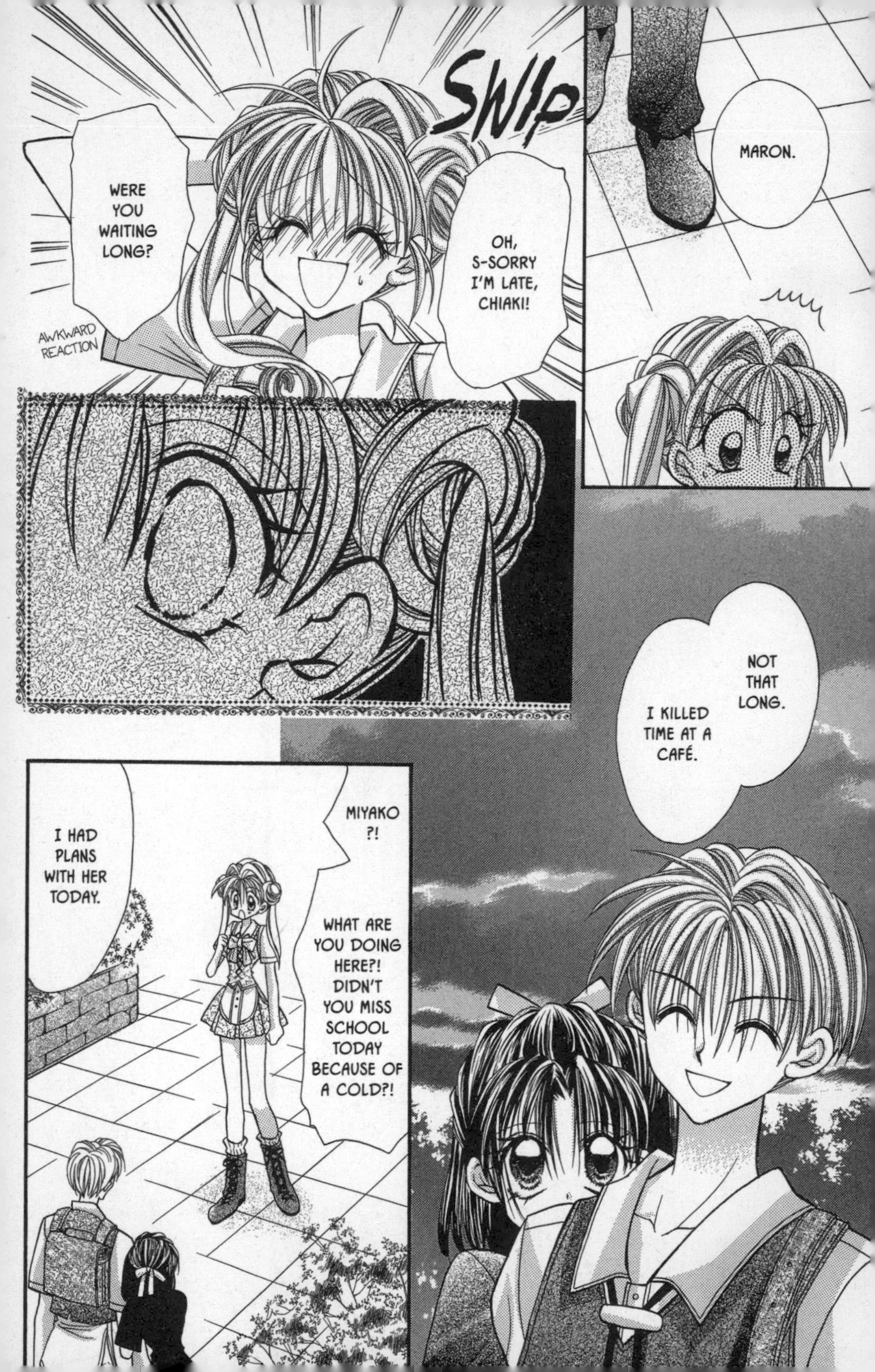
MARON.
SWIP
OH, S-SORRY I'M LATE, CHIAKI!
WERE YOU WAITING LONG?
AWKWARD REACTION
NOT THAT LONG.
I KILLED TIME AT A CAFÉ.
MIYAKO?!
WHAT ARE YOU DOING HERE?! DIDN'T YOU MISS SCHOOL TODAY BECAUSE OF A COLD?!
I HAD PLANS WITH HER TODAY.

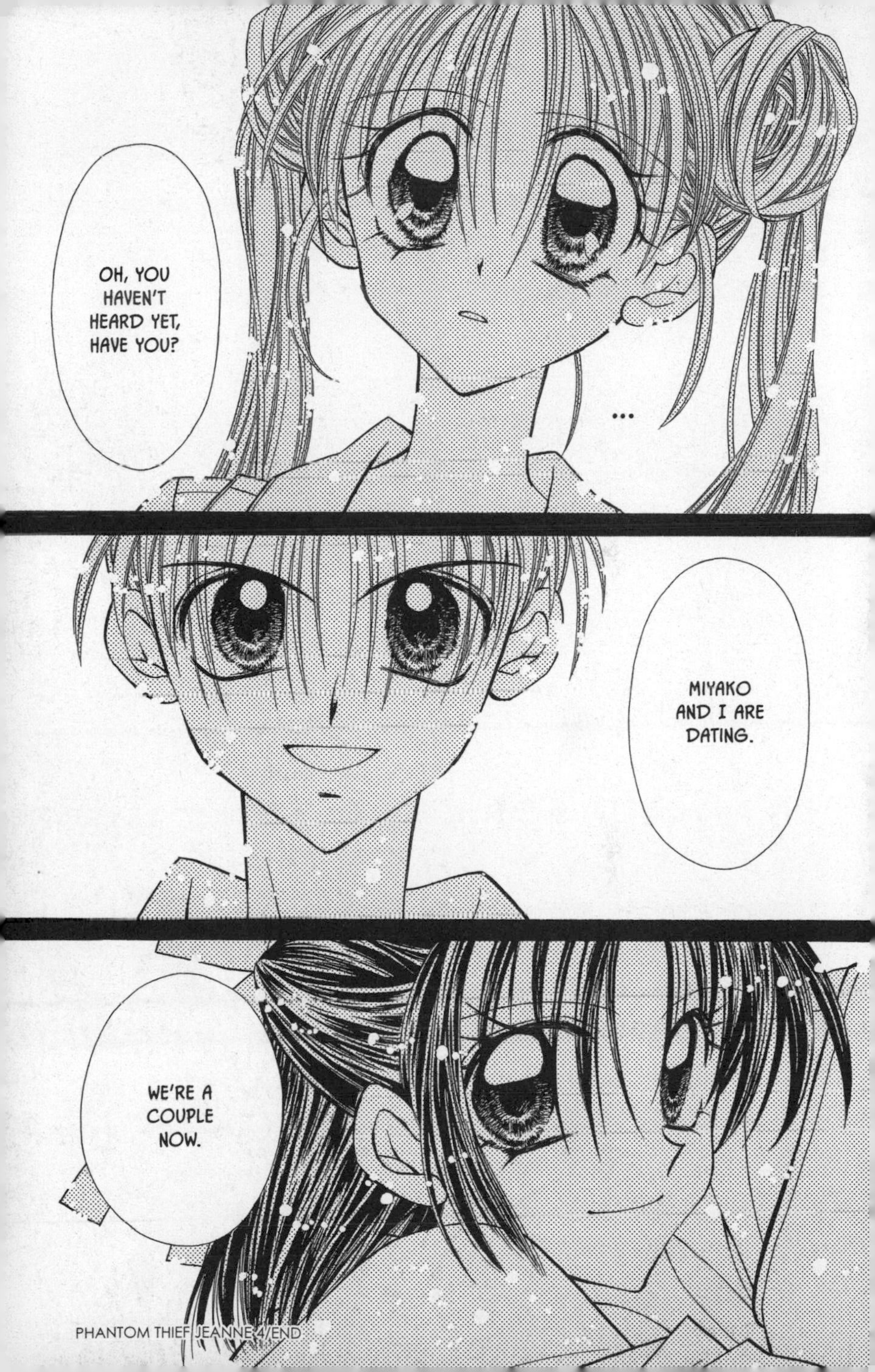
...
OH, YOU HAVEN'T HEARD YET, HAVE YOU?
MIYAKO AND I ARE DATING.
WE'RE A COUPLE NOW.
PHANTOM THIEF JEANNE 4/END

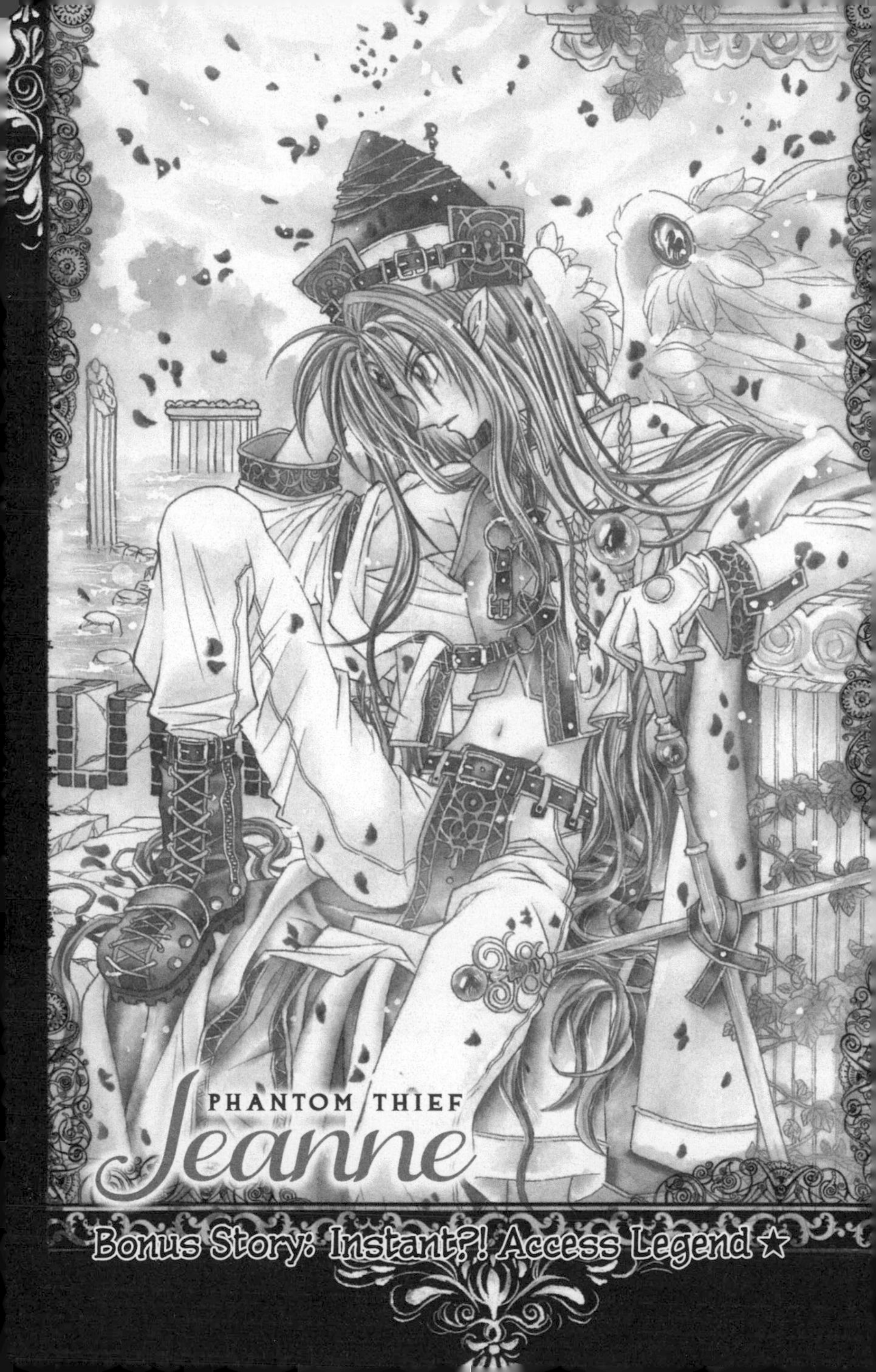
PHANTOM THIEF
Jeanne
Bonus Story: Instant?! Access Legend ★

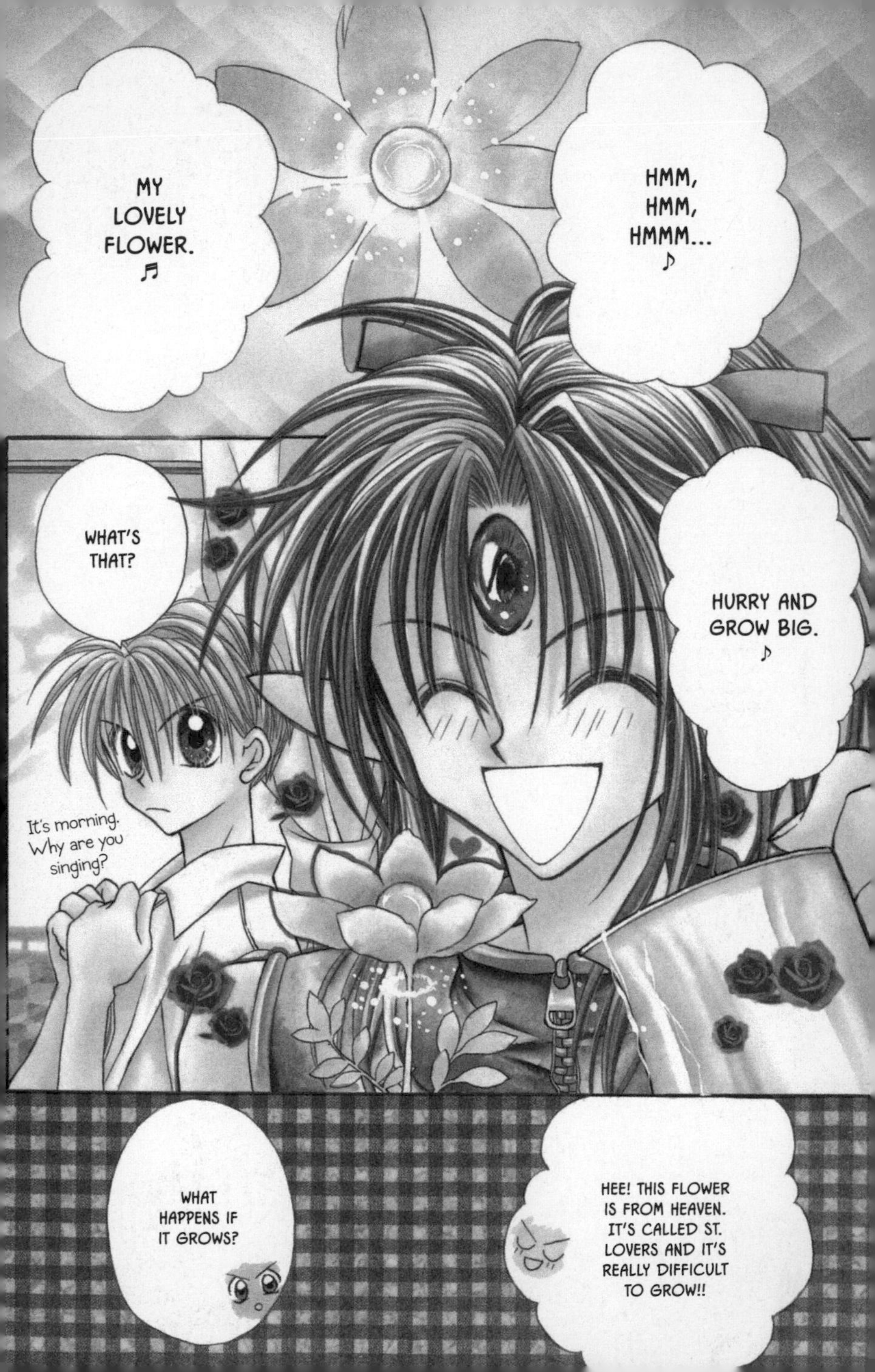
HMM, HMM, HMMM... ♪
MY LOVELY FLOWER. ♬
HURRY AND GROW BIG. ♪
WHAT'S THAT?
It's morning. Why are you singing?
HEE! THIS FLOWER IS FROM HEAVEN. IT'S CALLED ST. LOVERS AND IT'S REALLY DIFFICULT TO GROW!!
WHAT HAPPENS IF IT GROWS?

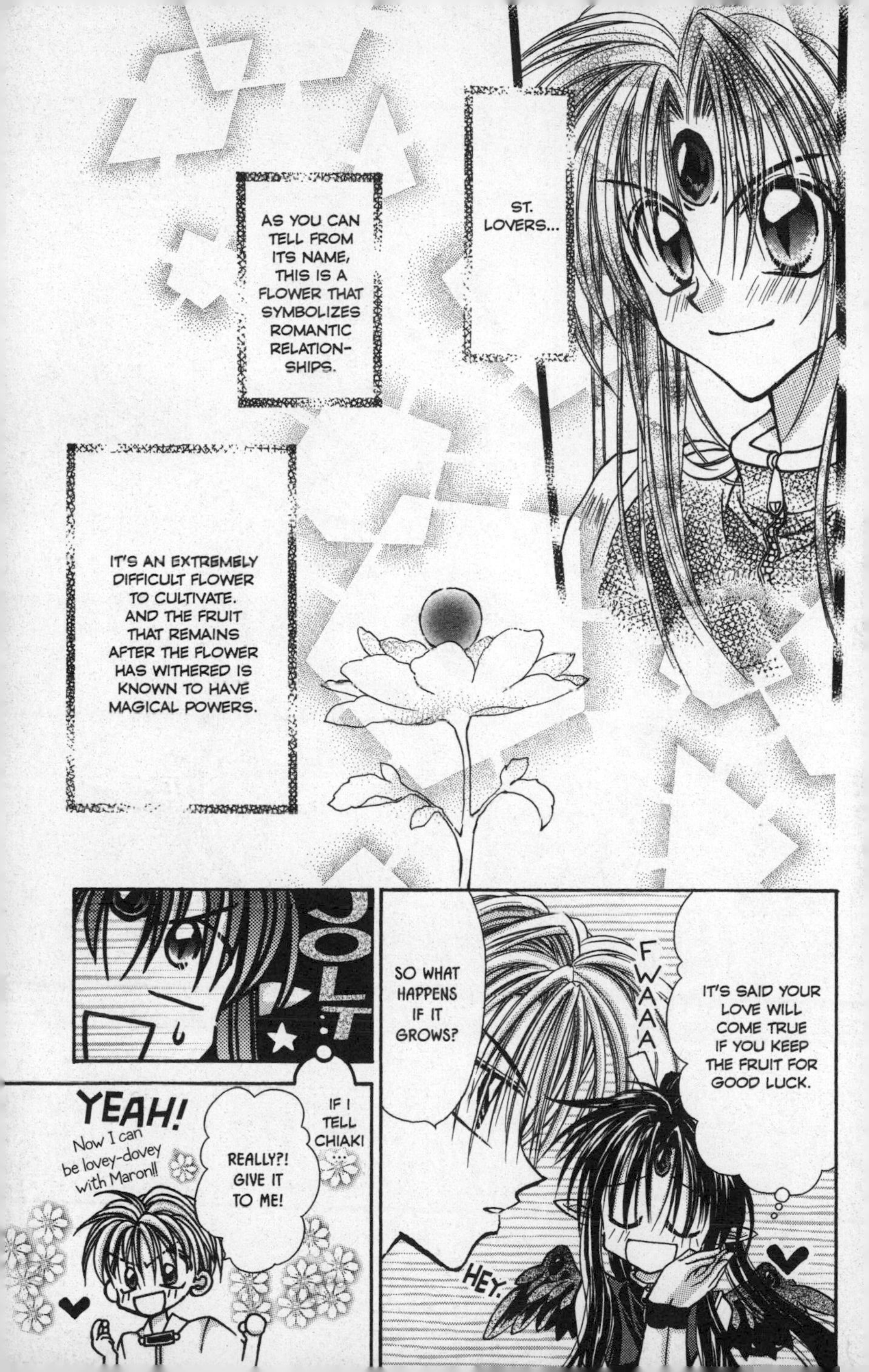
ST. LOVERS...
AS YOU CAN TELL FROM ITS NAME, THIS IS A FLOWER THAT SYMBOLIZES ROMANTIC RELATION-SHIPS.
IT'S AN EXTREMELY DIFFICULT FLOWER TO CULTIVATE. AND THE FRUIT THAT REMAINS AFTER THE FLOWER HAS WITHERED IS KNOWN TO HAVE MAGICAL POWERS.
IT'S SAID YOUR LOVE WILL COME TRUE IF YOU KEEP THE FRUIT FOR GOOD LUCK.
FWAAA
SO WHAT HAPPENS IF IT GROWS?
HEY.
JOLT
IF I TELL CHIAKI
REALLY?! GIVE IT TO ME!
YEAH!
Now I can be lovey-dovey with Maron!!

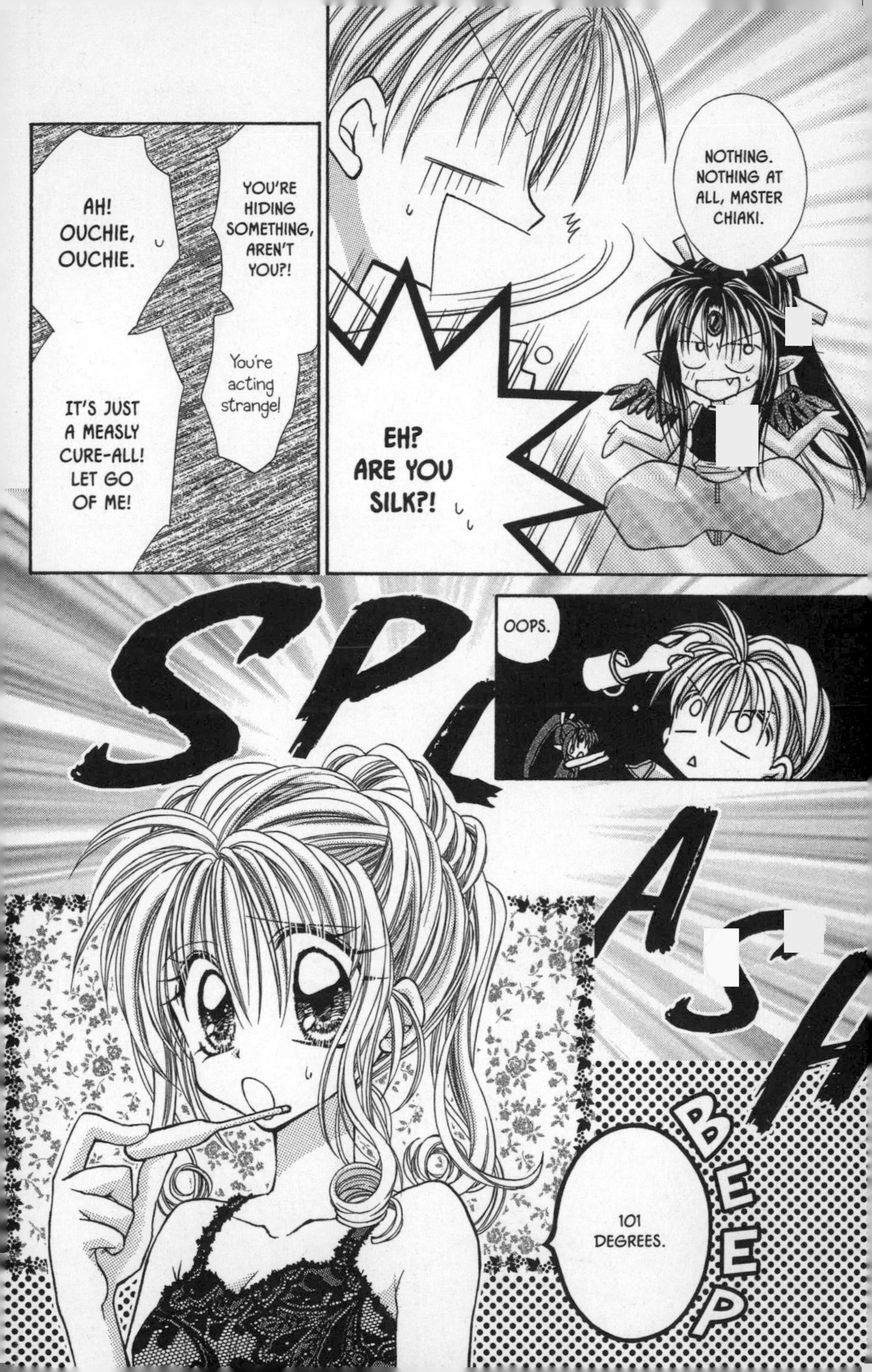
NOTHING. NOTHING AT ALL, MASTER CHIAKI.
EH? ARE YOU SILK?!
YOU'RE HIDING SOMETHING, AREN'T YOU?!
AH! OUCHIE, OUCHIE.
You're acting strange!
IT'S JUST A MEASLY CURE-ALL! LET GO OF ME!
OOPS.
SPLASH
BEEP
101 DEGREES.

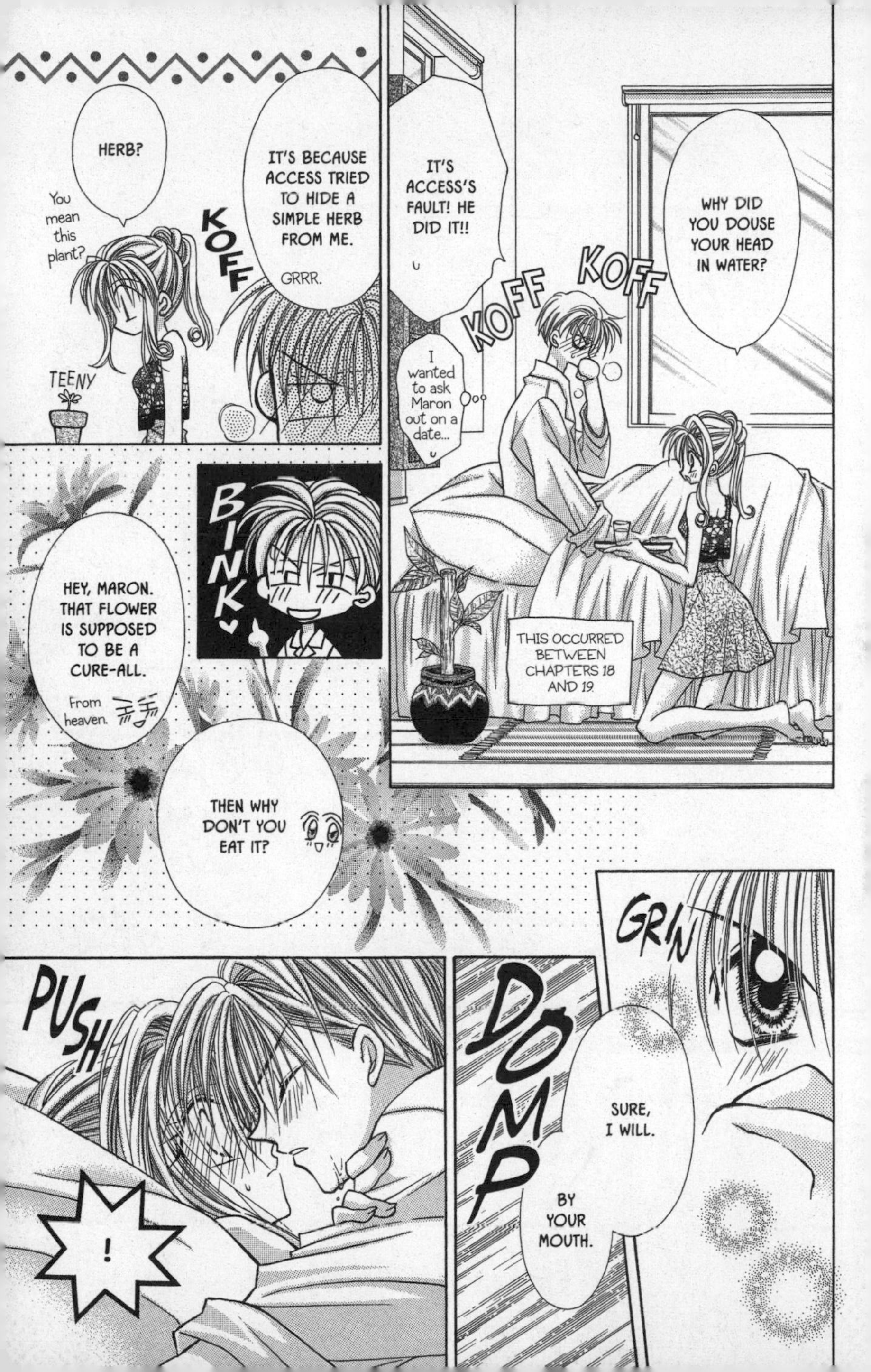
WHY DID YOU DOUSE YOUR HEAD IN WATER?
KOFF KOFF
KOFF
IT'S ACCESS'S FAULT! HE DID IT!!
I wanted to ask Maron out on a date...
THIS OCCURRED BETWEEN CHAPTERS 18 AND 19.
IT'S BECAUSE ACCESS TRIED TO HIDE A SIMPLE HERB FROM ME.
GRRR.
KOFF
HERB?
You mean this plant?
TEENY
BINK
HEY, MARON. THAT FLOWER IS SUPPOSED TO BE A CURE-ALL.
From heaven.
THEN WHY DON'T YOU EAT IT?
GRIN
SURE, I WILL.
DOMP
BY YOUR MOUTH.
PUSH
!

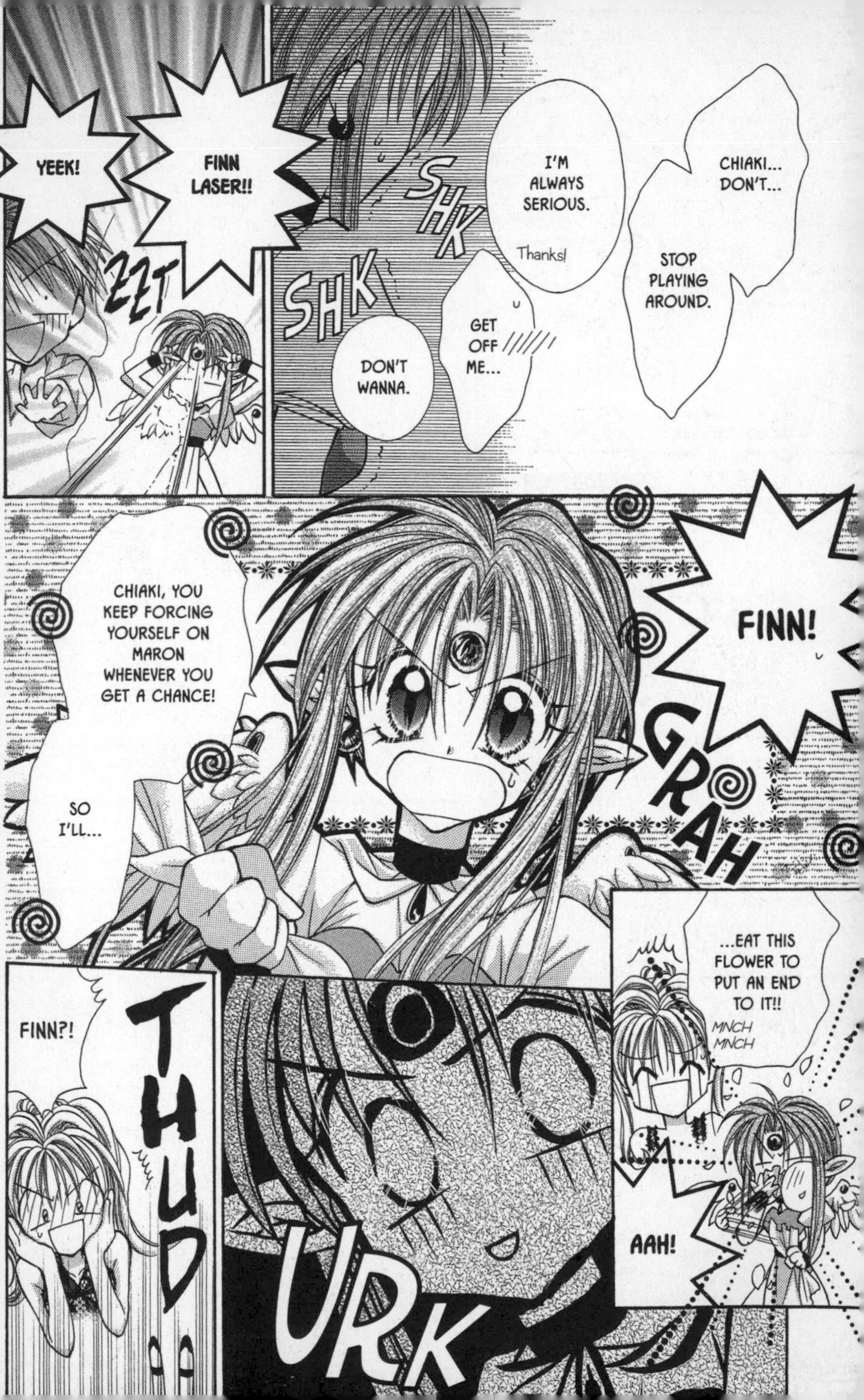
CHIAKI... DON'T...
STOP PLAYING AROUND.
I'M ALWAYS SERIOUS.
Thanks!
SHK
SHK
GET OFF ME...
DON'T WANNA.
FINN LASER!!
YEEK!
ZZZT
FINN!
GRAH
CHIAKI, YOU KEEP FORCING YOURSELF ON MARON WHENEVER YOU GET A CHANCE!
SO I'LL...
...EAT THIS FLOWER TO PUT AN END TO IT!!
MNCH MNCH
AAH!
URK
FINN?!
THUD

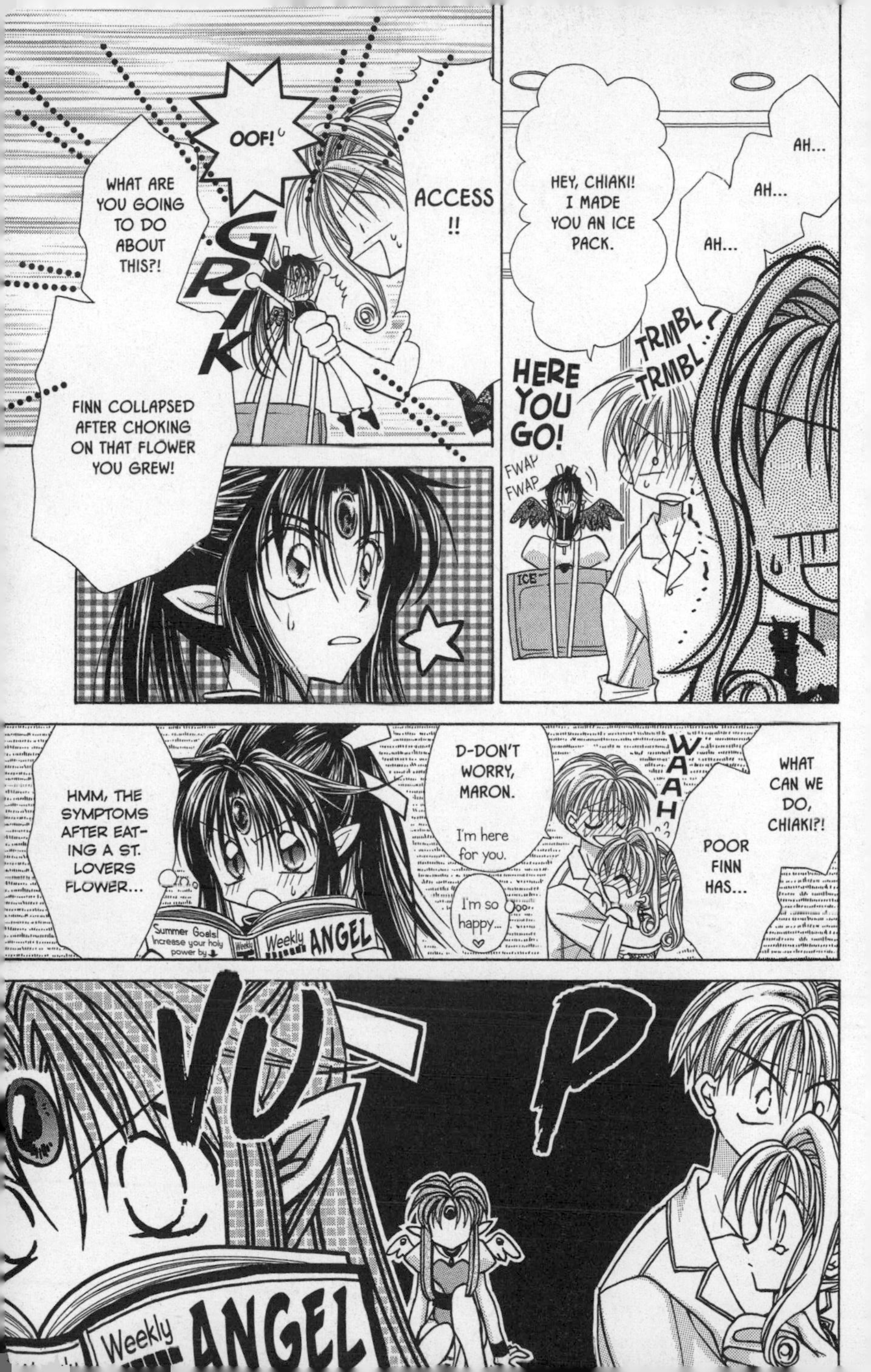
AH...
AH...
AH...
HEY, CHIAKI! I MADE YOU AN ICE PACK.
TRMBL TRMBL
HERE YOU GO!
FWAP FWAP
ICE
ACCESS !!
OOF!
WHAT ARE YOU GOING TO DO ABOUT THIS?!
GRIK
FINN COLLAPSED AFTER CHOKING ON THAT FLOWER YOU GREW!
WHAT CAN WE DO, CHIAKI?!
POOR FINN HAS...
WAAH
D-DON'T WORRY, MARON.
I'm here for you.
I'm so happy...
HMM, THE SYMPTOMS AFTER EATING A ST. LOVERS FLOWER...
Summer Goals! Increase your holy power by
Weekly ANGEL
VU-P
Weekly ANGEL

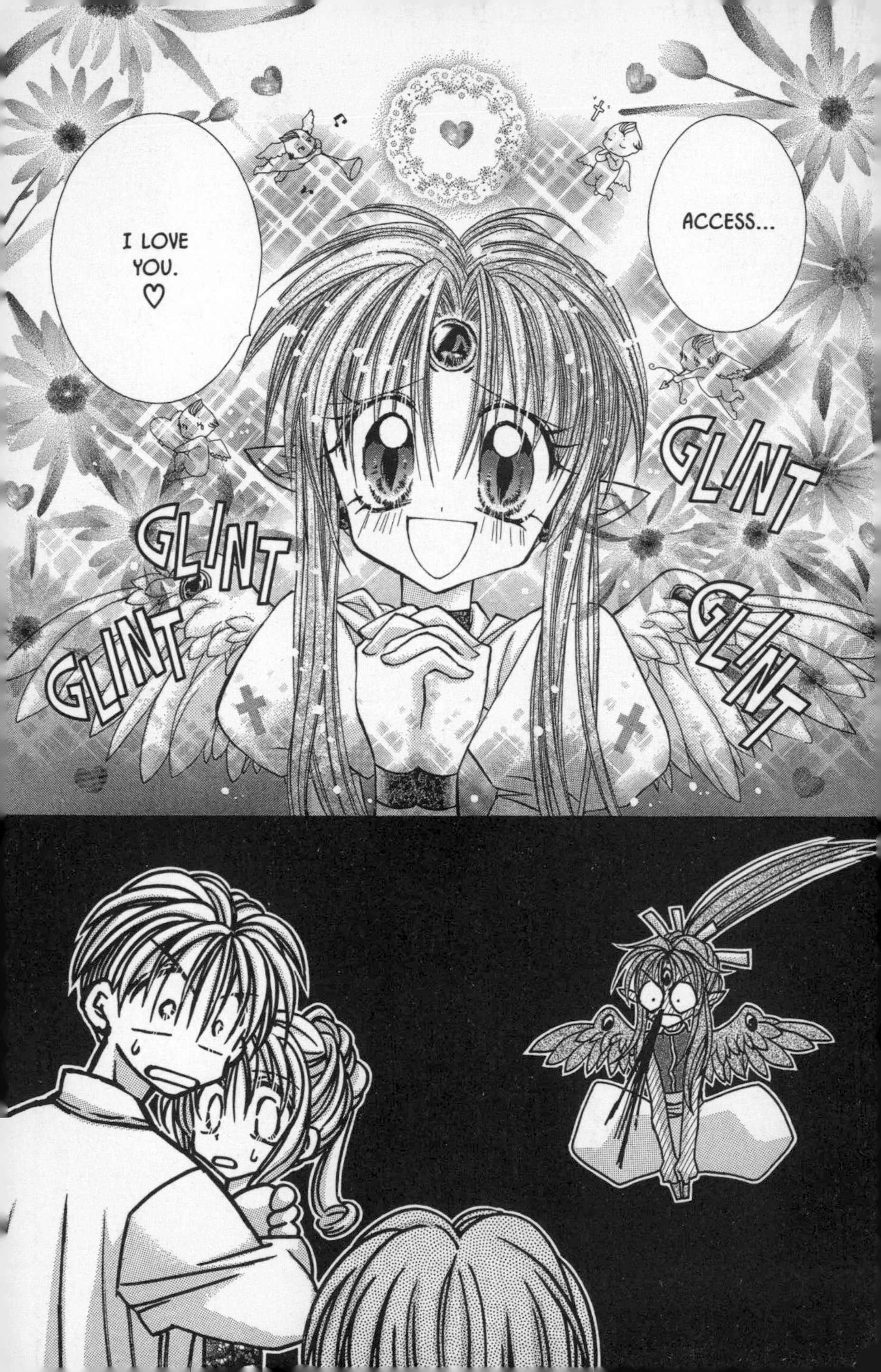
ACCESS...
I LOVE YOU. ♡
GLINT
GLINT
GLINT
GLINT

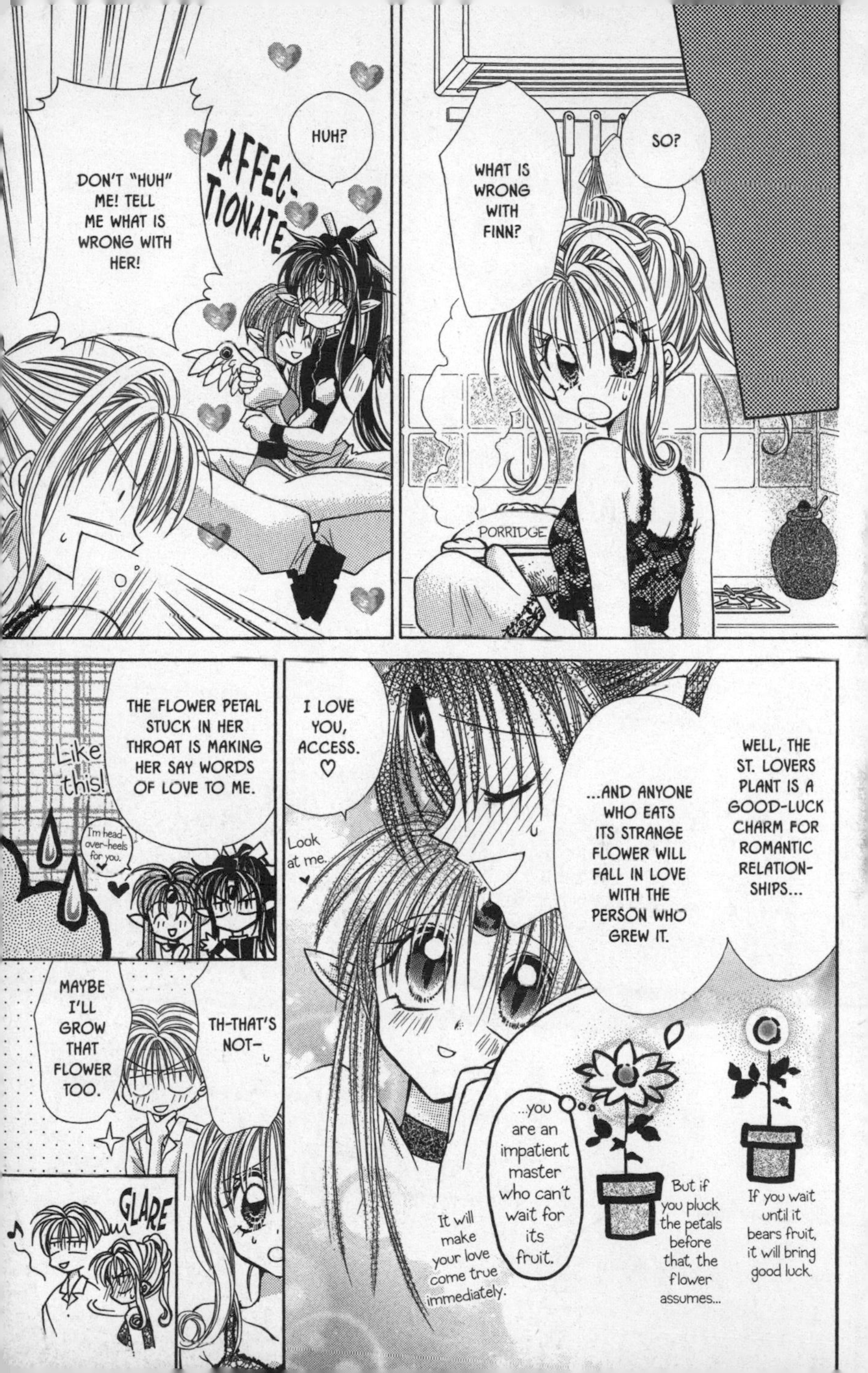
SO?
WHAT IS WRONG WITH FINN?
PORRIDGE
HUH?
DON'T "HUH" ME! TELL ME WHAT IS WRONG WITH HER!
AFFEC-TIONATE
WELL, THE ST. LOVERS PLANT IS A GOOD-LUCK CHARM FOR ROMANTIC RELATIONSHIPS...
...AND ANYONE WHO EATS ITS STRANGE FLOWER WILL FALL IN LOVE WITH THE PERSON WHO GREW IT.
I LOVE YOU, ACCESS. ♡
Look at me.
If you wait until it bears fruit, it will bring good luck.
But if you pluck the petals before that, the flower assumes...
...you are an impatient master who can't wait for its fruit.
It will make your love come true immediately.
THE FLOWER PETAL STUCK IN HER THROAT IS MAKING HER SAY WORDS OF LOVE TO ME.
Like this!
I'm head-over-heels for you.
TH-THAT'S NOT-
MAYBE I'LL GROW THAT FLOWER TOO.
GLARE

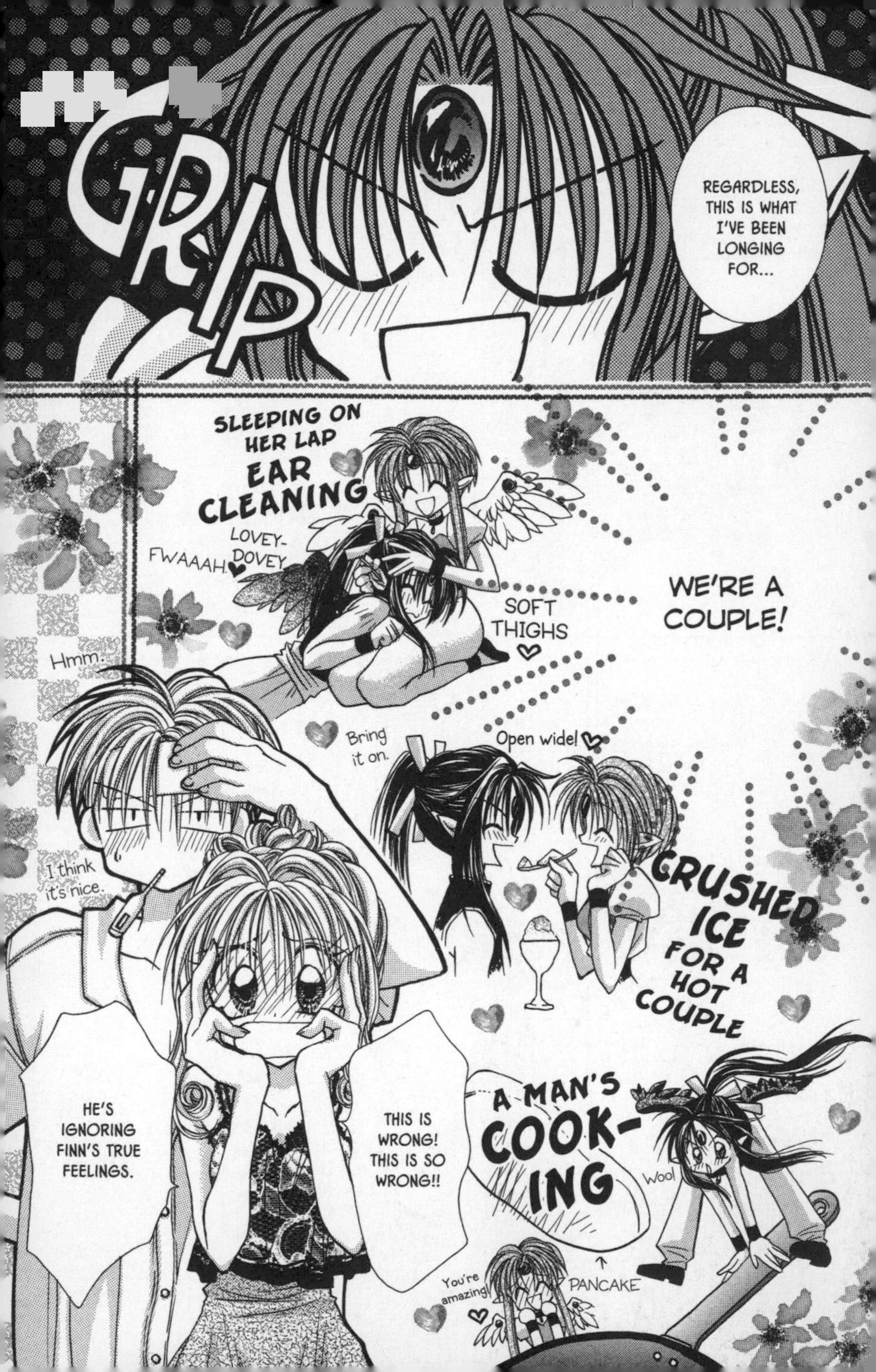
REGARDLESS, THIS IS WHAT I'VE BEEN LONGING FOR...
GRIP
WE'RE A COUPLE!
SLEEPING ON HER LAP
EAR CLEANING
LOVEY-DOVEY
FWAAAH.
SOFT THIGHS
Hmm.
Open wide!
Bring it on.
CRUSHED ICE FOR A HOT COUPLE
I think it's nice.
A MAN'S COOK-ING
Woo!
PANCAKE
You're amazing!
THIS IS WRONG! THIS IS SO WRONG!!
HE'S IGNORING FINN'S TRUE FEELINGS.

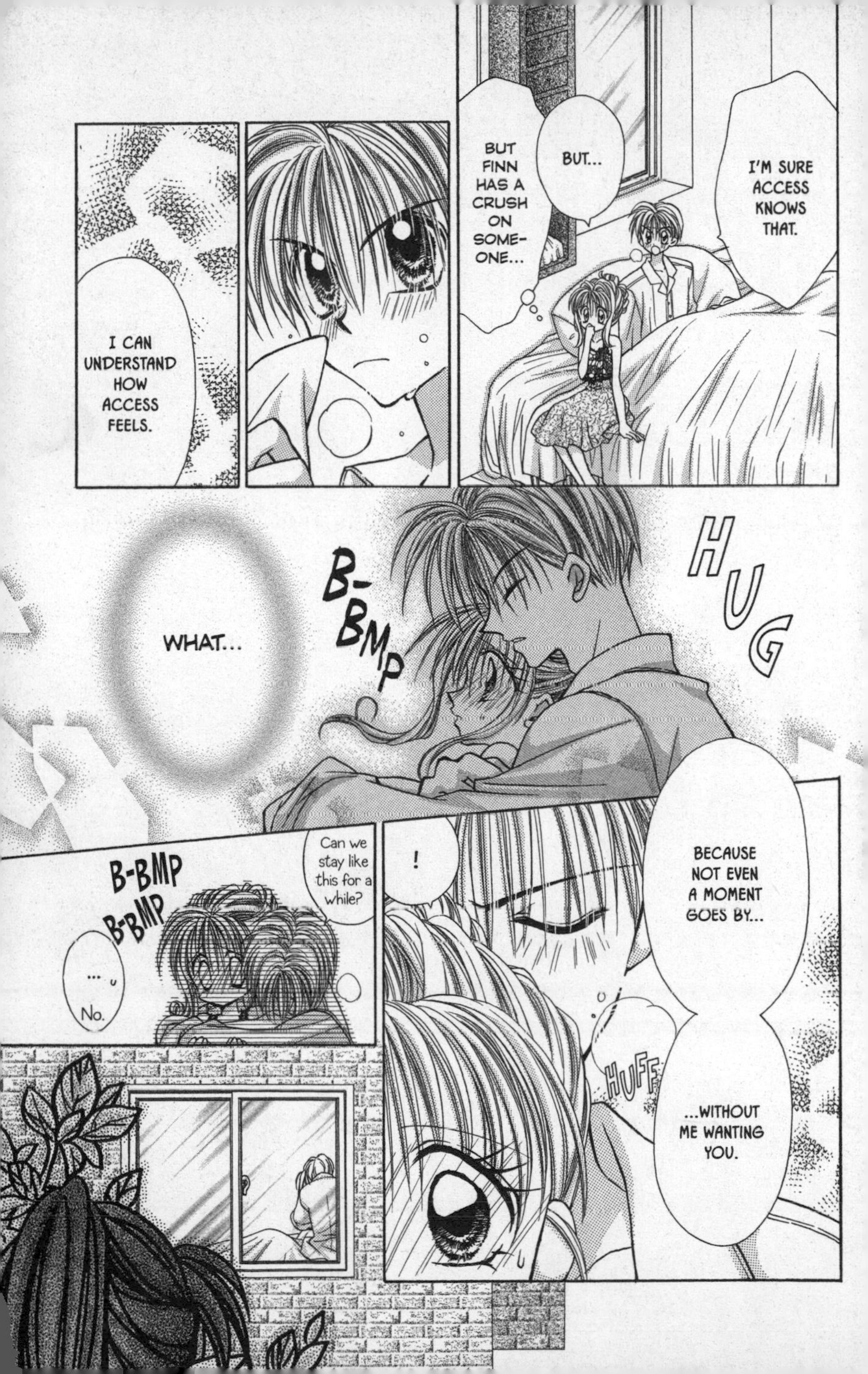
I'M SURE ACCESS KNOWS THAT.
BUT...
BUT FINN HAS A CRUSH ON SOME-ONE...
I CAN UNDERSTAND HOW ACCESS FEELS.
HUG
B-BBMP
WHAT...
BECAUSE NOT EVEN A MOMENT GOES BY...
!
HUFF
...WITHOUT ME WANTING YOU.
Can we stay like this for a while?
B-BMP
B-BMP
... No.

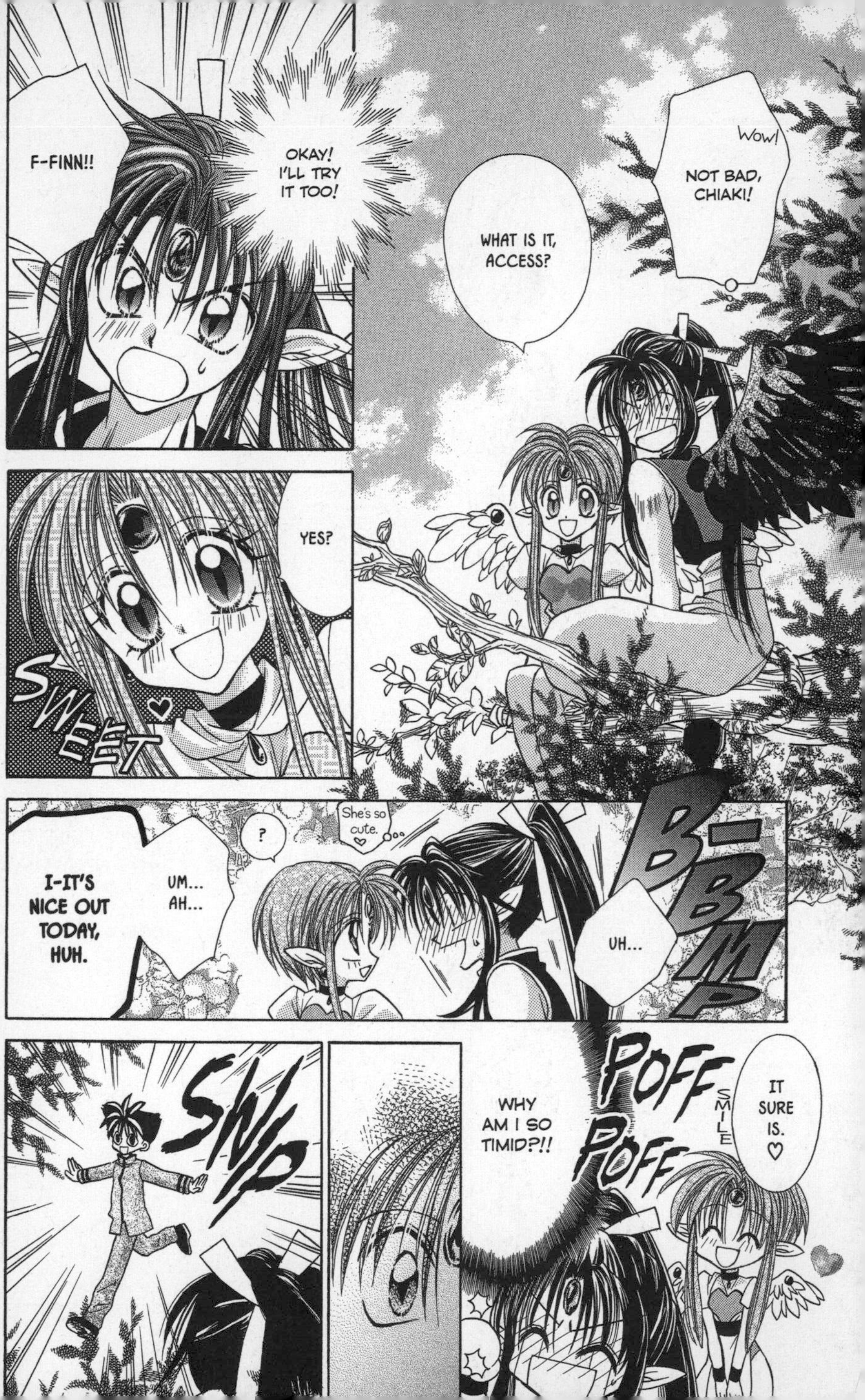
Wow!
NOT BAD, CHIAKI!
WHAT IS IT, ACCESS?
OKAY! I'LL TRY IT TOO!
F-FINN!!
YES?
SWEET ♡
B-BMMP
UH...
She's so cute. ♡
?
UM... AH...
I-IT'S NICE OUT TODAY, HUH.
IT SURE IS. ♡
SMILE
POFF POFF
WHY AM I SO TIMID?!!
SNIP

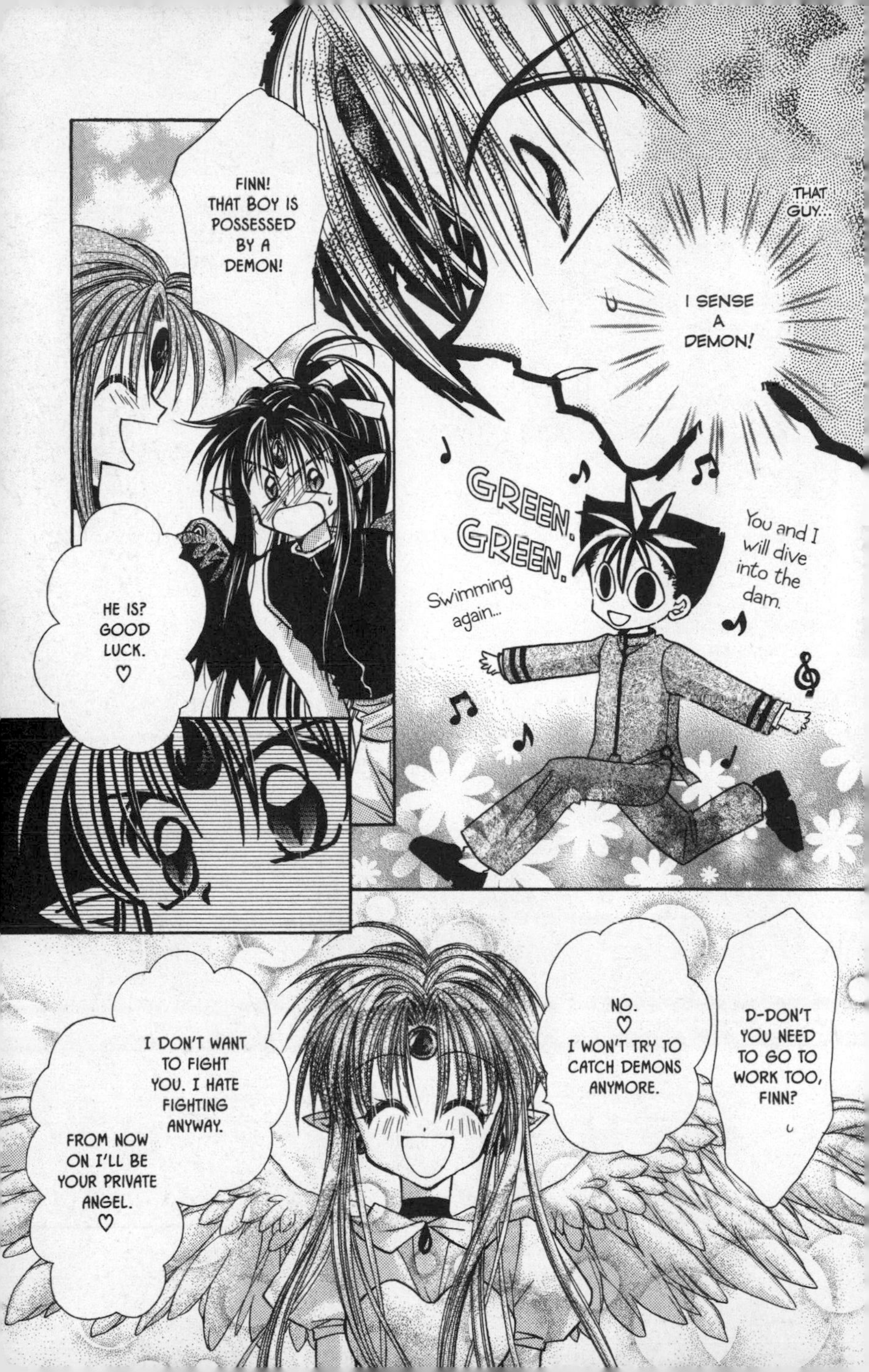
THAT GUY...
I SENSE A DEMON!
FINN! THAT BOY IS POSSESSED BY A DEMON!
GREEN. GREEN.
You and I will dive into the dam.
Swimming again...
HE IS? GOOD LUCK. ♡
D-DON'T YOU NEED TO GO TO WORK TOO, FINN?
NO. ♡ I WON'T TRY TO CATCH DEMONS ANYMORE.
I DON'T WANT TO FIGHT YOU. I HATE FIGHTING ANYWAY.
FROM NOW ON I'LL BE YOUR PRIVATE ANGEL. ♡

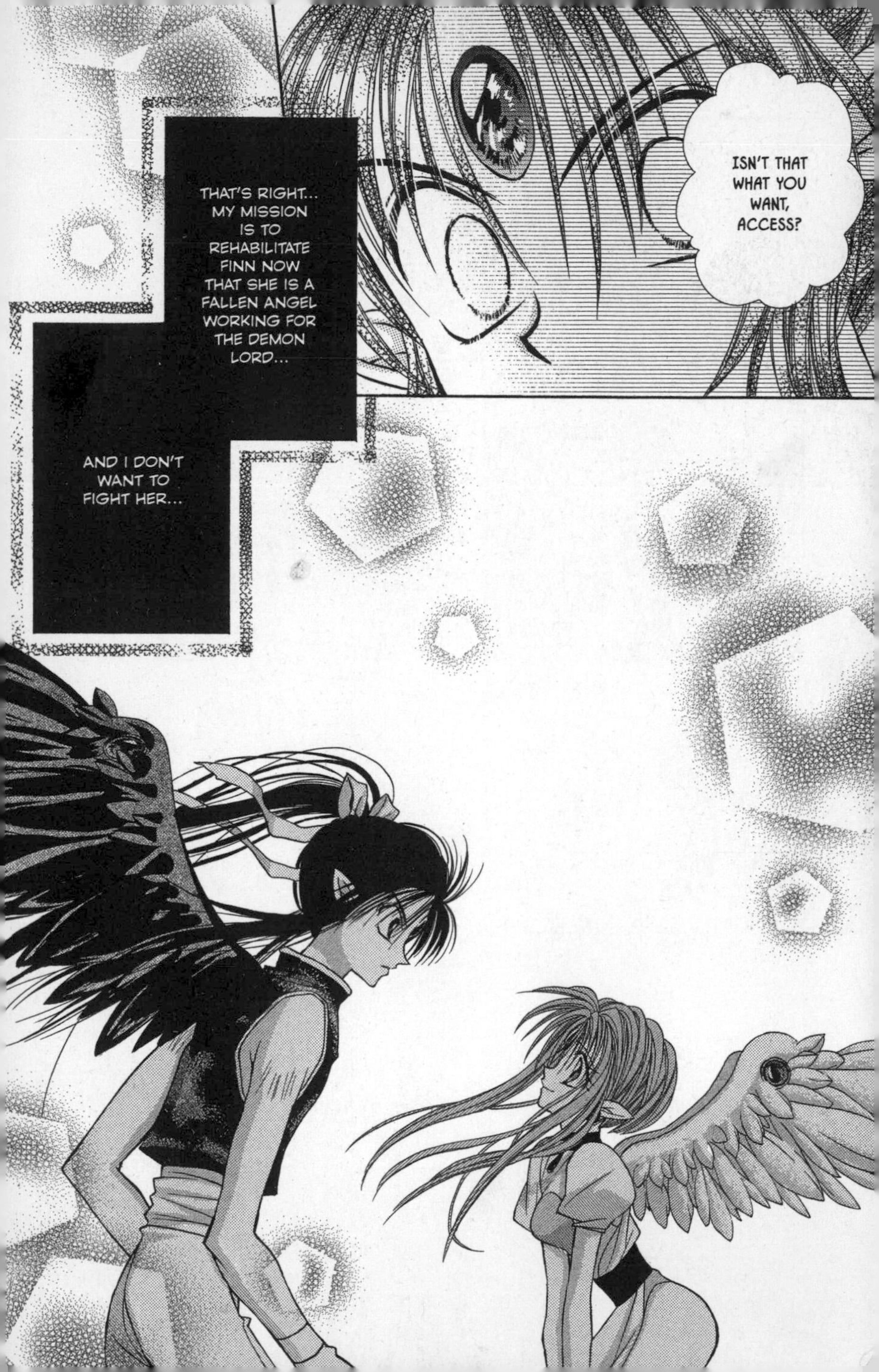
ISN'T THAT WHAT YOU WANT, ACCESS?
THAT'S RIGHT... MY MISSION IS TO REHABILITATE FINN NOW THAT SHE IS A FALLEN ANGEL WORKING FOR THE DEMON LORD...
AND I DON'T WANT TO FIGHT HER...

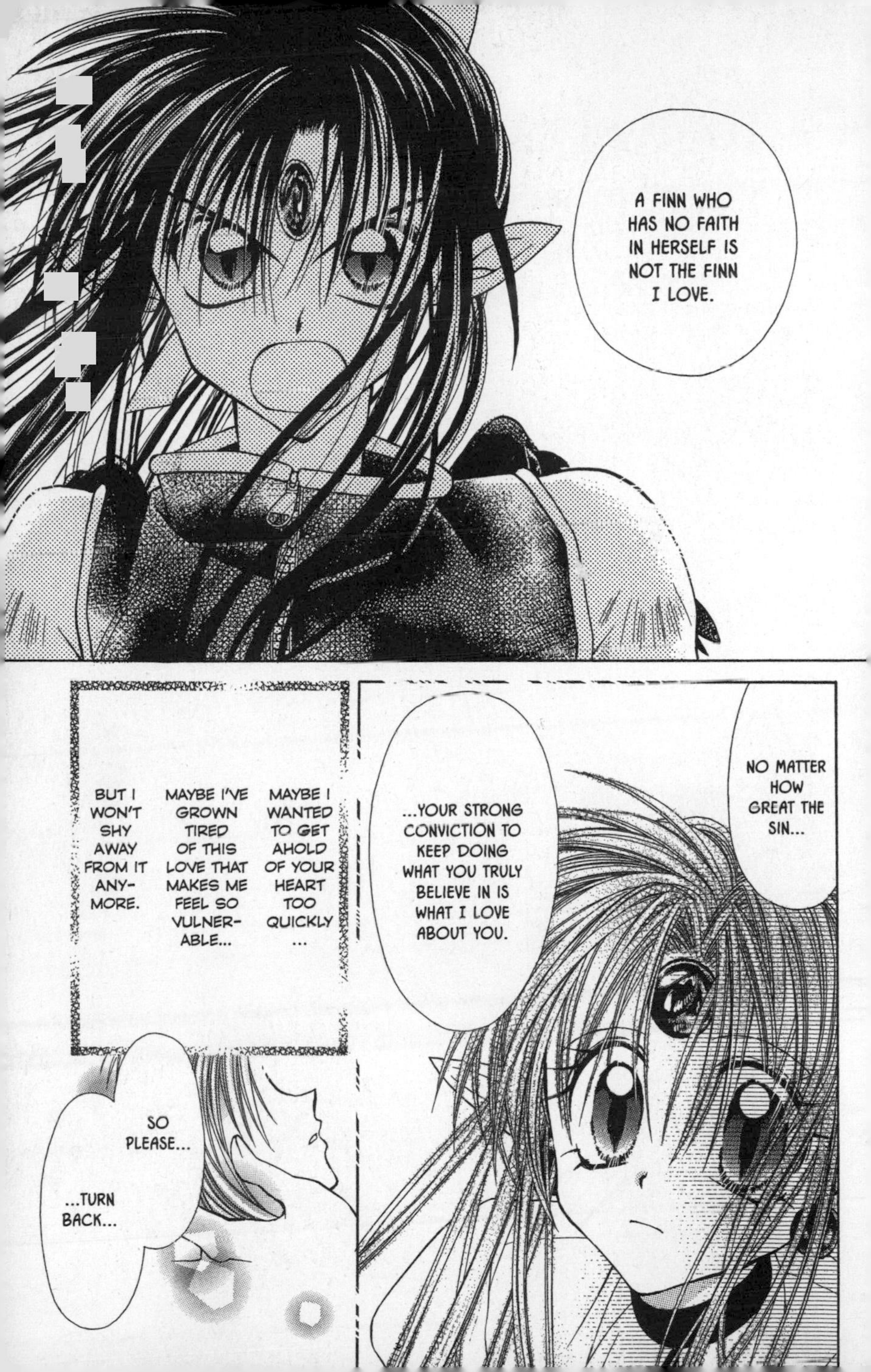
A FINN WHO HAS NO FAITH IN HERSELF IS NOT THE FINN I LOVE.
NO MATTER HOW GREAT THE SIN...
...YOUR STRONG CONVICTION TO KEEP DOING WHAT YOU TRULY BELIEVE IN IS WHAT I LOVE ABOUT YOU.
MAYBE I WANTED TO GET AHOLD OF YOUR HEART TOO QUICKLY...
MAYBE I'VE GROWN TIRED OF THIS LOVE THAT MAKES ME FEEL SO VULNER-ABLE...
BUT I WON'T SHY AWAY FROM IT ANY-MORE.
SO PLEASE...
...TURN BACK...

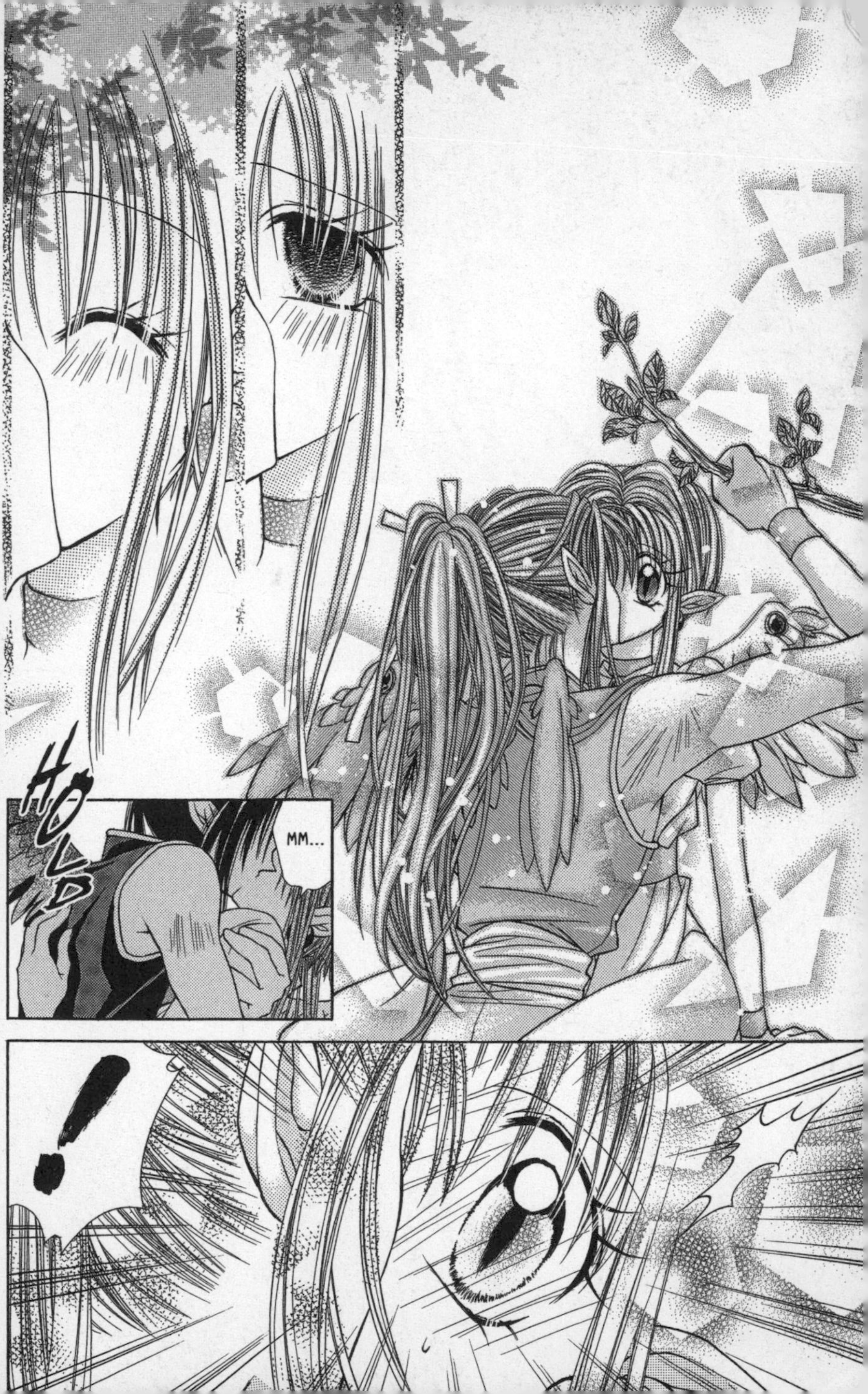
HOLD
MM...
!

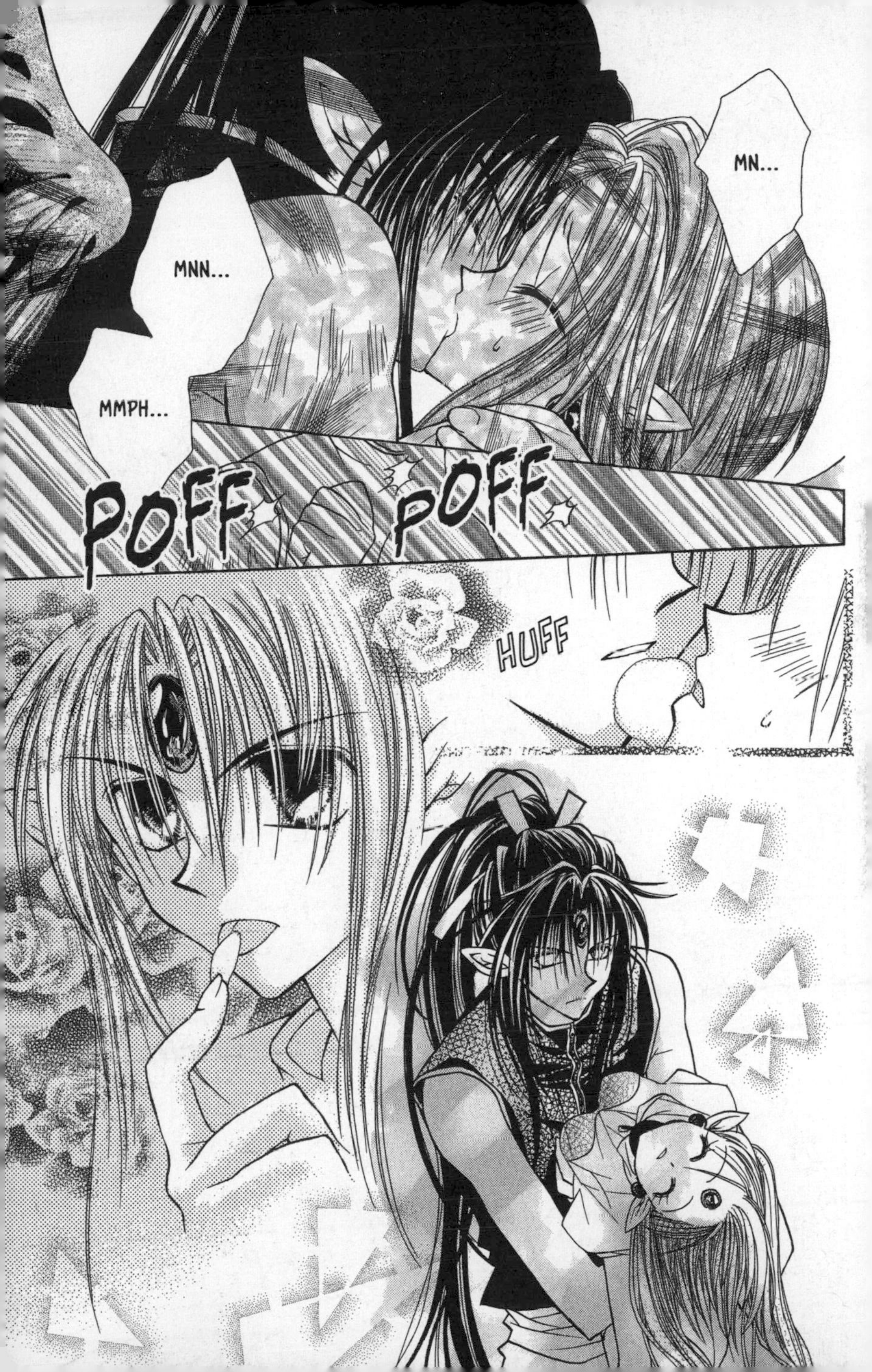
MN...
MNN...
MMPH...
POFF
POFF
HUFF

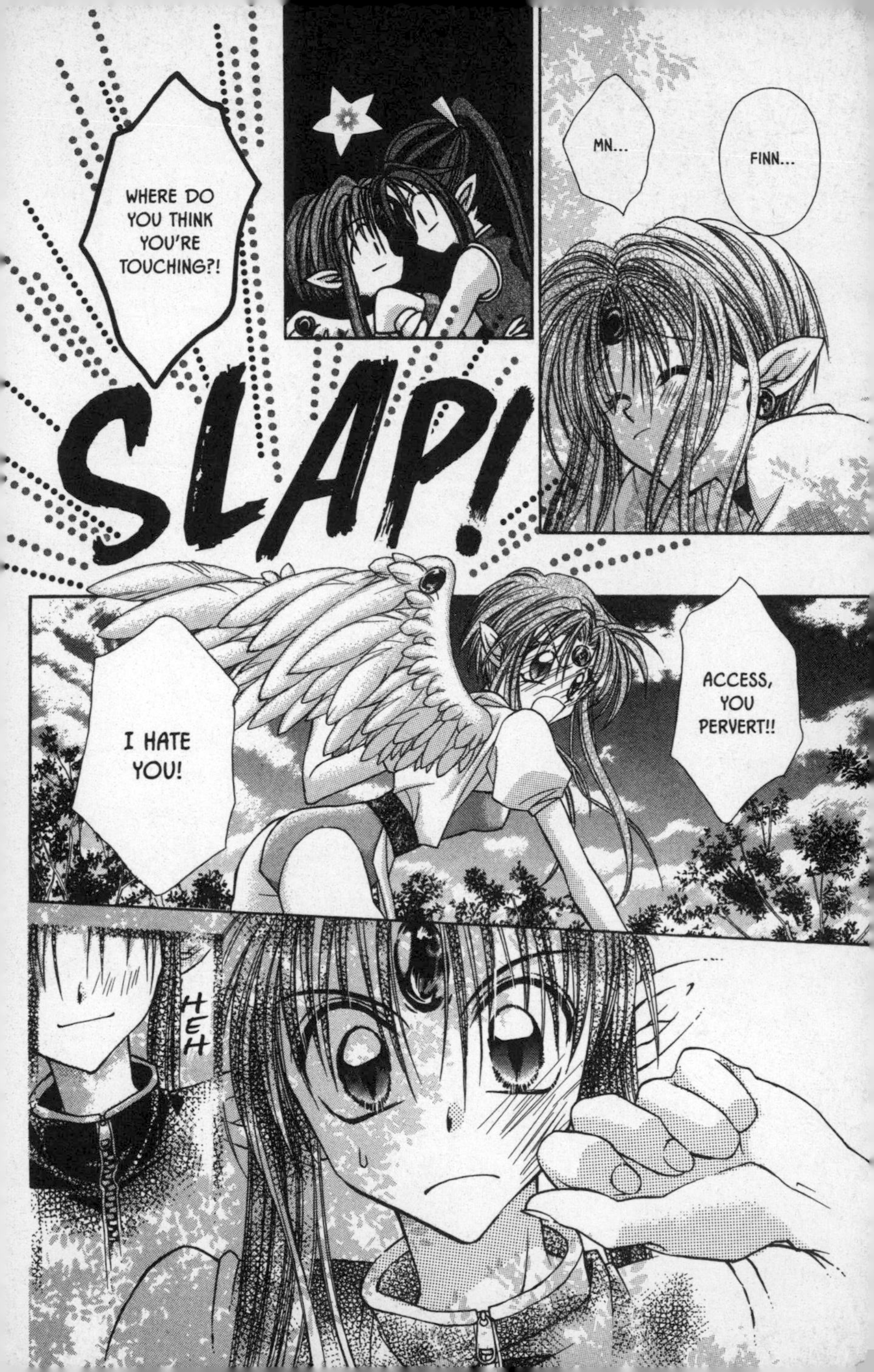
FINN...
MN...
WHERE DO YOU THINK YOU'RE TOUCHING?!
SLAP!
ACCESS, YOU PERVERT!!
I HATE YOU!
HEH

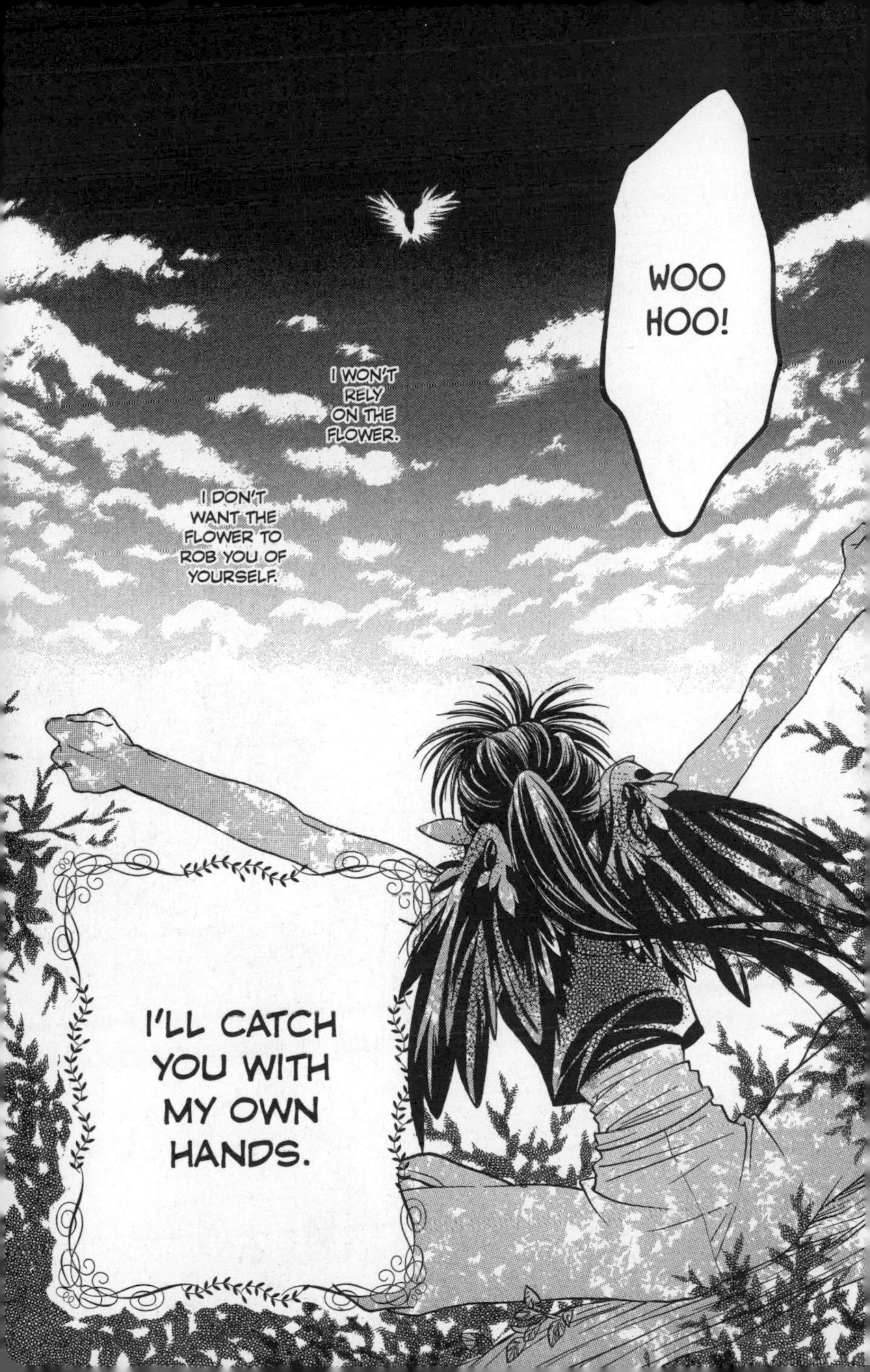
WOO HOO!
I WON'T RELY ON THE FLOWER.
I DON'T WANT THE FLOWER TO ROB YOU OF YOURSELF.
I'LL CATCH YOU WITH MY OWN HANDS.

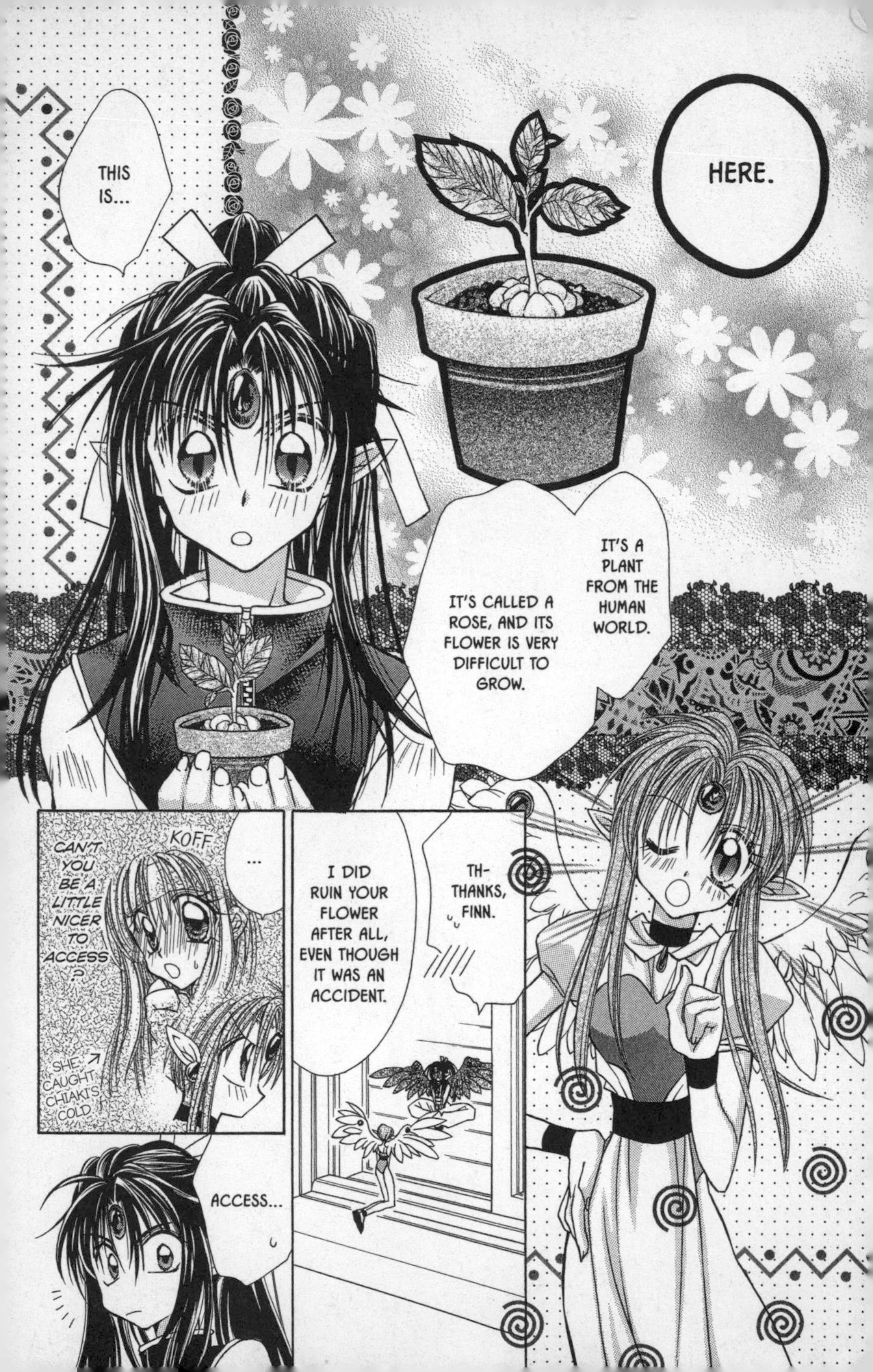
HERE.
THIS IS...
IT'S A PLANT FROM THE HUMAN WORLD.
IT'S CALLED A ROSE, AND ITS FLOWER IS VERY DIFFICULT TO GROW.
TH- THANKS, FINN.
I DID RUIN YOUR FLOWER AFTER ALL, EVEN THOUGH IT WAS AN ACCIDENT.
...
KOFF
CAN'T YOU BE A LITTLE NICER TO ACCESS?
SHE CAUGHT CHIAKI'S COLD
ACCESS...

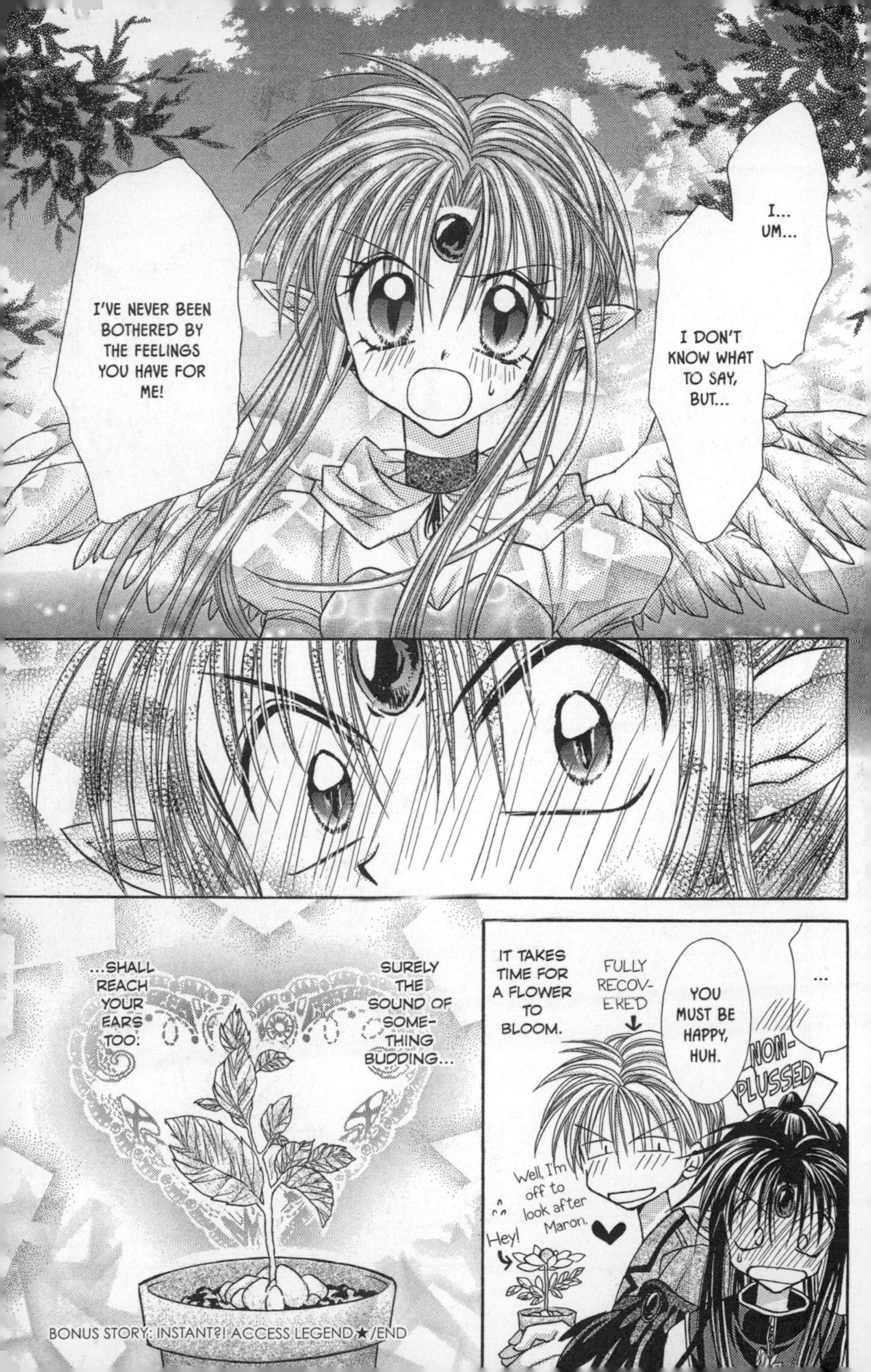
I... UM...
I DON'T KNOW WHAT TO SAY, BUT...
I'VE NEVER BEEN BOTHERED BY THE FEELINGS YOU HAVE FOR ME!
...
YOU MUST BE HAPPY, HUH.
NON-PLUSSED
FULLY RECOV-ERED
IT TAKES TIME FOR A FLOWER TO BLOOM.
Well, I'm off to look after Maron.
Hey!
SURELY THE SOUND OF SOME-THING BUDDING...
...SHALL REACH YOUR EARS TOO.

BONUS STORY: INSTANT?! ACCESS LEGEND★/END

Jeanne Special Illustrations

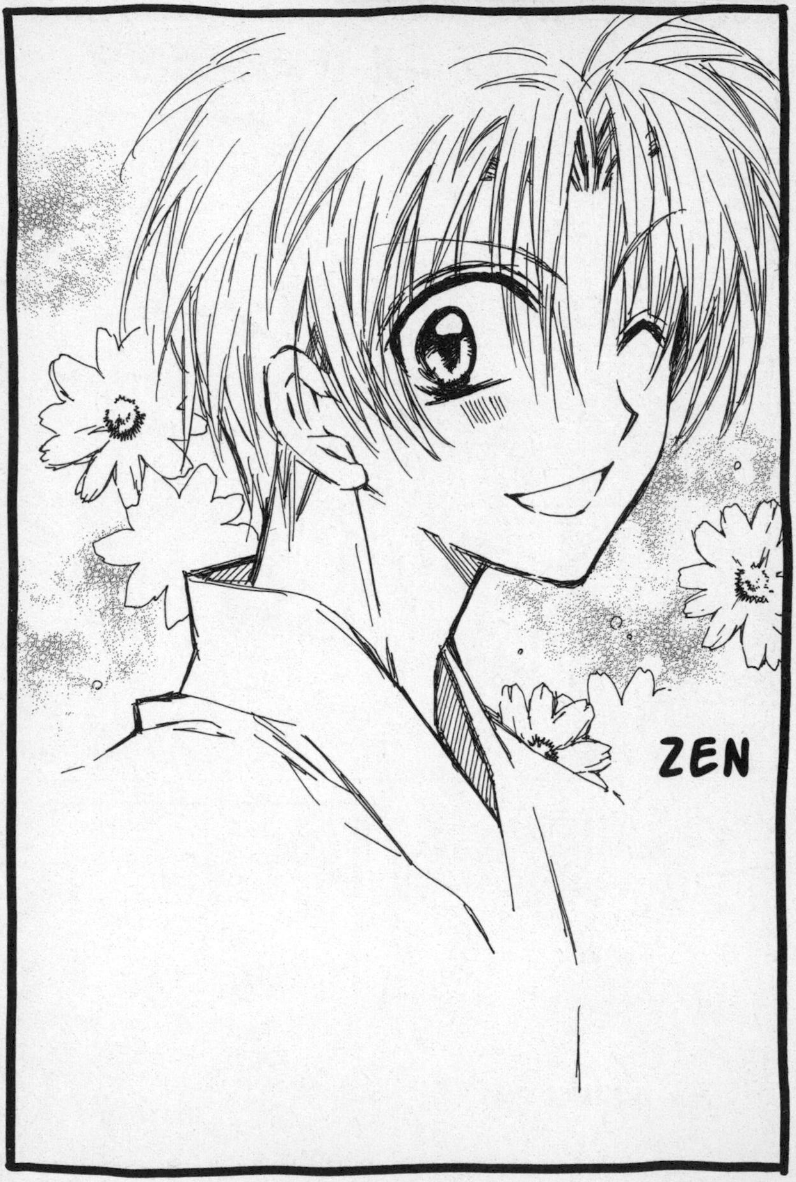
ZEN

FINN & ACCESS

ARINA TANEMURA

Arina Tanemura began her manga
career in 1996 when her short stories
debuted in *Ribon* magazine. She gained
fame with the 1997 publication of *I•O•N*,
and ever since her debut Tanemura
has been a major force in shojo manga
with popular series *Phantom Thief
Jeanne, Time Stranger Kyoko, Full Moon,*
and *The Gentlemen's Alliance †.* Both
Phantom Thief Jeanne and *Full Moon*
have been adapted into
animated TV series.

PHANTOM THIEF
Jeanne

VOLUME 4
SHOJO BEAT EDITION

STORY AND ART BY Arina Tanemura

TRANSLATION Tetsuichiro Miyaki
TOUCH-UP ART & LETTERING Inori Fukuda Trant
DESIGN Shawn Carrico
EDITOR Nancy Thistlethwaite

KAMIKAZE KAITO JEANNE © 1998 by Arina Tanemura
All rights reserved.
First published in Japan in 1998 by SHUEISHA Inc., Tokyo.
English translation rights arranged by SHUEISHA Inc.

The stories, characters and incidents mentioned
in this publication are entirely fictional.

Printed in the U.S.A.

Published by VIZ Media, LLC
P.O. Box 77010
San Francisco, CA 94107

10 9 8 7 6 5 4 3 2 1
First printing, September 2014

www.viz.com

www.shojobeat.com

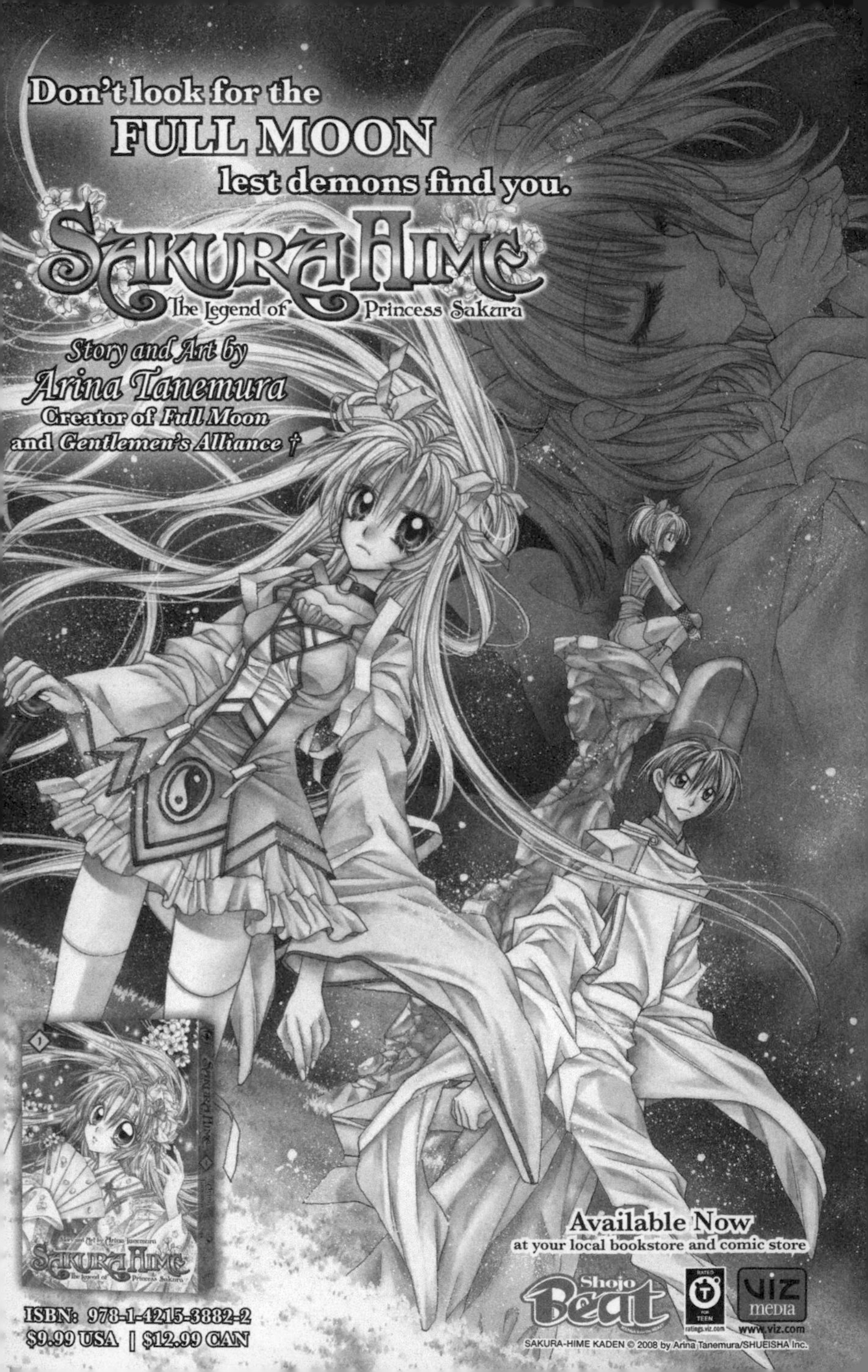
Don't look for the
FULL MOON
lest demons find you.
SAKURA HIME
The Legend of Princess Sakura
Story and Art by
Arina Tanemura
Creator of Full Moon
and Gentlemen's Alliance †
Available Now
at your local bookstore and comic store
ISBN: 978-1-4215-3882-2
$9.99 USA | $12.99 CAN
Shojo Beat
RATED T FOR TEEN
ratings.viz.com
VIZ media
www.viz.com
SAKURA-HIME KADEN © 2008 by Arina Tanemura/SHUEISHA Inc.

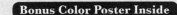

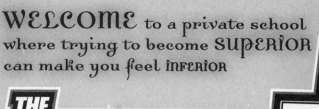

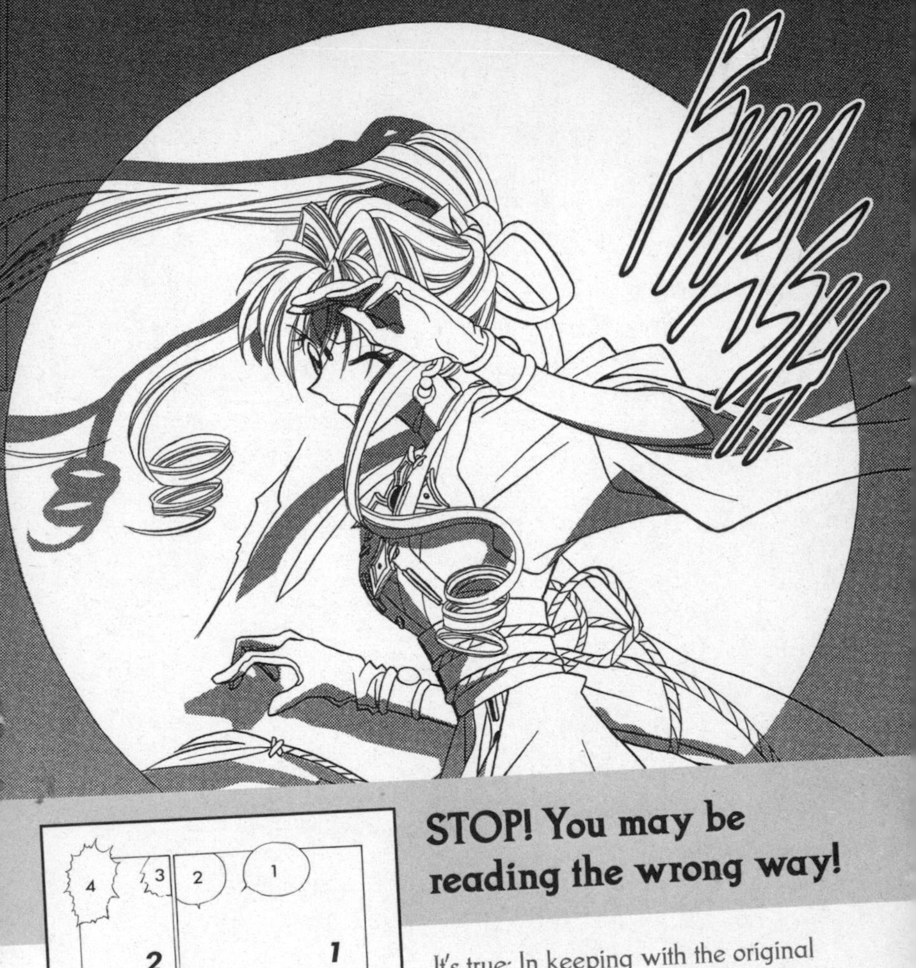

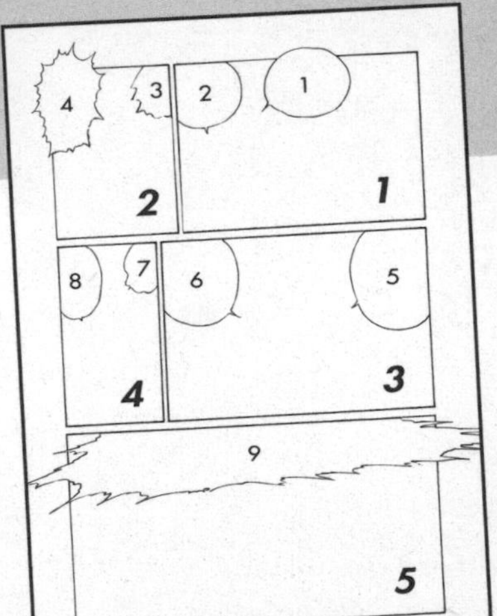

STOP! You may be reading the wrong way!

It's true: In keeping with the original Japanese comic format, this book reads from right to left—so action, sound effects, and word balloons are completely reversed. This preserves the orientation of the original artwork—plus, it's fun! Check out the diagram shown here to get the hang of things, and then turn to the other side of the book to get started!